CW00554496

The Uniformed Police Forces of the Third Reich
1933–1945

Other titles by Leandoer & Ekholm förlag:

Estländare i tysk tjänst (2005)
Pansar i Vinterkriget (2006)

Warszawa 1: Pansar i upproret (2006)

Original Title: The Uniformed Police Forces of the Third Reich 1933–1945.
Written by: Phil Nix and Georges Jerome
Quality control: Ulf Olsson
Map: Samuel Svärd
Picture sources: Phil Nix and Georges Jerome and if not noted otherwise
Cover: Magdalena Hagelind
Editor: Andy McHale, Andreas Leandoer and Ulf Olsson
Proof reading: Andy McHale
Corrections: Damco Ltd
Leandoer & Ekholm Publishing, Stockholm Sweden
www.leforlag.se

2nd edition, 3rd printing

Printed at: Spaustuve Spindulys, Kaunas

The Uniformed Police Forces of the Third Reich

1933–1945

Table of Contents

Acknowledgements

Phil Nix

This book was conceived following a request from our fellow author and friend Mark C. Yerger and it owes much to the seminal work on the subject written by Georg Tessin. Use has also been made of the report on the German Police issued by the Supreme Headquarters of the Allied Expeditionary Force Evaluation and Dissemination Section issued in April 1945. It has been Flushed out using original documentation from various archives in Germany and in Washington. My thanks must go to my fellow author Georges Jerome who has travelled to visit the various German archives and our friend Mark C. Yerger who did the same regarding the Washington archive.

My thanks also goes to Drs. Robin Lenman, Robin Clifton, Robin Okey and the late Professor Callum MacDonald, all of the University of Warwick, who provided inspiration during my studying for a degree in the 1990s. Thanks to Jost W. Schneider who, over a number of years, has supplied information on the post war fates of many of the personalities in the book and who supplied many of the original photos used. Peter Hertel too for his valuable information.

Jan Pra has supplied unique photos of her uncle, a Gendarmerie NCO, that are unique. Julie Cheswick and Kim Rose advised on basic structure while Harry Downes used his computer scanner to reproduce some of our photographic material. We both also thank Mark C. Yerger for many hours computer designing the text format.

Georges Jerome

Trained as a lawyer, I remain interested in primary sources and methods of investigation to gain any useful information. Between management duties and courses at the University institute of Technology of Metz, I found time to conduct research and entered into what has become a close and friendly relationship with Phil in 1978.

In addition special thanks must go to The Dean Guy Pedroncini, Director of the Revue "Guerres Mondiales." His influence and support in 1991 gave me access to the US Berlin Document Center.

Also my appreciation to André Boulanger, who allowed me access to his personal collection and gave me warm and kind support in my researches throughout years. I would like to thank the staff of the Bundesarchiv Koblenz, who provided me with advice and assistance during my visits over 15 years, and the U.S. Berlin Document Center for their valuable help. The Loan Department of Bibliothèque Universitaire (Metz) carried out research for me throughout Europe and the Archives Nationales d'Etat (Luxemburg) opened their Archives on German Police to me. The staff of Bibliothèque de Documentation Internationale Contemporaine (Paris) who was very helpful to me during my visits.

The Archives Départementales de la Moselle allowed me to use their microfilm printer for my research work and the Institut für Zeitsgeschichte (München) pointed me in the right direction with the extensive bibliography they provided me with and for the loan of primary sources. Ascomemo, the historical association of the Annexation of Lorraine 1940/1945, of which I'm a member, also opened its library and collection to me. Finally, individual thanks are extended to Philippe Wilmouth, Roger Munch, Jean Pierre Ehrmann, Emmanuel Lavocat, Guy Muller and Gerard Verhoef.

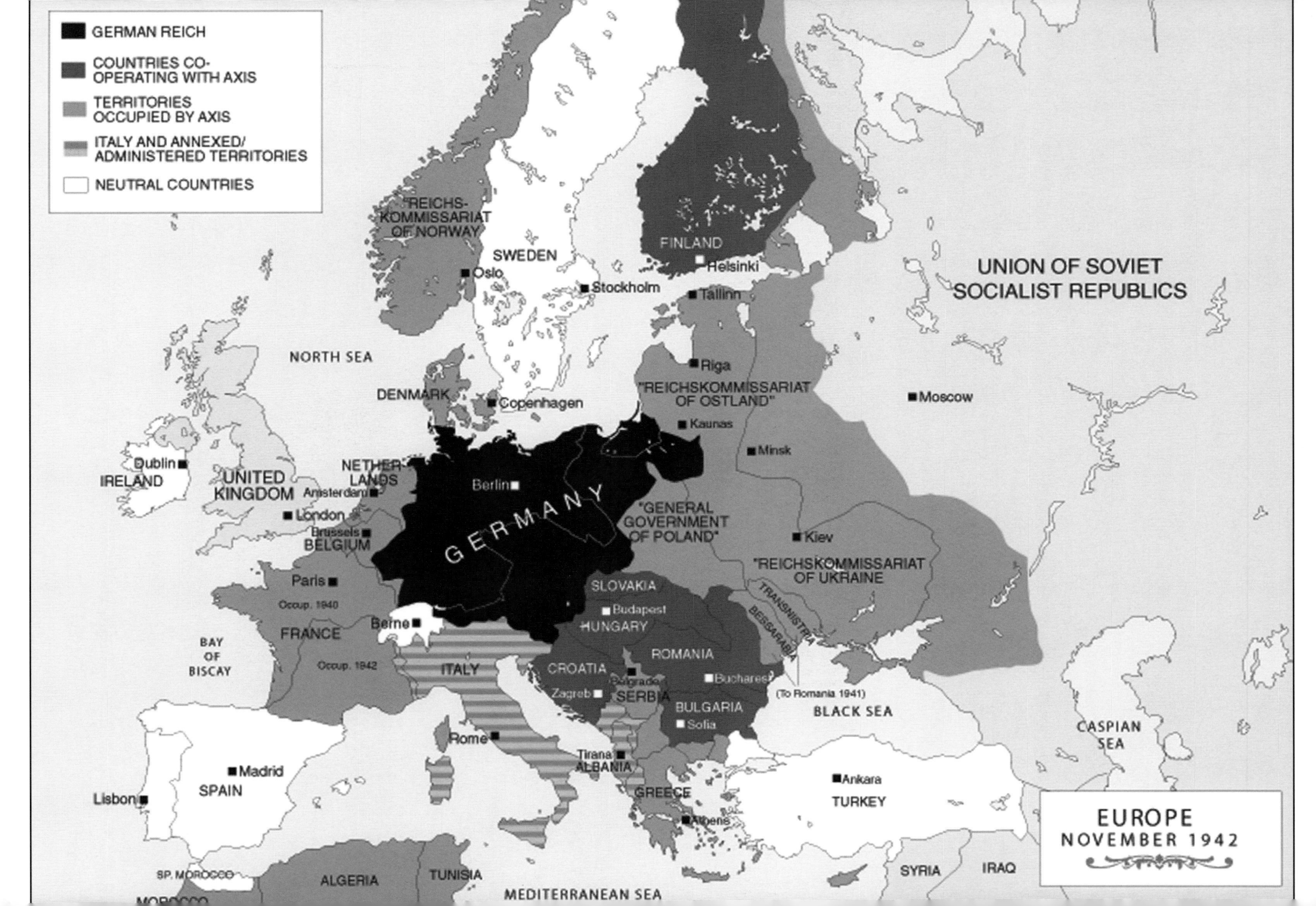
GERMAN REICH
COUNTRIES CO-OPERATING WITH AXIS
TERRITORIES OCCUPIED BY AXIS
ITALY AND ANNEXED/ ADMINISTERED TERRITORIES
NEUTRAL COUNTRIES
"REICHS-KOMMISSARIAT OF NORWAY"
SWEDEN
FINLAND
Helsinki
Oslo
Stockholm
Tallinn
UNION OF SOVIET SOCIALIST REPUBLICS
NORTH SEA
Riga
"REICHSKOMMISSARIAT OF OSTLAND"
Moscow
DENMARK
Copenhagen
Kaunas
Minsk
Dublin
IRELAND
UNITED KINGDOM
NETHER-LANDS
Amsterdam
Berlin
GERMANY
London
Brussels
BELGIUM
"GENERAL GOVERNMENT OF POLAND"
Kiev
"REICHSKOMMISSARIAT OF UKRAINE
Paris
Occup. 1940
SLOVAKIA
Budapest
HUNGARY
TRANSNISTRIA
BESSARABIA
Berne
BAY OF BISCAY
FRANCE
Occup. 1942
ITALY
CROATIA
ROMANIA
Bucharest
Zagreb
SERBIA
(To Romania 1941)
BLACK SEA
BULGARIA
Sofia
CASPIAN SEA
Rome
Tirana
ALBANIA
Madrid
SPAIN
Lisbon
GREECE
Athens
Ankara
TURKEY
EUROPE
NOVEMBER 1942
SP. MOROCCO
ALGERIA
TUNISIA
MEDITERRANEAN SEA
SYRIA
IRAQ

High Command of the Ordnungspolizei

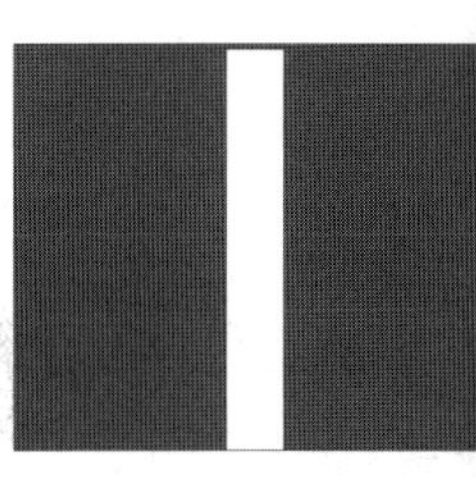

1.1 Hauptamt Ordnungspolizei

This headquarters was created with effect from 17 June 1936. The term "Hauptamt" (Main Office) was a new one to the German State machine, it is thought that it came from the SS which already had three such headquarters (SS-HA, RuSHA and SD-HA). Its role was to supervise all aspects of the uniformed police throughout the Reich. It absorbed offices from Abteilung III (Polizei) of the Reich Ministery of the Interior.

Chef

SS-Oberst-Gruppenführer und Generaloberst der Polizei
Kurt Daluege[1] 17.06.1936–08.05.1945

SS-Obergruppenführer und General der Polizei und Waffen-SS
Alfred Wünnenberg (m.d.F.b.)[2] 31.08.1943–08.05.1945

Hauptbüro (Main Desk): created in two groups to advise the Chef on all staff matters.

Gruppe 1: Personalangelegenheiten der Verwaltungsbeamten des Chefs (Personnel questions of the Police Administrative Officials). For Besoldungs Gruppe (Pay Groups) A 2b bis A 10b:
Ministerialrat Heinrich Meinecke

Gruppe 2: Alle übrigen Bürodirektorgeschäfte (All others leading administration duties):
Oberregierungsrat Johannes Klapper

In November 1943, those parts of the Büro concerned with economics were put under the Wirtschaftsverwaltungssamt. The remainder concentrated together into a new office called Stabsführer des Kommandoamts (Chief of Staff of Command Office) under Johannes Klapper.

Adjudantur: created in two parts to provide personal service to the Chef

Adjudantur 1: Persönlicher Dienst beim Chef der Ordnungspolizei
(Personal duties next to Chief of Ordnungspolizei)

General der Polizei, Alfred Wünnenberg greets members of the fire service during an inspection in the Ruhr. Behind him stands Generalmajor der Polizei Kurt Gohrum

SS-Oberst-Gruppenführer und Generaloberst der Polizei Kurt Daluege

Adjudantur 2: SS-Verbindungsoffizier und Pressestelle
(SS-liaison officer and Press Office)

[1] *Born on 15 May 1897 in Kreuzburg (Upper Schlesien). Served in the Great War from January 1916 and was wounded in the head and shoulder in 1918 suffering 25% disability. He ended the war as Vizefeldwebel. Studied engineering and achieved a diploma, he then worked in various concerns as a construction engineer. Joined the Party in 1922 left in the wake of the München Putsch of November 1923 and rejoined on the 12 March 1926. Served in the SA from 1 November 1926. Führer SA-Gruppe Berlin-Brandenburg from 1 November 1926 until 27 March 1930.*

He was also Stellvertreter-Gauleiter for Berlin from November 1926 until 1 November 1930. Gau SS-Führer Berlin-Brandenburg from March 1927. Joined the SS as Oberführer with effect from 25 July 1930. He headed all SS-units in Berlin and was a rival to Himmler for a time with Görings backing. Later he accepted Himmlers authority and led the SS-Main District Ost until 1 October 1933. Promoted Gruppenführer on 1 July 1932 and Obergruppenführer on 9 September 1934. He was appointed Leiter PolizeiAbteilung in the Prussian Ministry of the Interior on 11 May 1933 to 15 September 1933 and was given the civil service rank of Ministerialdirektor on 5 May 1933. Member of the Reichstag from November 1933. After serving in various other senior SA commands he devoted his time to Police service being given the rank of Generalmajor der Landespolizei on the 13 September 1933. Appointed Befehlhaber der Kasernierte Landespolizei from 13 September 1933 until 17 June 1936. Promoted Generalleutnant der Landespolizei on 20 April 1935.

Appointed Chef der Hauptamt rdnungspolizei on 17 June 1936 and promoted General der Polizei at the same time. Served as deputy Reichsprotektor for Böhmen-Mähren from 27 May 1942 until 14 October 1943. He was promoted SS-Oberst-Gruppenführer and Generaloberst der Polizei on the 20 April 1942. He was taken ill with a form of multiple sclerosis in the summer of 1943 and he gradually deteriorated to such an extent that Alfred Wünnenberg had to take over his Police post on 31 August 1943. He retained his police rank until the end of the war. Awarded the Knight's Cross of the War Service Cross on 6 September 1943. He was a married man with three sons and one daughter. Sentenced to death by the Czechs he was carried to the scaffold on a stretcher and was hanged whilst only semi-concious on 20 October 1946.

[2] *Born on 20 July 1891 in Saarburg (Lorraine). Joined the army as Fahnenjunker 25 February 1913. Served in the infantry until 13 June 1916. Commissioned Leutnant on 5 August 1914. Served in the flying corps to 17 November 1918. Promoted Oberleutnant on 6 November 1917. Left the army as Hauptmann on 26 October 1919. Joined the Schutzpolizei in Münster on 27 October 1919 with the rank of Oberleutnant. Served in Essen, Potsdam, Krefeld, and Cologne to 1 June 1932. Promoted Hauptmann on 13 July 1921 and Major on 1 April 1932. Kommandeur der Schutzpolizei in Hindenburg from 1 June 1932 to 1 August 1933, in Beuthen to 1934, in Gleiwitz to 1 May 1935, in Saarbrücken to October 1937, in Bremen then in Mannheim to December 1938. Promoted Oberstleutnant der Schutzpolizei 1 April 1937. Ia beim IdO Stuttgart to 1 October 1939. Kommandeur der Polizei-Schützen-Regiment 3 to 15 December 1941.*

Promoted Oberst der Schutzpolizei 1 January 1940 and Generalmajor der Polizei 1 October 1941. Kommandeur der Polizei-Division to 10 June 1943. Promoted Generalleutnant der Polizei on 11 July 1942 and General der Polizei on 1 July 1943. Kommandierender- General der IV. SS-Armee-Korps from 1 June 1943 to 31 August 1943. Acting Chief of the Hauptamt Ordnungspolizei from 31 August 1943 to the end of the war. Chef der Deutschen Polizei from 6 May 1945 to 17 May 1945 (Appointed by the Dönitz Government). Joined the Party on 1 May 1933 and the SS as Standartenführer on 1 January 1940. Promoted Oberführer on 9 November 1941, Brigadeführer on 9 December 1941, Gruppenführer on 1 July 1942 and Obergruppenführer on 1 July 1943. He was given the rank of General in the Waffen-SS on 1 July 1943. Awarded the Knight's Cross 15 November 1941 and the Oakleaves to the Knight's Cross 23 April 1942. He was a married man with a step-daughter. He died of a heart attack in Krefeld on 30 December 1963.

The Hauptamt was divided into a number of offices known as Amtsgruppen (Group Offices), Ämtern (Offices) and Inspekteurs (Inspectors). Minor changes took place on a regular basis but there was only one major reorganisation that took place in September 1943.

Amt Verwaltung und Recht (Administration and Legal Office)

Created on 30 June 1936 from Unterabteilung IIIa of the Polizei-Abteilung of the Reich and Prussian Interior Ministeries. It controlled budgets, economics, quarters and legal affairs.[3]

Chef

SS-Gruppenführer,
Ministerialdirektor Werner Bracht [4] 30.06.1936–15.09.1943

From 1 December 1940, this office was split into three Amtsgruppen as follows:
Amtsgruppen VuR I: Haushalt, Beamtenrecht, Versorgung
(Budget, Officials Law, Allowances and Pensions)
Chef
Ministerialrat,
Maximilian Rheins 01.12.1940–15.09.1943

Amtsgruppe VuR II: Organisation, Personalien, Gewerbepolizei, Verkehr (Organisation, Personnel matters, Police controlling handicrafts and trades, Traffic)
Chef
SS-Brigadeführer, Ministerialdirektor
Dr. Kurt Bader [5] 01.12.1940–01.06.1943

SS-Gruppenführer und Generalleutnant der Waffen-SS und der Polizei
Heinz Reinefarth [6] 01.06.1943–15.09.1943

Amtsgruppe VuR III: Unterkunfts und Bauangelegenheiten (Quartering, Billetting and Construction)
Chef
Ministerialdirektor,
Rudolf Scheidel 01.12.1940–15.09.1943

Amt Verwaltung und Recht was abolished with effect from 15 September 1943. The whole of Group Office VuR III and part of VuR I went to the Wirtschaftverwaltungsamt. Part of VuR I went to the Rechtsamt, part of VuR I and II to the Kommandoamt and part to the Reichssicherheitshauptamt (Security Police Main Office).

[3] *All the major offices are listed. For a full chart of the sub-offices of the Hauptamt Ordnungspolizei see "Die Stäbe und Truppeneinheiten der Ordnungspolizei" by Tessin, Neufeldt and Huck, Koblenz 1957.*

4 Born on 5 February 1888 in Berlin. He studied law and graduated as an administrative lawyer. Served in the cavalry during the Great War and then joined the Prussian Interior Ministry. Promoted Ministerialrat in 1927. Remained there until June 1936 having been in charge of the Police department from 1934. Served as Chef des Amtes Verwaltung und Recht in Hauptamt Ordnungspolizei from 26 June 1936 to 15 September 1943. Promoted Ministerialdirektor on 9 November 1940. He was dismissed in the general reorganisation of September/October 1943, he did not fit in with Himmlers new ideas of integration between the Police and the SS. He held a non police post in the Interior Ministry for the rest of the war. Joined the Party on 1 May 1933 and the SS as Oberführer on 30 January 1939. Promoted Brigadeführer with effect from 20 April 1939 and Gruppenführer on 20 April 1941. He was a married man with two sons and a daughter. He died in Eschweiler near Aachen on 21 September 1980

5 Born on 26 February 1899 in Mannheim (Baden). Served in the Great War being commissioned Leutnant der Reserve on 18 April 1917. Joined the Schutzpolizei in April 1920 and served until September 1922. Left the police and studied law. Graduated as an administrative lawyer in 1925. Served in the Baden Interior Ministry from 1929 until May 1934 and then transferred to the Reich Interior Ministry. Promoted Regierungsrat 8 December 1929, Oberregierungsrat 1 May 1933 and Ministerialrat 1 January 1934. Transferred to the Hauptamt Ordnungspolizei on 17 June 1936 and was promoted Ministerialdirigent on 31 October 1939. Appointed Deputy head of the Verwaltung und Recht (Administration and Law) office in Hauptamt Ordnungspolizei on 31 October 1939. Became Leiter of Amtsgruppe II in that department from 1 December 1940. He left both posts on 1 June 1943. Transferred to the Schutzpolizei on 1 April 1943 with the rank of Generalmajor der Polizei with seniority from 1 April 1942. BdO Wien from 1 September 1943 to 27 February 1944 and from 1 October 1944 until the end of the war (he was ill from February to October 1944). Joined the Party 1 May 1933 and the SS as Sturmführer on 20 December 1933. Promoted Obersturmführer 15 September 1935, Hauptsturmführer 20 April 1936 and Sturmbannführer and Obersturmbannführer in 1938 with seniority from 9 November 1936 and 20 April 1937. Promoted Standartenführer on 1 July 1938, Oberführer in 1940 and Brigadeführer on 20 April 1941. He was a married man with four children and died in Baden on 1 June 1959

6 Born on 26 December 1903 in Gnesen (Westpreussen). Studied law at the University of Jena and passed his Assessor exam. Practiced as a lawyer and notary public in Forst and Cottbus until 1939. Joined the Party on 1 August 1932 and the SS as Scharführer on 19 December 1932. Served as a Rechtsberater (legal official) in the Allgemeine-SS until 1939 when he joined the army. Commissioned Untersturmführer on 20 April 1934. Promoted Obersturmführer on 15 September 1935, Hauptsturmführer on 20 April 1937 and Sturmbannführer on 20 April 1939. Ranked Feldwebel in 1940 and served in an infantry regiment until June 1942. Awarded the Knight's Cross on 25 June 1940. Promoted Obersturmbannführer on 20 April 1940, Standartenführer on 20 April 1941, Oberführer on 30 January 1942 and Brigadeführer on 20 April 1942. Joined the Police as Generalmajor with effect from 20 April 1942. Generalinspekteur der Verwaltung beim Stellvertreter-Reichsprotektor in Böhmen-Mähren from June 1942 until 1 June 1943. Chef Amtsgruppe Verwaltung und Recht in Hauptamt Ordnungspolizei until 1 October 1943 and Chef Rechtsamt until 27 December 1943. After a period of training in Krakau, he was appointed Höhere SS und Polizeiführer in Wehrkreis XXI in Posen on the 29 January 1944. Promoted Generalleutnant der Polizei on the 1 August 1944. Promoted Gruppenführer on 1 August 1944 and was given the rank of Generalleutnant in the Waffen-SS on the same date. Appointed Gaustabsleiter für Volksturm in Gau Wartheland from August to November 1944. Kommandierender-General XVIII. SS-Armee-Korps from December 1944 until the 4 February 1945. Stadtkommandant in Küstin an der Oder from January to March 1945. Kommandieren der General XIV. SS-Armee-Korps from 1 March to 1 April 1945. He was arrested for abandoning Küstrin and was brought before a court martial. No sentence was passed. Awarded the Oakleaves to his Knight's Cross on 4 October 1944. Served as the Mayor of Westland-Sylt after the war. Died in that town on 7 May 1979.

Kommandoamt (Command Office)

This was the central Command Office for Organisation, Personnel, Training, Command functions, Uniformed Police employment and Medical matters. In the reorganisation of September 1943, the Kommandoamt took over responsibility for all police officials and for legal matters in connection with buildings and theatre policing. The Amtsgruppe responsible for Medical services was abolished on 1 October 1944 and its duties were put under a new independent Sanitätsamt.

Chef

SS-Gruppenführer und Generalleutnant der Polizei
Adolf von Bomhard [7] 30.06.1936–01.10.1942

SS-Obergruppenführer und General der Waffen-SS und der Polizei
Otto Winkelmann [8] 01.10.1942–01.03.1944

SS-Brigadeführer und Generalmajor der Polizei
Anton Diermann [9] 01.03.1944–31.07.1944

SS-Brigadeführer und Generalmajor der Polizei
Hans Flade [10] 31.07.1944–08.05.1944

With effect from 1 December 1940, three Amtsgruppen were created under the Kommandoamt.
Amtsgruppe Kommando I: Organisation, Ausbildung, Nachschubwesen (Organisation, Training, and Supply)

Chef

SS-Obergruppenführer und General der Waffen-SS und der Polizei
Otto Winkelmann 01.12.1940–01.10.1940

SS-Brigadeführer und Generalmajor der Polizei
Hans-Dietrich Grünwald 01.10.1942–31.07.1943

SS-Gruf. Generalleutnant Otto Winkelmann

SS-Gruf. Generalleutnant Arthur Mulverstedt

SS-Oberführer und Oberst der Schutzpolizei
Hans Müller-Brunkhorst 01.08.1943–30.11.1943

[7] *Born on 6 January 1891 in Augsburg (Bayern). Joined the Royal Bayern army and was commissioned Leutnant on 28 October 1912. Served in the Great War being promoted Oberleutnant on 9 July 1915 and Hauptmann on 19 August 1919. Joined the Bayrische Landespolizei in 1920. Served as deputy chief of staff to the training section of the Bayrische Landespolizei from 1924 until 1933. Promoted Major der Landespolizei on 1 May 1933 and appointed Chef des Stabes der Landespolizei Inspektion Bayern. Chef des Stabes der Landespolizei Inspektion Brandenburg from 1934 to 1935 then der Landespolizei Inspektion West from 1935 to June 1936. Promoted Oberstleutnant on 1 October 1934 and Oberst on 1 April 1936. In 1936, he became Chef des Reichstabes der Landespolizei until he was transferred to the Schutzpolizei on 30 June 1936. Chef der Kommandoamt in Hauptamt Ordnungspolizei from 30 June 1936 to 1 October 1942. Promoted Generalmajor on 1 April 1937 and Generalleutnant on 1 July 1940 with seniority from 20 April 1939. BdO Ukraine from 1 October 1942 to 1 November 1943. Inspekteur für die Weltanschauliche Schulung in Hauptamt Ordnungspolizei from 9 May 1942 to 1 January 1944. Generalinspekteur der Schulen in Hauptamt Ordnungspolizei from 31 October 1943 to 1 February 1945. Retired from the Police in February 1945. Joined the Party on 1 May 1937. Joined the SS on 20 April 1938 with the rank of Oberführer. Promoted Brigadeführer on 20 April 1939 and Gruppenführer on 9 November 1940. He was a married man with one child. He died in Prien-Cheimsee on 19 July 1973*

[8] *Born on the 4 September 1894 in Otterndorf (Schleswig Holstein). Joined the army in 1912 as Fahnenjunker. Served in the infantry to 5 December 1919. Commissioned Leutnant der Reserve. Joined the Schutzpolizei in Sennelager as Oberleutnant on 8 November 1919. Served in Altona, Düsseldorf then Dortmund to 1 February 1930. Promoted Hauptmann der Schutzpolizei on 16 May 1923. Transferred to Gemeindepolizei as Stadtpolizeidirektor Görlitz from 1 February 1930 to 22 November 1937 then served at Police Headquarters in Berlin to 16 November 1940. Promoted Major der Schutzpolizei in 1933, Oberstleutnant in 12 June 1938 and Oberst in 1 April 1940. Chef der Amtsgruppe Kommando I in Kommandoamtes der Hauptamt Ordnungspolizei from 1 December 1940 to 1 October 1942. Promoted brevet Generalmajor der Polizei 22 December 1941 and confirmed on 26 March 1942. Promoted Generalleutnant der Polizei on 9 August 1942. Chef des Kommandoamtes in Hauptamt Ordnungspolizei to 1 March 1944. Promoted General der Polizei on 15 March 1944. Joined the Party on 1 November 1932 and the SS as Sturmbannführer on 11 September 1938. Promoted Obersturmbannführer on 1 November 1938, Standartenführer on 1 April 1940, Oberführer on 9 November 1941, Brigadeführer on 26 March 1942, Gruppenführer on 9 November 1942 and Obergruppenführer on 15 March 1944. HSSPF Hungary from 19 March 1944 to the end of the war. Kampfkommandant von Budapest from December 1944 to February 1945. Stellvertreter-Chef der Ordnungspolizei Süd-Deutschland from 1 March 1945 to the end of the war. He was given the rank of General der Waffen-SS on 1 December 1944. Awarded the Knight's Cross of the War Service Cross on 21 December 1944. He was a married man with two sons. He died in Bordesholm near Kiel on 24 September 1977*

[9] *Born 25 February 1889 in Husten (Westfalen). Served in the army during the Great War and was commissioned Leutnant 18 May 1918. Joined the Schutzpolizei in March 1920 as Leutnant. He was promoted Oberleutnant 21 July 1921and Hauptmann 23 September 1923. He transferred to the Gendarmerie 12 May 1927 and was promoted Major 1 April 1930. He was promoted Oberstleutnant der Gendarmerie 1 November 1937. He served in Poland, France, Russia and Czechoslovakia and finally at the Police Headquarters in Berlin and was promoted Oberst 1 January 1942. He was promoted Generalmajor der Police 1 January 1944. Joined the SS on 1 September 1942 and appointed to the rank of Brigadeführer with effect from 30 January 1944. After leaving his post in Berlin he was without assignment until he took over the Police Administration duties. He retired 1 March 1945. He was a married man with two children. He died in Ettlingen 22 July 1982.*

[10] Born on 27 October 1898 in Zittau (Sachsen). Joined the army on 15 November 1916 and served in the infantry until 27 September 1919. Promoted Vizefeldwebel und Reserve Offizieraspirant on 23 February 1918. Joined the Schutzpolizei on 27 September 1919 and was commissioned Leutnant on 31 January 1921. Served in Görlitz until 15 November 1929. Promoted Oberleutnant on 1 January 1925. Transferred to the Prussian Gendarmerie (Landjägerei) on 1 January 1928 and was promoted Landjäger Hauptmann on 1 October 1929. Served in Briesen and Trier until 15 February 1925. Then, he was appointed Kommandeur der Gendarmerie in Lyck serving until 1 December 1936, in Saarbrücken until September 1937 and Hakin until November 1939. Promoted Major der Gendarmerie on 1 October 1936 and Oberstleutnant on 1 October 1940. Served on Commissions in the Generalgouvernment of Poland until January 1941 and then in the SS Race and Settlement Office until November 1943. Promoted Oberst on 1 April 1943.

Headed the Amtsgruppe Kommando I in Hauptamt Ordnungspolizei from November 1943 and the Kommandoamt in Hauptamt Ordnungspolizei from 31 July 1944. Promoted Generalmajor der Polizei on 1 June 1944. Joined the Party on 3 September 1939 and the SS as Obersturmbannführer on 20 April 1941. Promoted Standartenführer on 20 April 1943, Oberführer on 21 June 1944 and Brigadeführer on 21 August 1944. He was a married man with two sons. Died in Schmiden near Stuttgart on 4 November 1978.

SS-Brigadeführer und Generalmajor der Polizei
Hans Flade — 30.11.1943–31.08.1944
Oberst der Schutzpolizei
Johannes Rogalski — 31.08.1944–08.05.1945

Amtsgruppe Kommando II: Personalangelegenheiten (Personnel questions)

Chef
SS-Brigadeführer und Generalmajor der Polizei
Wilhelm von Grolmann — 01.12.1940–30.09.1942

SS-Brigadeführer und Generalmajor der Polizei
Paul Otto Geibel [11] — 01.10.1942–31.03.1944

Generalmajor der Polizei
Arthur Bahl [12] — 01.04.1944–09.1944
Oberst der SCHUPO
Rudolf Abesser [13] — 09.1944–08.05.1945

Amtsgruppe Kommando III: Sanitätswesens (Medical Service)

Chef
Generalarzt der Polizei
Dr. Wilhelm Kloster [14] — 01.12.1940–12.02.1942

SS-Brigadeführer und Generalarzt der Polizei
Dr. Ernst Wenzel [15] — 12.02.1942–01.09.1943

SS-Brigadeführer und Generalmajor der Waffen-SS und der Polizei
Dr. Oscar Hock [16] 01.09.1943–30.4.1944

Generalarzt der Polizei
Dr. Friedrich Becker [17] 01.05.1944–01.10.1944

[11] *Born 10 June1898 in Dortmund (Ruhr). Served in the Imperial Navy during the Great War and then worked in a Insurance Company. Member of the SA from December 1931 until April 1935 rising to the rank of Sturmbannführer. Transferred to the SS in December 1938, he rose to the rank of Brigadeführer with effect from 26 October 1944. Joined the Gendarmerie 1 April 1935 with the rank of Major. He served at Police Headquarters in Berlin until March 1944 when he was appointed SS und Polizeiführer in Warsaw. Promoted Oberstleutnant 1 April 1939 and Oberst der Gendarmerie 14 July 1942. During Polish assignment, he also performed Police Administration duties. He was promoted Generalmajor der Polizei 1 September 1944. He was transferred to Prague 1 February 1945 as Commander of the Ordnungspolizei. Sentenced to imprisonment by the Poles, he committed suicide in prison at Varsovia 12 November 1966.*

[12] *Born on 9 August 1893. Joined the army and was commissioned Leutnant on the 19 December 1912. Served in the Great War being promoted Oberleutnant on 22 March 1918. Transferred to the Baden Schutzpolizei in January 1921 Promoted Hauptmann der Schutzpolizei on 1 January 1923 and Major on 1 October 1933. As Kommandeur der Schutzpolizei in Karlsruhe promoted Oberstleutnant on 1 January 1937. Appointed as Kommandeur der Schutzpolizei Köln in 1937. Ranked Oberst der Schutzpolizei on 1 January 1940. Served as Kommandeur der Offizierschule der Ordnungspolizei in Oranienburg (then Mariaschein in Sudetenland) from 1943 to March 1944. Posted to Hauptamt Ordnungspolizei as Leiter Amtsgruppe Kommando II on 1 April 1944. Promoted Generalmajor der Polizei on 1 September 1944. Kommandeur der Schutzpolizei in Wien from 1 September 1944 until the end of the war. He joined the Party on 1 May 1933. He was a married man with one child. He died in March 1966*

[13] *This office was abolished on 1 October 1944.*

[14] *Born on 22 August 1891 in Mülheim (Ruhr). Attended the Kaiser-Wilhelm Akademie in Berlin from 1910 to 1914 studying miltary medicine. Served in the army medical service from 1914 and graduated with a doctorate in 1917. From August 1919 he served in the Prussian state service as Oberarzt and was promoted Stabsarzt in 1920. Served as Hilfsreferent und Referent in the Prussian Ministry of the Interior and was promoted Polizei-Medizinalrat in 1922. Promoted Regierungs-und Medizinalrat in 1925, Oberregierung und Medizinalrat in 1927 and Ministerialrat in 1933. He was promoted Generalarzt der Landespolizei on 1 April 1935 and transferred to the Ordnungspolizei in June 1936. Served as head of the Amtsgruppe Kommando III in Hauptamt Ordnungspolizei from 1 December 1940 to 12 February 1942. He was placed in retirement in September 1942. A married man, he was not a member of the Party but was a member of the Party Welfare Agency. He died on 10 February 1953.*

[15] *Born on 8 June 1891 in Frankfurt an der Oder (Preussen). Attended the University of Berlin Medical School from 1909 to 1914. Graduated as a Doctor in 1919. Served as a medical officer in the infantry from 1 April 1910 to 20 August 1920. Commissioned Unterarzt in August 1914. Promoted Oberarzt on 25 October 1916 and Stabsarzt on 1 April 1920. Left the army and joined the Schutzpolizei as Oberstabsarzt der Polizei on 4 October 1920. Transferred to the Landespolizei on 1 April 1934 and back to the Schutzpolizei 1 June 1936. Promoted Oberfeldarzt der Polizei on 1 June 1936. Facharzt für Innere und Kinderkrankheiten in Berlin-Lankwitz (Specialist for internal medicine and for pediatrics) to 12 February 1942. Direktor der Staatskrankenhaus der Landespolizei in Berlin-Lankwitz on 1 April 1934 to 1 June 1936. Direktor der Staatskrankenhaus der Polizei in Berlin-Lankwitz to 12 February 1942. Promoted Oberstarzt der Polizei on 1 February 1939 and Generalarzt der Polizei on 1 February 1942.*

Leiter Amtsgruppe Kommando III in Haptamt Ordnungspolizei to 1 September 1943. Generalinspekteur für das Sanitätswesens in Hauptamt Ordnungspolizei from 1 April 1942 to 1 September 1943. He was retired from the Police 29 February 1944 and he went to work in industry. Betriebsarzt in H.Rommler A.G. in Sprembuerg Niederlaustiz to 21 April 1945. Joined the Party on 1 May 1937 and the SS as SS-Mann on 22 October 1934. SS NCO's from 1934 until 1938. Ranked Obersturmbannführer on 11 September 1938. Promoted Standartenführer on 28 January 1939, Oberführer on 15 February 1942 and Brigadeführer on 20 April 1942. He was a married man with two sons and one daughter. Committed suicide in Halbe on 21 April 1945.

[16] *Born on 31 January 1898 in Babenhausen (Westfalen). Joined the army 31 December 1916 and served in signals until 20 January 1919 ending with the rank of Unteroffizier and Offizieraspirant. Studied medicine at the medical schools in Würzburg, Erlangen and Giessen. Graduated Doctorate in Medicine in 1923. Practiced in Regen-Bayernwald until 1934. Joined the Party 1 September 1928. Bezirksarzt in Landau 1 August 1934. Kreisamtsleiter und Verwaltung Stellvertrender-Leiter des Amts für Volksgesundheits from 1 August 1934 to 1 August 1936. Joined the SS as Sturmbannführer on 1 August 1936. Served as a medical officer in the SS-Verfügungstruppen from 1 August 1936 to 25 September 1938. Promoted Obersturmbannführer 12 September 1937. Truppenarzt I. SS-Standarte "Der Führer" to 19 October 1939. Chef Sanitätsinspektion der SS-Totenkopfstandarten from 16 January 1940 to 15 August 1940. Sanitätsinspekteur der Waffen-SS to 15 February 1941.*

Promoted Standartenführer on 30 January 1941. Divisionsarzt der SS-Totenkopf-Division from 15 February 1942 to 21 June 1943. Promoted Oberführer 9 November 1942. Chef Amtsgruppe Kommando III in Hauptamt Ordnungspolizei from 1 September 1943 to 30 April 1944. Chef Sanitätswesens in Hauptamt Ordnungspolizei from 1 September 1943 to 10 April 1944. Promoted Brigadeführer und Generalmajor der Waffen-SS 1 September 1943. Given the rank of Generalmajor der Polizei 1 September 1943. Chef Amt XIII (Sanitätswesens) in SS Führungshauptamt from 10 April 1944 to 23 August 1944. Korpsarzt XIII. SS-Armee-Korps to 15 November 1944 and Korpsarzt II. SS-Panzer-Korps from 15 November 1944 to April 1945. Chef Krankenhaus Karlsbad April 1945. He was a married man with two sons and one daughter. He died in Leverkusen on 24June 1976.

[17] *Born on 28 June 1891 in Karlsruhe (Württemberg). Studied medicine and was awarded a Doctorate on 31 July 1919. Served in the Great War in the 4 Regiment of Foot Guards and then as medical officer to the 2 Kurassierregiment. Promoted Assistentarzt on 22 August 1917 and Oberarzt on 25 September 1919. Joined the Schutzpolizei on September 1919 as Oberarzt. Served on the organisation staff of the Schutzpolizei in Münster until February 1920 then on the medical staff of the Police School in Münster until 30 September 1926.*

Promoted Stabsarzt der Sicherheitspolizei in February 1920, Polizei-Medizinalrat on 1 April 1920. Leitender Polizeiarzt (Leading Police Medical Officer) to the Police Presidency in Recklinghausen from 1 October 1926 until 1941. Transferred to the BdO staff in Krakau as Leitender Polizeiarzt on 1 February 1941 and appointed Leitender Arzt SS und der Polizei beim Höhere SS und Polizeiführer "Ost" on 25 September 1943. Promoted Oberfeldarzt der Polizei on 1 August 1936, Oberstarzt der Polizei on 1 December 1940 and Generalarzt der Polizei on 1 February 1943. He was transferred back to Police Headquarters in Berlin as Chef des Sanitätswesens and Leiter Amtsgruppe Kommando III on 10 April 1944. He was placed in retirement on 9 November 1944 after having been denied promotion to Generalstabsarzt der Polizei. Joined the SA as Sanitäts-Sturmführer in September 1933 and joined the Party on 1 May 1937. He died on 12 November 1954.

Sanitatsämt (Medical Office)

This office was created on 1 October 1944 as an independent office directly under Hauptamt Ordnungspolizei. It took over the duties formerly undertaken by Amtsgruppe Kommando III of the Kommandoamt.

Chef
Oberstarzt der Schutzpolizei
Dr. Gustav Döderlein 01.10.1944–17.11.1944
SS-Oberführer und Generalarzt der Polizei
Dr. Kurt Hoffmann 17.11.1944–08.05.1945

Kolonialpolizeiamt (Colonial Police Office)

After the fall of France in 1940 it was decided that an attempt be made to regain some of Germany's old colonies. Various steps were taken in preparation for running such colonies, such as a series of courses in colonial policing that were run in Italy by the Ministry of Italian Africa under Generale Attilio Teruzzi. These courses were for members of the Sicherheitspolizei and the SD and ran from 18 November 1940 to 31 March 1941. In January 1941, Himmler also ordered the setting up of a colonial police office under the Hauptamt Ordnungspolizei to prepare the policing in such colonies. After the disasterous defeat at Stalingrad in February 1943 and the reverses in North Africa, it was decided that colonisation would not take place and the office was closed down in March 1943.

Chef
SS-Obergruppenführer und General der Waffen-SS und der Polizei
Karl Pfeffer-Wildenbruch 14.01.1941–03.1943

Amt Feuerwehren (Fire Brigade Office)

This office was a part of the move to bring the Fire Service under the direct control of the Ordnungspolizei. It was set up in May 1941 to control voluntary, regular and factory fire services and to administer the independant Amt für Freiwillige Feuerwehren (Voluntary Fire Brigade Office). It was abolished in the general reorganisation of september 1943. Its functions were allocated to the, by now, Reichsamt.

Freiwillige Feuerwehren

Chef
Generalmajor der Polizei
Walter Schnell [18] 09.05.1941–15.09.1943

Amt Technische Nothilfe (Technical Emergency Corps Office)
This office was created along similar lines as the Amt Feuerwehren to administer the Reichsamt Technische Nothilfe. Created in December 1941, it was also abolished in the general reorganisation of September 1943.

Chef
SS-Gruppenführer und Generalleutnant der Polizei
Hans Weinreich 12.1941–15.09.1943

Wirtschaftsverwaltungsamt (Supply and Administrative Office)

This Office was created in the reorganisation of September 1943 to run the supply, budget, welfare, legal and administrative affairs of the police. It was split into three Amtsgruppen, taking over duties formerly run by Amtsgruppe VuR III and part of VuR I of the abolished Amt Verwaltung und Recht plus two groups from the Kommandoamt. In December 1943, it took over Amtsgruppe II from the abolished Rechtsamt, this becoming Amtsgruppe W IV. It, in turn, was abolished in April 1944 and all its duties, except control of the Gewerbepolizei, were given to others Amtgruppen in Wirtschaftsverwaltungsamt. The Gewerbepolizei was given to the Reichssicherheitshauptamt.

Chef
Obergruppenführer und General der Waffen-SS und der Polizei

25 September 1919. Joined the Schutzpolizei on September 1919 as Oberarzt. Served on the organisation staff of the Schutzpolizei in Münster until February 1920 then on the medical staff of the Police School in Münster until 30 September 1926. Promoted Stabsarzt der Sicherheitspolizei In February 1920, Polizei-Medizinalrat on 1 April 1920. Leitender Polizeiarzt (Leading Police Medical Officer) to the Police Presidency in Recklinghausen from 1 October 1926 until 1941. Transferred to the BdO staff in Krakau as Leitender Polizeiarzt on 1 February 1941 and appointed Leitender Arzt SS und der Polizei beim Höhere SS und Polizeiführer "Ost" on 25 September 1943. Promoted Oberfeldarzt der Polizei on 1 August 1936, Oberstarzt der Polizei on 1 December 1940 and Generalarzt der Polizei on 1 February 1943. He was transferred back to Police Headquarters in Berlin as Chef des Sanitätswesens and Leiter Amtsgruppe Kommando III on 10 April 1944. He was placed in retirement on 9 November 1944 after having been denied promotion to Generalstabsarzt der Polizei. Joined the SA as Sanitäts-Sturmführer in September 1933 and joined the Party on 1 May 1937. He died on 12 November 1954.

[18] *Born on 6 January 1895, he served in the army during the Great War being commissioned Leutnant der Reserve on 16 March 1917. After the war he joined the fire service in Hannover as Provinzialfeuerwehrführer. Promoted Hauptmann der Reserve on 27 August 1939. He served as Amtschef for Amt Feuerwehren and as Head of the Reichsamt Freiwillige Feuerwehren in Hauptamt Ordnungspolizei. Promoted Oberst der Feuerschutzpolizei on 1 January 1941, brevet Generalmajor der Polizei on 20 April 1942 and was confirmed as Generalmajor der Polizei on 1 June 1942. He joined the Party on 1 April 1933. He died on 7 May 1967.*

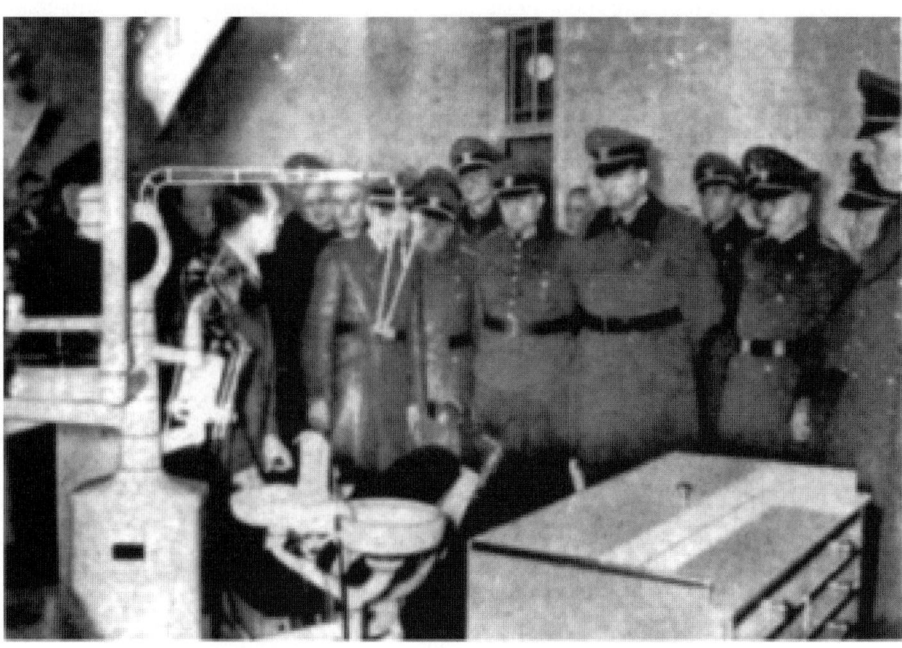

Inspection of a new Police Dental Hospital 1942, Kurt Daulege with SS-Obergruppenführer Dr. Ernst-Robert Grawitz and Oberstartz der Polizei, Dr. Otto Sitte.

August Frank [19] 15.09.1943–08.05.1945
SS-Oberführer, Ministerialrat Dr. Otto Diederichs i.V. 01.08.1944–08.05.1945
Amtsgruppe W I: Wirtschaft (Supply)

Chef
SS-Standartenführer und Oberst der Polizei
Hans Moser 15.09.1943–04.09.1944
Oberstleutnant der Schutzpolizei Eugen Hohmuth 04.09.1944–08.05.1945
Amtstgruppe WII: Verwaltung (Administration)

Chef
SS-Obergruppenführer und General der Waffen-SS und der Polizei
August Frank 15.09.1943–01.01.1944

SS-Oberführer, Ministerialrat Dr. Otto Diederichs 01.01.1944–08.05.1945
Amtstgruppe W III: Unterbringung (Quartering and Billetting)

Chef
Ministerialdirigent Rudolf Scheidel 15.09.1943–08.05.1945
Amtsgruppe **W IV**: Polizeirecht, Versorgung (Police Law, Allowances, and Pensions)

Chef
Ministerialrat
Georg Freiherr von Hohenastenberg gennant Wigandt 20.12.1943–08.05.1945

Rechtsamt (Legal Office)

This office was also created in the reorganisation of September 1943. Formed from six offices from the disolved Amt Verwaltung und Recht and one office from the Kommandoamt, the intention was to bring all police legal affairs under one man, however it did not work out and the department was abolished in December 1943. Divided into two Amtsgruppen, the first was absorbed partially by the Wirtschaftsverwaltungsamt and partially by a new post described as Jurist beim Chef der Ordnungspolizei. The second became Amtsgruppe W IV in the Wirtschaftsverwaltungamt.

Chef
SS-Gruppenführer und Generalleutnant der Waffen-SS und der Polizei
Heinz Reinefarth 15.09.1943–20.12.1943
Amtsgruppe R I: Polizeibeamtenrecht und Justitariat für die Ordnungspolizei (Police official rules and Legal matters)

Chef
Ministerialrat Maximilian Rheins 15.09.1943–20.12.1943
Amtsgruppe R II: Polizeirecht (Police legal matters)

Chef
Ministerialrat
Georg Freiherr von Hohenastenberg gennant Wigandt 15.09.1943–20.12.1943

Jurist beim Chef der Ordnungspolizei (Lawyer next to Chief of Ordnungspolizei)

This office was formed in December 1943 from Department I of Amtsgruppe RI and Departments 5,7 of the Amtsgruppe R II. It provided legal services to the whole of the Hauptamt Ordnungspolizei.

Chef
SS-Oberführer, Ministerialrat
Dr. Otto Diederichs 17.01.1944–08.05.1945

Technische SS und Polizeiakademie (Technical SS and Police Academy)

The Academy was created on 13 June 1942 from the Technical Police School in Berlin. Originally independent, it was put directly under Hauptamt Ordnungspolizei in September 1943 and its commander was ranked as an Amtschef. It was responsible for all research, development and the testing of police related technology.

Kommandeur
SS-Brigadeführer und Generalmajor der Polizei
Dr. Helmuth Gerloff 15.09.1943–30.09.1944

SS-Brigadeführer und Generalmajor der Polizei
Oskar Schmiedel [20] 30.09.1944–08.05.1945

[19] *Frank was appointed head of army Administration (Heeresverwaltung) on 1 August 1944. He retained his Police post but his duties were performed by his standing deputy, Dr. Otto Diedrichs.*

[20] *Born on 20 May 1897 in Dresden (Sachsen). Served in the Infanterie from 2 August 1914 to Autumn 1920. Commissioned Leutnant on 20 August 1915 and was promoted Oberleutnant on 9 August 1920. Worked in private business to 1934 and then joined the army as Oberleutnant January 1934. Promoted Hauptmann on 25 July 1934. Served as a company commander until 1938 and then transferred to the military transport department. Promoted Major on 1 June 1938. Chef der Amtsgruppe Motorisierung beim Generalbevollmächtigter der Rustungsamt beim Reichsministerium der Bewaffung und Munitions to 1 January 1943. Promoted Oberstleutnant on 1 April 1942. Transferred to the Schutzpolizei January 1943 as Oberst. Leiter Amt Kraftfahrwesens in Amtsgruppe Kommando I der Hauptamt Ordnungspolizei from 17 January 1943 to 15 September 1943.*

Generalinspekteur und Inspekteur

The first three General Inspectorates (Schutzpolizei des Reiches, Gendarmerie und Schulen) were formed in June 1936. A fourth one covering the Fire Service was added in June 1937. A fifth covering building and construction was added in January 1942 and a sixth and final one covering medical matters was created in April 1942. Three Inspectorates were created, the first covering Ideological Education in October 1939, the second covering Dentistry in July 1943 and the third covering the Waterways Protection Police in September 1943. A further six were added under the control of Amtsgruppe Kommando I in September 1943 and they were responsible for Air Raid protection, Fire Service Police, Signals, Motor Vehicles, Arms and Equipment and Veterinary Medicine. An independent Inspector of Cavalry was established in September 1943.

Generalinspekteur der Schutzpolizei des Reiches (Reich Protection Police)

This command was created in June 1936 as an Inspectorate. It was upgraded to General Inpector status on 1 September 1936. The command supervised the training of Schutzpolizei men and the provision of replacements, acting as a conduit between the Hauptamt and field formations. From September 1944, it was responsible for all police formations in Central and North Western Germany, including Denmark and the Benelux countries.

Generalinspekteur

Generalmajor der Polizei
Theodor Siebert — 17.06.1936 – 20.04.1937

SS-Gruppenführer und Generalleutnant der Polizei
Arthur Mülverstedt — 20.04.1937 – 01.04.1940

SS-Gruppenführer und Generalleutnant der Polizei
Georg Schreyer — 01.04.1940 – 30.06.1943

SS-Gruppenführer und Generalleutnant der Polizei
Herbert Becker — 01.07.1943 – 08.05.1945

Generalinspekteur der Gendarmerie und Schutzpolizei der Gemeinden (Rural Police and Municipal Protection Police)

This Inspectorate was formed in June 1936 as Inspector der Gendarmerie und Gemeindepolizei. It was upgraded to General Inspector status on 1 September 1936 and its name was changed on 28 September 1938. Supervising the training of Gendarms and Municipal Policemen and the provision of replacements, it was a conduit between the Hauptamt and field formations. From September 1944, it was responsible for all police formations in South and Southwestern Europe.

Generalinspekteur

SS-Obergruppenführer und General der Polizei
Jürgen von Kamptz — 17.06.1936 – 06.04.1937

SS-Brigadeführer und Generalmajor der Polizei
Wilhelm Roettig — 06.04.1937 – 10.09.1939

No Inspekteur appointed	10.09.1939 – 01.11.1940
SS-Obergruppenführer und General der Waffen-SS und der Polizei	
Rudolf Querner	01.11.1940 – 30.04.1941
SS-Obergruppenführer und General der Polizei	
Jürgen von Kamptz	30.04.1941 – 31.05.1943
SS-Gruppenführer und Generalleutnant der Polizei	
Emil Höring	01.06.1943 – 31.03.1944
SS-Gruppenführer und General der Polizei	
August Meyszner	01.04.1944 – 08.05.1945

Generalinspekteur der Schulen (General Inspector of Schools)

This Inspectorate was formed in June 1936. It was upgraded to General Inspector status on 1 September 1936, being responsible for supervising the speedy activation of Polizei-Regimenter (Police-Regiments) and Polizei-Schützen-Regimenter (Police-Rifle-Regiments). From September 1944, It was made responsible for all police formations in Eastern, North Eastern and Northern Europe.

Generalinspekteur

SS-Obergruppenführer und General der Waffen-SS und der Polizei	
Karl Pfeffer-Wildenbruch	17.06.1936 – 31.08.1943
No Inspector appointed	31.08.1943 – 31.10.1943
SS-Gruppenführer und Generalleutnant der Polizei	
Adolf von Bomhard	31.10.1943 – 01.02.1945
SS-Gruppenführer und Generalleutnant der Polizei	
Emil Höring	01.02.1945 – 08.05.1945

Generalinspekteur für die Feuerschutzpolizei und Feuerwehren (Fire Protection Police And Fire Brigades)

This Inspectorate was formed in January 1937 as Inspekteur des Feuerloschwesens (Fire Fighting forces) directly under the Reichs Ministry of the Interior. It was put under the Hauptamt Ordnungspolizei on 14 June 1937 and was upgraded to General Inspector status in March 1940. In July 1942 its title was changed to "Fire Police and Fire Brigade" (see above) and in the reorganisation of September 1943 it was split into two General Inspectorates. The first covered fire brigade training schools, factory fire brigades and the office responsible for investigating the causes of fires. The second covered professional and voluntary fire brigades, the fire service security police and the fire service officer school in Eberwalde.

Generalinspekteur

SS-Gruppenführer und Generalleutnant der Polizei	
Dr. Johannes Meyer	01.1937 – 15.09.1943

Generalinpekteur der Feuerschutzpoliei und Feuerwehren
(Fire Protection Police and Fire Brigades)

SS-Brigadeführer und Generalmajor der Polizei Hans Rumpf	15.09.1943 – 08.05.1945

Generalinspekteur der Feuerwehrschulen, Werkfeuerwehren und Brandschau (Fire Brigade Schools and Fires)

SS-Gruppenführer und Generalleutnant der Polizei
Dr. Johannes Meyer 15.09.1943 – 08.05.1945

Generalinspekteur für das Unterkunftswesens (Building and construtions)

This command was created in January 1942 to take over some of the duties carried out by Amtsgruppe III of Amt Verwaltung und Recht. It was responsible for the supervision of buildings and construction, was involved in the repair and administration of Police offices and living quarters and also for the establishment of new building programs. The command was abolished in September 1943 and its duties absorbed by Amtsgruppe WIII of the Wirtschaftsverwaltungsamt.

Generalinspekteur
Ministerialdirigent Rudolf Scheidel 01.01.1942 – 15.09.1943

Generalinspekteur für das Sanitätswesens (Medical matters)

Created in April 1942 to supervise all areas concerned with medical matters in conjunction with Amtsgruppe kommando III. The Generalinspekteur was also the head of Amtgruppe Kommando III until 15 September 1943.

Generalinspekteur
SS-Brigadeführer und Generalarzt der Polizei
Dr. Ernst Wenzel 04.1942 – 15.09.1943
SS-Obergruppenführer und General der Waffen-SS
Dr. Ernst Robert Grawitz 15.09.1943 – 20.04.1945

Generalinspekteur für Spezialabwehr (Special Defence)

This command was created in September 1944 to coordinate the Werwolf operation at a national level. It had previously operated as a decentralised organisation under individual Höhere SS und Polizeiführers. It was directly controlled by the Reichsführer-SS and only appeared under Hauptamt Ordnungspolizei for administrative and financial purposes.

Generalinspekteur
SS-Obergruppenführer und General der Waffen-SS und der Polizei
Hans-Adolf Prützmann 19.09.1944 – 08.05.1945

Inspekteur für die Weltanschauliche Erziehung (Ideological Training)

This Inspectorate was formed in October 1939 along the lines established by the Schulungsamt of the SS-Hauptamt. It was responsible for the ideological training of all police school commanders, tutors and speakers with a view to bringing the correct political indoctrination to all students in the police. It worked in conjunction with the Weltanschauliche Erziehung office in the Kommandoamt. To emphasis the connection with SS ideological training, the first inspector was also head of the Schulungsamt of the SS-Hauptamt and was a paid Allgemeine-SS officer and not a police officer. The last holder of the post was also from the Allgemeine-SS and did not have a police background.

Inspekteur

SS-Oberführer Dr. Joachim Caesar 17.10.1939 – 09.05.1942

SS-Gruppenführer und Generalleutnant der Polizei
Adolf von Bomhard 09.05.1942 – 01.01.1944

SS-Brigadeführer und Generalmajor der Waffen-SS
Ernst Fick 01.01.1944 – 29.04.1945

Inspekteur für den Zahnarztlichen Gesundheitsdienst (Dentistry)

This Inspectorate was created on 1 July 1943 to supervise all matters concerned with dentistry under the control of Amtsgruppe Kommando III. However, after only three months it was found to be unnecessary and in the reorganisation of September 1943 was abolished and its functions absorbed by the general medical office.

Inspekteur

SS-Standartenführer und Oberstarzt der Polizei Dr. Otto Sitte 01.07.1943 – 15.09.1943

Inspekteur der Wasserschutzpolizei (Waterways Protection Police)

This command was created in September 1943 to manage all water bourne police units and the water police schools in Lauterbach and Stettin. The headquarters of the Inspectorate was in Kiel but it maintained a working office at the Hauptamt Ordnungspolizei in Berlin.

Inspekteur

SS-Brigadeführer und Generalmajor der Polizei
Bruno Krumhaar 15.09.1943 – 30.06.1944
Oberst der Schutzpolizei Ernst Schröter 30.06.1944 – 08.05.1945

Inspekteur Amtsgruppe Kommando I

These six Inspectorates were created in September 1943 from the relevant offices in Office Group I. Unlike the above General Inspectorates and Inspectorates they were not independent offices directly under the Hauptamt but they remained under Amtsgruppe I leadership.

Inpektion Luftschutz (Air Raid Protection)

This command was formed from the air raid protection office within the Amtsgruppe. The department within the Inspection dealing with fire fighting was transferred to the Technische SS und Polizei Akademie in September 1944.

Inspekteur

Unknown 15.09.1943 – 08.05.1945

Inspektion Feuerschutzpolizei (Fire Protection Police)

The command was formed from the Amt Feuerschutzpolizei which was created within Amtsgruppe Kommando I in November 1937 to provide supervision over a security force protecting the fire service whilst they were fighting fires. The head of this office was Oberbaurat Walter Goldbach.

Inspekteur
Oberstleutnant der Feuerschutzpolizei
Johannes Schmidt 15.09.1943 – 08.05.1945

Inspektion Nachrichtenverbindungswesen (Signals Matters)

This command was formed from Amt für Nachrichtenverbindungswesen that was created as part of a group of offices within the Technisches Amt in June 1936. It became a separate office in Amtsgruppe Kommando I in December 1940 when the Technische Amt was abolished. Its task was to supervise all signals and communication pertaining to the Ordnungspolizei.

Inspekteur
SS-Brigadeführer und Generalmajor der Polizei
Robert Schlake 15.09.1943 – 08.05.1945

Inspektion Kraftfahrwesen (Motor Vehicles)

This command was formed from Amt Kraftfahrwesen and its history and background is the same as the Signals Inspectorate (above). Its task was to supervise all vehicular transport for the Ordnungspolizei.

Inspekteur
SS-Brigadeführer und Generalmajor der Polizei
Oskar Schmiedel 15.09.1943 – 08.05.1945

Inspektion Waffen und Gerätewesen (Arms and Equipment)

This command was formed from Amt Waffen und Gerätewesen and its history and background was similar to the Signals Inspectorate. Its task was to supervise the provision and use of weapons and munitions pertaining to the Ordnungspolizei.

Inspekteur
SS-Brigadefühter und Generalmajor der Polizei
Karl Fischer 15.09.1943 – 08.05.1945

Inspektion Veterinärwesen (Veterinary Medicine)

This command was formed as the Veterinary Office on 30 June 1936 and it became part of the Amtsgruppe Kdo I in December 1940. It was transferred to Amtsgruppe Kdo II in October 1942 and returned to Amtsgruppe Kdo I on the formation of the Inspectorate in September 1943. Its task was to supervise all veterinary matters pertaining to the Ordnungspolizei.

Inspekteur
Generalveterinär der Polizei
Dr. Wilhelm Kries 15.09.1943 – 01.10.1944
SS-Oberführer und Oberstveterinär der Polizei
Dr. Karl Pfragner 01.10.1944 – 08.05.1945

Inspektion der Kavallerie (Cavalry)

Little is known about this Inspectorate, presumably it was to supervise any cavalry with a police connection but it does not appear under any of the Group Offices. It was probably connected with Inspektion 3 Reit und Fahrwesen in Amtsgruppe C of the SS-Führungshauptamt.

Inspekteur
SS-Obersturmbannführer und Oberstleutnant der Schutzpolizei
Rudolf Ruge 09.43 – 08.05.1945

Reichsämter (Reich Offices)

Two Offices were listed under the umbrella of the Hauptamt Ordnungspolizei. The reason for the distinction was that all Offices were controlled by the Kommandoamt or Verwaltung und Recht Amt (after September 1943 Wirtschaftsverwaltungsamt). The two Offices listed below were given the title Reichs Ämter (Reich Offices) to show that they were independent of the Hauptamt. They are shown under formal authority of the Hauptamt Ordnungspolizei because it was responsible for personnel matters and they came within the Main Office's pay structure. As both were considered part of the General Ordnungspolizei structure, they were subject to orders applied to Ordnungspolizei as a whole. Further than that they retained their independence.

Reichsamt Technische Nothilfe (Technical Emergency Corps)

This office was created in 1934 and its history and scope can be found in the chapter on the Technische Nothilfe.

Leiter
SS-Gruppenführer und Generalleutnant der Polizei
Hans Weinreich 24.04.1934 – 15.10.1943
SS-Gruppenführer und Generalleutnant der Polizei
Willy Schmelcher 15.10.1943 – 08.05.1945

Reichsamt Freiwillige Feuerwehren (Fire Brigades)

This office was created in March 1942. Its history and scope can be found in the chapter on the fire service.

Leiter
Generalmajor der Polizei Walter Schnell 11.03.1942 – 08.05.1945

In December 1943, a Reichsinspektion der zivil Luftkriegsmassnahmen (Inspection for Civil Air War Tasks) was created as a Party office under the Gauleiter for South-Hannover-Braunschweig, SS-Obergruppenführer Hartmann Lauterbacher. It was formed to centralize the battle against air raids. At the same time, the Reichsführer-SS appointed a beauftragter (representative) to co-ordinate efforts by the police and the fire service in this battle. He operated under the aegis of Hauptamt Ordnungspolizei and had a staff of six officers, three from the Schutzpolizei and three from the Feuerschutzpolizei.

Beauftragter
SS-Gruppenführer und Generalleutnant der Polizei Herbert Becker

Stab Schutzpolizei
Oberst der Schutzpolizei Herbert Melchior
SS-Standartenführer und Oberst der Schutzpolizei Hermann Fuchs
Oberst der Schutzpolizei Hauser

Stab Feuerschutz
SS-Sturmbannführer und Major der Feuerschutzpolizei Josef Steiner
Major der Feuerschutzpolizei Adam
SS-Standartenführer und Oberst der Feuerschutzpolizei Georg Schetzker.

Adolf Hitler greets H. Himmler

Branches of the Ordnungspolizei

2.1 Landespolizei (Barracked Territorial Police)

After the end of the Great War, one of the articles of the Versailles Treaty was that the German army would be reduced to 100,000 officers and men. As a result a large number of former soldiers suddenly found themselves without a job. So, the new republic, which was undergoing violent birth pains, found itself short of trained men to protect the new state. In the summer of 1919, in an attempt to deal with the situation, barracked security police (kasernierte Sicherheitspolizei) were set up employing former soldiers. The first units appeared in Preussen with other Länder quickly following and Kommandostab (command staffs) were set up in Berlin, Kassel, Magdeburg, Breslau and Königsberg. They controlled forces with the size of a brigade commanded by a former army general. Although this new force was set up to combat general lawlessness in the Republic, the Allied Control Commission decided that it contravened the treaty and the new force was banned by the Decree of Boulogne dated 22 July 1920. This state of events remained until the National Socialists took power in 1933.

On the 1 April 1933, the Ministerpräsident of Preussen, Hermann Göring, issued a ministerial decree which set up a new barracked police unit separate from the Schutzpolizei. Göring stated that "in complete devotion to the Führer" the new unit would be capable and willing to stamp out any spark of resistence before it could become a threat to the new regime. The formation of this unit was entrusted to Major der Schutzpolizei Walter Wecke on the 23 February 1933. Two days later, Wecke reported that Polizei-Abteilung z.b.V "Wecke" (Special Police Battalion Wecke) with a strength of 14 officers and 400 men had been established. They were initially billeted in the barracks in Kreuzberg (Berlin District), the former barracks of the 4 Guards Grenadier Regiment "Queen Augusta".

They later moved to Berlin Charlottenburg, to the former barracks of the 3 Guards Grenadier Regiment "Queen Elizabeth". In May 1933, the unit moved to the Lichterfelde Barracks alongside the SS-Stabswache Berlin (SS-Staff Guard Berlin). On 17 June, the unit was renamed Landespolizeigruppe "Wecke" z.b.V (Territorial Police Group Wecke at special disposal) becoming the first Landespolizei unit in Germany. On 13 September 1933, Göring presented the unit with a new flag and at the presentation ceremony he stated "It is my objective to transform the Prussian Police Force into a sharpedged weapon equal to the Reichswehr, which I can deliver to the Führer when the day comes for us to fight our external enemies". On 22 December 1933, the unit was again retitled being called Landespolizeigruppe "General Göring" and command was passed to Oberstleutnant der Schutzpolizei Friedrich Jakoby on the 6 June 1934. With effect from 1 October 1935 this unit was transferred to the Luftwaffe following the formation of the forgoing unit, Göring decided to establish a barracked police for the whole of Preussen. On 13 September 1933, Kurt Daulege was appointed Befehlhaber der Kasernierte Landespolizei (Commander of Barracked Territorial Police). Seven Landesinspektions (District Inspections) were set up covering the whole Preussen.

General der Polizei Kurt Daulege

Landesinspektion Südost (Breslau)
Generalmajor der Polizei Heinrich Niehoff

Landesinspektion Brandenburg (Berlin)
Generalmajor der Polizei Richard Baltzer until June 1934
Oberst der Landespolizei Walter Wecke from June 1934

Landesinspektion Mitte (Magdeburg)
Generalmajor der Polizei Georg von dem Knesebeck

Landesinspektion Nord (Stettin)
Oberst der Landespolizei Karl Strecker (promoted Generalmajor 1 April 1934)

Landesinspektion West (Düsseldorf)
Generalmajor der Polizei Hans Stieler von Heydekampf to June 1934
Generalmajor der Polizei Richard Baltzer from June 1934 until 16 March 1936

Landesinspektion Südwest (Frankfurt am Main)
Generalmajor der Polizei Georg Poten

Landesinspektion Ost (Königsberg)
Oberst der Landespolizei Georg Bertram
A decree dated from 15 November 1933 gave authority to the Prussian Inspections over the small Landespolizei forces of the Länders through a Reich Zwichenbefehlstelle
(Reich Liaison Command)

Landesinspektion Südwest covered States Hessen and Thüringen
Landesinspektion Nord covered State Mecklenburg and the Hanseatic Free Town Lübeck
Landesinspektion Mitte covered States Anhalt, Braunschweig and Oldenburg

Police conference Berlin 1934, left to right: Otto Dilenburger, von Levetzow (civilian),Landespolizei Kurt Daulege, Generalmajor der Landespolizei Ferdinand von Zepelin, Richard Baltzer, Oberst der Landespolizei

Generalleutnant der Landespolizei Hans Steiner von Heydekamp

A new Liaison Command was set up in Stuttgart to co-ordinate the Landespolizei of States Württemberg and Baden. It was placed under Oberst der Landespolizei Wolfgang Schmidt-Logan who also commanded the Landespolizei in Württemberg, the Landespolizei in Baden was under the command of Oberst der Landespolizei Franz Vaterrodt who also commanded the Gendarmerie of State Baden.

The larger Länder had their own command structure called Landesbefehlstellen (State Command):
Landesbefehlstelle State Bayern (München)
Generalmajor der Landespolizei Heinrich Doehla

Landesbefehlstelle State Sachsen (Dresden)
Oberst der Landespolizei Hans Meissner

Landesbefehlstelle Hanseatic Free Town Hamburg (Hamburg)
Oberst der Landespolizei Werner Hüber
Göring also decided that the police troop emblems from the former German colonies should be revived and would be worn by a current police unit in honour of past duties. Emblems were allocated as follows:

The emblem for Deutsch Südwest Afrika (German South West Africa) was given to the Landespolizei in Bremen.

The emblem for Deutsch Ost Afrika (German East Africa) was given to Landespolizeigruppe General Göring.

On the 30 January 1934, with the decree about the rebuilding of the Reich, all the Länder governments came under centralised authority of Berlin. As a result Oberst der Landespolizei Erich Lüdke was appointed "Generalinspekteur und Befehlhaber der Landespolizei" (General Inspector and Commander of Landespolizei) for the whole Germany. He feuded with Hermann Göring and consequently he was transferred to the post of Leiter der Ausbildung der Polizeieinheiten in Reichswehrministerium (Head of Police Training in the War Ministry) on 1 February 1934. Göring took over direct command of the Landespolizei with the title of Supreme Commander of the German Police "Oberbefehlhaber der Gesamten Deutschen Polizei" and appointed Kurt Daluege as "Befehlhaber der Gesamten Deutschen Polizei" (Commander of the whole German Police).

Landespolizei units were listed in the mobilisation organisation alongside the Schutzpolizei and the Gendarmerie for military training. They were also used for protection duties and for coastal security. The internal organisation of a territorial inspection was:

Landesinspektion/Landesbefehlstellen equivalent to an infantry division in size

Generalmajor der Landespolizei, Erich Lüdke, shown as General der Infanterie in Denmark

Gruppen equivalent to a regiment
Abteilungen equivalent to a battalion
Hundertschaften equivalent to a company

A decree of the Defense Ministry dated 8 February 1934 co-ordinated the police forces and put them under the orders of the army in case of outbreak of war. The Inspection level was to be used to oversee this change and the Landespolizeibrigaden were formed. They were to be subordinated to the Wehrkreis (army Districts).
The former Ausbildungsleitung der Landespolizei (Training office of the Landespolizei) which was equivalent to a regiment headquarters in size was organized into 29 Landespolizeigruppen. (Landespolizei Groups)

The Order of battle of the Landespolizei groups from the 1 October 1934 was:

State Preussen	16 Groups
(including Landespolizeigruppe	"General Göring" in Berlin)
State Württemberg	1 Group
State Baden	1 Group
State Mecklenburg	1 Group
Free Town Bremen	1 Group
State Thüringen	1 Group
State Hessen	1 Group
State Bayern	3 Groups
State Sachsen	2 Groups
Free Town Hamburg	2 Groups

Landespolizei battalions consisted of cavalry and infantry battalions.
The infantry battalions were made up of:
three infantry companies
one machine gun (Maschinengewehr or MG) machine gun company
one (Minenwerfer) light company
and one (Panzerabwehr) anti-tank company.

On 21 May 1935, the Reichstag passed a law called the Wehrgesetz (Defence Law) which covered general questions of organisation. It laid down specific conditions governing the duration and size of the conscription programme and determined the liability of individuals for service. A secret law called Reichsverteidigungsgesetz (Reich Defence Law) was also passed. This conferred upon Hitler the power of declaration of war, mobilization and creation of a 'state of defence'. These Laws introduced re-armament and created the Wehrmacht (Armed Forces) to oversee the army, Navy and Air Force.

As a result of these laws the Landespolizei was transferred to the army. A Cabinet meeting which took place during the afternoon of the 16 March 1935, discussed the transfer of the Landespolizei to the army. Hermann Göring, as Minister President of Preussen, was reluctant to surrender complete control of any of his forces. The Reichswehr Minister, General Werner von Blomberg, argued with him and a compromise was reached: the Landespolizeigruppe "General Göring" was transferred as a regiment into Luftwaffe and the remainder of the Landespolizei went to the army. On the 21 March 1935, Hitler announced that the central staff of the Landespolizei was to pass from the command of the Minister of the Interior to the Commander-in-Chief of the army. The various units of the police were to pass into the army, while their police functions were to be taken over by the local police.

An important exception to this transfer besides the "General Göring" regiment was the Landespolizei force which was stationed in the demilitarized zone (the Rhineland and the fifty kilometer strip on the eastern bank of the Rhine). On 1 August 1935, the officers of the Landespolizei were transferred directly into the army. A small number of such officers transferred directly into the SS, to give one example; Wilhelm Hartenstein who held the rank of Colonel and had commanded the 1 Landespolizeiregiment in Hamburg joined the Allgemeine-SS as SS-candidate on the 18 June 1934. He rose to the rank of Brigadeführer and commanded the 1. SS-Infanterie-Brigade in Russia. He died on the 27 January 1944. On the 1 October 1935, the various units of the Landespolizei were completely incorporated into the army. This increased the strength of the army by 58 battalions (53 infantry, 2 signales, 2 cavalry and 1 despatch rider) plus 6 Police schools. 28 battalions, all located all in the demilitarized zone, remained under the official control of the Minister of the Interior. A total of 60,000 officers and NCO were transferred to the army to become the framework of staff s and field units. Following the return of the demilitarized zone to Germany in 25 March 1936, the Landespolizei units were incorporated into the local Military District or were disbanded.

The Landespolizei and the Wehrmacht

The General Corps of the army included 15 Generals, 84 Generalleutnants and 160 Generalmajors who had served in the Landespolizei. The former Landesinspektion Commanders served as follows:

Richard Baltzer Born 1 June 1886 in Danzig. Transferred to the staff of the 26 Infantry Division (Ostpreussen) on 16 March 1936. Commander of the Reserve army of Allenstein (Preussen) on 1938. Promoted Generalleutnant on 1 October 1939. Commander of the 217 Infantery Division from 1939 until 1942. Commander of the Depot Division 156 until end 1943. He commanded the 182 Training Division on march 1944. Awarded German Cross in Gold. He was killed in Prague 10 May 1945.

George Bertram Born 31 August 1882 in Danzig. Transferred to the army as Commander of Stettin on 15 October 1935 as Generalmajor with seniority from 1 October 1935. Promoted Generalleutnant on 1 August 1939. He served on the Reich War Court from September 1939 until September 1942. He held rear area commands until the end of the war. He was awarded the German Cross in Silver. Died in Bad Pyrmont 27 October 1953.

Heinrich Doehla Born 3 November 1881 in München. Transferred to the army as Generalmajor on 1 August 1935. Garrison Commander of München until December 1939 when he took over command of the 537 Infantery Division. Promoted Generalleutnant on 1 February 1941. He served as a rear area commander until 12 November 1943. Retired on 31 March 1944. Died in Stuttgart 14 July 1956.

Generalmajor der Landespolizei
Bernhard Graf von Poninski 1928
Source: Josef Wotka

George von dem Knesebeck Born 25 July 1881 in Hameln. Transferred to the army on 15 October 1935 as Garrsion Commander of Münster and ranked Generalmajor. On 1 April 1937 he became Inspector of the Recruiting for Münster until 28 February 1945 when he retired. He was promoted Generalleutnant on 1 February 1941. Died in Münster 2 June 1955.

Erich Lüdke Born 20 October 1882 in Naumburg. Transferred to the army on 15 June 1935 as Generalmajor. Commanded the 9 Infantry Division until March 1936 and then 34 Infantry Division. Promoted Generalleutnant on 1 November 1935. Commander of the Wehrkreis X (Hamburg) until 1 June 1940 and then Militärbefehlhaber (Commander in Chief) in Denmark until 27 September 1942. Promoted General der Infanterie on 1 December 1940. Retired on 31 January 1944. Died as a Russian prisoner of war in 1946.

Heinrich Niehoff Born 20 November 1882 in Bochum. He transferred to the Luftwaffe as Generalmajor and Vice-President of the Luftschutzbundes in February 1936. He was promoted Generalleutnant on 30 January 1938 and was retired on 31 March 1938. He was recalled to the army as an Field HQ Commander in North France in February 1941. Then he was Commander of the army Group Rear Area South France until he retired in August 1944. Died as a Russian prisoner 19 February 1946.

Georg Poten Born 14 December 1881 in Berlin. Transferred to the army as Generalmajor on 16 March 1936. Served as Inspector for Recruiting at Koblenz. He was promoted Generalleutnant on the 'at Disposal' list on 1 June 1941. Retired on 31 December 1941. He died in Hannover 4 May 1965.

Wolfgang Schmidt-Logan Born 8 September 1884 in Ludwigsburg. Transferred to the army as Generalmajor on the 1 April 1936. Garrison Commander at Pforzheim until 31 March 1938. He was placed in retirement. Recalled on the 10 September 1939 and served as a rear area commander until the 31 October 1943 when he was retired again. Promoted Generalleutnant on the 'at Disposal' list on 1 February 1941. Committed suicide at Schliersee 4 May 1945.

Hans Stieler von Heydekampf Born 24 August 1880 in Berlin. He was retired from the Landespolizei on the 1 October 1934. Recalled to the army on 1 February 1937 as Inspector for the Supplies in Wehrkreis IX. Equipment Inspector in Wehrkreis III on 6 February 1940. Promoted Generalleutnant on 1 February 1941. He served as Equipment Inspector in East. Retired on 30 November 1942. Died as a Russian Prisoner of War 31 December 1946.

Karl Strecker Born on 20 September 1884 in Radmannsdorf in Westpreussen. Transferred to the army on 14 June 1935 as Commander of Infantery Regiment 4. He was promoted Generalleutnant on 1 June 1940 and General der Infanterie on 1 April 1942. He served as Commander of the Infantery Division 79 from September 1939 until January 1942. Commander of the XVII. Army Corps from April to June 1942. He was captured in Stalingrad on 2 February 1943 as Commander of the IX. Army Corps. He was promoted Generaloberst by wireless-message but had already been captured. He was awarded the Knight´s Cross and the German Cross in Gold. He returned from captivity on the 9 October 1955. He died in Idar Oberstein 10 April 1973.

Generalmajor der Landespolizei Karl Strecker (here as General der Infantry and a Knight´s Cross Holder)

Franz Vaterrodt Born 29 April 1890 in Diedenhofen. Transferred to the army as Oberstleutnant on 1 August 1935. Served as a regiment commander until March 1941. Wehrmachtkommandant of Strassburg from 1941 until 25 November 1944 when he was captured by the Americans. Promoted Oberst on the 1 March 1937 and Generalmajor on 1 March 1941.

Walther Wecke Born 30 September 1885 in Nennhausen in Westhavelland. Transferred to the army on 1 October 1935 as Generalmajor, he was transferred to the Luftwaffe on 16 September 1937. Commander of the Reichsluftschutzschule (Air Raid Protection School). He served as Commander der Luftwaffen-Übungsplatz Malacki (Luftwaffe Training Camp) in Slovakia. Promoted General der Luftwaffe on the 'at Disposal' list on 1 December 1942. Died 16 December 1943

Ferdinand von Zepelin Born 12 April 1886 in Berlin. Transferred to the army as Generalmajor 1 October 1935 with senority from 1 April 1938. Inspekteur der Wehrersatzinspektion Hannover until 1 May 1942. Promoted brevet Generalleutant 1 June 1940 and was confirmed in that rank 1 June 1942. Retired 31 July 1942. He died in Hannover 6 November 1962.

Generalmajor der Landespolizei Richard Baltzer

The Landespolizei and the Ordnungspolizei

A minority of the Landespolizei officers was transferred to the Schutzpolizei. They provided a trained cadre that formed the basis of the new Ordnungspolizei. First of all Kurt Daluege, the former Commander of the Landespolizei took over the head of the ORPO on 1936, he took with him a group of former Landespolizei officers to set up the new Uniformed Police Main Office. First in Germany in 30's then during the war in occupied countries, most of these officers held Senior Field Command: Inspekteur der ORPO, Befehlhaber der ORPO, Kommandeur der ORPO or Regimentkommandeur. Another group of former Landespolizei officers took command in the Police Divisions in the Waffen-SS

The Landespolizei and the Waffen-SS

The first units of the militarized SS known as Politische Bereitschaft (Political Barracked units) were created on 1933 in Württemberg then in Bayern. Organised into battalions of 3 infantry companies and 1 Motor Gun company these units were renamed Verfügungstruppen (Troops at disposal known as SS-VT). 2 SS-Officers Schools were created for the training of the merging leader corps. The SS-recruited officers and NCO of the Landespolizei to instruct its own barracked units in the SS-VT Regiment "Deutschland" in München, Georg Ritter von Hengl set up 1 Battalion on 1934, followed by Georg Keppler another Landespolizei officer in 1935. Heinz Bertling took over this battalion on 1938. Karl Maria Demelhuber used the 2 battalion of the SS-VT Regiment "Deutschland" to create the new SS-VT Regiment in Hamburg during 1936. In the staff of the SS-VT, Walter Neblich took over the Department "Transport" and August Frank served as a skilled administrative staff officer. In the Leibstandarte SS "Adolf Hitler", no less than 4 officers of the Landespolizei became junior officers in 1934. Two of them became noteworthy in the Waffen-SS: Kurt Meyer better known as "Panzermeyer" and Walter Bestmann. During the war, 8 officers of Landespolizei became Commanders of Field Units of the Waffen-SS (Brigade, Division, Army Corps) and 7 officers took over staff duties as Majors.

The Landespolizei and the Luftwaffe

The Landespolizeigruppe "Hermann Göring" as a whole joined the Luftwaffe on September 1935 to become Regiment "General Göring". 5 of its officers rose to General rank. 29 Landespolizei officers who joined Luftwaffe after 1936 rose to the rank of General. Few of them served in Field Units, they served in Technical Units (Signals, Medical, Equipment, Recruiting, School), administrative duties (Luftgau administration) or were involved into Air Raid Protection duties.

Machinegun training for the Landespolizei

2.2 Schutzpolizei (Uniformed Protection Police)

Based upon model of the " Schutzmannschaft " and " Stadtgendarmeriekorps, " the Gemeinde Polizei (Municipal Police) was created in the middle of the 19th Century relative to development of the population in urban zones. After the Great War, in regard to the rising insecurity, the German States developped Sicherheitspolizei or SIPO (Security Police) in large towns for public safety. During the Weimar, Sicherheitspolizei became Schutzpolizei (Protection Police). In small towns, the Municipal Police remained responsible for public safety and security.

2.2.1 Schutzpolizei des Reich (State Protection Police)

Staff organisation of the Schutzpolizei
The State Protection Police was the executive police arm in uniform of the Police Administrations (See chapter "Police Administrations"). At the head of the Schutzpolizei, a Kommandeur der Schutzpolizei (Commander of the Schutzpolizei) had rank based upon size of the town: Generalmajor der Polizei, Oberst der Schutzpolizei, Oberstleutnant der Schutzpolizei or Major der Schutzpolizei. The staff was organised as a Kommando der Schutzpolizei or KdSCHUPO (Commando of the Protection Police) with the following offices:

Organisation
Clothing, Equipment, Weapons
Personnel
Air Raid Protection

Units of a Kommando der Schutzpolizei

Polizei-Kompanie (Police Company)

The Police companies were barracked units of the Schutzpolizei including the youngest policemen. They were employed as reserve for Revierdienst (Police station duties), staff for accident brigades, street safety and security around airraid or accident damage. The size of a company depended on the size of the Police District. For service abroad, companies were organized into Polizei-Bataillone. In areas incorporated into the Reich (West Poland, East France, etc.), a Police Battalion had a headquarters in the suburbs of the major towns and companies had various duties. These included service with Police Administration, control of the boundaries, providing support to the SIPO during actions against partisans and transfer of population. They also served as warders in POW camps and Polizeigefängnis (Police prisons). For its duties in the control of motor traffic, Police Companies had an Überfallkommando (Accident Brigade) attached with technical and emergency cars. The Wasserschutzpolizei (Waterways police) was a special branch of the Schutzpolizei involved in the control of the waterways and harbours (see Chapter "Wasserschutzpolizei"). Reiterstaffel (Mounted Sections) were created in State Police Administrations for special use.

The size is depended on the Police District: in Berlin and Wien, the mounted unit had the size of a Reiterabteilung (Mounted Battalion). Their employment was generally in outareas of the town: urban areas, woods and fields. The Kraftfahrstaffel (Motor Section) was organized into Kraftfahrbereitschaft (car park), Mot. Vehrkehrbereitschaft (Motorized Traffic Police) and Vehrkehr Unfall Bereitschaft (Motorized Accident Brigade) The Motorized Section was involved in the management of the motorized units of the Police Administration. The Nachrichtenstaffel (Signal Section) took over the

signals of the Schutzpolizei and provided staff for Radio, Phone and and Telegraphy posts of the Police Adminstration. The Schutzpolizei was connected to the Reich Police Network. The staff of the Sanitätsdienst
(Medical Office) assisted the Police Medical Officers of the Sanitätsstellen (Medical Posts). Police Veterinary Officers were next appointed to Reiterstaffel. Other administrative units existed as follows: Waffenmästerei (Weapons and ammunitions), Bekleidungstelle (Clothing), Polizeikantine (Police Restaurant).

Field organisation of the Schutzpolizei

Until the unification of the Reich, each State developed its own organisation of Schutzpolizei. Later the number of Schutzpolizei commands was based upon the creation or disbanding of Police Administrations.

In Alt Reich (Old Reich):
State Preussen: 42 KdSCHUPO in 1944 (three were situated in the annexed areas of Memeland and Polish Schlesien),
State Bayern: 6 KdSCHUPO
State Sachsen: 5 KdSCHUPO
State Württemberg: 15 KdSCHUPO
State Baden: 13 KdSCHUPO
State Thüringen: 6 KdSCHUPO
State Hesse: 5 KdSCHUPO
States Mecklenburg, Oldenburg, Braunschweig, and Anhalt: 1 KdSCHUPO
Hanseatic Towns Hamburg and Bremen: 1 KdSCHUPO
Reichsgau Westmark: 4 KdSCHUPO
2 small states (Lippe and Schaumburg Lippe) without 1.
In Annexed Areas:
Österreich: 11 KdSCHUPO
Sudetenland: 5 KdSCHUPO
West Poland (Danzig Westpreussen and Wartheland): 9 KdSCHUPO
France and Luxemburg: 4 KdSCHUPO

The organisation for 1942/1943:

Kommando der Schutzpolizei	**Kommandeur**
Preussen	
Königsberg	Oberst der Schutzpolizei Hübert Sapp
Memel (*)	Major der Schutzpolizei Otto Günthe
Berlin	Generalmajor der Polizei Otto Klinger
Tilsit	Major der Schutzpolizei Paul Kärnbach
Potsdam	Major der Schutzpolizei August Kautsch
Frankfurt an der Oder	Major der Schutzpolizei Robert Schmidt
Stettin	Oberstleutnant der Schutzpolizei Paul Wolff
Breslau	Oberst der Schutzpolizei Hermann Crux

Waldenburg	Major der Schutzpolizei Dudler
Gleiwitz	Oberstleutnant der Schutzpolizei Küllmer
Kattowitz (*)	Oberst der Schutzpolizei
	Maximillan Himmelstoss
Sosnowitz (*)	Oberstleutnant der Schutzpolizei Hermann Balke
Oppeln	Major der Schutzpolizei Karl-Wilhelm Lange
Magdeburg	Oberstleutnant der Schutzpolizei Gerhard Hoppe
Wittenberg	Major der Schutzpolizei Leo Dalmann
Halle an der Saale	Major der Schutzpolizei Klaus
Bitterfeld	Major der Schutzpolizei Paul Fydrich
Weisenfels	Oberstleutnant der Schutzpolizei Buscher
Erfurt	Major der Schutzpolizei Wehlow
Sühl	Hauptmann der Schutzpolizei Gies
Flensburg	Major der Schutzpolizei Paulus Meier
Kiel	Oberstleutnant der Schutzpolizei Fritz-Karl Wirths
Lübeck	Oberstleutnant der Schutzpolizei Joachim von Funcke
Hannover	Oberstleutnant der Schutzpolizei Ferdinand Heske
Wesermünde	Major der Schutzpolizei Stark
Cuxhaven	Major der Schutzpolizei Roth
Münster	Oberstleutnant der Schutzpolizei Ernst Zicklam
Recklinghausen	Oberst der Schutzpolizei Kurt Göhrum
Bochum	Oberst der Schutzpolizei Werner Volkerling
Dortmund	Oberst der Schutzpolizei Wilhel Stöwe
Hamm	Major der Schutzpolizei Stolzenberg
Kassel	Oberst der Schutzpolizei Wilhelm von Thaden
Hanau	Major der Schutzpolizei Josef Oberresch
Frankfurt am	Main Oberstleutnant der Schutzpolizei Hamel
Wiesbaden	Major der Schutzpolizei Richard von Coelln
Koblenz	Major der Schutzpolizei Heinrich Steffen
Düsseldorf	Oberstleutnant der Schutzpolizei Hermann Fuchs
Duisburg	Oberstleutnant der Schutzpolizei Timaeus
Essen	Oberst der Schutzpolizei Edmund Krause
Wuppertal	Oberst der Schutzpolizei Martini
Mönchengladbach-Rheydt	Oberstleutnant der Schutzpolizei Bruch Oberhausen
	Oberstleutnant der Schutzpolizei Taute
Köln	Oberst der Schutzpolizei Max Daume
Aachen	Oberst der Schutzpolizei Richard Weber
Luxemburg (*)	Oberstleutnant derSchutzpolizei Kalden
Bayern	
München	Oberst der Schutzpolizei Ludwig Mühe
Regensburg	Major der Schutzpolizei Röckner
Nürnberg-Fürth	Oberst der Schutzpolizei Otto Kuschow
Hof	Oberstleutnant der Schutzpolizei Meyer-Spelbrink
Würzburg	Oberstleutnant der Schutzpolizei Herzog
Augsburg	Major der Schutzpolizei Stäb

Sachsen	
Dresden	Oberst der Schutzpolizei Hermann Keuper
Leipzig	Oberst der Schutzpolizei Schleich
Chemnitz	Oberstleutnant der Schutzpolizei Gerhard Walther
Zwickau	Major der Schutzpolizei Sernan
Plauen	Major der Schutzpolizei Wahl
Württemberg	
Stuttgart	Oberst der Schutzpolizei Erich Süss
Heilbronn	Major der Schutzpolizei Kuhlemann
Ulm	Major der Schutzpolizei Kerner
Friedrichshafen	Major der Schutzpolizei Thomas
Esslingen	Major der Schutzpolizei Ganser
Baden	
Karlsruhe	Oberstleutnant der Schutzpolizei von der Mosel
Mannheim	Oberstleutnant der Schutzpolizei Gotthold Witkugel
Freiburg	Major der Schutzpolizei Bieser
Heidelberg	Oberstleutnant der Schutzpolizei Werner Kuhn
Pforzheim	Major der Schutzpolizei Vossberg
Baden-Baden	Major der Schutzpolizei Hensen
Strassburg (*)	Oberstleutnant der Schutzpolizei Richard Hepperle
Mülhausen (*)	Oberstleutnant der Schutzpolizei Wilhelm Schwertschlager
Thüringen	
Weimar	Oberstleutnant der Schutzpolizei Ludwig Velte
Gera	Major der Schutzpolizei Wilhelm Kurth
Jena	Major der Schutzpolizei Heizmann Gotha
	Oberstleutnant der Schutzpolizei
Altenburg	Wilhelm Stock
Hessen	Unknown
Darmstadt	Oberstleutnant der Schutzpolizei
	Franz Jürgens
Mainz	Major der Schutzpolizei Wieprecht
Offenbach	Major der Schutzpolizei Erich Holtey-Weber
Worms	Major der SchutzpolizeiErnst Schmidt
Giessen	Oberst der Schutzpolizei Harri Hellwege Emden
Mecklenburg	
Rostock	Oberstleutnant der Schutzpolizei August Werner
Oldenburg	
Wilhelmshaven	Major der Schutzpolizei Hewitz Braunschweig
Braunschweig	Oberstleutnant der SchutzpolizeiHermann Stührmann
Anhalt	
Dessau	Major der Schutzpolizei Eduard Orthmann
Hamburg	
Hamburg	Generalmajor der Polizei Max von Heimburg
Bremen	
Bremen	Oberst der Schutzpolizei Ziller

Westmark	
Saarbrücken	Oberst der Schutzpolizei Ernst Weigand
Ludwigshafen	Oberstleutnant der Schutzpolizei Max Baltersee
Kaiserslautern	Major der Schutzpolizei Geisler
Metz (*)	Major der Schutzpolizei Arthur Fladrich
Österreich	
Wien	Oberst der Schutzpolizei Paul Schuster
Klagenfurt	Major der Schutzpolizei Arved Kröger
Wiener-Neustadt	Major der Schutzpolizei Sturm
Sankt Polten	Major der Schutzpolizei Robert Franz
Znaim	Major der Schutzpolizei Schlitt
Linz	Oberstleutnant der Schutzpolizei Dr. Herbert Krögler
Salzburg	Oberstleutnant derSchutzpolizei Reinisch
Graz	Oberstleutnant der Schutzpolizei Adolf Haan
Marburg am Drau	Major der Schutzpolizei Robert Buchholz
Leoben	Major der Schutzpolizei Kratzenberg
Innsbruck	Major der Schutzpolizei Georg Hahn
Sudetenland	
Karlsbad	Oberstleutnant der Schutzpolizei Rieckhoff
Aussig	Oberstleutnant der Schutzpolizei Richard Illas
Brüx	Oberstleutnant der Schutzpolizei Richard Dressler
Reichenberg	Oberstleutnant der Schutzpolizei Dühmig
Troppau	Oberstleutnant der Schutzpolizei Grundig
Danzig-Westpreussen (*)	
Danzig	Oberstleutnant der Schutzpolizei Harald Wilcke
Gotenhafen	Major der Schutzpolizei Johannes Wedermann
Elbing	Oberstleutnant der Schutzpolizei Spieker
Graudenz	Oberstleutnant der Schutzpolizei Roggenbrück
Bromberg	Oberstleutnant der Schutzpolizei Tausenfreund
Thorn	Oberstleutnant der Schutzpolizei Ebel
Posen	Oberstleutnant der Schutzpolizei Kurt Feukert
Leslau	Major der Schutzpolizei Leschke
Litzmannstadt	Oberst der Schutzpolizei Willy Dressler

(*) Foreign area annexed to the Reich.

2.2.2 Schutzpolizei der Gemeinden (Municipal Police)

The Municipal Police (Gemeinde Polizei) was responsible for public order and safety in the towns with over 2,000 inhabitants that did not have a Police Administration. Its organisation was similar to the State Police Administration. The Municipal Administrative Police dealt with trade, regulations on punishable offences, control of foreigners, etc. Municipal Criminal Police was responsible for the fight against crime (only in towns with over 10,000 inhabitants). Municipal Protection Police were used to maintain order and control traffic.

The Gemeinde Polizei was under the authority of the Mayor (Bürgermeister or Oberbürgermeister in larger towns and in Preussen Amtsbürgermeister or Amtsvorsteher). The executive head of this force was a professional Police Administrator.

In towns with over 50,000 inhabitants, the Municipal Police was led by a Municipal Police Director (Stadtpolizeidirektor), in towns between 30,000 and 50,000 inhabitants by a Police Senior Inspector (Polizeioberinspektor) and in towns between 20,000 and 30,000 inhabitants by a Police Commissar (Polizeikommissar). In towns under 20,000, the Municipal Police were under direct command of the District Commander of the Protection Police. During the war, the Municipal police in towns with under 5,000 inhabitants was the responsibility of the Gendarmerie.

Command of the Municipal Protection Police

The General Inspector of the Gendarmerie and the Municipal Protection Police (Generalinspekteur der Gendarmerie und der Schutzpolizei der Gemeinde) supervised the activities of the Municipal Police in the Ordnungspolizei Headquarters. In each Wehrkreis, the Befehlhaber der Ordnungspolizei controlled Municipal Police forces that were at the disposal of the Mayor. The Stabsoffizier der Schutzpolizei attached to the Senior Police Authority (District President) was also on the staff of the Befehlhaber der Ordnungspolizei. He acted as a liason as well as being in charge of personal, training and economics matters in connection with the Municipal Police.

Organisation of the Municipal Protection Police

The command of the Schutzpolizei der Gemeinde is based upon the size of the town. The units of the Municipal Protection Police were organized like State Protection Police with a staff and a network of Police stations (revier).

Size of Town:

27 towns with over 50,000 inhabitants
Kommandeur der Schutzpolizei der Gemeinde (Commander of Schutzpolizei) with the rank of Oberstleutnant/Major der Schutzpolizei (Lt Col/Major)

88 towns with over 30,000 inhabitants
Führer der Schutzpolizei Dienstabteilung (Leader of Department of Schutzpolizei) with the rank of Hauptmann der Schutzpolizei (Captain)

106 towns with over 20,000 inhabitants
Führer der Schutzpolizei Dienstabteilung with the rank of Revier Oberleutnant (Police Precinct first Lieutenant)

1,117 towns with 5,000 to 20,000 inhabitants
Führer der Schutzpolizei Dienstabteilung with the rank of Meister/Revier Leutnant (NCO/Police Precinct second lieutenant)

Members of the Schutzpolizei der Gemeinde were technically municipal civil servants and were made subject to the same regulations as the members of the State Protection Police. The staff of the Municipal Protection Police came from State Protection Police. During his career a member of the Schutzpolizei could be transferred from State to Municipal Protection Police and vice versa. Revier Oberleutnant and Revier Leutnant ranks were created during the war to replace the young officers who had been mobilised for service in the Armed Force or Police Battalions in occupied territories. These officers, who served only in precincts, were trained Police NCOs or Police reservists too old to be appointed to normal commissioned post.

Strength of Municipal Protection Police as at the 1 November 1944

+ Active officers and NCOs	15 152 (*)
+ Reservist policemen	8 152
- Retired and shown as 'at disposal'	58
Appointed to State SCHUPO, Gendarmerie, Gemeinde SCHUPO in Eastern and Western Territories	5 187
- Mobilised in Wehrmacht, Waffen-SS, Feldgendarmerie and Marineküstenpolizei	540
	= 17 635

53.4 % of the Municipal Protection Police serving in Old Reich were active officers and NCO.

Oberst der SCHUPO, Ernst Zicklam

Police Guard at the entrance of SCHUPO post in Kattowitz

2.3 Gendarmerie (Rural Police)

As a result of the June 1920 decree, the rural police was the oldest of the state police forces. The word "Gendarmerie" came from France where "Gens d'armes" were the personal guards of French kings. The Gendarmerie was set up in Preussen and other Länder at the beginning of the 18th century and it was organised like a military force. It was responsible for public safety in the countryside. Following the Great War, the State Gendarmerie in Preussen changed its name to "Landjägerei" by a decree dated 26 June 1920 to emphasise its military status. The Gendarmerie of the others states like Bayern, Sachsen, Württemberg remained "Landesgendarmerie."

The Prussian Rural Police 1920–1934

Landjägerei (State Foot Gendarmerie) 1920–1934

The Office of the Chief of the Gendarmerie was disbanded. The Gendarms became Landjäger (Foot Gendarm) and the Officers became Landjägerrat (Foot Gendarm Councillors) with the status of a civil servant. From 1926, a new organisation was set up: a staff officer involved in Landjägerei matters was appointed to the Abteilung II (Polizei) of the Ministery of Interior of Preussen and Landjäger ranks were created based upon Police ranks with " Landjägerei " added, i.e Leutnant der Landsjägerei. At Administrative District level, the chief of Landjägerei was the Senior Inspector (Oberaufsichtsbeamte) attached to the District President. The district organisation of the Landesjägerei was as follows:

Regierungsbezirk — Oberaufsichtsbeamte (Senior Inspector)
The Senior Inspector was also the chief of the department on the staff of the District President.
He was responsible for employment and personal matters,

Inspektionbezirk — Landesjägereiinspekteur (Inspector)
He was involved in training, personal and economic matters. During police actions he led Kreis (district) units.

Kreis — Landesjägerei Kreisleiter (Kreis Chief)
He was involved in training and was the advisor to the relevant Landrat

Abteilung (Kreis unit) — Landesjägerei Abteilungsleiter (Unit Chief)
Amtsbezirk (Kreis division) — Landjägermeister (Senior NCO)

In May 1933, the Landjägerei was reorganized at the highest level, bringing it closer to the former Gendarmerie organisation. The former chief of department (referent) in the Prussian Ministery of Interior Paul Schoepplenburg became "Chief of Landesjäger units". He was ranked Landjägerkommandeur (equivalent to General rank). A deputy (stabsoffizier) and an adjutant assisted him. The District Chief became Commander of Landjäger units (Kommandeur der Landjägerei). The Inspector became Leader of the Inspection (Führer der Landjägerinspektion). From 28 August 1933 the Director (Leiter) of the Landjägerei School Allenstein took the military term of "Kommandeur."

The Prussian Gendarmerie 1934

By a decree issued by the Prussian Minister of Interior dated 25 January 1934, the Landjägerei was renamed "Gendarmerie." The territorial organisation had the following changes:

Gendarmeriepost	Führer der Gendarmeriepost
Gendarmerieamtsbezirk	Führer der Gendarmerieamtsbezirk
Gendarmerieabteilung	Führer der Gendarmerieabteilung
Gendarmeriedistrikt (former inspektion)	Führer der Gendarmeriedistrikt
Regierungsbezirk	Kommandeur der Gendarmerie

Equivalent rank table

Landjägerei ranks	Gendarmerie ranks
Landjäger	Gendarm
Oberlandjäger	Wachtmeister der Gendarmerie
Landjägermeister	Oberwachtmeister der Gendarmerie
Oberlandjägermeister	Hauptwachtmeister der Gendarmerie
Kreisoberlandjägermeister	Stabswachtmeister der Gendarmerie
Landjägeroberleutnant	Oberleutnant der Gendarmerie
Landjägerhauptmann	Hauptmann der Gendarmerie
Landjägermajor	Major der Gendarmerie
Landjägeroberstleutnant	Oberstleutnant der Gendarmerie
Landjägeroberst	Oberst der Gendarmerie
Landjägerkommandeur	General der Gendarmerie

Members of Municipal Police on Exercise

The Reich Gendarmerie 1934–1945

Central Command of the Gendarmerie

Department III " Police " of the Ministry of Interior 1934–1936

The decree creating unity between Reich and State administration dated 30 January 1934 gave authority for centralising all police forces under the Reich. The newly created Reich and Prussian Ministery of Interior became the overall command centre for the German police. The chief of the Gendarmerie was Oberst der Gendarmerie Jürgen von Kamptz, newly appointed referent "Gendarmerie" in Department III "Polizei" under General Daluege. On 1 April 1936, von Kamptz was promoted Generalmajor der Gendarmerie. He was in communication with the Department "Gendarmerie" of all the German States with a view to developing common organisational rules and practices throughout Germany.

Generalinspekteur der Gendarmerie 1936–1945

On 17 June 1936 with the creation of the Hauptamt Ordnungspolizei (Police Headquarters), the Gendarmerie Central Command rose to the status of General Inspection for Rural Police and Municipal Police. It remained under Jürgen von Kamptz whose rank changed to Generalmajor der Polizei. The General Inspector was responsible for personal matters and developed training regulations. A network of police schools was created throughout Germany to provide the future officer material for the new force. A decree dated 4 February 1937 detailed von Kamptz's responsibilities as weapons, clothing, equipment, organisation and personnel matters.

Organisation of the Gendarmerie

The Gendarmerie was divided into two main branches:
Territorial Brigade (Gendarmerie des Einzeldienstes or " Gendarmerie ")
Motorised Units of the Gendarmerie (Motorisierte Gendarmerie or Mot. Gend.)

Territorial Brigades of Gendarmerie

In towns with under 2,000 inhabitants, villages and in the countryside, public safety was the responsibility of the Gendarmerie. The Gendarmerie played a major role in the local communities. In addition to their executive police duties, they were trained to " help and advise" in matters of general administration. At the level of each Wehrkreis, an Inspector of Order Police was appointed to co-ordinate activities of the whole uniformed police. A staff officer (Sachsbearbeiter) was responsible for Gendarmerie matters. The commander of Gendarmerie was the advisor to the Senior Police Authority (Regierungspräsident District President) and he was also the head of Gendarmerie forces in the Administrative District. He was responsible for technical matters, weapons, clothing, police regulations, welfare and economics. By a decree dated 26 July 1939, a new organisation was set up as follows:

Territorial Organisation (1939)

Senior Administrative District–(Land, Reichsgau, Regierungsbezirk)
(Kommando der Gendarmerie under a Kommandeur der Gendarmerie)

Administration area	Gendarmerie area	Size	Commander
Senior administrative district (Land, reichsgau)	Command of Gendarmerie (Kommando der Gendarmerie)	_	Commander of Gendarmerie (Kommandeur der Gendarmerie)
Administrative district (Regierungsbezirk)	Company of Gendarmerie (Gend. Hauptmannschaft)	140	Chief of the Company (Führer der Gend. Hauptmanschaft)
Main Rural circle Grössere Landkreis)	Gendarmerie Circle (Gend. Kreis)	40	Chief of the Circle (Gend. Kreisführer)
Small Rural circle (Klein Landkreis)	Gendarmerie Detachment (Gend. Abteilung)	15-20	Chief of Detachment (Gend. Abteilungsführer)
Group of Village (Ortkreis)	Gendarmerie Group of stations (Gend-Gruppenposten up to 10 Gend. posten)	_	Chief of Group (Gend. Gruppenpostenführer)
Village (ort)	Gendarmerie Station (Gend. post)	> 1	Chief of station (Gend. Postenführer)
Village (ort)	Gend. Einzelpost)	1	Gendarmerie NCO (Gend. Meister)

Organisation of Kommando der Gendarmerie in Great Reich (1942/1943)

State Preussen	
Aachen	Oberst Gotthilf Oemler
Allenstein	Oberstleutnant Eberhard Lueg
Arnsberg	Oberstleutnant Weigert
Aurich	Major Bolte
Breslau	Major Giebel
Düsseldorf	Oberstleutnant Hans Köllner
Erfurt	Oberstleutnant Wilhelm Meier
Frankfurt an der Oder	Oberst Kreuth
Gumbinnen	Oberstleutnant Franz Walter
Hannover	Major Otto Bruchmüller
Hildesheim	Oberst Pücher
Kassel	Oberst Johannes Overbeck
Koblenz	Major Palm
Köln	Major Bergauer
Königsberg	Major Rudat
Köslin	Oberstleutnant Fritz Goede
Liegnitz	Major Kreutzahler
Lüneburg	Major Nilsson
Magdeburg	Major Kindler
Halle Merseburg	Major Alfred Seeger
Minden	Major Zutz
Münster	Oberstleutnant Dr. Anton Barfuss
Osnabrück	Major Boos
Potsdam	Oberstleutnant Hans von Bredow

Schleswig	Oberst Claus
Schneidemühl	Major Müller
Sigmaringen	Hauptmann Hans Seeling
Stade	Major Richard Böhlke
Stettin	Major Schwieger
Trier	Oberstleutnant Helmut Ribstein
Wiesbaden	Major Johann Mullner
Zichenau	Oberst Johannes Krause
State Bayern	
München	Oberst Hans Dauwel [1]
Regensburg	Oberstleutnant Dr. Karl Kreml
Ansbach	Oberst Ludwig Niedermayr
Würzburg	
Augsburg	Oberstleutnant Josef Wachter
State Sachsen	
Dresden	Oberst Erich Klein
State Württemberg	
Stuttgart	Oberst Martin Hammerf
Karlsruhe	Oberstleutnant Dr. Held

Chef der Zivilverwaltung Alsace

Strasbourg	Oberst Anton Diermann
State Thüringen	
Weimar	Oberstleutnant Otto Zanker
State Hessen	
Darmstadt	Oberst Fritz Schüberth
State Mecklenburg	
Schwerin	
State Oldenburg	
Oldenburg	Oberstleutnant Gentz
State Braunschweig	
Braunschweig	Major Max Wittzang
State Anhalt	
Dessau	Hauptmann Kroker
State Lippe and Schaumburg Lippe	
Detmold	Hautpmann Petznick
Reichsgau Kärnten	
Klagenfurt	Oberst Rudolf Handl
Reichsgau Nieder-Donau	
Wien	Oberst Grahamer
Reichsgau Ober-Donau	
Linz	Oberst Vahlkampf

[1] *Born 25 August 1884 in Grunstadt (Pfalz). Served in the Great War as Hauptmann. Then he joined the Gendarmerie. He commanded Gendarmerie units in Speyer until the 31 January 1937 and then he was transferred to München as Kommandeur der Gendarmerie on 1 February 1937. Promoted Oberst der Gendarmerie 31 October 1937 He retired in 1942 and then was reactived as Oberst der Schutzpolizei a.W. Ranked Generalmajor der Polizei a.W. in September 1943 and remained Kommandeur der Gendarmerie für Oberbayern (München) until the end of the war. Joined the Party on 1 May 1933. Died 29 June 1958.*

Reichsgau Salzburg	
Salzburg	Oberst Reinisch
Reichsgau Steiermark	
Graz	Oberst Hugo Nowotny
Reichsgau Tirol Voralberg	
Innsbruck	Major Bernhard Hutmacher
Reichgau Sudetenland	
Aussig	Oberst Hans Georg Hirschfeld
Karlsbad	Oberst Harald Heink
Troppau	Oberst Josef Matros
Reichsgau Danzig-Westpreussen	
Danzig	Oberstleutnant Harald Wilcke
Bromberg	Oberstleutnant Bandlin
Marienwerder	Oberstleutnant Werner Kuhn
Reichsgau Wartheland	
Hohensalza	Oberst Dr. Walter Gudewill
Litzmannstadt	Oberst Hans Podzun
Posen	Oberst Lothar Mackeldey
Reichsgau Oberschlesien	
Kattowitz	Oberst August Matt
Oppeln	Oberst Friedrich Scholz
Reichsgau Westmark	
Saarbrücken	Oberst Alois Menschik
	Chef der Zivilverwaltung Lothringern
Metz	Oberst Werner Meltzer

High Mountain Gendarmerie

Following the Anschluss, large mountainous areas situated in Österreich came under the juridiction of the German Gendarmerie. The Austrian Gendarmerie with specialized training had been esponsible for these areas and, following the German takeover, were retained. The staffs of the units situated in the mountain areas were trained in the Police Ski Schools at Kitzbühel, Südelfeld and Oberjoch and at the Hochgebirgsschule (High Mountain School) at Innbruck. They became mountaineers for mountains less than 1,500 meters in height, high mountaineers for mountains over 1,500 meters or mountain guides. On 4 August 1941, all units of the Alps Gendarmerie took the name of High Mountain Gendarmerie (Hochgebirgsgendarmerie). The decree gave the list of mountain Gendarmerie areas as Austrian Reichsgau Salzburg, Tirol Voralberg, and Kärnten, Mountainous Gendarmerie districts of Reichsgau Ober und Niederdonau, and Oberbayern. During the war a High Mountain Gendarmerie Platoon was created in Neumark (District Krakau) in the General Gouvernement. Leutnant Hans Lanig, a former guide and ski instructor, was attached to Befehlhaber der ORPO in Oslo to conduct training of Gendarmerie appointed to the mountains and snowy areas of Norway.

Motorised Units of the Gendarmerie

A decree dated 30 June 1937 created Motorised Gendarmerie as special service branch of the Gendarmerie operating throughout the entire territory of the Reich, with the control of traffic both on first class roads (Landstrassen) and on the national highways (Autobahnen) as its main function. Most of its members came from the Feldjägerkorps.

Feldjägerkorps (1933–1935)

The Feldjägerkorps or FJK was created on 1 October 1933 in Preussen and in Sachsen. They served as a provost corps for the Party being responsible for order and discipline during meetings of the Party. They acted too as Hilfspolizei, helping the Gestapo and other police units during actions. The Feldjägerkorps was organized in battalions (Abteilungen) with three to nine companies (Bereitschaft) each. Eight battalions were set up in Preussen.

Feldjägerabteilung I	Königsberg
Feldjägerabteilung II S	tettin
Feldjägerabteilung IIIa	Breslau
Feldjägerabteilung IIIb and Staff	Berlin
Feldjägerabteilung IV	Magdeburg
Feldjägerabteilung V	Frankfurt am Main
Feldjägerabteilung VIa	Hannover
Feldjägerabteilung VIb	Düsseldorf

Membership of the Feldjägerkorps in (1935):

SA-men and NSKK men (former Mot. SA)	813
SS-men	224
Others (Hitlerjugend, Stahlhelm, etc.)	122
Total	3 159

On 1 April 1935, the Feldjägerkorps was incorporated into Schutzpolizei. In August 1936, the first highway police training for the Gendarmerie was started. It consisted of theoretical courses in the Schutzpolizei barracks in Berlin Schöneberg and practical courses at the former Feldjägerschule Sühl now known as the Kraftfahrschule der Gendarmerie headed by Oberstleutnant Deumich then Major Fuchs. Two thirds of FJK members were trained to join the motorised Reich Traffic Police.

Motorized Gendarmerie 1937–1945

In 1937, former Feldjäger members involved in traffic duties were transferred into the newly created motorized Gendarmerie. The Motorized Gendarmerie (Motorisierte Gendarmerie) was a barracked force organized into 26 Motorized Commands (Motorisierte Bereitschaften) which later rose to 32 units:

2 Bereitschaften of 144 men
12 Bereitschaften of 108 men
18 Bereitschaften of 72 men
10 Bereitschaften of 36 men

In each Wehrkreis (army District), a Motorised Gendarmerie Unit was attached to the Senior Police Authority. In July 1938, the two largest commands in Potsdam and München took the name of Motorised Battalions (Motorisierte Gendarmerie Abteilung). Following the enlargment of the Reich, Motorised Commands were set up in Österreich and the Sudetenland was covered by the Saxon Gendarmerie. Changes in training followed the development of motorised units. Next to the Gendarmerie Motor School (Kraftfahrschule der Gendarmerie) Suhl and the Motor and Traffic school (Kraftfahr und Verkehrsschule der Gendarmerie), two other Traffic schools (Vehrkehrschule der mot. Gendarmerie) were created at Deggingen in Württemberg and at Hollabrunn in Niederdonau. A further Motorized Gendarmerie was set up in Wien-Mödling under Oberst Kurt Albrecht. At the outbreak of the war, numerous members of the Motorised units, sometimes the whole unit, were mobilised into the military Provost Corps (Feldgendarmerie) (see chapter "Feldgendarmerie"). With a view to replacing them, motorised reserve units were set up in July 1940. Motorised companies were stationed in the newly annexed territoires in the East (Reichgau Wartheland, Oberschlesien, Westpreussen) and in the West, in Lorraine, a motorised company "Lothringen" was created at Lubeln under the Kommandeur der Gendarmerie in Metz. On 28 November 1940, the Motorised Gendarmerie adopted military terms for organisational purposes:

Motorised Gendarmerie Battalion	Large Gendarmerie Companies (Motorized)
Motorised Gendarmerie Commands	Gendarmerie Companies (Motorized)
Gend. Motorised Platoon	Gendarmerie Platoon (Motorized)
Motor and Traffic School Suhl Gendarmerie School Suhl	
Traffic School Deggingen	Gendarmerie School Deggingen
Traffic School Hollabrunn	Gendarmerie School Hollabrunn
Motor School Wien-Mödling	Gendarmerie School Wien-Mödling

2.4 Kriminalpolizei (Criminal Police)

The Kriminalpolizei or KRIPO (Criminal Police) had existed for many years in Germany. It performed the normal functions of a detective force common in other countries, being responsible for the detection of crime and the arrest of criminals. Until the NSDAP took power, the criminal police operated under the administration of the various Länder (States) and was not centralized although it was well organised and co-ordinated. It was responsible to the "Staatliche Polizeiverwaltung" (state Police Administration).

Each city and town had a criminal police office being responsible for crime in that area, working in close co-operation with the Schutzpolizei in urban areas and the Gendarmerie in rural areas. There was no Reich criminal police and there was no official structure for co-ordinating interstate crime fighting. In 1897 Land representatives met in Berlin to increase co-ordination among the states and free cities for identifying criminals, but controversy over the methods to be used prevented a fully comprehensive solution being found. In 1912 it was decided to create a Reich information centre on crime but it took so long to set up that the Great War intervened and the plan was abandoned. The need for a centralising authority became more urgent in the Weimar period with the heightened rate of crime in the post war years and the assassination of some prominent political leaders like Walter Rathenau, provided special impetus.

In 1922 the Reichstag passed a law to create a criminal police office under the Reichs Ministry of the Interior to combat interstate crime and to provide for liason among the state police. Problems again arose with several states led by Preussen and Bayern blocking final implementation. The Reich Ministry of Finance also created obstacles and since the Reich government could not effectively press its case, it had to emasculate its Law for the Protection of the Reich and abandon the Reich Criminal Police Office. As a result of these efforts some states did at least rationalise their own criminal police forces. In 1921 Sachsen went the furthest by bringing all municipal criminal police, formerly independant of state authority, into its state police system and by 1925 all states had state criminal police forces co-ordinated by a central office. Forces like that in Berlin had large forces of plain clothes officers, this was scaled down according to the size of the state to the extent of Schaumburg-Lippe which had a total of two officers.

Following a police conference in Karlsruhe during the early summer of 1925 the first attempt at centralization occurred with the creation of a German Criminal Police Commission. This body was made up of police technicians who made recommendations to state governments and this became a fairly efficient if informal form of co-operation. Also intelligence centres, laboratories and technical facilities in the various states which were used for combating specialised aspects of crime became responsible for interstate liason in their specilaities. On the 1 June 1925 a "Landeskriminalpolizeiamt" or LKPA

1934 member of Fäldjägerkorps meeting Gauleiter Gustav Simon

(State Criminal Police Direction) was created in Berlin to standardize Criminal Police techniques in all the provinces for the State of Preussen. It also acted as a clearing house for information on criminal activities through subordinate " Landes-kriminalpolizeistellen" (State Criminal Police Offices) within the state. A final task allocated to it was to maintain liaison and to give assistance to similar offices in other German states, especially in areas covering forgery, pickpocketing, bank and train robberies, white slavery and pornography. It also maintained a central fingerprint file. Other states also specialised, the München office in Bayern was responsible for controlling Gypsy excesses and the Dresden office in Sachsen became the central office for missing persons and for indentifying unknown bodies, their specialties were made available for general use. The first head of the State Criminal Police Direction in Berlin was Dr. Bernard Weiss. He was a trained lawyer whose promising career in the judiciary had been interrupted by military service during World War I. Following the war he joined the Berlin Police as Deputy Head of the KRIPO. He became head of the Berlin KRIPO in 1924 and in this capacity helped build the system of State Criminal Police from 1925 and to modernize the entire detective force. Appointed head of the State Criminal Police Direction on its formation, he was promoted Regierungsdirektor in 1927. He was made Deputy Police President of Berlin during the same year. Politically he sympathized with German Nationalists in the company with Social Democrats and Trade Unionists.

Highly competent and industrious, he was also remarkably versatile. He tried to know all his immediate subordinates and took part in many of their organized activities. Detectives found him always ready to accompany them on field trips. He was not popular with other civil servants because they threatened the authority and integrity of his police command. His one big problem as regards the Nazi's was that he was Jewish and they carried out a malicious campaign of ridicule against him. Following the dismissal of the Prussian government of Otto Braun by Chancellor Franz von Papen on 20 July 1932, the Commander of Wehrkreis III, Lieutenant General Gerd von Rundstedt moved on the Police Presidency and deposed the Police President Albert Gazesinski, the Schutzpolizei commander Colonel Magnus Heimannsberg and Dr. Weiss. The post of head of the LKPA was given to Regierungsdirektor Scholz. Unsuccessful, it was said he showed little interest or aptitude for political cases and he was replaced by Erich Liebermann von Sonnenberg in July 1933. He had become a detective officer candidate in 1912 and by 1915 was frozen in rank. As an outspoken advocate of forced sterilization to prevent crime and reduce burdens on society, he put himself at odds with the regime. During January 1932, he became the unofficial representative of the higher criminal police officials in the National Socialist Fellowship of Civil Servants. There,

A unit of motorcycle Gendarmerie

his theories found approval and he joined the NSDAP. He specialized in robbery and counterfeiting, remaining head of the LKPA until April 1934 when a significant change took place, Reinhard Heydrich took over the LKPA. After 1936, von Sonnenberg's status declined. He served obscurely in the Gestapo and died after a short illness in 1941. Heydrich 's move to the LKPA was one in a series that culminated in Reichsführer-SS Himmler being appointed Head of the German Police. From the formation of the Nazi government in January 1933, everyone wanted to see a unified police force in Germany. This meant a unified Criminal Police. The problem was that the Minister of the Interior, Wilhelm Frick, wanted such a force under his Ministery's control and not merged with the SS. Heydrich 's move to Berlin and take-over of the LKPA meant an actual, if not official merger, with the Party Security Service (SD).

The result of proposals and counterproposals which took over two years was a decree from Adolf Hitler dated 17 June 1936 appointing Himmler head of the German Police. One consolation given to Frick was that in this post he was subordinate to the Ministry of the Interior with the rank of State Secretary. On 20 June 1936 Himmler issued two decrees reorganizing and centralizing the Police. The KRIPO was removed from the State Police Administration and was put under the head of the Security Police. At Ministry level a Hauptamt Sicherheitspolizei (Main Office Security Police) was created and the KRIPO became one of three departments in this headquarters. On the 16 July 1937, the KRIPO was centralized by the creation of the Reichskriminalpolizeiamt or RKPA (Reich Criminal Police Direction). From this date, when acting as a Ministry authority, it used the title "Hauptamt Sicherheitspolizei" and when acting as an executive administrative authority it used the title "Reichskriminalpolizeiamt." The division of the police force as a whole into two main branches, Ordnungspolizei (Uniformed Police) and Sicherheitspolizei meant that the Criminal Police was drawn into the sphere of influence of the Political Police. One of the practical outcomes was that because the Security Police had no powers of arrest it could now use the KRIPO to carry out this task. In January 1935 a further change in command of the KRIPO took place when Arthur Nebe took over from Heydrich. Nebe was born in Berlin of 13 November 1894 the son of a schoolteacher. After service in World War I when he served in the Engineers and rose to the ranks of Lieutenant, he joined the Criminal Police in Berlin.

He reached the status of Police Commissar by 1924. His career was slow and he did not make a reputation for himself until 1931 when he solved the murder of a chauffeur and helped capture Franz Spernau, a major criminal. He was head of the KRIPO in Berlin from 1928 to 1931, working in both the narcotics and murder squads. He joined the NSDAP in 1931, serving as police liaison with SS-Gruppe "Ost" from 1931 to April 1933. He was very successful in convincing the Party of his dedication to their political ideals and not just to the jobs they could offer. Nebe made good use of his record as a former Freikorps units (Free Corps) soldier and his early admiration for the virtues of patriotism, militarism and anti-Semitism. He proved his long ideological affinity with National Socialism and as a result did not loose his job in the purges of 1932/1933. Nebe was quickly promoted achieving the rank of Oberregierungs-und Kriminalrat by the 29 September 1933. He took over the LKPA from January 1935 and the RKPA from July 1937. He joined the SS on 2 December 1936 with the rank of Sturmbannführer. He was promoted Obersturmbannführer on the 20 April 1938, Standartenführer on the 1 August 1938, Oberführer on the 20 April 1939, Brigadeführer on the 1 January 1941 and Gruppenführer on the 9 November 194. He was given the rank of Generalmajor der Polizei on the 1 January 1941 and was promoted General-leutnant der Polizei on the 9 November 1941. On 27 September 1939, a further reorganization of the police took place with the merger of the Hauptamt Sicherheitspolizei (a State organization) and the Sicherheitshauptamt or SD Hauptamt (a Party organization) to form the Reichsicherheitshauptamt or RSHA (Security Direction for the Reich). In this r eorganization the KRIPO became Amt (Office) V and resulted in the merger of the KRIPO Abteilung (Department) of Hauptamt Sicherheitspolizei with the RKPA.

The new office was called "Verbrechensbekämpfung" (Combating of Crime) and it was headed by Arthur Nebe. He remained in this post until September 1944. In July 1941 he volunteered for duty with the SIPO/SD in Russia and took command of Einsatzgruppe "B" operating behind army Group "Center." Nebe remained in Russia until October 1941 and then resumed his duties in Berlin. He systemized the KRIPO's methods and increased its efficiency, priding himself on being more competent than the Gestapo. His objectives were reached by research and logic rather than by crude violence. This was evident in the investigation of Reinhard Heydrich 's assassination in May-June 1942. The Gestapo failed and the culprits weren't found until a KRIPO squad under Kriminalrat Pannwitz arrived from Berlin. A complex personality, Nebe had serious qualms about the direction the Nazi's were taking and he cultivated friends in the anti-Hitler circle. He acted as a watchdog for them through the actions of the SIPO. He regularly passed on SD reports on leading conspirators to Hans Oster and Hans von Donnanyi of the Abwehr. In the assassination attempt of 20 July 1944, he led a trusted group of KRIPO officials ready to arrest Party and SS-leaders in Berlin. After the failure of the coup he covered his tracks and, although not under suspicion, chose to go into hiding.

A warrant was issued for his arrest on 24 July 1944 and an investigation was conducted by his deputy in Amt V, SS-Oberführer Paul Werner. Nebe evaded capture until 16 January 1945 when he was betrayed by a former mistress. Tried before the Peoples Court on 25 February 1945, he confessed and was sentenced to death on 2 March. He was hanged in Berlin on 21 March 1945. Nebe was succeeded as head of Amt V by Friedrich Panzinger, and not as he hoped by Paul Werner. Panzinger, born in München on the 1 February 1903,was a lawyer who joined the KRIPO in München in 1919. He remained in this post until the 1 October 1937 being promoted Regierungsassessor on the 1 December 1934 and Regierungsrat on the 1 April 1937.

Transferred to the Gestapo in Berlin on the 1 October 1937, he led Gruppe IVA in the Reichs Security Headquarters (RSHA) from August 1940. He was promoted Oberregierungsrat on the 12 September 1940 and Regierungsdirektor on the 1 December 1942. He joined the Party on the 1 May 1937 and the SS, as Hauptsturmführer on the 20 April 1939. He achieved rapid promotion reaching the rank of Oberführer on the 24 September 1943. He commanded Einsatzgruppe A of the Security Police in Northern Russia from the 4 September 1943 to the 20 May 1944 and he was Befehlhaber der SIPO und SD for Ostland (Commander of the Security Police for the Baltic States) at the same time. Returning to Berlin, he took over his old post of head of Gruppe IVA in RSHA on the 20 May 1944.

He also acted as standing deputy for Heinrich Müller the head of Amt IV. It is interesting that the investigation into Nebe's disappearance was given to his office in the Gestapo and not to the KRIPO but strictly speaking it was correct as Nebe's crime was political. His appointment to head Amt V was as a result of Dr. Ernst Kaltenbrunner, the head of the RSHA and Heinrich Müller not knowing who could be trusted in the KRIPO office. Panzingers promotion to Oberführer in the SS was not made until the 21 May 1944 with senority from the 24 September 1943 to give him senority over Paul Werner. Panzinger was captured by the Russians in 1945 and he remained a prisoner until October 1955. He then served in the Bundesnachrichtendienst (West German Security Service) with the rank of Regierungsrat. He was dismissed during the summer of 1949 and was indicted for war crimes. He died of a stroke in München on the 31 August 1959.

KRIPO offices existed throughout Germany. The capitals of the German Länder and the Prussian Provincial capitals had the main branch offices or KRIPO-(Leit)-Stellen smaller cities and towns had Kripo-Stellen and outlying areas had branch offices under the control of Leitstellen or Stellen They were known as KRIPO-Aussendienststellen (Out offices) and KRIPO-Aussenposten (Out posts) the difference between the last two was one of size, an Aussendienstelle had a staff of 10 or more whereas Aussenposten had a staff of 9 or less. This relationship between the Leitstellen and Stellen was one of independence. Stellen were not subordinate to Leitstellen. Until September 1943 KRIPO offices were subordinated to the RKPA for executive matters and to the Staatliche Polizeiverwaltungen for administrative purposes. In this regard the individual Police Presidents and Police Directors had the title of "Chef der KRIPO-(Leit)-Stelle". The day-to-day operating of the offices was the responsibility of a professional detective and they had the title of "Leiter der KRIPO-(Leit)-Stelle". In towns which had a Police President or Director but no KRIPO office, a KRIPO department was created within the Police Presidency/Directorate and it was directly under the Police President/Director. In localities without a Staatliche Polizeiverwaltung, the Gemeindepolizei (Municipal Police) took charge of KRIPO activities through Gemeinde Kriminalpolizei Abteilungen (Municipal Criminal Police Department). In a decree dated 7 September 1943, Himmler, in a far-reaching reorganization of the Police, completely separated the KRIPO from the Staatliche and Gemeinde Polizeiverwaltungen and incorporated all KRIPO headquarters into the structure of the Reich's Criminal Police. As a result, the KRIPO-(Leit)-Stellen and Stellen were made independent headquarters within the chain of command of the SIPO. The "Leiter" of KRIPO offices, formerly administrative subordinates to Police President/Directors, now only had to submit routine reports. All former Gemeinde Kriminalpolizei Abteilungen and Staatliche Kriminalabteilungen were transformed into Aussendienststellen of the Reich's Criminal Police. For financial and economic administration, KRIPO offices became dependent on the nearest Gestapo office. Throughout the war the KRIPO offices were under the operational supervision of the Inspekteur (and later Befehlhaber) der Sicherheitspolizei und SD. As various cities and towns were approached by the allies the relative offices were closed together with the Gestapo and SD offices and all were put under one man titled Kommandeur der Sicherheitspolizei. It is significant that the known officers appointed to the new posts of Kommandeur der Sicherheitspolizei all came from the Gestapo and the SD and none from the KRIPO. KRIPO Offices did not exist outside Germany, Österreich and the Protectorate of Böhmen-Mähren. In occupied territories KRIPO activities and personnel came under relevant Kommandeur der Sicherheitspolizei und des SD.

International Kriminal-Polizei Kommission I.K.P.K. (International Criminal Police Commission)

Within the KRIPO framework there existed a number of semi-independent of departments. In order to prosecute international criminals an International Criminal Police Commission was created in Paris in 1923. Originally known as the Commission Internationale de la Police Criminelle, by 1940 it was dominated by the Nazi's and its headquarters were moved first to Wien and then to Berlin. Austrian SS-Oberführer Otto Steinhäusl served as President of the Commission from May 1938 until his death on the 20 June 1940. The first German Head of the Commission was Reinhard Heydrich who took over on 20 June 1940. After his death, Dr. Ernst Kaltenbunner took over and it was agreed that the head of RSHA would also hold the position of President of the Commission. The vice-presidency was to be vested in the head of the German Criminal Police. Day-to-day running of the Commission was the responsibility of the Chairman, SS-Standartenführer Dr. Karl Zindel, assisted by the General Secretary. The General Secretary was SS-Standartenführer Dr. Bruno Schultz until 1 August 1942 and then Regierungs und Kriminal Direktor Dr. Dressler. An organization chart of the RSHA dated 1 March 1941 shows that the Commission was directly under the command of the Chief of RSHA. From 2 January 1942, the RSHA took over the commission radio offices in Bukarest, Budapest, Pressburg and Zurich. It also set up new radio offices in Oslo, Den Haag and Brussels.

Weibliche Kriminalpolizei
(Female's branch of the Criminal Police)

There had been a female department in the criminal police for many years and it was reorganized in 1935. It was responsible for the registration and supervision of children and females who were exposed to criminal and immoral influence, crime prevention with regard to females and the invitation of educational and welfare programs for those brought to the notice of the KRIPO. Known as "Weibliche Kriminalpolizei" it was Gruppe VA-e in Amt V of RSHA and was run by Kriminaldirektor Wieking. Its personnel did not wear a uniform and were not armed but they were trained in the handling of weapons.

Kriminal Institut der Sicherheitspolizei
(Scientific Institutes of the Security Police)

By the end of the war, three scientific institutes existed for use by the Security Police. They all came under the control of Amt V of RSHA. The first was the Kriminaltechnisches Institute der Sicherheitspolizei located at Werderscher-Markt 5-6 in Berlin. It was founded in 1938 for the purpose of handling technical and scientific investigations essential for the discovery and solution of crimes. The institute had at its disposal 27 laboratories equipped with the most modern types of apparatus for experiments and forensic research. It also had Kriminaltechnische Untersuchungsstellen attached to all KRIPO-(Leit)-Stellen staffed by specialists. This institute became Gruppe VD in RSHA and was headed by Standartenführer Dr. Heess. A doctor of chemistry, he also held a doctorate in physics. He had worked as a chemist in the Police Administration in Stuttgart and headed the institute from its formation. The second institute was the Kriminalbiologisches Institute der Sicherheitspolizei (Criminal Biology Institute) located at the same address as the Technical Institute in Berlin. A central office of this kind had existed from 1937 and it took over a collecting station of criminal biological data in München that had existed since 1924. The Institute was established in December 1941. Its functions included maintenance of indexes on all anti-social and criminal family groups in the Reich, the establishment of an observation office in cooperation with the National Health Bureau [Reichsgesundheitsamt]. The Institute compiled records from the point of view of criminal biology and took part in research into the heredity of the German people, working with the Reichsgesundheitsamt and the SS Race and Settlement Main Office.

It was also responsible for the biological aspect of forensic science and is this area it had been given the task on establishing the means of effectively killing large numbers of people. Experiments showed that carbon monoxide was the most efficient method and, therefore, the system of gas vans was created. This Institute also came under Gruppe V D of RSHA and it was headed by SS-Untersturmführer Dr. Robert Widmann, a chemical engineer who was head of Referat VD2 in RSHA. The final institution was the Kriminalmedizinisches Zentralinstitute der Sicherheitspolizei (Criminal Medicine Institute) which was created in September 1943. It provided scientific research into forensic medicine, forensic examination of criminal cases and training of KRIPO personnel. It also provided training for replacements for medical sections of the police excluding those serving in the Waffen-SS. This Institute was under the direct control of the Leitender-Artz der RSHA (Doctor in Chief), Obersturmbannführer Dr. Werner Kirchert. All three of these Institutes although basically part of the Criminal Police also provided the same services for the Gestapo and the ORPO. The members of the KRIPO were closely connected to the SS but unlike other groups in RSHA, not all held SS-rank. There was great rivalry between it and the Gestapo and SD, KRIPO personnel were not completely trusted politically by members of the other two, primarily because they were professionals and the others were not. A survey of the chiefs of KRIPO-Leitstellen shows that of those who held rank in the SS only five reached the rank of Standartenführer or above. The rank structure of the KRIPO was as follows:

KRIPO	SS	Pay Group
Kriminalassistentanwärter	Scharführer	
Kriminalassistent	Oberscharführer	8c2
Kriminaloberassistent	Hauptscharführer	7c
Kriminalsekretär	Untersturmführer	7a
Kriminalobersekretar	Untersturmführer	5b
Kriminalkommissar zur Probedienstleistung	Obersturmführer	4c1
Kriminalkommissar	Obersturmführer	4c2
Kriminalinspektor	Hauptsturmführer	3b
Regierungs und Kriminalrat	Sturmbannführer	2c2
Kriminaldirektor	Sturmbannführer	2d
Oberregierungs und Kriminalrat	Obersturmbannführer	2b
Reichskriminaldirektor	Standartenführer	1b

Organization of the KRIPO Office in Reich's Security Headquarters

With the transfer of the KRIPO from the State Police Administration to the Security Police on 20 June 1936, an office was created under the Hauptamt Sicherheitspolizei to supervise the KRIPO. A chart from early 1938 shows the following:

Amt Kriminalpolizei [S-Kr]	SS-Obergruppenführer Reinhard Heydrich
Vertreter	SS-Gruppenführer Arthur Nebe
Referent S-Kr1	Ministerialrat Krause
Referent S-Kr2	SS-Sturmbannführer Dr. Karl Zindel
Refrent S-Kr3	SS-Brigadeführer Johannes Thiele

A desk covering KRIPO personnel matters came under Amt Verwaltung und Recht (Administration and Law). Known as Referent V04 it was under Johannes Thiele. On 27 September 1939 the Reichssicherheitshauptamt (Reich Security Main Office known as RSHA), was created and the KRIPO Office became Amt V. A chart from 1 February 1940 shows its organization as follows:

Amt V–Verbrechensbekämpfung (Combatting of Crime)
SS-Gruppenführer und Generalleutnant Polizei Arthur Nebe.

Geschäftsstelle (Administration Office)
SS-Sturmbannführer, Regierungs und Kriminalrat Walter Hasenjaefer

Amt VA–Aufbau, Aufgaben und Rechtsfragen der Kriminalpolizei (Creation, Duties and Law matters of the Criminal Police)
SS-Oberführer und Oberst der Polizei Paul Werner

Amt VB–Vorbeugung (Prevention)
SS-Sturmbannführer, Oberregierungs und Kriminalrat Dr. Friedrich Riese

Amt VC–Einsatz (Employment)
Oberregierungs und Kriminalrat Galzow

Amt VD–Erkennungsdienst und Fahndung (Identification and search for wanted persons)
Oberregierungs und Kriminalrat Dr. Josef Wächter

Amt VE–Kriminaltechnisches Institut der Sicherheitspolizei
SS-Standartenführer, Regierungs und Kriminaldirektor Dr. Walter Heess

Amt VF–Wirtschaftsangelegenheiten, Sonderbeschulung und Ausrustung der KRIPO
(Economics matters, special Education, Equipment)

SS-Sturmbannführer, Oberregierungs und Kriminalrat Wolfgang Berger.

By 1941 changes had occurred, Amt VB duties were put under Amt VA and Ämter VC to VE became VB to VD as a result. Amt VF was dissolved and its duties were put under Amt I and II A chart for 1 March 1941 shows the new organization as follows:

Amt V–Verbrechenbekämpfung (Combatting of Crime)
SS-Gruppenführer und Generalleutnant der Polizei Arthur Nebe

Geschäftsstelle (Administration Office)
SS-Sturmbannführer, Regierungs und Kriminalrat Walter Hasenjaeger

Amt VA–Kriminalpolitik und Vorbeugung (Criminal Policy and Prevention)
SS-Oberführer und Oberst der Polizei Paul Werner

Amt VB–Einsatz (Employment)
Oberregierung und Kriminalrat Galzow

Amt VC–Erkennungsdienst und Fahndung (Identification and search for wanted persons)
SS-Sturmbannführer, Oberregierung und Kriminalrat Wolfgang Berger

Amt VD–Kriminaltechnisches Institut der Sicherheitspolizei
SS-Standartenführer Regierungs und Kriminadirektor Dr. Walter Heess

Little is known of further changes to this office. It is known that it absorbed Group 2 Haushalt KRIPO (Finances) Group 5 Personalien der KRIPO (Personnel) and Group 9 Angelegenheiten der Gesamtpolizei (Matters of the whole Police) from Amtsgruppe Verwaltung und Recht of Hauptamt Ordnungspolizei (Main Group "Administration and Law" of the ORPO Main Office) in September 1943. A chart of 15 December 1944 shows the following organization:

Amt V–Verbrechenbekämpfung (Combatting the crime)
SS-Oberführer und Oberst der Polizei Friedrich Panzinger

Stellvertreter–Chef (deputy)
SS-Oberführer und Oberst der Polizei Paul Werner

Geschäftstelle (Administration Office)
SS-Sturmbannführer, Regierungs und Kriminalrat Rudolf Kant

Amt VA–Kriminalpolitik und Vorbeugung (Criminal Policy and Prevention)
SS-Oberführer und Oberst der Polizei Paul Werner

Amt VB–Einsatz (Employment)
SS-Sturmbannführer, Oberregierungs und Kriminalrat Dr. Rudolf Schneider

Amt V Wi.–Wirtschaftsangelegenheiten (Economics duties)
SS-Obersturmbannführer, Oberregierungs und Kriminalrat Dr. Alfred Filbert

Note: Personnel matters for the KRIPO were always under Amt I of RSHA and were run by SS-Standartenführer, Regierungs und Kriminaldirektor Georg Schraepel.

1940 Jose Conde de Maydale with SS-Oberführer Arthur Nebe at the Reichskripo office Berlin

Kriminalpolizei Leitstellen (Criminal Police Main Branches)

Berlin: was under the command of the IdS Berlin. It supervised the KRIPO Stellen in Frankfurt an der Oder and Potsdam.

SS-Gruppenführer und Generalleutnant der Polizei Arthur Nebe	1928–1931
Regierungsdirektor Scholz	1931–07.1933
Regierungsdirektor Erich Liebermann von Sonnenberg	07.1933–15.04.1937
SS-Oberführer, und Regierung und Kriminaldirektor Max Haertel	15.04.1937–31.03.1943
SS-Obersturmbannführer, Oberregierungsrat Dr. Robert Schefe	31.03.1943–end

Bremen: was under the command of the IdS Hamburg. It supervised the KRIPO-Stelle in Wilhelmshaven and Wesermünde. It was abolished February 1945 when a KdS was created.

SS-Oberführer und Oberst der Polizei Paul Schmitz-Voigt	08.1939–01.03.1940
Oberregierungsrat Paul König	01.03.1940–13.09.1941
Regierungs und Kriminalrat Hahn	13.09.1941–end

938 A KRIPO inspector t the scene of a crime

Breslau: was under the command of the IdS Breslau. It supervised the KRIPO-Abteilung in Waldenburg. It was abolished on 5 October 1944 when a KdS was created under Dr. Wilhelm Scharpwinkel.

SS-Oberführer, Regierungs und Kriminaldirektor Max Haertel	01.09.1936–15.04.1937
SS-Obersturmbannführer, Oberregierungs und Kriminalrat Max Wielen	15.04.1937–05.10.1944

Note: This officer was named Max Wilotzki until June 1941.

Danzig: was under the command of IdS Danzig. It supervised the KRIPO-Stellen in Bromberg, Graudenz, Elbing and Gotenhafen. It was abolished 17 August 1944 when a KdS was created under Dr. Günther Venediger.

Oberregierungs und Kriminalrat Friedrich Greiner	01.10.1914–10.01.1942
Regierungs und Kriminalrat Erich Kroll	10.01.1942–11.04.1942
SS-Obersturmbannführer, Oberregierungs und Kriminalrat Heinz Hermann	11.04.1942–17.08.1944

Dresden: was under the command of IdS Dresden. It supervised the KRIPO-Stellen in Karlsbad, Reichenberg, Chemnitz, Leipzig and Zwickau. From 1943 it controlled KRIPO Stelle Halle which had been downgraded from Leitstelle status. This post was abolished 17 August 1944 with the creation of a KdS under Paul Zapp.

Oberregierungs und Kriminalrat Paul König	13.09.1941–17.08.1944

Düsseldorf: was under the command of IdS Düsselford. It controlled the KRIPO-Stellen in Bochum, Dortmund, Essen, Recklinghausen, Wuppertal, and Mönchengladbach. It was abolished February 1945 when a KdS was created.

SS-Oberführer und Oberst der Polizei Paul Schmitz-Voigt	03.1930–01.03.1936
SS-Obersturmbannführer, Oberregierungs und Kriminalrat Rudolf Momberg	01.03.1936–21.02.1942
SS-Sturmbannführer, Oberregierungs und Kriminlrat Friedrich Riese	21.02.1942–19.09.1942
SS-Obersturmbannführer, Oberregierungs und Kriminalrat Rudolf Momberg	19.09.1942–09.01.1944
SS-Sturmbannführer, Regierungs und Kriminalrat Friedrich Class	09.01.1944–.02.1945

Frankfurt am Main: was under the command of IdS Wiesbaden. It supervised the KRIPO-Stelle in Darmstadt. Until 1940 it controlled the KRIPO-Stelle in Köln which was raised to Leitstelle status and Trier which was put under Köln.

Until 1944 it also controlled the KRIPO Stelle in Kassel which was also raised to Leitstelle status. The post was abolished February 1945 when a KdS was created.

Regierungs und Kriminalrat Evert	1936–28.02.1942
SS-Sturmbannführer, Oberregierungs und Kriminalrat Wolfgang Berger	28.02.1942–.02.1945

Halle an der Saale: was under the command of IdS Dresden. It was down-graded to KRIPO Stelle status June 1944. Until then it controlled KRIPO Stellen in Dessau (transferred to Hannover), Erfurt (transferred to Kassel), Magdeburg (transferred to Hannover) and Weimer (transferred to Kassel).

SS-Obersturmbannführer, Oberregierungs und Kriminalrat Otto Fell	1941–1941
Kriminalrat Marquardt	1941–1942
SS-Sturmbannführer, Oberregierungs und Kriminalrat Max Bunger	1942–1943
SS-Hauptsturmführer, Kriminaldirektor Dr. Karl Fehl [i.V.]	1943–25.03.1944
SS-Sturmbannführer, Oberregierungs und Kriminalrat Max Bunger	25.03.1944–06.1944

Hamburg: was under the command of IdS Hamburg. It supervised the KRIPO-Stellen in Flensburg, Kiel and Cuxhaven. It was abolished February 1945 when a KdS was created..

Kriminaldirektor Purucker	"-"–01.02.1937
SS-Brigadeführer und Generalmajor der Polizei Dr. Walter Bierkamp	01.02.1937–15.02.1941
SS-Brigadeführer und Generalmajor Polizei Johannes Thiele	01.03.1941–12.09.1942
SS-Obersturmbannführer Oberregierungs und Kriminalrat Philipp Greiner	12.09.1942–06.02.1943
SS-Oberführer und Oberst der Polizei Max Haertel	06.02.1943–02.1945

Hannover: was under the command of IdS Braunschweig. It controlled the KRIPO Stelle in Braunschweig and from June 1944 those in Dessau and Magdeburg transferred from the down-graded office in Halle. It was abolished in February 1945 when a KdS was created.

Regierungs und Kriminalrat von Kulick	1938–1940
SS-Obersturmbannführer Regierungs, und Kriminaldirektor Felix Linnemann	1940–02.1945

Karlsruhe: was under the command of IdS Stuttgart. It had KRIPO Stelle status under the KRIPO-(Leit)-Stelle Stuttgart until 1944. It was abolished on the 9 December 1944 when a KdS Baden/Elsass was created under Josef Gmeiner.

SS-Obersturmbannführer, Oberregierungs und Kriminalrat Günther Braschwitz	1944–10.06.1944
SS-Sturmbannführer, Kriminaldirektor Peter Liesabeths	10.06.1944–12.08.1944

Kassel: was a KRIPO Stelle under the KRIPO-(Leit)-Stelle Frankfurt am Main until June 1944. It was then upgraded to Leitstelle status under the command of IdS Kassel. It was abolished in February 1945 when a KdS was created.

Kriminalrat Nitsche	”-”–03.1942
SS-Sturmbannführer, Regierungs und Kriminalrat Friedrich Weber	03.1942–02.1945

Kattowitz: was a KRIPO Stelle under the KRIPO-(Leit)-Stelle Bresl was until 10 November 1941 when it was upgraded to Leitstelle status under the command of IdS Breslau. It took over the supervision of the KRIPO-Stelle Oppeln and Troppau from Breslau and it also supervised the KRIPO Stellen in Gleiwitz and Sosnowitz. It was abolished in August 1944 when a KdS was created under Dr. Johannes Thümmler.

SS-Obersturmbannführer, Oberregierungs und Krminalrat Max Rausch	10.05.1941–08.1944

Köln: was a KRIPO Stelle under the KRIPO-(Leit)-Stelle Frankfurt am Main until 1940 when it was upgraded to Leitstelle status under the IdS Düsseldorf. It supervised the KRIPO-Stellen in Aachen, Koblenz and Trier.

SS-Obersturmbannführer, Oberregierungs und Kriminalrat Franz Sommer	1940–11.11.1944
SS-Obersturmbannführer, Oberregierungs und Kriminalrat Max Wielen	11.11.1944–end

Königsberg: was under the command of IdS Königsberg. It supervised the KRIPO Stellen in Tilsit and Zichenau. It was abolished on 17 August 1944 when a KdS was created under Kurt Gornig.

Oberregierungs und Kriminalrat
Paul Elsner ”-”–10.08.1940
zur zeit unbesetzt (office vacant) 10.08.1940–21.09.1940

SS-Obersturmbannführer, Oberregierungs und Kriminalrat
Dr. Horst Barth 21.09.1940–10.05.1941

SS-Sturmbannführer, Oberregierungs und Kriminalrat
Harry Schulze 10.05.1941–12.09.1942

SS-Obersturmbannführer, Oberregierungs und Kriminalarat
Dr. Kamillo Brichta 12.09.1942–28.11.1942

SS-Sturmbannführer, Regierungs und Kriminalrat
Helmuth Müller 28.11.1942–17.08.1944

München: was under the command of IdS München. It supervised the KRIPO-Stelle in Augsburg. Until the late 1930's it had supervised the KRIPO Stellen in Nürnberg (upgraded to Leitstelle), in Regensburg and in Wüzburg (both transferred to the supervision of Nürnberg).

SS-Standartenführer, Regierungs und Kriminaldirektor
Hans Kaphengst 20.09.1937–15.03.1941

SS-Sturmbannführer, Regierungs und Kriminalrat
Hans Klamp 15.03 1941–19.04.1941

SS-Oberführer und Oberst der Polizei Paul Schmitz-Voigt 19.04.1941–12.09.1942

SS-Sturmbannführer, Regierungs und Kriminalrat
Dr. Hans Pokorny 12.09.1942–06.02.1943

SS-Obersturmbannführer, Oberregierungs und Kriminalrat
Philipp Greiner 06.02.1943–end

Nürnberg: was a KRIPO Stelle under the supervision of the KRIPO-(Leit)-Stelle München until the late 1930's when it was upgraded to Leitstelle status. It was under the command of IdS Nürnberg and supervised the KRIPO Stellen in Regensburg, Würzburg and Karlsbad. It was abolished in February 1945 when a KdS was created under Erich Naumann.

Oberregierungs und Kriminalrat Friedrich Greiner 01.10.1933–01.10.1941

SS-Obersturmbannführer, Oberregierungs und Kriminalrat
Philipp Greiner 01.10.194–19.09.1942

SS-Sturmbannführer, Oberregierungs und Kriminalrat Dr. Friedrich Riese	19.09.1942–.02.1945

Posen: was under the comand of IdS Posen. It supervised the KRIPO Stellen in Hohensalza and Litzmannstadt. It was abolished on the 9 September 1944 with the formation of a KdS under Dr. Karl Putz.

Regierungs und Kriminalrat Wilhelm Weitzel	11.1939–1943
SS-Sturmbannführer, Regierungs und Kriminalrat Hugo Krüger	1943–09.09.1944

Prag: was under the command of BdS Prague. It supervised the KRIPO Stelle in Brünn. It was abolished 23 December 1944 when a KdS was created under Dr. Ernst Gerke.

SS-Oberführer, und Oberst der Polizei Paul Schmitz-Voigt	01.08.1939–19.04.1941
SS-Standartenführer, Regierungs und Kriminaldirektor Friedrich Sowa	19.04.1941–23.12.1944

Salzburg: originally a KRIPO Stelle, it was upgraded to Leitstelle status in 1940. It was under the command of IdS Salzburg. It supervised the KRIPO Stellen in Graz, Klagenfurt and Innsbruck. The KRIPO Stelle Innsbruck was transferred as an independent KRIPO Stelle and was put under the BdS Verona in 1943.

SS-Sturmbannführer, Kriminalrat Dr. Anton Bohmer	29.06.1940–12.08.1944
SS-Obersturmbannführer, Oberregierungs und Kriminalrat Günther Braschwitz	12.08.1944–end

Stettin: was under the command of IdS Stettin. It supervised the KRIPO Stelle in Schneidemühl and Schwerin.

SS-Standartenführer, Regierungs und Kriminaldirektor Friedrich Sowa	01.06.1939–15.01.1940
Regierungs und Kriminalrat Eduard Holters	15.01.1940–11.04.1942
Regierungs und Kriminalrat Erich Kroll	11.04.1942–26.02.1944
Kriminaldirektor Gatzke (i.V)	26.02.1944–12.08.1944
SS-Sturmbannführer, Kriminaldirektor Peter Liesabeths	12.08.1944–end

Stuttgart: was under the commmand of IdS Stuttgart. It controlled the KRIPO Stellen in Ludwigshafen, Karlsruhe and Saarbrücken. It was abolished February 1945 when a KdS was created under Friedrich Mussgay.

Oberregierungsrat Ernst Lauer	01.10.1936–01.07.1940
Oberregierungs und Kriminalrat Paul Elsner	01.07.1940–11.11.1944
SS-Obersturmbannführer, Oberregierungs und Kriminalrat Heinz Hermann	11.11.1944–.02.1945

Wien: was under the command of IdS Wien. It supervised the KRIPO Stelle in Salzburg until 1940 when that office was upgraded to Leitstelle status. It also supervised the KRIPOStellen in Graz, Innsbruck and Klagenfurt until 1940 when those three offices passed to the new Leitstelle in Salzburg. The KRIPO Stelle in Linz remained in Wien's jurisdiction until the end. It was abolished on the 16 December 1944 when a KdS created on the 1 December 1944 under Dr. Edmund Trinkl took over its duties. The KdS was enlarged and command passed to Dr. Rudolf Mildner on the 16 December 1944

SS-Brigadeführer und Generalmajor der Polizei Johannes Thiele	12.04.1940–01.03.1941
SS-Standartenführer, Regierungs und Kriminaldirektor Hans Kaphengst	01.03.1941- 16.12.1944

Notes; The dates of sucession are only approximate, they are the issue dates of the Befehlsblatt der Chef der Sicherheitspolizei und des SD. These orders purport to show each mans rank, however errors are not uncommon, i.e. in all orders Paul Elsner is shown with the SS-rank of Sturmbannführer, however his name does not appear in any SS rank list. It is not the only case and the rank list is more accurate. Of a total of 48 officers who served as heads of Leitstelle, 34 had SS-rank and 15 did not.

2.5 Feuerschutzpolizei (fire police protection)

During the Weimar period in Germany fire fighting and fire protection was organised on two levels. In the larger cities professional fire brigades (Beruffeuerwehren) existed under the control of the relevant city administration. In the smaller towns and villages voluntary fire brigades (Freiwilligen Feuerwehren) existed also under the control of the local administration. The professional fire brigades were manned by civil servants trained as fire engineers who were employed by city administrations and the voluntary brigades were manned by members of the community who were not trained engineers and were not paid. It is assumed that volunteers were given some training by professionals but most learnt as they worked. During this period fire fighting was not considered part of the police.

The decree of the 30 January 1934 called the Law for the Reconstruction of the Reich effectively abolished the federal system. The state governments remained in existence but they were subordinated to the Reich authorities. This meant that all fire fighting whilst still controlled by local authorities was now under Reich authority. The decree of the 17 June 1936 creating a Chief of the German Police within the Ministry of the Interior brought the fire service within the Police Administration, it became part of the Staatliche Polizeiverwaltung (state Police Administration) as a specialised unit but its manpower remained as before. In January 1937 an Inspektion für Feuerlöschwesen (Inspector of Fire Fighting Services) was created within the ORPO headquarters. It was headed by SS-Gruppenführer und Generalleutnant der Polizei Dr. Johannes Meyer, a trained fire fighting engineer and its task was to supervise the technical aspects of the service, including the professional and voluntary levels. It evaluated the executive corps and was concerned with training, material and equipment. The Inspector made recommendations on fire fighting methods to the head of the ORPO and details on the development of the Inspectorate can be found in the chapter on the ORPO headquarters. On the 25 November 1937 an Amt Feuerschutzpolizei (Office for Fire Protection Police) was created under the Kommandoamt of the ORPO headquarters. It was organised as follows:

Amt Feuerschutzpolizei.
Oberbaurat der Feuerwehr Walter Goldbach

Sachgebiete F1 (General Organisation, Administration)
Oberbaurat der Feuerwehr Walter Goldbach

Sachgebiete F2 (Action, Disposal, Material
Baurat der Feuerwehr Dr. Wilhelm Kalass

Sachgebiete F3 (Personnel, Training)
Baurat der Feuerwehr Fritz Gunderloch

Sachgebiete F4 (Construction, Water, Signals, Press)
Baurat der Feuerwehr Georg Bergmüller to 1940
Oberbaurat der Feuerwehr Helmut Schikorr

With the creation of Amtsgruppen within the Kommandoamt in December 1940 the Amt Feuerschutzpolizei was put under Amtsgruppe Kommando I and its title was changed to Gruppe Feuerschutzpolizei. In the major reorganisation of the Hauptamt in September 1943 the office was upgraded to Inspectorate status but it remained under Amtsgruppe Kommando I. The Inspector was Oberstleutnant der Feuerschutzpolizei Johannes Schmidt. It will be noted that this office was, from its creation, called a Polizei office. However it was a decree of 23 November 1938 which gave the professional fire service the status of "vollzugpolizeibeamten" (police executive officials). A decree of September 1939 made the professional fire service a "Technische Polizeitruppe" (Technical Police Force) and it was ranked alongside the Schutzpolizei, Gendarmerie etc. At this time its total complement consisted of 213 engineers and leaders and 9423 men. Moving to the voluntary sector the decree of 23 November 1938 separated the voluntary from the professional fire services and on the 24 October 1939 the voluntary fire service became a "Technische Auxiliary Polizei" (Technical Auziliary Police). Part 6 of the November 1938 decree, which was published on the 3 January 1940, provided for the creation of the Amt für Freiwilligen Feuerwehren (Office of the Voluntary Fire Service) under Generalmajor der Polizei Walter Schnell. This office was put under the Hauptsamt ORPO on the 9 May 1941 and it was disolved following the major reorganisation of the Hauptamt on the 15 September 1943, its duties and tasks were transferred to the Generalinspekteur der Feuerschutzpolizei und Feuerwehren (General Inspector of the Fire Service Police and the Voluntary Fire Service) under Generalmajor der Polizei Hans Rumpf. To emphasize the separation of the voluntary from the professional fire service a Reichsamt Freiwillige Feuerwehren (National Office for Voluntary Fire Services) was created by order of the Reichsführer-SS and Chef der Deutschen Polizei on the 11 March 1942 (1) (O-VuR RII 321/42). It came under the umbrella of the Hauptamt ORPO but was an independant office except for personnel matters and pay structure. It was subject to orders as applied to the ORPO as a whole but was not under a specific office in the Hauptamt, to that extent it retained a measure of independence being directly under the Ministry of the Interior. I suppose that the whole matter was academic as the Ministry of the Interior was shortly after given to the Reichsführer-SS thereby nullifying any sense of independence. The head of this new office was Generalmajor der Polizei Walter Schnell.

Organisation of the Fire Protection Police

The decree of September 1939 established a command structure for the professional fire services in the major towns and cities of the Reich. Those towns and cities listed in the decree had to transfer what fire services they had into the new organisation and all members of the service became Police Executive Officials. The decision whether a town had to form a professional fire service not only depended on the size of the population but also on certain characteristics and conditions founded in the locality such as the type and volume of such a towns industrial activity, its buildings and construction, its potential exposure to air raids etc. The local head of the fire service police was designated Kommandeur and he was responsible for the organisation and operation of the entire unit. He allotted operational areas to the various subsections of his command and issued orders concerning fire prevention. He was tactically subordinate to the relevant Kommandeur der Schutzpolizei. The local fire service was divided into Abschnittkommandos (District Commands) and these, in turn, were divided into Wachbezirk (Ward Areas). Each Wachbezirk had a number of Feuerlöschzug (Fire Fighting Platoons). In the cities of Berlin, Wien and Hamburg an additional level of command was imposed between the Kommandeur level and the Abschnitt level called Gruppenkommando (Group Command).

Chart of Command of Fire Services for Berlin, Hamburg and Wien

Kommandeur der Feuerschutzpolizei

Gruppenkommando

Abschnitt Kommandeur

Wachbezirk

Loschzug

Chart of Command of Fire
Kommandeur der Feuerschutzpolizei
Abschnitt Kommandeur
Wachbezirk
Loschzug

Sachbearbeiter "Feuerschutzpolizei" beim IdO/BdO

At the regional level (Wehrkreis) a staff officer was appointed to the Befehlhaber der Ordnungspolizei. He was called Sachbearbeiter Feuerschutzpolizei beim IdO/BdO (special advisor to the Schutzpolizei Inspector) and his task was to advise the Inspector on all matters concerning fire fighting. After the outbreak of war such officers were appointed to the police inspectorates in the occupied territories. To emphasise the connection with the police it was the duty of all members of the Feuerschutzpolizei to exercise full police powers in matters outside their technical sphere, whenever officials of the Schutzpolizei or Gendarmerie could not be reached.

Sachbearbeiter Feuerschutzpolizei beim IdO/BdO (1943)

Kommandoamt der Hauptamt ORPO
SS-Standartenführer, Generalmajor der Polizei Walter Goldbach

Wehrkreis I Königsberg
SS-Sturmbannführer, Oberstleutnant der Feuerschutzpolizei Wilhelm Braun

Wehrkreis II Stettin
Oberstleutnant der Feuerschutzpolizei Elfreich

Wehrkreis III Berlin
Oberstleutnant der Feuerschutzpolizei Kadow

Wehrkreis IV Dresden
Unknown

Wehrkreis V Stuttgart
Unknown

Wehrkreis VI Münster
Oberstleutnant der Feuerschutzpolizei Senf
Oberstleutnant der Feuerschutzpolizei Roesner

Wehrkreis VII München
SS-Obersturmbannführer und Oberstleutnant der Feuerschutzpolizei Rolf Weinmayer

Wehrkries VIII Breslau
Oberstleutnant der Feuerschutzpolizei Richard Gribow
Oberstleutnant der Feuerschutzpolizei Hammerstein

Wehrkreis IX Kassel
Major der Feuerschutzpolizei Isenbart
Oberstleutnant der Feuerschutzpolizei Oberbaurat Dr. Freiesleben
Oberstleutnant der Feuerschutzpolizei Noehl

Wehrkreis X Hamburg
Oberstleutnant der Feuerschutzpolizei Drews
Oberstleutnant der Feuerschutzpolizei Stoll

Wehrkreis XI Hannover
Oberstleutnant der Feuerschutzpolizei Bange
Major der Feuerschutzpolizei Effenberger

Wehrkreis XII Wiesbaden
Oberstleutnant der Feuerschutzpolizei Hans
Oberstleutnant der Feuerschutzpolizei Noehl

Wehrkreis XIII Nürnberg
Oberbaurat Fahrner

Wehrkreis XVII Wien
SS-Obersturmbannführer und Oberstleutnant der Feuerschutzpolizei Gerhard Kattenstroth

Wehrkreis XVIII Salzburg
Oberstleutnant der Feuerschutzpolizei Holsten
Oberstleutnant der Feuerschutzpolizei Abrell

Wehrkreis XX Danzig
SS-Obersturmbannführer und Oberstleutnant der Feuerschutzpolizei Heinrich Engelhardt
Oberstleutnant der Feuerschutzpolizei Papke

Wehrkreis XXI Posen
SS-Obersturmbannführer und Oberstleutnant der Feuerschutzpolizei Kurt Günter
Oberstleutnant der Feuerschutzpolizei Sauer

Protektorat Böhmen-Mähren
Oberstleutnant der Feuerschutzpolizei Garski
Major der Feuerschutzpolizei Mobius
SS-Sturmbannführer und Major der Feuerschutzpolizei Gerhard Haase

Generalgouvernement Polen
Oberstleutnant der Feuerschutzpolizei Garski
SS-Obersturmbannführer und Oberstleutnant der Feuerschutzpolizei Heinz Günther
Oberstleutnant der Feuerschutzpolizei Assmann
SS-Sturmbannführer und Major der Feuerschutzpolizei Wilhelm Gabbert
Major der Feuerschutzpolizei Sopp

Paris
Major der Feuerschutzpolizei Adam
Oberstleutnant der Feuerschutzpolizei Friedrich Seifert

Brussels
Unknown

Den Haag
Oberstleutnant der Feuerschutzpolizei Hertell
Oberstleutnant der Feuerschutzpolizei Assmann

Kopenhagen
Unknown

Oslo
Oberstleutnant der Feuerschutzpolizei Johannes Westphal
SS-Obersturmbannführer und Oberstleutnant der Feuerschutzpolizei Heinz Günther

Riga
SS-Obersturmbannführer und Oberstleutnant der Feuerschutzpolizei Heinrich Engelhardt

Rowno/Kiew
Oberstleutnant der Feuerschutzpolizei Richard Gribow
Oberstleutnant der Feuerschutzpolizei Anton Heupel

Simferopol
Unknown

Belgrad
Oberstleutnant der Feuerschutzpolizei Hammerstein

Athen
Unknown

Esseg
Unknown

Gardasee Verona
Oberstleutnant der Feuerschutzpolizei Richard Gribow

Trieste
Unknown

Slowakei
Unknown

Minsk
Oberstleutnant der Feuerschutzpolizei Hammerstein

As has already been mentioned, the decree of the 23 November 1938 separated the non-professional from the professional fire brigades and on the 24 October 1939 the voluntary sector became part of the police. This sector consisted of three separate types of fire service. Firstly the Freiwilligen Feuerwehren (Voluntary Fire Brigades) which was set up in any town which was not compelled by decree to set up a professional fire brigade. The town council had to form a fire brigade trained and equipped to combat fires in the town. The difference was that the members had other duties and were only required when fires occurred. The second type of brigade was the Pflichtfeuerwehren (Compulsory Fire Brigades) and this type of brigade was set up in towns where voluntary enlistment did not suffice.

The relevant Bürgermeister (Mayor) in his town or the local Landrat (Rural Councillor) in his Landkreis (Rural District) could establish a compulsory fire brigade by drafting suitable personnel for service. The difference between these brigades and the voluntary brigades was the compulsory nature of them. They received the same training as the voluntary brigades. Wartime manpower shortages went far in depleting the ranks of the voluntary brigades and the authorities had to resort more and more to the employment of Pflichtfeuerwehren to fill the gaps. Even though a Feuerschutzpolizei may already exist in a town the Ortspolizeibehörde (Local Police Authority) could have decided that it was inadequate to meet all contingencies and therefore they could supplement the professionals by establishing a voluntary or compulsory brigade to serve alongside the professionals. Such brigades retained administrative independence but for all tactical purposes they were operationally attached to the professional brigade and for training and employment they were subordinated to the local Feuerschutzpolizei commander. Recruits for both of these non-professional brigades must, in addition to the required minimum physical qualifications, have been known to have been at "The disposal of the National Socialist State at all times and without reservations". They could not be drawn from the Technische Nothilfe, the German Red Cross or a works fire brigade but except for these limitations all Germans between the ages of 17 and 65 were eligible for service in these brigades. The last of these voluntary services were the Werkfeuerwehr (Factory Fire Brigades), these units were established by the management of industrial concerns and were staffed by employees.

Also the relevant Regierungspräsident (District Administrator) in conjunction with the Reich Ministry of the Interior and the local air raid protection headquarters in the Reichsgruppe Industrie (National League for Industry) could determine where factory brigades were to be established. Similarly a factory desiring to organise a Werkfeuerwehr could seek the approval of the above mentioned authorities by submitting a request through the local air raid protection unit and the local police authority. Each factory unit must consist of at least eighteen members and must have been equipped with a minimum of one power driven pump. They would, obviously, be the first brigade to attend any emergency but they could quickly call on local professional brigades for assistance. To counter the increased wartime manpower shortage within the ranks of both the professional and voluntary fire brigades, use was made of the HJ Feuerwehrscharen (Hitler Youth Fire Fighting Platoons). This service was founded as the Jugendfeuerwehrschar (Youth Fire Defense Service) in 1938 as a result of co-ordination between the Reichsjugendführung and the Reichsführer-SS in an effort to further develop the air defense plans of Germany which naturally included fire fighting. Volunteers were under HJ leadership and consisted of units of various sizes, depending on the number of available volunteers, organised into groups and platoons, they were trained in the basic technical elements of fire fighting. A definitive fire fighting training plan was devised including theoretical as well as practical elements. A meeting between the General Inspector for the Fire Service and the Fire Service Police, Dr. Johannes Meyer and HJ Leaders in June 1939 resulted in the creation of the HJ Feuerlöschdienst (Hitler Youth Fire Fighting Service).

A directive from the Reichsjugendführung dated the 30 June 1939 specified that the HJ Fire Fighting Volunteers be subordinated to the HJ Streifendienst (Hitler Youth Patrol Service) and in March 1941 it was decided to change the designation to Feuerwehrscharen im Hitlerjugend Streifendienst. It was further decreed that such units would become part of the Feuerlöschdienstreserve (Fire Fighting Reserve). The fire fighting plan was implemented on the 1 September 1940 and participants in the Feuerwehrscharen since the 1 October 1940 were the first to received the "K-Schien der Hitler-jugend" the K-Certificate of the Hitler Youth. These units played a significant role during the war especially considering the extensive Allied incendiary attacks on industrial targets. The demands for manpower became so acute that the age limitation was waived and the younger Deutsche Jungvolk members became involved. All expenses of the Fire Protection Services, both professional and voluntary, were met entirely by the local community. In the case of works brigades the cost was shared with the factory that organised them. Only for the maintenance of Fire Brigade Schools in the Länder and the Prussian Provinces was the cost shared between the Länder and the Provinces and the Reich Government. An exception was the Reichsfeuerwehrschule in Eberswalde, commanded by Oberstleutnant der Feuerschutpolizei Walter Hans from the 27 October 1941, which was fully under the control of the Reich Government and was, therefore, funded by them. For purely technical matters the fire fighting organisations relied on the specialised knowledge of the Reichsverein Deutscher Feuerwehringingenieure (National League of German Fire Protection Engineers).

Kommandeur der Feuerschutzpolizei

Aachen

Oberstleutnant der Feuerschutzpolizei Senf ”-”–1943

Augsburg

Baurat der Feuerwehr Hammer ”-”–01.10.1940

SS-Obersturmbannführer und Oberstleutnant der Feuerschutzpolizei Ernst Schilling 01.10.1940–end

Berlin

Generalleutnant Gustav Wagner ”-”–.05.1943

SS-Standartenführer, Generalmajor der Polizei Walter Goldbach 05.1943–26.04.1945

Beuthen

“ -”

Bielefeld

“ -”

Bochum

Major der Feuerschutzpolizei Effenberge ”-”–1943

SS-Sturmbannführer und Major der Feuerschutzpolizei Dr. Werner Kurth 1943–end

Bonn

Major der Feuerschutzpolizei Krause 01.1943–end

Brandenburg
" -"

Braunschweig

Major der Feuerschutzpolizei Worman	"-"–1943
Major der Feuerschutzpolizei Stude	1943–end

Bremen

SS-Standartenführer und Oberst der Feuerschutzpolizei	
Georg Schetzker	"-"–1943
Oberstleutnant der Feuerschutzpolizei Kissling	1943–end

Bremerhaven " -"

Breslau

SS-Obersturmbannführer und Oberstleutnant der Feuerschutzpolizei	
Heinz Günther	"-"–1943
Oberstleutnant der Feuerschutzpolizei Hammerstein	1943–1944
Oberst der Feuerschutzpolizei Hoffmann	1944–end

Bromberg

Oberstleutnant der Feuerschutzpolizei Patelt	1941 -1943
SS-Sturmbannführer und Major der Feuerschutzpolizei	
Heinrich Schläfer	1943–end

Chemnitz

Oberstleutnant der Feuerschutzpolizei Haase	"-"–02.1944
" -"	02.1944–end

Danzig

Oberstleutnant der Feuerschutzpolizei Winchenbach	28.06.1939–31.01.1944
" -"	31.01.1944–end

Darmstadt

" -"	"-"–end

Dessau

SS-Sturmbannführer und Major der Feuerschutzpolizei	
August Eilert	1942–1943

Dortmund

Oberst der Feuerschutzpolizei Firsbach	03.1941–1944

Dresden

Oberbaurat Leithold	"-"–1939
Oberstleutnant der Feuerschutzpolizei Wolff	1939–1943
Major der Feuerschutzpolizei Dabbert	1943–1944
Oberstleutnant der Feuerschutzpolizei Wolff	1944–end

Duisburg

Oberbaurat Fritz Zingler	"-"–1943
Major der Feuerschutzpolizei Bongartz	1943–1944
Major der Feuerschutzpolizei Frosch	1944–end

Düsseldorf

Oberstleutnant der Feuerschutzpolizei Senf	1943–1944
Oberstleutnant der Feuerschutzpolizei Eller	1944–1944

Elbingen

" -"

Erfurt

" -"

Essen

SS-Sturmbannführer und Major der Feuerschutzpolizei Walter Todt	"-"–10.1940
Oberstleutnant Hin	10.1940–01.1943
SS-Obersturmbannführer und Oberstleutnant der Feuerschutzpolizei Friedrich Gaarz	01.1943–12.1943

Members of fire service regiment 2 "Hannover" take a meal break 1943

Oberstleutnant der Feuerschutzpolizei, Oberbaurat
Dr. Freiesleben 12.1943–end

Flensburg
SS-Sturmbannführer und Major der Feuerschutzpolizei
Arnold Harms ”-”–1943

Frankfurt am Main
Major der Feuerschutzpolizei
Sopp ”-”–1943
SS-Obersturmbannführer und Oberstleutnant der Feuerschutzpolizei
Dr. Georg Langbeck 1943–end

Frankfurt an der Oder
Oberstleutnant der Feuerschutzpolizei
Freese 1943–end

Gelsenkirchen
Oberstleutnant der Feuerschutzpolizei
Scholten 1938–1940
Oberst der Feuerschutzpolizei
Manskopf 1940–end

Gleiwitz
“ -”

Görlitz
Major der Feuerschutzpolizei Sadeck ”-”–1944
Hauptmann der Feuerschutzpolizei Schrader 1944–end

Gotenhafen
Major der Feuerschutzpolizei Hertell 01.03.1939–.04.1943
SS-Sturmbannführer und Major der Feuerschutzpolizei
Helmut Knies 04.1943–end

Graz
SS-Sturmbannführer und Major der Feuerschutzpolizei
Arnulf Schreiner ”-”–end

Guben
Hauptmann der Feuerschutzpolizei Geilenberg 1941–end

Hagen
Major der Feuerschutzpolizei Ulrich ”-”–”-”

Halle an der Saale

SS-Sturmbannführer und Major der Feuerschutzpolizei Helmut Leymann	”-”–1944
SS-Obersturmbannführer und Obertstleutnant der Feuerschutzpolizei Walter Zettner	1944–end

Hamburg

Generalmajor Dr. Otto Zaps	01.02.1937 – end

Hannover

Oberstleutnant der Feuerschutzpolizei Hans Schmidt	1933–29.11.1940
Major der Feuerschutzpolizei Isnenghi	29.11.1940–14.06.1943
Oberstleutnant der Feuerschutzpolizei Hans Schmidt	14.06.1943–15.09.1943
Oberstleutnant der Feuerschutzpolizei Witzler	15.09.1943–end

Heidelberg

SS-Obersturmbannführer und Oberstleutnant der Feuerschutzpolizei Karl Kargl	01.05.1939–end

Hindenberg

“ -”

Innsbruck

Major der Feuerschutzpolizei Stoltz	03.1938–end

Karlsruhe

Major der Feuerschutzpolizei Effenberger	1944–end

Kassel

“ -”

Kattowitz

“ -”

Kiel

SS-Sturmbannführer und Major der Feuerschutzpolizei Josef Steiner	”-”–1942
Oberstleutnant der Feuerschutzpolizei Siber	1942–end

Köln

Oberst der Feuerschutzpolizei Baurat Walter Hans	1938–1939
SS-Obersturmbannführer und Oberstleutnant der Feuerschutzpolizei Rolf Weinmayer	1939–1942
Major der Feuerschutzpolizei Krause	1943–1944
Oberstleutnant der Feuerschutzpolizei Drews	1944–end

Königsberg

Oberstleutnant der Feuerschutzpolizei Stoll	1939–1944
Oberstleutnant der Feuerschutzpolizei Scholten	1944–end

Königshütte

SS-Sturmbannführer und Major der Feuerschutzpolizei	
Ludwig Smutny	03.1941–end

Krefeld-Uerdingen

Major der Feuerschutzpolizei Bongartz	”-”–1943
Major der Feuerschutzpolizei Glenz	1943–end

Leipzig

Oberbaurat Bange	”-” -12.1939
Oberstleutnant der Feuerschutzpolizei Scholten	01.1940–1944
Oberstleutnant der Feuerschutzpolizei Fritz Gunderloch	

Liegnitz

“ -”

Linz

“ -”

Litzmannstadt

Oberstleutnant der Feuerschutzpolizei Mikus	09.1939–end

Lübeck

Major der Feuerschutzpolizei Sachers	”-” -1944
SS-Sturmbannführer und Major der Feuerschutzpolizei	
Wilhelm Gabbert	01.1944–end

Ludwigshafen

“ -”

Magdeburg

Oberbaurat Fahrner	”-”–1939
Oberstleutnant der Feuerschutzpolizei Bieck	1939–02.1944
SS-Obersturmbannführer und Oberstleutnant der Feuerschutzpolizei	
Heinz Günther	02.1944–end

Mainz

Oberstleutnant der Feuerschutzpolizei Noehl	”-”–12.1943
Major der Feuerschutzpolizei Kirchner	12.1943–end

Mannheim

Major der Feuerschutzpolizei Kohle ”-”–1944

Memel

Hauptmann der Feuerschutzpolizei Lebius 03.1939–1943

SS-Sturmbannführer und Major der Feuerschutzpolizei
Wilhelm Gabbert 1943–1944

Metz

Major der Feuerschutzpolizei Hawalka 07.1940–end

Mönchengladbach

Major der Feuerschutzpolizei Eller ”-”–1941

SS-Sturmbannführer und Major der Feuerschutzpolizei
Walter Todt 1941–end

Mülheim

SS-Sturmbannführer und Major der Feuerschutzpolizei Alfred Freter ”-”–”-”

München

Oberstleutnant der Feuerschutzpolizei Abrell ”-” -1942

SS-Obersturmbannführer und Oberstleutnant der Feuerschutzpolizei
Ernst Wittmann 1942–end

Münster

Major der Feuerschutzpolizei Boll 1944–end

Neumünster

“ -”

Nürnberg

Oberstleutnant der Feuerschutzpolizei Rudolf Bethke 23.11.1938–1941

Major der Feuerschutzpolizei Bumiller 1941–1942

Major der Feuerschutzpolizei Winkler 1942–1943

Oberhausen

“ -”

Offenbach

“ -”

Oldenburg

SS-Sturmbannführer und Major der Schutzpolizei Hanns Spohn 1944–end

Osnabrück

“ -”

Plauen in Vogtland

Major der Feuerschutzpolizei Roessler	"-"–1943

Posen

Oberstleutnant der Schutzpolizei Kurt Müller	10.1939–17.01.1941
Oberstleutnant der Feuerschutzpolizei Heising	17.01.1941–01.1943
Oberstleutnant der Feuerschutzpolizei Hin	01.1943 -1944
SS-Sturmbannführer und Major der Feuerschutzpolizei Georg Bergmüller	1944–end

Potsdam

SS-Obersturmbannführer und Oberstleutnant der Feuerschutzpolizei Willi Kohrs	"-"–1942
SS-Sturmbannführer und Major der Feuerschutzpolizei Karl Lurf	1942–end

Prag

Oberst der Feuerschutzpolizei Petersen	"-"–08.1943
Oberstleutnant der Feuerschutzpolizei Garski	08.1943–02.1944

Regensburg

" -"

Remscheid

SS-Sturmbannführer und Major der Feuerschutzpolizei Dr. Walter Fehle	"-"–1943
Major der Feuerschutzpolizei Winkler	1943–end

Rostock

Hauptmann der Feuerschutzpolizei Thoms - end

Saarbrücken

" -"

Schwerin

Major der Feuerschutzpolizei Rönning	1941–end

Sosnowitz

SS-Sturmbannführer und Major der Feuerschutzpolizei Walter Todt	10.1940–1941

Stettin

Stadtbaurat Roesner	"-"–"-" 1939
SS-Sturmbannführer und Major der Feuerschutzpolizei Wilhelm Gabbert	1939–12.1943

Stralsund

Hauptmann der Feuerschutzpolizei Schmidt	1939–1944
Hauptmann der Feuerschutzpolizei Margies	1944–end

Strassburg

Major der Feuerschutzpolizei Vaulmont	21.06.1940 -1941
Major der Feuerschutzpolizei Schweighauser	1941–end

Stuttgart

Oberbaurat Reutlinger	"-"–1940
Oberstleutnant der Feuerschutzpolizei Hammerstein	1940–1943
SS-Sturmbannführer und Major der Feuerschutzpolizei Rudolf Reiss	1940–end (i.V until 1943)

Thorn

" -"

Tilsit

" -"

Wesermünde

Major der Feuerschutzpolizei Druhmel	1939–1941

Wien

Oberstleutnant der Feuerschutzpolizei Friedrich Seifert	1939–1941
Generalmajor der Polizei Dr. Paul Bernaschek	1941–03.1944
SS-Standartenführer und Oberst der Feuerschutzpolizei Johann Stanzig	03.1944–end

Wiesbaden

" -"

Wilhelmshaven

SS-Sturmbannführer und Major der Feuerschutzpolizei Hanns Spohn	1939–1944

Wuppertal

Baurat Zehlein	- 1943
Oberstleutnant der Feuerschutzpolizei Riedel	1943–end

Zwickau

" -"

Note: It is obvious that these listings are incomplete, they are based on records from the Archiv in Berlin that was formerly controlled by the East German Government.

Fire representatives in State Governments

Representatives for the fire service existed in all state governments. They advised on all matters concerning fire fighting and helped with financial support for fire brigades. Liaison existed between state governments and the Hauptamt ORPO through these officials.

Anhalt Abteilung II of the Landesregierung
Ministerialrat Ackermann

Baden Abteilung Va in the Staatsministerium des Innern
Regierungsdirektor Schneider

Bayern Abteilung IV in the Staatsministerium des Innern
Regierungsdirektor Freiherr von Schwerin

Böhmen/Mähren Abteilung I of the Office of the Reichsprotektor
Ministerialrat Dr. Rossler

Braunschweig Abteilung III in the Staatsministerium des Innern
Landrat Sievers

Danzig/Westpreussen Abteilung I in the Office of the Reichsstatthalter
Regierungsdirektor Weber

Hamburg Abteilung III in the Staatsverwaltung
SS-Gruppenführer und Generalleutnant der Polizei Georg Graf von Bassewitz-Behr

Hessen Abteilung II in the Office of the Reichstatthalter
Regierungsdirektor Stier

Kärnten Abteilung I in the Office of the Reichstatthalter
Regierungsdirektor Dr. von Burger-Scheidlin

Lippe Abteilung I in the Landesregierung
Regierungsdirektor Dr. Oppermann

Mecklenburg in the Staatsminsterium des Innern
Ministerialdirektor Dr. Studemund

Niederdonau Abteilung I in the Office of the Reichstatthalter
Regierungsdirektor Dr. Vogel

Oberdonau Abteilung I in the Office of the Reichstatthalter
Regierungsdirektor Dr. Stoger

Oldenburg Abteilung C in the Staatsministerium des Innern
Ministerialrat Eilers

Sachsen Abteilung VI in the Staatsministerium des Innern
SS-Gruppenführer und Generalleutnant der Polizei Ernst Hitzegrad

Salzburg Abteilung I in the office of the Reichstatthalter
Regierungsdirektor Dengler

Steiermark Abteilung I in the office of the Reichstatthalter
Regierungsdirektor Dr. Mayrhofer

Sudetenland Abteilung I in the Office of the Reichstatthalter
Regierungsdirektor Kellner

Thüringen Abteilung P in the Staatsministerium des Innern
Oberregierungsrat Dr. Schmidt

Tirol-Vorarlberg Abteilung I in the Office of the Reichstatthalter
Regierungsdirektor Dr. Schuler

Wartheland Abteilung I in the Office of the Reichstatthalter
Regierungsdirektor Weber

Westmark Zentralreferat für Verkehr
Oberregierungsrat Dr. Schlessmann

Wien Abteilung I in the Office of the Reichstatthalter
Regierungsdirektor Dr. Kramer

Württemberg Abteilung VII in the Staatsministerium des Innern
Regierungsdirektor Richard Drautz

Note. This list dated from 1943 comes from the Taschenbuch für Verwaltungsbeamte issued by the Reich Ministery of the Interior. It will be noted that the Hamburg post was held by the Higher SS and Police Leader and the post for the Saxon government was held by the BdO for Dresden

Feuerwehren (Non professional fire units)

Until approximately 1939, leaders of fire fighting units did not hold police rank, they were titled "Baurat der Feuerwehr" and " Oberbaurat der Feuerwehr" (Building and Senior Building Councillors in Fire-Fighting). From 1939/1940 all were accorded police ranks followed by "der Feuerschutzpolizei". The voluntary sector had its own regional organisation and rank structure. Each unit was led by a brigade leader (Wehrführer) appointed by the relevant police authority. Initially there were three levels:

Provinzialfeuerwehrenführer	Sub-District Commander
Kreisfeuerwehrenführer	District Commander
Landesfeuerwehrführer	Sector Commander

On the 23 November 1939, the structure was changed to:

Kreisführer der Freiwilligen Feuerwehr	Middle level administrative authorities (Bürgermeister)
Bezirksführer der Freiwilligen Feuerwehr	Senior level administrative authorities (Reg Pdt)
Abschnittsinspekteur der Freiwilligen Feuerwehr	Land level authorities and HSSPF

As the war progressed, the rank structure changed again and ranks then conformed to the Technische Nothilfe rank structure as follows:

Landesführer der Feuerwehr	Oberst
Oberabteilungsführer der Feuerwehr	Oberstleutnant
Abteilungsführer der Feuerwehr	Major
Bereitschaftsführer der Feuerwehr	Hauptmann
Oberzugführer der Feuerwehr	Oberleutnant
Zugführer der Feuerwehr	Leutnant

In 1944, the following Feuerwehr leaders were given rank in the Feuerschutzpolizei on the Reserve:

"4" Promoted Oberst der Feuerschutzpolizei
Landesführer der Feuerwehr für München Bimeslehner
Landesführer der Feuerwehr für Posen Gustav Kilian
Landesführer der Feuerwehr für Magdeburg Scholz
Landesführer der Feuerwehr für Düsseldorf Wolf
Landesführer der Feuerwehr für Stolp Zander
Landesführer der Feuerwehr für Braunschweig Hans Helmke
"4" Promoted Oberstleutnant der Feuerschutzpolizei
Landesführer der Feuerwehr für Baden-Baden Kurt Bürkle
Landesführer der Feuerwehr für Oldenburg Fortmann
Landesführer der Feuerwehr für Mainz Müller
Landesführer der Feuerwehr für Münster Querfeld
Landesführer der Feuerwehr für St Wendel Kassemeyer
Landesführer der Feuerwehr für Güstrow Hans Richter
Landesführer der Feuerwehr für Breslau Sauerbier
Landesführer der Feuerwehr für Dobberpfuhl Otto Richter
Oberabteilungsführer der Feuerwehr für Klagenfurt Kohla

The voluntary fire brigades were a major component of the emergency system in Germany. When its 1,750,000 members became technical auxiliary police in 1939, they represented 79% of the total strength of the ORPO. The attack on Poland revealed the need for professional firemen to be used in newly occupied areas. Initially it was thought that the task could be covered by members of the Wehrmacht but it was soon realised that their expertise was in the area of engineering with no fire-fighting experience. As a result a "Schnellbrief" was issued by the Reichsführer-SS und Chef der Deutschen Polizei dated 20 December 1939 which stated that "In the interest of defence it is decided to create a regiment of fire fighters". As a result 131 qualified officials were selected as skeleton staff for the new regiment. This regiment became Feuerschutzpolizei- Regiment 1 "Sachsen" and it was followed in 1941 by Feuerschutzpolizei-Regiment 2 "Hannover" and the Feuerschutzpolizei-Regiment 3 "Ostpreussen". In the early summer of 1943 a further three regiments were established called "Niederlande" "Ukraine" and "Böhmen-Mähren". Details of these regiments can be found in the chapter on Polizei-Regiments. Following the abolishment of the regiments in June/July 1943 the units were reformed into Selbständige Feuerschutzpolizei-Abteilung (Motor) (Independent Fire Service detachments- motorised). By the end of the war a total of nine such units had entered service. They had a membership of between 450 and 520 men split into a staff with three companies. A typical detachment was manned as follows:

Abteilung (Detachment Staff)	67 men	31 vehicles
1 Kompanie	130 men	37 vehicles
2 Kompanie	130 men	37 vehicles
3 Kompanie	130 men	37 vehicles
Total	457 men	142 vehicles

The men were given basic infantry training combined with technical fire fighting training at the Feuerwehrschule Kurmark bei Beeskow and they were established at the Feuerschutzpolizei-Lager Burgdorf, the headquarters of the Feuerschutzpolizei-Abteilung 2. For supply and accommodation they came under the Truppen-Wirtschaftslager der Waffen-SS (Troop economic camp of the Waffen-SS). In February 1945 all Abteilungen were retitled SS-Feuerschutzpolizei-Abteilungen (Motor) and all officers and men were given SS-pay books and were tattooed, under the left arm, with their blood group. At the end of the war the Abteilungen were situated as follows:

SS-Feuerschutzpolizei-Abteilung 1 "Sachsen" in Rumania
SS-Feuerschutzpolizei-Abteilung 2 "Hannover" in Burgdorf Hannover
SS-Feuerschutzpolizei-Abteilung 3 "Ostpreussen" in the Wien area
SS-Feuerschutzpolizei-Abteilung 4 in the Bochum area
SS-Feuerschutzpolizei-Abteilung 5 in the München area
SS-Feuerschutzpolizei-Abteilung 6 in the Nürnberg area
SS-Feuerschutzpolizei-Abteilung 7 in the Berlin area
SS-Feuerschutzpolizei-Abteilung 8 in Holland
SS-Feuerschutzpolizei-Abteilung 9 in training for the Graz area.

Although by the end of the war the fire service was officially a fully integrated part of the SS many of its officers never took up SS-membership. From the list of known Feuerschutzpolizei commanders totalling 173 officers only 32 held SS rank ranging from Standartenführer to Sturmbannführer. Only two Lieutenant-Generals existed from the fire service and only five Major-Generals and from these totals one Lieutenant-General and two Major-Generals held SS rank.

2.6 Technische Nothilfe (Technical Emergency Corps)

The Technische Nothilfe (Technical Emergency Corps) was founded in 1919 under the auspices of Generaloberst Hans von Seeckt, the founder of the Reichswehr. The intention was to provide a technical organisation to be used in national emergencies and for the whole of its life it was known as the "TENO". During the initial years of the Weimar Republic it was mainly used to keep the public utilities and essential industries running during the wave of strikes and general political unrest instigated by various political parties from both the right and left wing. In effect it became a strike breaking organisation serving the Government in power. From 1925 until 1930, when the political scene had settled down, the organisation lost much of its importance although it remained in existence. In 1930 a gas and air protection service was introduced and the emergency service branch (Bereitschaftsdienst) was enlarged to become an organisation equipped to fight natural catastrophes. After Hitler became Chancellor of Germany in January 1933 the service was reorganised to serve the National Socialist Party as Government.

In 1934 it was converted into a fully fledged Party organisation named "Reichsamt Technische Nothilfe" under the aegis of the Reich Ministry of the Interior and from the 13 October 1936 it was put under the Reichsführer-SS und Chef der Deutschen Polizei. On the 18 June 1937 the Reichsamt became a permanent technical auxiliary corps of the police (Ständiges Technisches hilfsorgan der Polizei) and it came under the aegis of the ORPO although it was not directly subordinated to the Headquarters of the ORPO (1). At the end of December 1941 an Amt Technische Nothilfe (Office for Technical Emergency Services) was formed under the Hauptamt ORPO (2). This office was to provide assistance and liaison between the Hauptamt ORPO and the Reichsamt TENO and the head of the office was the same man as the head of the Reichsamt. The office was abolished in the general reorganisation of September 1943 when the Reichsamt lost its independent status and was put directly under Hauptamt ORPO where it remained until the end of the war. In 1936 a training school was opened in Belzig in Mark Brandenburg to train officers between the ages of 30 and 55. In March 1939 members of the TENO were given the right to carry sidearms and firearms. The law laying down the basic functions of the TENO was made public in 1939 and it stated that the TENO was to render technical assistance in the following three fields;

1) Keeping essential public utilities operating under all circumstances.
2) Air raid protection work.
3) Dealing with major emergencies.

This law also changed the organisation from a Verein (Membership organisation) to a Körperschaft des Offentlichen Rechtes (a legally registered state controlled corporation). In 1942 TENO was put directly under the SS und Polizeigerichtsbarkeit (SS and Police Jurisdiction and Disciplinary code).
Notes: (1) Rd Erl.d.RFSS, u.Ch. d. Dt. Pol. von 15.12.1937–O-VuR RIII 4975-37
(2) Erl.d.Chefs ORPO von 30.12.1941-O-HB 367 Nr2/41

The TENO was a corps of engineers, technicians and skilled and semi-skilled specialists in construction work. They specialised in public utilities operations, communications, metal salvage and other related fields and they were used after national catastrophes in the fields of rescue, demolition and restoration. During the war it was the primary force brought in to combat the after effects of air raids and, in this area, it made extensive use of prisoners of war as manpower often in tasks that were contrary to the Geneva convention. This authors uncle by marriage, Private Charles Lane of the Sherwood Foresters Regiment, who was captured in North Africa was one such man being employed in the Dresden area. The Wehrmacht also made extensive use of the corps from March 1938 and during the war Technische Abteilungen were attached to army

Groups to provide the same functions as in their civilian role. A depot for these field formations called "Ersatz-Abteilung der Technische Nothilfe" was set up in Köln-Dunnwald and each Abteilung was divided into specialist sections such as:

Bautrupp–Construction Section
Brücken und Schleusentrupp–Bridges and Water Locks
Leitungstrupp–Electrical section
Krantrupp–Crane section
Rohrtruppe–Pipeline section
Wasserwerktrupp–Waterworks maintenance section

In army rear areas, TENO units were allocated to the Higher SS and Police Leaders for their use in tasks of a technical nature. The overall organisation of the corps was that Germany was divided up into Landesgruppen. Each Landesgruppe was, if large enough, split into Bezirksgruppen which in turn were split into Ortsgruppen. They in turn were divided into Zweigstellen. In some areas the Landesgruppen which were smaller were divided directly into Ortsgruppe. Each Ortsgruppe was split into four departments Technischer Dienst (Technical Service), Bereitschaft Dienst (Emergency Service), Allgemeiner Dienst (General Service) and Luftschutz Dienst (Air Raid Protection Service). The latter involved the normal Luftschutz Dienst personnel who were considered part of the TENO during each emergency. Members of the TENO were generally men over military age, aged 45 to 70 who joined the organisation voluntarily. After the outbreak of war such volunteers found that they could no longer leave at will. They must also be politically reliable and must be able to prove their reliability to the National Socialist State.

No one who had been expelled from the Party could be accepted into the TENO. They must also be Germans or racial Germans (ethnic Germans from foreign countries). Only key positions in higher headquarters were filled by full time officers, the manpower generally served in the corps only during emergencies and they were known as "Notdienstpflichtige" (persons required to serve in an emergency on the home front). At the end of such emergencies such persons would return to their own jobs. In addition specialists could be appointed, both from within and from outside the corps. Called Sonderführer (Special Leaders) they could be given rank in the corps commensurate with their abilities. As the war progressed the corps started to bring in young men with the correct political and engineering background and they were trained to become professional TENO leaders. Those born in 1901 and after received their initial training with the Polizei-Lehr-Bataillon II in Iglau and upon completion they were posted to police units in the field as TENO leaders. As a state corps TENO was organised along military lines with its own uniform and ranks. From 1943 the rank badges underwent a major change emerging as almost identical to the SS reflecting its close association with that organisation. Finally the Germans created native organisations in some occupied countries.

In Norway a branch of the TENO was set up called "Tekniske Nödhjelpe" and it was put under the Norwegian "Ordenspoliti" (ORPO). In France the "Secours Technique" was set up in competition to the Organisation Todt. It recruited French technicians and was attached to the Luftwaffe. It wore a blue-grey uniform with black TENO ranks and other insignia although it is not known if the French national emblem was allowed. In Holland a "Technische Noodhulp" was introduced in July 1941 as a semi civilian, uniformed formation using technicians and engineering specialists. About 60 to 70 units of varying sizes were quartered in Holland under the control of the Luftwaffe and the members wore either the blue-grey Luftwaffe uniform or the black TENO uniform. Again it does not seem that any national emblem was worn and often the uniform consisted of nothing more than white overalls with the TENO badge. Some officers also held rank in other organisations such as the SS and Police and although the rank of Landesführer was equal to the police rank of Colonel some Landesführer held the rank of Major-General

Technische Nothilfe Organisation

Technische Nothilfe ranks:

Gemeinschaftsführer	2nd Lieutenant
Kameradschaftsführer	2nd Lieutenant
Gefolgschaftsführer	Lieutenant
Bereitschaftsführer	Captain
Hauptbereitschaftsführer	Major
Bezirksführer	Lieutenant-Colonel
Landesführer	Colonel

Chef

Ingenieur Lummitzsch — 1919–24.04.1934

SS-Gruppenführer und Generalleutnant der Polizei
Hans Weinreich (1) — 24.04.1934–15.10.1943

SS-Gruppenführer und Generalleutnant der Polizei
Willy Schmelcher — 15.10.1943–end

Stellvertretender Chef

Generalmajor Erich Hampe (2) — 1939–20.05.1941
Landesführer, Generalleutnant der Polizei Theodor Siebert — 20.05.1941–end

Chef des Stabes (formed on the 17 January 1943)

Generalmajor der Polizei Walter Junecke — 17.01.1943–end

Chef Adjutant

Hauptbereitschaftsführer, Major der Schutzpolizei Walter Troschke

Chef Führerverwaltung

Hauptbereitschaftsführer, Major der Schutzpolizei Walter Troschke

Personal Adjutant

Gemeineschaftsführer Probst

Pressestelle

Hauptbereitschaftsführer, Major der Schutzpolizei Paul Fischer

Bildung und Filmstelle

Hauptbereitschaftsführer, Major der Schutzpolizei Dr. Kröncke

Inspekteur 1

Landesführer, Generalmajor der Polizei Josef Fornoni ”-”–21.01.1943

Unknown 21.01.1943–09 06 1943

Landesführer, Generalmajor der Polizei
Josef Fornoni 09.06.1943–24.01.1944

Landesführer, Oberst der Polizei a.D.
Schongarth 24.01.1944–end

Inspekteur 2

Landesführer, Generalmajor der Polizei Dr. Ludwig Röthenmeier

Reichsschule Belzig

Hauptbereitschaftsführer Hugendubel

Chef Amt I

Landesführer, Generalmajor der Polizei Josef Fornoni 01.04.1929 -”-”

Landesführer, Generalleutnant der Polizei Theodor Sieber ”-”–end

Feldeinsatzführer und Generalinspekteur für Auswärtigen Einsatz der TENO–

Landesführer Dr. Etmer

Allgemeiner Chefangeleinheiten–Hauptbereitschaftsführer, Major der Schutzpolizei Dr. Kröncke

- Gruppe A Einsatz, Organisation
- Gruppe B Ausrüstung
- Gruppe C Propaganda
- Gruppe D Ausbildung

Chef Amt II

Bezirksführer, Major der Schutzpolizei Malicke

- Gruppe II Personalen

Chef Amt III

Bezirksführer Major der Schutzpolizei Malicke Gruppe III Rechts und Versicherungs–Generalmajor der Polizei Helmuth Gerloff

Chef Amt IV

Landesführer, Oberstleutnant der Schutzpolizei Ramthun

- Gruppe Haushalt Finanzwesen
- Gruppe Verwaltung Beschaffung
- Gruppe Prüfwesen

Chef Amt V Abnahmeamt

Generalmajor der Polizei a.D. Osswald

Reichsschule TENO Dresden

Generalmajor der Polizei Richard Buban

Note (1) Hans Weinreich was born on the 5 September 1896 in Merseburg an der Saale. He served in the army during the Great War and was a British prisoner of war from October 1917. After his return to Germany he joined the police in Berlin. Leaving in the wake of the Kapp Putsch of July 1920 he worked in agriculture and then in industry. He served in the SA from 1922 until December 1936 rising to the rank of Gruppenführer. From December 1936 he served as a Gruppenführer in the SS. He was given the rank of Generalmajor der Polizei 1 January 1941 and was promoted Generalleutnant on the 1 June 1942. He served in the TENO from the 24 April 1934. He left the service in disgrace. He was a married man with one daughter and he had been openly consorting with a prostitute. He caught veneral disease and then promised to marry the girl. As a result of the disgrace his wife and daughter committed suicide on the 15 November 1942. He was brought before an SS-Honour Court was found guilty of conduct prejudicing the good order and discipline of the SS, was demoted to SS-Mann and was dismissed from all his posts with effect from 25 November 1943 (Reichsführer-SS Tagebuch Nr III 10/43g). He survived the war and died in Düsseldorf on the 23 December 1963.

Note (2) Erich Hampe was born on the 17 December 1889 in Gera in Thüringen. Joined the army as 2nd Lieutenant in Jäger-Bataillon 4 on the 17 August 1909. After service in the Great War he joined the TENO and served until 20 May 1941 when he rejoined the army with the rank of Oberstleutnant. Served as an Abteilungschef in OKH until 25 August 1942 and then as General der Technische Truppen in OKH. Promoted Oberst on the 1 February 1942 and Generalmajor on the 1 April 1945. He served as director of emergency operations in Dresden in February 1945 and was awarded the German Cross in Silver on the 22 July 1944.

Gebietsgliederung (District Organisation)

Landesgruppe I Ost Preussen HQ Königsberg	
Landesführer Oberst der Schutzpolizei Ehrbar	"-"–941
Landesführer Oberst der Schutzpolizei Schriever	1941–end
Bezirksgruppe I Südost Kameradschaftsführer Polkehn	
Landesgruppe II Nord HQ Stettin	
Landesführer, Hauptmann der Schutzpolizei Hermann	"-"–1940
Landesführer, SS-Obersturmbannführer Ernst Schilling	1940–04.1944
Hauptbereitschaftsführer Oberstleutnant der Schutzpolizei Langjahr	04.1944–end
Bezirksgruppe II Pommern-Ost	zur zeit unbesetzt
Landesgruppe III Mark Brandenburg -Berlin HQ Berlin	

Landesführer Generalmajor der Polizei Josef Fornoni	01.04.1921–01.04.1929
Unknown	01.04.1929–1937
SS-Brigadeführer und Generalmajor der Polizei Helmuth Gerloff	1937–1939
Landesführer, Oberst der Schutzpolizei Schröder	1939–22.01.1943
Landesführer, Generalmajor der Polizei Josef Fornoni	22.01.1943–08.05.1943
Landesführer, Oberst der Schutzpolizei Schröder	08.05.1943–end
Landsgruppe, IV Ober-Elbe HQ Dresden	
Landesführer, Generalmajor der Polizei Richard Buban	1927–end
Bezirksgruppe Sudetenland-Nord	
Kameradschaftsführer Hentsch	1939–1943
Kameradschaftsführer Wagner	1943–end
Bezirksgruppe Sachsen-West	zur zeit unbesetzt 1941
Hauptbereitschaftsführer Keiselt	1943
Bezirksgruppe Halle-Leipzig	
Bereitschaftsführer Rudolph	
Bezirksgruppe Sachsen-Ost	
Bereitschaftsführer Dr. Brehmer	
Landesgruppe V Südwest HQ Stuttgart Bezirksführer SS-Obersturmbannführer und Oberstleutnant der Schutzpolizei Ernst Oelker	05.1941–end
Bezirksgruppe Elsass	
Hauptbereitschaftsführer Schmidt	1941
Gefolgschaftsführer Brendow	1943

SS-Gruppenführer Willy Schmelcher

Bezirksgruppe Baden	zur seit unbesetzt 1941 and 1943
Landesgruppe VI Westfalen-Niederrhein HQ Köln	
Landesführer, Oberst der Schutzpolizei Friedrich Prüssner	1939–end
Bezirksgruppe Niederrhein	
Gefolgschaftsführer Romany	1941
Hauptbereitschaftsführer Vollmer	1943
Bezirksgruppe Westfalen	
Bezirksführer Beil	
Hauptbereitschaftsführer Sellquist	1941–end (i.V.whilst Beil was absent on other duties)
Bezirksgruppe Weserland	
Bereitschaftsführer Leidenberg	1941
Gefolgschaftsführer Romany	1943
Landesgruppe VII Bayern-Süd HQ München	
Bezirksführer Oberst der Schutzpolizei Düll	1939–end
Landesgruppe VIII Schleisen HQ Breslau	
Landesführer Berger	1938–end
Bezirksgruppe Kattowitz (became independent Befehlstelle VIIIA Oberschlesien)	
Hauptbereitschaftsführer Kuna	1941–1942

Meeting of the Leadership corps of Technische Nothilfe 1939, Frontrow, Stell. Chef Hampe

Bezirksgruppe Sudetenland-Ost	zur zeit unbesetzt 1941
Bezirksführer Heberer 1943	
Bezirksgruppe Oppeln (became part of Befehlstelle VIII A)	
Gemeineschaftsführer Nitzek	1941
Landesgruppe IX Hessen-Thüringen HQ Kassel	
Landesführer, Oberstleutnant der Schutzpolizei Höpker	1938–end
Bezirksgruppe Thüringen-Erfurt	
Bereitschaftsführer, Hauptmann der Schutzpolizei Leutloff	1941
Bezirksführer von Zastrow	1943
Landesgruppe X Nordwest HQ Hamburg	
Landesführer Curtze	1939–1942
Landesführer, Oberst der Schutzpolizei Dr. Maack	1942–1944
Landesführer Kollmeyer	1944–end
Bezirksgruppe Hansestadt Hamburg	
Hauptbereitschaftsführer Rump	1941
Bezirksführer Magnus	1943
Gefolgeschaftsführer Paul other	1943 (i.V.whilst Magnus was absent on duties)

Bezirksgruppe Weser-Ems

Generalmajor der Polizei, Richard Buban

SS-Gruppenführer Hans Weinrich

Hauptbereitschaftsführer, Major der Schutzpolizei Condereit	1941–end
Landesgruppe XI Mitte HQ Hannover	
Landesführer Schläger	1938–1942
Hauptbereitschaftsführer Major der Schutzpolizei Langjahr	1942–end
Bezirksgruppe Magdeburg-Anhalt	
Bereitschaftsführer Schulze	1941–end (Promoted Bezirksführer by 1943)
Landesgruppe XII Westmark HQ Frankfurt am Main	
Landesführer, Generalmajor der Polizei Franz Wenzel	1938–end
Bezirksgruppe Saarpfalz	
Bereitschaftsführer Grim	1941–end (Promoted Bezirksführer by 1943)
Bezirksgruppe Moselland	
Bezirksführer Wier	
Bezirksgruppe Lothringen	
Gemeinschaftsführer Dick	1941–end (Promoted Gefolggeschafsführer by 1943)
Landesführer XIII Nordbayern-Egerland HQ Nürnberg	
Landesführer, SS-Standartenführer und Oberst der Schutzpolizei	

Members of the Technische nothilfe awarded Iron Cross 2. class by a naval Kapitän-zur-See and Harbour Commandant

Leo Meier	1939–1943
Bereitschaftsführer, SS-Sturmbannführer Hans Zimmer	(i.V.whilst Meier was absent on other duties) 1943–end
Bezirksgruppe Egerland	
Gemeineschaftsführer Löbermann	1941–end (Promoted Gefolgschaftsführer by 1943)
Landesgruppe XVII Ostmark-Nord HQ Wien	
Landesführer, Generalmajor der Polizei Walter Junecke	1938–17.01.1943
Bezirksführer, Oberstleutnant der Schutzpolizei Carl Stauss	17.01.1943–.07.1944
Unknown	07.1944–end
Bezirksgruppe Wien	
Landesführer, Generalmajor der Polizei Walter Junecke	1938–17.01.1943
Gefolgschaftsführer Bakalar	17.01.1943–end
Bezirksgruppe Oberdonau	
Gefolgschaftsführer Rumpf	1941
Bezirksführer Lohma	1943
Gefolgschaftsführer Schüffl	1944 (kommis. whilst Lohmar was absent)
Bezirksgruppe Niederdonau	
Landesführer, Generalmajor der Polizei Walter Junecke	1938–17.01.1943

France 1941, a member of Technische Nothilfe assists a navy diver in mine clearance at a channel port

Bezirksführer, Major der Schutzpolizei Kunzig	17.01.1943–end
Gemeinschaftsführer Mairhofer	(i.V.whilst Kunzig was absent on other duties).
Landesgruppe XVIII Ostmark-Süd HQ Salzburg	
Bezirksführer, Oberstleutnant der Schutzpolizei Carl Stau	1939–end
Bezirksgruppe Steiermark	
Bereitschaftsführer Erich Schmidt	1941–end (Promoted Bezirksführer by 1943)
Bezirksführer Tirol-Vorarlberg	zur zeit unbesetzt 1941–end
Bezirksgruppe Kärnten	
Bereitschaftsführer Emil Tazoll	1941–end (Promoted Hauptbereitschaftsführer by 1943)
Befehlstelle Böhmen-Mähren HQ Prag	
Bezirksführer, Major der Schutzpolizei Oskar Hölzle	1939–end
Bezirksgruppe Böhmen	
Bezirksführer, Major der Schutzpolizei Oskar Hölzle	1941

Members of the Technische Nothilfe working on Bridge repairs

Bezirksführer Eichner	1943
Bezirksgruppe Mähren	
Bereitschaftsführer Johann Krotschak	1941–end (Promoted Bezirksführer by 1943)
Landesgruppe XX Danzig-Westpreussen HQ Danzig	
Hauptbereitschaftsführer Willibald Kamm 1	941–end
Bereitschaftführer Hoffmann	(i.V.whilst Kamm was absent on other duties)
Landesgruppe XXI Wartheland HQ Posen	
Landesführer, Oberstleutnant der Schutzpolizei	
Adalbert Schulze	1938–end
Bezirksgruppe Wartheland-Ost	
Hauptbereitschaftsführer Kuna	1943–end
Befehlstelle VIIIa Oberschlesien	
Bezirksführer, Oberstleutnant der Schutzpolizei Haust	1943–end
Bezirksgruppe Oberschlesien	
Gefolgschaftsführer Nitzek	1943
Befehlstelle Generalgouvernment HQ Krakau	
Gefolgschaftsführer von Zastrow	1941
Gefolgschaftsführer Schuler	1943
Befehlstelle Niederlande HQ Den Haag	
Hauptbereitschaftsführer, Major der Schutzpolizei Dr. Beck	1943
Befehlstelle Norwegen HQ Oslo	
Bereitschaftsführer Dr. Schmitz	1940–1943
Bezirksführer Dr. Konrad Thaler	1943–end

2.7 Polizei Schulen der Ordnungspolizei (Police schools of the ORPO)

Generalinspekteur der Schulen (General Inspection of Schools)

On 30 June 1936, the office of Inspection of Schools (Inspektion der Schulen) was created in Ordnungspolizei Headquarters. From 1 September 1936 the office was upgraded to Generalinspekteur status. The General Inspector was closely connected with the Training Office of the Ordnungspolizei (Ausbildungsamt). By a decree dated 14 January 1941, the Generalinspekteur, Generalleutnant der Polizei Karl Pfeffer Wildenbruch was appointed chief of the newly created Colonial Police Office (Kolonialpolizei Amt). He retained his post as Generalinspekteurand kept control of the following schools:

Polizei Offizierschule Berlin Köpenick
Polizei Offizier und Schutzpolizei Schule Furstenfeldbrück
Polizei Reitschulen Rathenow und Bendzin
Wasserschutzpolizeischule Stettin

Polizei Offizier Schulen (Officers Schools)

Polizei Offizier Schule Berlin Köpenick established on the 1 February 1936, moved to Oranienburg in 1943 and to Mariaschein in the Sudetenland in 1944.

SS-Gruppenführer und Generalleutnant Reiner Liessem	02.1936–11.03.1938
SS-Brigadefürer und Generalmajor der Polizei Konrad Ritzer	11.03.1938–21.02.1939
SS-Brigadefürer und Generalmajor der Polizei Fritz Freitag	20.04.1939–30.10.1939

Kurt Daulege takes the salute at a march past at the police officers school at Berlin Köpernick, Generalmajor der Polizei Adolf von Bomhard stands to Dauleges left.

Generalmajor der Polizei Hans-Dietrich Grunewald	30.10.1939–30.09.1942
SS-Brigadefürer und Generalmajor der Polizei Fritz Freitag	30.09.1942–08.05.1943
Oberst der Schutzpolizei Albert Buchmann	08.05.1943–end

Polizei Offizier-und Schutzpolizeischule Furstenfeldbrück was established in 1933 as the Bayern Polizeihauptschule. It became the Polizei Offizier-und Schutzpolizeischule Furstenfeldbruck in 1936 then in 1942 became the Offiziersschule der Ordnungspolizei.

Kommandant

SS-Gruppenführer und Generalleutnant der Polizei Gerret Korsemann .	04.1939–30.10.1939
SS-Brigadeführer und Generalmajor der Waffen-SS und der Polizei Fritz Freitag	10.1939–12.1940
Oberst der Schutzpolizei Arno Hagemann .	12.1940–-..-

Schutzpolizei der Gemeinden (Municipal Protection Police)

The Gemeindepolizei had no special schools, Schutzpolizei staff were trained in Schutzpolizei Schools (Schutzpolizei der Gemeinde) and the KRIPO in Criminal Police schools. Officers were trained in the Police Officer Schools Berlin Köpenick and Furstenfeldbrück.

Schutzpolizei des Reich (State Protection Police)

Polizeischule für Leibesübungen Berlin-Spandau
Polizei Ski Schule Kitzbühel (Österreich)
Polizei Ski Schule Südelfeld (Österreich)
Polizei Ski Schule Oberjoch (Österreich)
SS-Polizeigebirgschule Oberstein
Hochgebirgschule der Ordnungspolizei Innsbruck (Österreich)
Polizeischule für Skiausbildung Zakopane in der Generalgouvernment
Kolonialpolizeischule (former Polizeischule für Auslandverwendung) Oranienburg
Kolonialpolizeischule Wien Strebersdorf
Schutzpolizei Nachrichtenschule Eilenburg Ost (formerly the Lager der Ordnungspolizei, it changed in November 1941)
Polizei-Lehr Bataillon Dresden-Hellerau
Staatliche Lehr- und Versuchsanstalt für das Polizei Hundwesen Gründheide (Mark.)
Polizeireitschule Bensburg near Kattowitz in Upper Schlesien
Polizeireitschule für Reit-und Fahrwesen Magdeburg formed 1937. It moved to Rathenow (GG Poland)
Pferdedepot der Ordnungspolizei Litzmannstadt (Wartheland)
Pferdedepot der Ordnungspolizei Rennbahn Ruda Pubianicka
Polizei Lehrschmied der Ordnungspolizei Rathenow
Polizeiverwaltungschule Wendefurt Harz established November 1940

Polizeiverwaltungschule München Haar established October 1941
Schutzpolizei Schule Kattowitz (Upper Schlesien)
Schutzpolizei Schule Jena
Schutzpolizei Schule Frankfurt am Main
Schutzpolizei Schule Heidenheim
Schutzpolizei Schule Bottrop
Schutzpolizei Schule Gnesen
Schutzpolizei Schule Hamburg

Gendarmerie
Gendarmerie Schule Alexandrowo
Gendarmerie Schule Bad Ems
Gendarmerie Schule Breslau
Gendarmerie Schule Hildesheim
Gendarmerie Schule Wien Mödling (Österreich)
Gendarmerie Schule Fraustadt established 1 January 1941
Gendarmerie Schule Freiburg
Gendarmerie Schule Brünn
Gendarmerie Schule Allenstein
Gendarmerie Schule Brieg
Gendarmerie Schule Darmstadt
Gendarmerie Schule Marburg/Lahn
Gendarmerie Schule Trier
Gendarmerie Schule Schonwalde

Hochgebirgschule der Gendarmerie Innsbruck became the Hochgebirgschule der Ordnungspolizei
Kraftfahr und Verkehrschule der Gendarmerie. Later Gendarmerie Schule (mot) Suhl
Verkehrschule der Motor Gendarmerie. Later Gendarmerie Schule (mot.) Hollabrunn (Österreich)
Schule der Motor Gendarmerie. Later Gendarmerie Schule (mot.) Deggingen-Nordalb b. Geislingen
Gendarmerie Schule (mot.) Köln

Oberst der Schutzpolizei Karl Heinrich Brenner. Commander sport school of Police

Major der Gendarmerie Hermann Fuchs Commander of Gendarmerie motor school Suhl.

Landespolizei (Militarized Barracked Police) 1933 – 1936

The former Landespolizeischulen or LPS were disbanded in 1935/1936 and incorporated as battalions into the army in their local Wehrkreis (Military District).

Landespolizeischule Eiche (Wehrkreis III)
Landespolizeischule Brandenburg (Wehrkreis III)
Landespolizeischule Frankenstein (Wehrkreis VIII)
Landespolizeischule Treptow (Wehrkreis II)
Landespolizeischule Sensburg (Wehrkreis I)
Landespolizeischule Bonn (Wehrkreis VI)
Landespolizeischule Wesel (Wehrkreis VI)
Landespolizeischule Burg (Wehrkreis XI)
Technische Landespolizeischule Berlin became Technische Polizei Schule for the Schutzpolizei.

Feldjägerkorps (SA/SS-Provost Corps) 1933 – 1935

Feldjägerschule Schule became Kraftfahrschule der Gendarmerie
Landjägerei (Prussian Foot Gendarmerie) 1922 – 1934
Landjägerei Schule Allenstein became Gendarmerie Schule Allenstein

Techniches Polizei Schulen (Technical Police Schools)

Polizei Kraftfahrschule Dresden
Polizei Kraftfahrschule Eisenstadt (Oberdonau)
Technichen Polizei Schule Berlin formerly Polizei Schule für Technik und Verkehr
Technische SS und der Polizei Akademie Berlin Zehlendorf
Technische SS und der Polizei Akademie Brünn
Polizei Waffen Schule I
Kraftfahr – Panzerschule der Ordnungspolizei Wien-Purkersdorf

Feuerschutz (Fire Police)

Professional Fire Brigades (Feuerschutzpolizei)
Reichsfeuerwehrschule Eberwalde became Offizierschule der Ordnungspolizei in 1942
Polizeischule für Luftschutzführer became Polizei Akademie für Luftschutzführung Berlin-Schöneberg and moved to Oranienburg on 29 March 1944
Feuerschutzpolizeischule Beeskow /Markt

Volunteer Fire Brigades (Freiwilligen Feuerwehren)

A decree from 24.10.1939 stated that the creation of Feuerwehrpolizei (volunteer fire brigades) was a duty of the States and Provinces in Preussen. As a result the following schools were created by the relevent state:

Feuerwehrschule Celle
Feuerwehrschule Linz
Feuerwehrschule Regensburg
Provinzialfeuerwehrschule Königsberg

Technische Nothilfe (Emergency Technical Corps)
Reichsschule der Technische Nothilfe Belzig/Markt

Wasserschutzpolizei (Waterways Police)

Wasserschutzpolizei Schule Stettin moved to Lauterbach Isle of Rügen on 19 July 1944

Hilfspolizei Schulen (Auxilliary Police Schools)

Hilfspolizei Schule Pelplin + Hipo Ausbildung Bataillon Pelplin became Schutzpolizei Schule (BdO Danzig) in 1941

Hilfspolizei Schule Gnesen + Hipo Ausbildung Bataillon Alexandrow became Schutzpolizei Schule (BdO Posen) in 1941

Hilfspolizei Schule Kattowitz + Hipo Ausbildung Battaillon Kattowitz became Schutzpolizei Schule (BdO Breslau) in 1941

Hilfsgendarmerie Schule became Gendarmerie Schule Stolpmünde in 1941

Hilfsgendarmerie Schule became Gendarmerie Schule Alexandrowo in 1941

Hilfsgendarmerie Schule became Gendarmerie Schule Breslau 1941

Hilfsgendarmerie Schule became Gendarmerie Schule Schönwalde in 1941

Hilfsgendarmerie Schule became Gendarmerie Schule Marburg/Lahn in 1941

Commanders of the main Police Schools (1942)

Polizei Schule für Technik und Verkehr Berlin	Oberst der Schutzpolizei Wilhelm Kasten
Polizei Schule für Reit und Fahrwesen Rathenow	Oberstleutnant der Schutzpolizei Arnold Hartmann
Polizei Schule für Reit und Fahrwesen Bendsburg	Oberst der Gend Felix Bauer
Polizei Schule für Leibesübungen Berlin Spandau	Oberst der Schutzpolizei Hans Egon Russel
Polizei Schule für Kraftfahrwesen Wien	Oberst der Schutzpolizei Kurt Albrecht
Wasserschutzpolizei Schule Stettin	Major der Schutzpolizei Franz Gröning
Reichsfeuerwehrschule Eberswalde	Oberstleutnant der FeuerschupoWalter Hans
Kolonialpolizeischule Oranienburg	Oberst der Schutzpolizei Herbert Jilski
Polizei Verwaltungsschule München Haar	Oberregierungsrat Otto Ziedrich
Polizei Verwaltungsschule Wendefurt (Harz)	Polizeirat Riesenberg
Polizei Akademie für Luftschutzführung Oranienburg	Oberst der Schutzpolizei Herbert Melchior
Staatliche Lehr und Versuchsanstalt für das Polizei	Hundwesen Gründheide (Mark) Oberst der Schutzpolizei Rudolf Belleville
Reichsschule der TENO	Hauptbereitschaftsführer Hugendubel
Gendarmerie Schule Hildesheim	Oberst der Gendarmerie Kurt Petersdorf

2.8 Polizei-Reiterstaffen (Mounted units of the Ordnungspolizei) The Command Structure of Police Mounted Units

In July 1936, an office called "Physical Education, Cavalry and Riding duties" (Körperschulung, Reit und Fahrwesen) was created and put under the Command Office of the Hauptamt ORPO. It was known as Office "K/R" and was responsible for all mounted matters to do with the police. In December 1940, the Office "K/R"' was disbanded. The Group "Organisation" of the Command Office took over mounted police matters as Untergruppe O 8 then O 5 "Reit und Fahrwesen". During the war a field inspection unit was set up in Lemberg (Galicia) to supervise mounted battalions and mounted schools in Eastern territories. It was under Oberstleutnant der SCHUPO Rudolf Ruge, the former Commandant of the Police Mounted School Rathenow (for Police Cavalry Inspection see chapter "Hauptsamt ORPO"). An inspection for veterinary matters in Eastern territories was also created under Chief Veterinär attached to BdO Cracow (Leitender Veterinar beim BdO Krakau) Dr. Alfred Dasch.

The Mounted Troops of the Protection Police (Reiterstaffeln der SCHUPO)

Until 1937 the mounted squad (Berittene Bereitschaft) was the basic unit of the SCHUPO Mounted Force within the State Police Administration. It was subordinated to the relevant Kommandeur der SCHUPO. From 1937 its name changed to mounted troops of the Protection Police. The mounted troops were involved in patrolling parks, woods and lakes areas adjacent to towns. They also served on the motorway (autobahn) service.

Prussian Mounted Squads (from 1937 Troops) were organised into:

Mounted Squads: In Berlin 3 mounted squads were combined into an Inspection (from 1937 mounted section (Reiterabteilung) and after 1938 Wien had a similar arrangement.

Mixed Squads: 2/3 mounted platoons, plus 1/3 foot platoons existed in Frankfurt am Main, Bochum, Düsseldorf, Halle and Magdeburg. Mixed Squads consisting of 1/3 mounted platoons and 2/3 foot platoons existed in Tilsit, Elbing, Schneidemühl, Oppeln, Erfurt, Kassel, Koblenz, Aachen. Finally a mixed squad consisting of ½ mounted platoons, ½ foot platoons existed in Wiesbaden. On 28 April 1941, the Mounted Troops of the SCHUPO (Reiterstaffeln der SCHUPO) became known as Police Mounted Troops (Polizei-Reiterstaffeln). The mounted units of the Prussian Landespolizei had short life, as early as 1934, the 90 horses were transferred to the SCHUPO and were incorporated into the Inspection of Mounted Police in Berlin.

Mounted Police Squadrons and Battalions (Polizei Reiter Schwadrons and Abteilungen)

During the war, independant police mounted units underwent limited expansion. Some additional battalions and squadrons were created, mainly in the East. On the other hand, some Polizei-Regiments had a mounted troop (Polizei-Regiments 10 and 18 in 1944).

Poland 1939/40

In September 1939, two mounted police battalions were set up alongside the 21 ordinary police battalions to take part in security duties in the rear area of the German army. The Mounted Police Battalion 5 (consisting of 4 companies numered 5 to 8) was attached to Police Group 5 and saw action in Pomerania behind the 4 army. A second unit, the Mounted Police Battalion Albrecht (4 companies numered 1 to 4) was set up in September 1939 under the command of Oberstleutnant der

Schutzpolizei Kurt Albrecht. The strenght of the units in May 1940 was:

Mounted Battalion in the Generalgouvernement (Berittene Abteilung in GG)	4 officers and 270 men
Mounted Battalion in annexed former Polish territories	3 officers and 230 men

Both were disbanded in the Summer of 1940.

Eastern territories 1941/44

After the beginning of the invasion of the Soviet Union, mounted units were set up as follows:

1. Mounted Police Battalion I headed by Major Hahn. This unit was attached to Verband z.b.V Kaukasus under the HSSPF Gerret Korsemann. In 1942/43, it was involved in security duties under HSSPF Russland-Süd and Höchster SSPF Ukraine. Later, it served with Kampfgruppe "Prützmann" in South Ukraine and in 1944 it served in Galicia.

2. Mounted Police Battalion II. It served in Ukraine in 1942 and fought against partisans in the Pripjet area during 1943. It also served with Kampfgruppe "Prützmann" in 1944.

3. Mounted Police Battalion III. It was created in Posen in the Wartheland but little additional information is available.

Also set up were Police Mounted Squadrons in Galicia and Lublin.
Non German auxiliary police forces also had mounted units formed from the Cossacks as follows:
Cossack Mounted Front Battalions 68, 72, 73 and 74 in Bielorussia and a Cossack mounted troop in Cracow.

South East

Several Mounted units were created in Balkans area:

- A Police Mounted Battalion in Serbia with 4 squadrons
- A Police Mounted Squadron in Greece as part of the Police Voluntary Battalion Greece
- A Police Mounted Squadron in Croatia

In May 1943, the Mounted Police Battalions were given the prefix "SS".

Police Mounted Schools

Police Mounted School Rathenow

On the 24 August 1937, the training battalions of purchased horses (Ausbildung Abteilung für Ankaufpferde) in Magdeburg was transferred to Rathenow. It became known as the Polizei-Reitschule Rathenow.

Kommandant:

Oberstleutnant der SCHUPO Arnold Hartmann	1940–08.42
Oberstleutnant der SCHUPO Rudolf Ruge	08.42–15.09.43
Oberst der SCHUPO Werner Voelkerling	15.09.43–1944

Police Mounted School Bendsburg (Polizeischule für Reit und Fahrwesen Bendsburg)

On 1 April 1941, a police mounted school was created at Bendsburg near Kattowitz in Upper Schlesien. The school was involved in training horses for use by the SCHUPO and the Gendarmerie.

Kommandant: Major der Gendarmerie Heinrich Baumann	1941
Oberstleutnant der Gendarmerie Felix Bauer	1942

Three Police Mounted Schools were created in the Eastern territories at Mosty, Postawy and in the Ukraine. One Police Mounted School was set up at Esseg (Croatia). It included a riding department, a remount department, a driving departement and a stables.

Police Training Farrier Unit (Polizei Lehrschmiede) Rathenow

Alongside the Mounted School Rathenow, a farrier training unit for candidate officers, NCO's and men was set up and alongside a remount depot.

Horse Depot of the ORPO

This depot for horses was set up at Hermannstahl to provide facilities for horses to rest and recover after disease and injury when they could be returned to duty with mounted police units.

Portrait of a leader of the Mounted Police

Rudolf RUGE was born on 31 January 1895. He joined Allgemeine-SS in June 1933 with the number 90 266 and was member of the NSDAP (2 728 849). From 1934, he served as an instructor at SS-Junkerschule Bad Tölz. Promoted Untersturmführer 09.11.1933, Obersturmführer 20.04.1935, Hauptsturmführer 15.09.1935, Sturmbannführer 12.09.1937. In September 1939, he joined the newly created Totenkopf Reiterstandarte as chief Reiterstaffel 2 of the 3 Schwadron of the Totenkopf Reiter Standarte. From November 1939, he took over the 2 schwadron serving until June 1940. From June to December 1940 he led 1 schwadron of the 2 SS-Reiterstandarte. He moved back to Junkerschule Bad Tölz then served with Gebirgs Jäger Ersatz Abteilung before joining 6. SS-Gebirgs Division Nord. He was promoted SS-Obersturmbannführer on 30.01.1942. He left Waffen-SS duties for Police with rank of Oberstleutnant der SCHUPO. He took command of the Police Mounted School Rathenow in August 1942. Then he supervised Mounted units in East until he was appointed Inspector of the Mounted units of the ORPO.

2.9 Polizei Fliegerstaffel (Flying units of the Police)

Short history of the Flight Police forces (1919–1939)

Flying units of the Police (Fliegerpolizei) are created in Länders in 1919 and organized into Flying Police Groups (Polizei Fliegergruppe). They are involved in Air Police Watch-Service (Luftpolizei überwachungsdienst) into the Airport areas: traffic on airport, passengers and lugages, fire protection, flight schools, pilots licences. On October 1920, they are organised into Flight Police Battalions (Luftpolizei Abteilungen) but soon disbanded (1921). On 1926, the allied control commission allowed a force of 50 pilots (former airforces pilots) but without planes and involved in administrative duties. New Police forces were organised into Police Flight platoons (Polizei Flieger Staffeln). From 1933, the Flight police went under Göring authority in Air Ministery (Reichskommissar für Luftaufsicht later Luftmachtministerium -RLM-). The following staff was in charge of police duties: Police Major Karl Angerstein from 15.04.1933 as Inspector of the Prussian Air Police (Inspizienten der Luftpolizei) in Office of the Prussian Minister President. Police Major Ernst Exss as chief of department Air Police Watch-Service (Referent für Luftüberwachung) and Police Major Wilhelm Haenschke as Department chief in RLM and commander of the Luftschutz and Luftpolizeischule in Berlin. By decree from 1 April 1935, the Flight Watch Service of the Landespolizei (Landespolizei Flugüberwachungsdienstellen) created in 1933, came under Reich Air Ministery too. By 1936 the order and security matters came definitively under Luftfahrt administration and Police duties were known as " Reichsluftaufsichtsdienst or RLAD ". 4 Police Flight districts were created on 1939 in West Germany (Aachen, Trier, Palatine, Bade). Police airplanes of the RLAD were involved in the control of Boundaries areas. These planes held the symbol " D-Pol " on the left side. At the outbreak of the war the police flight units were disbanded and incorporated into Luftwaffe.

The command of the flight units in Hauptamt ORPO

On september 1939, the flight duties came under Organisation Office of the ORPO Main Office. End 1940, the flight duties moved into department O2 (traffic and flight duties) of the Group " Organisation ". From December 1942, this department went to Group K (Transport duties) were flight affaires became the Sachsgebiete K 5.

The flight units of the ORPO during the war (1939–1945)

On september 1939, a Polizei Flieger Abteilung was created into Hauptsamt ORPO headed by Oberstlt. Carl Kuring, former commander of the Fliegerstaffel of the Chief of ORPO. It include the Pilot Group at special disposal 7 (Fliegergruppe z.b.V) stationed in Berlin Tempelhof. A police flight platoon (Polizei Fliegerstaffel) saw action during the Poland Campaign. The unit served for mail transport between Berlin, Posen, Lodz and Cracow. It was then stationned in Cracow. A new platoon was created during the western campaign and stationed in Netherlands. At the beginning of eastern offensive police flying units were attached to the 3 HSSPF appointed in Russia. Others flying units saw actions in Balkan area, Norway and Italia. The various platoons had the following duties:

anti partisans support (air reconnaissance, transport of wounded…) and fights
(Fieseler storch, Fw 189)
medical duties
transport duties (Ju 52, Si 104, 204, Fw 58)
mail (Si 104, 204, Fw 58)
action in air raid duties (Luftschutz)
inspection flights (Fieseler Storch)

A collaboration was developped between water Protection police and police airplanes for the control of the waterways and coasts.

Police aircraft, marking, D-Pol-98

Specialised Police Services

3.1 Kolonialpolizei

This service was established in January 1941 following the commencement of the Italian campaign in North Africa. The-National Socialist government had always had colonial aspirations and a colonial political office was set up by the Party under Reichsleiter Franz Ritter von Epp on the 15 June 1936. With the unification of the German Police in 1936 certain Schutzpolizei units were charged with the continuation of the colonial tradition. The Schutzpolizei in Bremen was selected to represent the police of the former German South West Africa, the Kiel office represented the Cameroon and the Hamburg office represented Kiautschau in China. Officers and men were identified by a shield badge called "Kreuz des Südens", the Southern Cross badge. As a result of the formation of the Colonial Police, a Colonial Police Office was created in Hauptamt ORPO under SS-Obergruppenführer Karl Pfeffer-Wildenbruch and a Colonial Police School was set up at Oranienburg under Oberst der Gendarmerie Herbert Jilski who was succeeded by Oberstleutnant der Schutzpolizei Karl Elstermann von Elster. Officers were also trained at the SS-Führerschule der Sicherheitspolizei in Berlin-Charlottenburg and some were sent on courses to the Italian Colonial Police College at Tivoli near Rome. At the completion of such training candidates were returned to their normal duties but they were earmarked for colonial service when required. This force was never advanced beyond the planning stage and following the defeats in North Africa and at Stalingrad, the whole idea was abandoned. The Colonial Police office was closed down in March 1943.

3.2 Wasserschutzpolizei

This was a branch of the Schutzpolizei used to police inland waterways and harbour traffic. Following an agreement between the Reichsführer-SS Heinrich Himmler and the Reichsverkehrsministerium (Ministry of Transport–Julius Dorpmüller) on the 21 January 1937, the Schutzpolizei took over the responsibilities of the existing Schiffahrtpolizei (Water Traffic Police), Strompolizei (River Police) and the Hafenpolizei (Harbour Police) including Hafen und Schiffahrtpolizei Hamburg, Rheinpolizei, Bodenseepolizei. A decree of the 26 July 1937 declared the Wasserschutzpolizei (Waterways Protection Police) "A special service branch of the Schutzpolizei with the abbreviation SW". Its principal task was to maintain law and order on waterways, in harbours and in harbour approaches. Its units were at the disposal of the relevant local authorities for technical assistance and they could also act on behalf of the security police. The force was organised into:

group command	Wasserschutzpolizei-Gruppe
command	Wasserschutzpolizei-Kommando
sector	Wasserschutzpolizei-Abschnittskommando
precinct	Wasserschutzpolizei-Revier
stations	Wasserschutzpolizei-Station
squad	Wasserschutzpolizei-Wache
patrol	Wasserschutzpolizei-Fliegende Wache
post	Wasserschutzpolizei-Post

Tivoli 1941, A german NCO of the Kolonialpolizei with an Italian police NCO

In 1940/1945, the SW had the following formations:

General der Flakartilleri Friedrich Hirschhauer

Authorities

Inspekteur der ORPO in Königsberg
SW Kommando Östliche Ostsee
Reichstathalter Danzig-Westpreussen
SW Kommando Weichsel
Polizeipräsident Stettin
SW Abschnittkommando Stettin
Oberpräsident in Kiel
SW Kommando Westliche Ostsee
Polizeipräsident in Hamburg
SW Gruppenkommando Hamburg
Polizeipräsident in Bremen
SW Abschnittkommando Bremen
Befehlhaber der ORPO in Posen
SW Revier Warthe/Netze
Inspekteur der ORPO in Breslau
SW Kommando Oder
Polizeipräsident Berlin
SW Abschnittkommando Berlin
Polizeipräsident Potsdam
SW Revier Potsdam
Oberpräsident in Sachsen
SW Kommando Elbe
Polizeipräsident in Recklinghausen
SW Revier Recklinghausen
Oberpräsident in Rhein
SW Kommando Rhein
Reichstattalter in Wien
SW Kommando Donau
Württemburg Innernministerie

SW Kommando Bodensee
Befehlhaber der ORPO Den Haag
SW Kommando Niederlande
Militäriebefehlhaber Serbien
SW Flottille Serbien
Befehlhaber der ORPO Riga
SW Kommando Ostland
Befehlhaber der ORPO Kiew
SW Kommando Asowsches Meer
SW Kommando Schwarzes Meer
Befehlhaber der ORPO Kopenhagen
SW Kommando Dänemark
Befehlhaber der ORPO Oslo
SW Kommando Norwegen
Befehlhaber der ORPO Triest
SW Kommando West-Adria
SW Kommando Ost-Adria
Befehlhaber der ORPO Budapest
SW Kommando Ungarn

The service was supervised by the Inspector of Waterways Protection Police in the Hauptamt ORPO under SS-Brigadeführer Generalmajor der Polizei Bruno Krumhaar from September 1943 and before that date it was Gruppe O7 in the Kommandoamt of the Hauptamt. The service headquarters were in Kiel until July 1944 when they moved to Berlin. Each waterway or harbour had a Wasserschutzpolizei section of various size (see above). The former "Kommandeur der Wasserschutzpolizei" cover a waterway area under authority of the Senior Police Authority or the SCHUPO Commander. The daily work of the service was carried out by foot and cycle patrols alongside canals and rivers and on the waterways themselves, small patrol boats (Hafenboote) were used. Major service commands based at the largest ports used long range boats (Streckenboote) which were capable of carrying out coastal and even sea patrols. Close co-operation existed between the Wasserschutzpolizei and the Marine-Küstenpolizei (Naval Coastal Police), the latter was under the command of the Oberkommando der Kriegsmarine or OKM (Naval High Command) and its manpower was from that arm. An agreement was reached between the OKM and the Reichsführer-SS on the 26 April 1940 which laid down the terms of employment of officers and men from the Wasserschutzpolizei for use by the Marine-Küstenpolizei. When so used these men were temporarily classed as naval personnel and were subject to naval regulations. They were mainly used to provide specialised police experience and to supervise the Marinesoldaten (Marines). The NSKK (National Socialistische Kraftfahr Korps–National Socialists Motor Corps) also operated motorboat units on inland waterways and lakes and they were used as auxiliaries by the Wasserschutzpolizei. Finally in the larger ports the service was reinforced by specialised units from the Allgemeine-SS called SS-Hafensicherungstruppen (port security troops). Such units existed in the SSOberabschnitt Nordsee, Nordwest, Nordost and Ostsee and they were use in co-operation with the Wasserschutzpolizei and the SD especially in the wake of major air raids.

A group of security and assistance service members, later replaced by Luftspolizei

3.3 Luftschutzpolizei (Air Raid Police)

This was the Air Protection Police. On the 29 April 1933 the Reichsluftschutzbund (Reichs Association for Air Raid Precautions) was founded and its existence was made known to the public on the 24 June 1933. Initially a private organisation which had the backing of the Party and the Ministry of War, it was taken over by the Air Ministry in the Spring of 1935, It was run on a voluntary basis until the Air Protection Law of the 26 June 1935 made membership compulsory for most citizens and infractions of this law were punished by severe prison sentences. It organised a net-work of air raid wardens who were responsible for the safety of an apartment block or a group of houses.

Präsident des Reichsluftschutzbundes

General der Flakartillerie (charakterisiert) Hugo Grimme	29.04.1933–30.03.1936
General der Flakartillerie (charakterisiert) Karl von Roques (1)	29.04.1936–23.05.1939
SS-Gruppenführer, General der Flakartillerie Ludwig von Schröder (2)	23.05.1939–28.07.1941
General der Flakartillerie Friedrich Hirschauer	28.07.1941–30.04.1945

Notes (1) He returned to the army and was appointed General der Infanterie (charakterisiert) 22 April 1940

(2) He served in the navy rising to the rank of Vice Admiral by 1937.
Transferred to the Luftwaffe he died from injuries received in an air crash on 28 July 1941

On the outbreak of war the professional nucleus of all defensive ARP services was the Sicherheits-und Hilfsdienst (security and assistance service). It had been formed in 1935 under the control of the police presidencies of 106 of the largest German cities which were regarded as the most vulnerable in the event of air attack. It formed the mobile civil defence for those towns and was responsible for the execution of all major tasks arising in emergencies caused by air raids. By 1939 it was a conscripted force of men housed in barracks on a rota system, they were allowed to sleep at home on alternate nights, air raids permitting.

Service in the Sicherheits-und Hilfsdienst (SHD) was a form of reserved occupation in that its members were exempted from having to serve in the Wehrmacht. They were also exempt from physical training or rifle drill, though they were not permitted to pursue any other occupation whilst serving in the SHD. In 1940 a mobile strategic reserve of some three of four battalions was formed to provide reinforcements in towns being heavily attacked. Each town having an SHD unit had to find a quota of men as a nucleus for these mobile battalions, which were self supporting and were capable of rapid transfer. Their equipment included pile-drivers, hydraulic jacks, cutting equipment and wrecking tools. The SHD was divided into five branches as follows:

I Entgiftungsdienst (Decontamination Service)
II Feuerwehrdienst (Fire Fighting Service)
III Instandsetzungsdienst (Repair Demolition and Rescue Service)
IV Veterinärdienst (Veterinary Service)
V Sanitätsdienst (Medical Service).

As a result of attacks on Lübeck and Rostock, an overhaul of the air raid protection organisation came about. The Lübeck raid took place during the night of 28/29 March 1942 and resulted in 62% of the town being destroyed or damaged with 320 persons being killed and 784 injured. The Rostock raid took place during the night of 26/27 April 1942, it was the last of four raids and it resulted in 60% of buildings being destroyed with 204 persons being killed and 89 injured. The casualty figures would have been higher but most people fled before the raid. The raid led to the first use of the term "Terrorangriff" by Dr. Josef Goebbels of the Propaganda Ministry. The air raid service totally collapsed and this highlighted the fact that reorganisation was essential. At the end of April 1942 the SHD was re-named the Luftschutzpolizei (Air Protection Police) and the new force took over all the functions and personnel of the SHD with authority vested jointly with Hermann Göring as Air Minister and Heinrich Himmler as head of the police.

Himmler was responsible for administration and Göring for operations. The force worked closely with the Technische Nothilfe (TENO) and the Feuerschutzpolizei. The mobile battalions of the SHD were transferred to the Luftwaffe and were re-named Motorised Air Protection Battalions and they were confined to fire-fighting, rescue and debris clearance duties with decontamination and first aid playing only a minor role. The training of the Luftschutzpolizei was the responsibility of the local ORPO commander and the size of the unit alloted to a town was roughly proportional to the size of the population. As a reflection of its status as auxiliary police service, a section covering the service was created within Hauptamt ORPO. An office called Amt für Reichsverteidigung was formed on the 30 June 1936 within the Hauptamt, it was responsible for all civil defence matters with police connections. In December 1937, the Amt became Reichsverteidigung und Luftschutz under the control of the Kommandoamt in the Hauptamt. Now it consisted of two Untergruppen as follows;

Untergruppe RV	Reichsverteidigung (Civil Defence)
Untergruppe L	Luftschutz (Air Raid Protection)

During the summer of 1939 Untergruppe L was expanded to control the Sicherheits-und Hilfsdienst. It was also provided with its own medical and veterinary services and was given a fire service and technical department. In December 1942 the Untergruppe Reichsverteidigung was abolished (Amtsbefehl 22 December 1942) and the Untergruppe Luftschutz was raised to Gruppen status (Amtsbefehl 29 December 1942). In the major reorganisation of September 1943 the Gruppe Luftschutz became the Inspektion der Luftschutz remaining under Amtsgruppe Kommando I in the Kommandoamt. Finally, in September 1944, the fire service office in the Inspectorate was transferred to the Technischen SS und Polizei Akademie. After the re-naming the force was organised as follows;

I Feuer-und Entgiftungsdienst (Fire and Decontamination Service)
II Instandsetzungsdienst (Repair, Demolition and Rescue Service)
III Luftschutzsanitäts-und Veterinärdienst (Medical and Veterinary Service)
IV Fachtruppen (Specialised Technical Squads)

The personnel in department I were trained by the fire service. Department II provided emergency engineering as well as bomb disposal work and it was originally the Luftschutzdienst of the Technische Nothilfe. The Fachtruppen Department was originally part of the Bereitschaftdienst (Emergency Service) branch of the Technische Nothilfe and was used to repair damaged gas and water mains, electrical installations, sewers and drains. The Luftschutzpolizei, in its capacity as a technical police service, was considered as an aid to the Ordnungspolizei and as such was under the command of the relevant police commander during air raids, which thereby was able to command and employ all auxiliary air raid protection services. Most members of the service were recruited from the police reserve and unless members were also of the regular police, they were not subjected to the jurisdiction of the SS and Police judicial system. The service had its own training school for officers called the Polizeischule für Luftschutzführung at Berlin-Schönberg, it was renamed Polizeiakademie für Luftschutzführung (Police Academy for Air Raid Precaution Tactics) and it was moved to Oranienburg near Berlin. The commander in 1943 was Oberst der Schutzpolizei Herbert Melchior. As a result of increasing manpower shortages, a decision was taken to employ women where possible so that men could be released for active field service. As bombing raids increased mobile Luftschutzpolizei units were formed known as LS Abteilungen (Motor) and these were used throughout Germany and even in non German strategic potential targets such as the oil fields in Ploesti in Rumania. The service could call on various auxiliary air raid protection services as follows:

Werkluftschutzdienst (Factory Air Raid Protection Service) organised in all larger and war essential plants as designated by the Reichsgruppe Industrie (National League of Industry) of the Reich Economic Chamber. It was supervised by the factory management and was staffed by the workers.

Werkschutzpolizei (Factory Protection Police) organised in all factories having a Werkluftschutzdienst. It was formed to provide for maximum protection of such factories and their employees. Workers were conscripted for this service and were registered with the Luftschutzpolizei. The force was also used for the protection of factories against sabotage and theft and worked closely with the SS-Werkpolizei that was run by the relevant SS-Oberabschnitt.

Selbstschutz (Self-Protection Service) this covered all air raid wardens, block wardens, roof spotters etc. There was an Erweiterer Selbstschutz (Extended Self Protection Service) used in offices, hotels restaurants, theatres, cinemas, department stores and any other place were large crowds congregated and its members were conscripted from the employees. There was also a Landsluftschutzgemeinschaft (Rural Air Protection Fellowship) which provided fire fighting and rescue squads in rural area too small to be served by any of the other services.

Luftschutzwarndienst (Air Raid Warning Service) operated in the same way as the Royal Observer Corps of Great Britain. It was organised to observe approaching enemy aircraft and to place threatened populations on alert, it also analysed incoming reports from other LSW posts, from the police and from the Luftwaffe Flugmeldedienst units on the progress of enemy bomber formations over Germany.

Their conclusions led to the sounding of air raid warnings and they worked in close unison with the police during the co-ordinating of air raid and post air raid services. Finally they were responsible for giving the all clear signal. Service in all these organisations was compulsory but on a part-time, unpaid basis and they also made extensive use of foreign workers and prisoners of war. All these civilian services were supervised and trained by the Luftschutzpolizei thereby giving the police complete control in air raids and other emergencies. On 1 February 1944 a Reichsinspektion der Zivil Luftkriegsmassnahmen was created to centralise the battle against air raids (see chapter on Hauptamt Ordnungspolizei for details).

Special Police (Sonderpolizei)

4.1 Bahnpolizei (Railways Police)

The German railway system was unified in 1920 and individual rail companies were merged into the Deutsche Reichsbahn that came under the control of the Reichsverkehrsministerium (Reich Transport Ministry). The Reichsminister was Paul Freiherr von Eltz-Rubenach from 1 June 1932 until succeeded by Julius Dorpmüller on 2 February 1937. On 17 July 1928 an entirely new version of the Reichsbahn-Betriebsordnung (Railway Statutory Regulations) was passed. It included a uniform railway police code equally applicable to all parts of the Reich and it resulted in the formation of the Bahnpolizei, which, with the Postschutz, became the first unified national police force in Germany. The force consisted of part-time and fulltime members. The part-time members were all railway staff who, in addition to their normal duties, were responsible for the maintenance of law and order on railway property. Full time members were organised into two departments as follows:

Bahnschutzpolizei (Railway Protection Police)
This was a regular guard and patrol service. Created in April 1921 it had the folowing duties;
to secure the railway network (track, bridges, tunnels etc)
to guard railway installations and buildings.
to protect railway staff.

(Railway Protection Police)

This was a regular guard and patrol service. Its members were uniformed and were armed with pistols and truncheons. They patrolled station platforms and trains with the task of maintaining law order.

Reichsbahnfahndungsdienst (Railway Criminal Investigation Service)

This was a plain clothes service formed to combat corruption among railway personnel and to prevent and investigate the theft of goods carried by the railways and the embezzlement of funds held by the railways. The service was given wider powers in March 1943 following an agreement between the Transport Minister and the Reichsführer-SS. Under this agreement the Gestapo and the KRIPO could request the help of the service to assist in the investigation of any civil or political crime. This meant that the service acquired the status of Hilfspolizei (Auxiliary Police) and as such, while still remaining under the control of the Transport Ministry, they became operationally attached to the RSHA (Reich Security Headquarters) and thereby assumed regular police powers of arrest. They were supervised by Amt V Gruppe C-2 of the RSHA under Kriminaldirektor Dr. Baum. The Bahnpolizei were all accorded the status of Hilfspolizei after the outbreak of war and as such they received operational instructions from the head of ORPO through the Kommandoamt of the Hauptamt. In special emergencies the service was placed at the disposal of the Reichsführer-SS and to facilitate this, a Verbindungsreferent (Liaison officer) was appointed to establish liaison between the Ministry and the SS and Police. The latter were responsible for giving specialised training in security police functions and methods. Each Reichsbahndirektion (Regional Railway Headquarters, 31 of which existed in 1943) had a Fahndungsdezernent (Search for wanted persons official) who was responsible for the Bahnpolizei. For security duties he would receive his orders from the relevant KRIPO-(Leit)-Stelle who maintained constant liaison through a special member of his staff. Day to day supervision and administration came under Abteilung E-IV of the Transport Ministry under Ministerialdirektor Prang. An SS-Bahnschutz was formed in 1942 under the SS-Hauptamt being put directly under the Hauptamt Chief SS-Obergruppenführer Gottlob Berger. Its duties were similar to the Bahnpolizei but with SS emphasis.

4.2 Postschutz and Funkschutz (Postal Guard and Radio Guard)

These two services performed the same functions as the Bahnpolizei but applied to the postal service and the broadcasting authority. Both were under the Reichspostministerium (Postal Ministry) led by Paul Freiherr von Eltz-Rubenach from 1 June 1932 until succeeded by Wilhelm Ohnesorge on 2 February 1937. The same operational rules applied as to the Bahnpolizei.

4.3 Landwacht und Stadtwacht (Auxiliary Police for Rural and Urban areas)

Landwacht: the head of the Ordnungspolizei, Kurt Daluege created this service, in January 1942. It assisted the Schutzpolizei der Gemeinden and especially the Gendarmerie. It covered the smaller towns and the rural areas and its membership came from the SA Wehrmannschaften (SA Military Training Defense Units). This force was created by a Hitler decree dated 19 January 1939 to provide pre and post military training for the entire male population of Germany between the ages of 18 and 65. It included those considered unfit for military duty with the armed forces. It was also responsible for co-ordinating all political defense organisations (Allgemeine-SS, SA, NSKK, NSFK and HJ). Training consisted of two evenings per week and six hours on a Sunday and extra training was given to specialised personnel such as medics, signallers and those concerned with flight. The service was under SA-Gruppenführer Georg von Neufville, a 56 year-old former army Colonel. Those selected for service in the Landwacht originally served as volunteers on a part time basis. Later the service was made compulsory. They wore civilian clothes distinguished by a white armband with the inscription "Landwacht" in black and they were armed with pistols and rifles. When on duty they were allocated to Gendarmerie posts and were under the orders of the relevant Gendarmerie commander. They were especially useful in supervising the activities of the almost 12 million foreign workers.

Stadtwacht: This service was formed in January 1943 to assist the Schutzpolizei in the cities and major towns. Its background and training was the same as for the Landwacht. In October 1943 the Reichsführer-SS issued a decree for the expansion of the Landwacht and Stadtwacht and as a result it was split into three classes. The active Landwacht and Stadtwacht consisted of personnel who were liable for duty for extended periods and were subject to immediate call. The Reserve I consisted of personnel who, because of their official occupations, were not immediately available for duty but who could be called in on special occasions. The Reserve II included all personnel who, owing to the special importance of their normal duties, were only available during extreme emergencies. An example of this would be a "Grossfahndungen" (National Search) such as took place after the escape of 76 prisoners of war from Stalag Luft III, the Luftwaffe controlled camp at Sagan, during the night of 24/25 March 1944. Both services were submerged on 17 January 1945 in the "Volkssturm," the People Militia created on 18 October 1944 for the defence of the Reich.

The man appointed to head the Landwacht and Stadtwacht was SS-Obergruppenführer Friedrich Alpers. Born in Sonnenburg in the State of Braunschweig on 25 March 1901, he was a trained industrial lawyer who joined the Allgemeine-SS in February 1931. He rose in this service in Braunschweig to command the 49. SS-Standarte in 1932/1933 and after becoming involved in political intrigue in Braunschweig he was moved to the headquarters of the SS-Oberabschnitt (Main District) in Braunschweig as a special duties officer in 1933. He remained there until November 1937 when he moved to the staff of the Reichsführer-SS as a "nebenamtlicher SS-Führer" (part time unpaid SS-Leader). He also served as General Hunting and Forestry Master in the Forestry department of the Office of the Four Year Plan.

He met Hermann Göring and as a result he joined the Luftwaffe in January 1937. Alpers became a reconnaissance pilot, rising to command long range reconnaissance group Fernaufklarungsgruppe 4 in Southern Russia in January 1942 with the rank of Major on the Luftwaffe Reserve with effect from 1 July 1942. He was awarded the Knight's Cross of the Iron Cross on 20 October 1942. He left full time service with the Luftwaffe in October 1942 to take up the post of head of the Landwacht (having been appointed head on 17 January 1942) and Stadtwacht (appointed head in January 1943). Alpers was still holding both posts, having been promoted SS-Obergruppenführer with effect from 21 June 1943, when he returned to full time service in the Luftwaffe on 1 March 1944. He joined the Fallschirmtruppen (Parachute Troops) with his old rank of Major of the Reserve and commanded Fallschirmjäger-Regiment 9 in the 3. Fallschirmjäger-division. Serving on the Western front, he was captured on 1 September 1944 near Lille in France and he committed suicide near Mons in Belgium on 3 September 1944.

Volunteers in the Landwacht with a Regular from the Gendarmerie

Hilfspolizei

5.1 Hilfspolizei (Auxilliary Police)

This term, meaning Auxiliary Police, was used throughout the period of the Third Reich to cover those men from Party para-military organisations who were used to assist the regular police in their duties. They were never part of the regular police and remained under the control of their parent organisations. The regular police had operational control while such men served as Hilfspolizei. The first time the term was used was in February 1933. During this period the National Socialists main concern was the elimination of all rivals in the coming election and their real concern was the para-military organisations of the Social Democrats, the Reichsbanner, and the Communists, the Rote Frontkämpfer Bund. Before January 1933 the regular police had stood aside whilst the SA and the SS fought streets battles with both the Reichsbanner and the Rote Frontkämpfer Bund and as this would not show the new government in a good light internationally it was decided that such actions should cease.

Hermann Göring, the Ministerpräsident of Preussen, established the post of Höherer Polizeiführer West (Higher Police Leader West) on the 11 February 1933 with Generalmajor der Landespolizei Hans Stieler von Heydekampf being given the post. On the 14 March 1933 a Höherer Polizeiführer Ost was created under Oberst der Landespolizei Hans Ruhle von Lilienstern. The intention was to moderate the civil war atmosphere and, by creating the illusion of official police presence, to lull the Social Democrats and others into a postponment of serious resistance until it was too late. In effect the first Hilfspolizei were in effect a kind of SA and SS military police and the only distinguishing mark they wore was a Hilfspolizei armband. The two senior police posts were abolished on the 10 June 1933 On the 22 February 1933 Göring created a semi-official Hilfspolizei of 50,000 men from the SA, SS and the Stahlhelm and their employment was reserved for the Prussian Ministry of the Interior. They were under the command of police officials who were gradually replaced by trusted SA and Party officials. They wore their SA etc. uniforms with the addition of a white

NSKK man on Traffic control duties.

An SA man appoints an Auxiliary Policeman 1933

armband with Hilfspolizei in black on it. A decree from 21 April 33 split the Hilfspolizei into two categories: Members of the SA working for regular police precinct stations, and members of the SS working with political police. Hilfspolizei also appeared in the states of Bayern, Braunschweig, Bremen, Hamburg, Württemberg and Thüringen. But states like Hessen and Sachsen had no Hilfspolizei due to the fact that they were still under the control of the Socialists. Following the burning of the Reichstag on the 28 February 1933 Hilfspolizei were rapidly mobilised to assist the regular police in raids and arrests of anti-nazi elements. Also on the 28 February the German Minister of the Interior, Wilhelm Frick, and the Justice Minister, Franz Gürtner, issued the decree "Verordnungs zum Schutz von Volk und Staat (Decree for the Protection of the People and State) and this provided for the Hilfspolizei, when acting on the orders of the Reich Government, to arrest persons, stop public meetings, raid homes, businesses and meeting places, seize property and intercept mail and telephone calls. This decree also meant that Hilfspolizei could be raised anywhere in Germany.

They were rushed into service as guards at public buildings, power plants and frontier outposts. An atmosphere of public emergency was created for the March elections and intimidation was extended beyond the Communists to the Social Democrat Party, the Centre parties and even the German National Peoples Party, estwhile allies of the National Socialists. The election of the 5 March resulted in the National Socialists receiving 43.9% of the vote and they needed the Centre parties votes to enable them to govern legitimately. This meant that they could anticipate future problems and the Hilfspolizei system was retained. Wilhelm Frick, using paragraph two of the 28 February decree, appointed Reich Police Commissars to maintain peace and order. None of these men were members of the SS and none were professional policemen. Some were high ranking SA leaders like Dietrich von Jagow in Württemberg and Manfred von Killinger in Sachsen and some were Party leaders like Robert Wagner the Gauleiter of Baden. These posts were quickly altered until they eventually became the Reichstatthalter (Reich Governors).

Other senior SA men in the Hilfspolizei quickly became Police Presidents surplanting politically non-acceptable holders of such posts. In Preussen, auxiliary police forces were disbanded in October 1933: Members of the SA joined newly created SA-Feldjägerkorps and members of the SS formed SS-Rollkommando Gestapa headed by SS-Brigadeführer Max Henze. On the 6 February 1933 Göring appointed Kurt Daluege "Preussische Staatskommissar zur besonderer Verwendung" (Special Commissar for the Police) and this was to lead to his appointment as head of the ORPO in 1936. On the 2 April 1933 Himmler was appointed "Politischer Polizeikommandeur Bayern" (Political Police Commander for Bayern) and this led to his becoming the Chief of the German Police on the 17 June 1936. By this time the term Hilfspolizei had been abandoned. The term was used later to cover assistance given to the regular police by various Party organisations.

5.2 NSKK Verkehrshilfsdienst (Traffic Control Service)

armband with Hilfspolizei in black on it. A decree from 21 April 33 split the Hilfspolizei into two categories: Members of The NSKK (National Socialist Motor Corps) created the NSKK Verkehrshilfsdienst (Traffic Control Service) on 28 November 1938 and this became an auxiliary to the regular police (Hilfsorganisation der Polizei) by decree from 7 September 1939. Because of the increase in military traffic and because of the demands on the regular police personnel as more and more of the latter were called up to serve in the Wehrmacht and the Waffen-SS. The service was organised into zones within the relevant NSKK Motorgruppe and it acted as a road traffic accident reporting system which also arranged for specialised services to be called to accidents. During Polish campaign in September/October 1939, 9 NSKK companies from NSKK Motorobergruppe Ost (Schlesien) were mobilised for use in road traffic control. In 1942 the NSKK Motorgruppe Hessen (under NSKK-Gruppenführer Prinz Richard von Hessen) reported that it controlled 525 such posts divided into 35 zones covering 30 main roads and 2,650 kilometres of secondary roads. This would be the rule for all Motorgruppen. In addition the NSKK was charged with "Transportkontrolle des Motorisierten Transportes der Kriegswirtschaft" (Cargo Inspection Service for Motorised Wartime Transport). This meant that drivers of commercial vehicles had to obtain permits from a NSKK Fahrbereitschaftleiter for journeys exceeding certain distances, this official was also responsible for the proper utilisation of vehicles as well as for the efficient employment of the most suitable means of transport. The NSKK was entrusted with the task of issuing drivers licences and with the testing of applicants exclusively from the 10 June 1944 (published in the Reichsverkehrsblatt for 10 June 1944).

5.3 HJ Streifendienst (HJ Local Patrol Service)

The Hitlerjugend (Hitler Youth) also provided assistance to the regular police by use of the HJ Streifendienst (Local Patrol Service) which came under Hauptamt I (Organisation Administration) of the Reichsjugendführung under the command of Obergebietsführer Heinz Hugo John. It was created on the 7 March 1935 and a decree dated 12 December 1936 further defined its role as a policing element to control and protect HJ members. An agreement between the HJ and the SS dated 26 August 1938 put the training of members under the control of the SS and as a result the Streifendienst became a supplementary SS and Police force which worked in close co-operation with regular police. The obvious intention was that members would automatically transfer to the SS when time came to perform their military service. Members of this force wore the regular HJ uniform but with the addition of a black cuff title with yellow-gold machine woven "HJ Streifendienst" in Gothic letters which was worn on the lower left sleeve, in addition each member was issued a special ausweis (identity card). A Rollkommando (Mobile Emergency Unit) was created within the Streifendienst, this was a motorised patrol section which was at the constant disposal of the regular police in readiness to assist, or take the place of, regular policemen in traffic control in any emergency. They were used to attend accidents and to provide manpower for general traffic duties thereby releasing regular policemen for other duties. They were given basic training in such matters by the Schutzpolizei in the cities and by the Gendarmerie in the rural areas. As the war neared its end, members of the military police could also be called upon to act as Hilfspolizei operating under the control of the regular police on an ad-hoc basis. To the general public they were in evidence mainly at road blocks.

Field organisation of the Ordnungspolizei in Great Reich

6.1 Höhere Polizeibehörden (Higher Police Authorities)

The police in Germany was a state service rather than a Party service and we think it would be beneficial to show how the state was organisated during this period. When Hitler was appointed Chancellor on the 30 January 1933 Germany consisted of 13 Länder (states) plus 2 Hansestadt (Hanseatic city states). The Länder were administered by state governments under the overall control of the Reich Government. They, in turn, were split into smaller administrative units. Preussen was divided into 12 provinces and they were sub-divided into Regierungsbezirk (administrative districts). Hessen was divided into 3 provinces which also sub-divided into Regierungsbezirk, Bayern and Sachsen were divided into Regierungsbezirk, Baden was divided into 4 Landeskommissariats (equivalent to Regierungsbezirk) and the remaining 8 Länder were divided into Landkreis and Stadtkreis (rural and urban counties). It will be noted that the Regierungsbezirk in Preussen, Hessen, Bayern, Sachsen and Baden were also sub-divided into Landkreis and Stadtkreis. The Prussian provinces of Sachsen and Hessen-Nassau were separate from the states of Sachsen and Hesse.

After the National Socialist takeover moves were made to centralise the government. The post of Reichsstatthalter (Reich Governor) was created by the 2. Law for the co-ordination of the Federal States under the Reich of the 7 April 1933 and they acted as representatives with the task of fulfilling the principles of politics laid down by the Federal Chancellor. It will be noted that in each case the post was given to the relevant Party leader (Gauleiter). The Gauleitung did not follow the state demarcation lines and this accounts for some of the appointees holding more than one post. The post of Ministerpräsident or Landespräsident was given to civil servants and they were the actual head of the state governments. This obviously led to conflict between Party and State which seemed to be the exact state of affairs desired by Hitler. On the 30 January 1934 the decree for the re-construction of the Reich (Gesetz über den Neuaufbau des Reiches) was published. Article 2 of this law laid down that the sovereign rights of the Länder were to be transferred to the Reich. All state governments were henceforth subordinated to the central government in Berlin, state governments were, therefore, only retained to implement and administer laws and decrees enacted by the central government. This centralisation meant that the police was also centralised being put under the Reichs Ministry of the Interior, it did, however, take two years to complete the task. It was completed with the appointment of the Reichsführer-SS Heinrich Himmler to the post of Chief of the German Police with effect from the 17 June 1936.

Polizei Wachbataillone

These were a strictly wartime innovation and they must not be confused with the pre-war barracks police. Police Guard Battalions were orgainsed by each army Wehrkreise and their principal task was to maintain order and to direct and re- route traffic in bombed-out areas. About four or five battalions existed in each Wehrkreis and they were designated by arabic numerals followed by the roman numeral of the Wehrkreis i.e. 4. Polizeiwachtbataillon VI/Köln. These units were almost exclusively composed of civilians of post conscription age classes, who had been drafted into the police as Polizei-Reservisten for the duration of the war. The average age in the battalions was reported to be 52. Only the officers and cadre were trained policemen; the rest were draftees who received only short, basic police training. There were 3 to 4 companies in each battalion and 2 to 3 platoons per company and 4 sections in each platoon. The total strength of a battalion ranged from 350-500 men. In the major cities they were constantly kept on alert for duty in case of air raids. They were not motorised but received the necessary vehicles from the Schutzpolizei Kommando of the relevant town or city where they were located. Their armanent consisted of rifles and a few light machine guns. In constrast to other barrack police units they could not be considered fully fledged infantry as the regular police could due to their ages and their lack of training. One battalion was sent into the front line near Aachen and it was wiped out in a day.

Preussen Capital Berlin

Reichstatthalter
Führer Adolf Hitler
Stellvertreter:
Reichsmarschall, SA-Obergruppenführer Herman Göring 30.01.1935–end
Ministerpräsident
Reichsmarschall, SA-Obergruppenführer Hermann Göring 11.04.1933–end

Provinces

Ostpreussen
Oberpräsident
Gauleiter Erich Koch 13.09.1933–end
Regierungsbezirk: Allenstein, Gumbinnen, Königsberg, Zichenau

Mark Brandenburg
Oberpräsident
Gauleiter, SS-Gruppenführer Wilhelm Kube 25.03.1933–01.09.1936
Gauleiter, NSKK-Gruppenführer Emil Stürtz 01.09.1936–end
Regierungsbezirk: Frankfurt an der Oder, Potsdam

Pommern
Oberpräsident
Gauleiter, SA-Obergruppenführer Franz Schwede-Coburg 01.08.1934–end
Regierungsbezirk: Köslin, Schneidemühl, Stettin

Schlesien
Oberpräsident
Gauleiter, SA-Gruppenführer Hellmuth Brückner 25.03.1933–25.12.1934
Gauleiter, SA-Obergruppenführer Josef Wagner 12.06.1935–09.01.1941
Regierungsbezirk: Kattowitz, Oppeln, Breslau, Liegnitz
This province was divided into two separate provinces called Oberschlesien (Upper Schlesien) and Niederschlesien (Lower Schlesien) with effect from the 9 January 1941.
Oberschlesien
Oberpräsident
Gauleiter, SA-Obergruppenführer Fritz Bracht 01.02.1941–end
Regierungsbezirk: Kattowitz, Oppeln
Niederschlesien
Oberpräsident
Gauleiter, SS-Obergruppenführer Karl Hanke 01.02.1941–end
Regierungsbezirk: Breslau, Liegnitz

Stadt Berlin

Stadtpräsident

SA-Gruppenführer Dr. Julius Lippert	01.05.1934 -..1943
SS-Brigadeführer, Oberleutnant der Reserve Ludwig Steeg	1943–end

Sachsen

Oberpräsident

Dr. Kurt Melcher	01.03.1933–01.12.1933
SA-Obergruppenführer Curt von Ulrich	01.12.1933–01.04.1944

Regierungsbezirk: Erfurt, Magdeburg, Merseburg

This province was divided into two separate provinces called Magdeburg and Halle-Merseburg on the 1 April 1944. The Regierungsbezirk called Erfurt was made semi-independent and was administered by the Land Thüringen .

Magdeburg

Oberpräsident

Gauleiter, SA-Obergruppenführer Rudolf Jordan	18.04.1944–end

Regierungsbezirk: Magdeburg

Halle-Merseburg

Oberpräsident

Gauleiter, SS-Obergruppenführer Joachim Eggeling	18.04.1944–end

Regierungsbezirk: Merseburg

Hessen-Nassau

Oberpräsident

SA-Obergruppenführer Philip Prinz von Hessen	16.06.1933–01.04.1944

Regierungsbezirk: Kassel, Wiesbaden

This province was split into two separate provinces called Kurhessen and Nassau with effect from the 1 April 1944.

Kurhessen

Oberpräsident

SA-Obergruppenführer Philip Prinz von Hessen	01.04.1944–01.07.1944
Erich Kurt von Monbart	01.07.1944–13.12.1944
Gauleiter, SS-Gruppenführer Karl Gerland	13.12.1944–end

Regierungsbezirk: Kassel

Nassau

Oberpräsident

SA-Obergruppenführer Philip Prinz von Hessen	01.04.1944–01.07.1944
Gauleiter, SA-Obergruppenführer Jakob Sprenger	01.07.1944–end

Regierungsbezirk: Wiesbaden

Rhein

Oberpräsident

Hermann Freiherr von Lünick	03.1933–05.02.1935
Dr. Nikolaus Simmer (i.V.)	05.02.1935–01.02.1936

Gauleiter, SA-Obergruppenführer Josef Terboven 01.02.1936–end
Regierungsbezirk: Aachen, Düsseldorf, Koblenz, Köln, Trier, Sigmaringen

Schleswig-Holstein

Oberpräsident
Gauleiter, SA-Obergruppenführer Hinrich Lohse 01.06.1933–end
Regierungsbezirk: Schleswig (including the Hanseatic port of Lübeck)

Hannover

Oberpräsident
Dr. Carl von Halfern 06.1930 – 03.1933
Stabschef der SA Viktor Lutze 25.03.1933–01.04.1941
Gauleiter, SS-Obergruppenführer Hartmann Lauterbacher 01.04.1941–end
Regierungsbezirk: Aurich, Hannover, Hildesheim, Stade, Lüneburg, Osnabrück

Westfalen

Oberpräsident
Ferdinand Freiherr von Lünick 07.1933–17.11.1938
Gauleiter, SA-Obergruppenführer Dr. Alfred Meyer 17.11.1938–end
Regiertungsbezirk: Arnsberg, Minden, Münster

Hohenzollerische Lande

Oberpräsident
This area was administered by the Oberpräsident of Rheinprovinz (See Rheinprovinz)
Regierungsbezirk: Sigmaringen
Notes; The Oberpräsident in Ostpreussen, Rhein, Schleswig-Holstein and Westfalen were absent on other duties throughout the war. Erich Koch was Reichskommisar for the Ukraine, Josef Terboven held the same post in Norway and Hinrich Lohse in Ostland (the Baltic States). Alfred Meyer was State Secretary in the Ministry of Eastern Territories. Standing deputies covered the duties in these provinces as follows: Ostpressen Dr. Hoffmann, Rhein SS-Brigadeführer Karl-Eugen Dellenbusch, Schleswig-Holstein SA-Standartenführer Vöge and Westfalen Herr Frundt.

Bayern capital München

Reichsstatthalter
SA-Obergruppenführer General der Infanterie
a.D. Franz Ritter von Epp 10.04.1933–end
Ministerpräsident
SA-Gruppenführer Ludwig Siebert 04.1933–.11.1942
Gauleiter, SA-Obergruppenführer Paul Giesler 11.1942–end
Regierungsbezir: Oberbayern (in München), Schwaben (in Augsburg), Niederbayern (in Regensburg) Bayerische-Pfalz (in Speyer, administered by the Reichsgau Westmark), Ober-und Mittelfranken (in Ansbach) and Mainfranken (in Würzburg).

Sachsen capital Dresden

Reichsstatthalter
Gauleiter, SS-Obergruppenführer Friedrich Hildebrandt 26.05.1933–end
Staatsminister this title was changed to Ministerpräsident in October 1934

Mecklenburg-Schwerin

SS-Oberführer Hans Egon Engell	09.07.1933–10.1934
SS-Oberführer Dr. Friedrich Scharf	10.1934 – 12.1936

Mecklenburg-Strelitz

Dr. Fritz Stichtenoth	29.05.1933 – 12.1936
Mecklenburg	
SS-Oberführer Dr. Friedrich Scharf	01.01.1937–end

Oldenburg capital Oldenburg

Reichsstatthalter	
Gauleiter Carl Röver	05.05.1933–15.05.1942
Gauleiter, SS-Obergruppenführer Paul Wegener	15.05.1942–end
Ministerpräsident	
Gauleiter Carl Röver	16.06.1932 – 05.05.1933
Befehlsleiter, SA-Brigadeführer Georg Joel	05.05.1933–end

Braunschweig capital Braunschweig

Reichsstatthalter	
Gauleiter, SS-Gruppenführer Wilhelm Loeper	05.05.1933–23.10.1935
Gauleiter, SS-Obergruppenführer Joachim Eggeling (i.V.)	01.11.1935–20.04.1937
Gauleiter, SA-Obergruppenführer Rudolf Jordan	20.04.1937–end
Ministerpräsident SS-Obergruppenführer Dietrich Klagges	..1933–end

Anhalt capital Dessau

Reichsstatthalter	
Gauleiter, SS-Gruppenführer Wilhelm Loeper	05.05.1933–23.10.1935
Gauleiter, SS und SA-Obergruppenführer Fritz Sauckel	23.10.1935–20.04.1937
Gauleiter, SA-Obergruppenführer Rudolf Jordan	20.04.1937–end
Ministerpräsident this title was changed to Staatsminister on the 5 May 1933	
SS-Gruppenführer, Leutnant der Reserve Alfred Freyberg	05.1932–21.08.1939
Gauleiter, SA-Obergruppenführer Rudolf Jordan	21.08.1939–end

Lippe capital Detmold

Reichsstatthalter	
Gauleiter, SA-Obergruppenführer Dr. Alfred Meyer	16.05.1933–end
Staatsminister	
SS-Gruppenführer, Ministerialdirektor Hans Joachim Riecke	22.05.1933–31.01.1936
Gauleiter, SA-Obergruppenführer Dr. Alfred Meyer	31.01.1936–end

Schaumburg-Lippe capital Detmold

Reichsstatthalter	
Gauleiter, SA-Obergruppenführer Dr. Alfred Meyer	16.05.1933–end
Landespräsident this title was changed to Staatsminister	
Karl Dreier	22.05.1933–end

Westmark capital Saarbrücken.

Former Saarland return to Germany in 1935 and was added to Rheinprovinz. Headed by a Reichskommissar for Saarland (Bürckel). On 08.04.1940, the Regierungsbezirk Pfalz was separate from Bayern to create "Saar Pfalz" under Bürckel administration. Then on 1941, the Reichsgau Westmark was created, including Civil Administration in occupied Lorraine.

Reichsstatthalter	
Gauleiter, SS-Obergruppenführer Josef Bürckel	11.03.1941–28.09.1944
Gauleiter, HJ-Oberbannführer Willi Stöhr	28.09.1944–end
Allgemeine Vertreter	
Fritz Barth	11.03.1941 – end
Chef der Zivilverwaltung in Lothringen	
Gauleiter, SS-Obergruppenführer Josef Bürckel	02.08.1940 – 28.09.1944
Gauleiter, HJ-Oberbannführer Willi Stöhr	28.09.1944 – end

Freien und Hansestadt Bremen

Reichsstatthalter	
Gauleiter Carl Röver	05.05.1933–15.05.1942
Gauleiter, SS-Obergruppenführer Paul Wegener	15.05.1942–end
Regierender Bürgermeister	
Dr. Richard Markert	18.03.1933 – .10.1934
SS-Brigadeführer Otto Heider	23.10.1934 – .04.1937
SA-Obergruppenführer Johann-Heinrich Böhmcker	16.04.1937–16.06.1944
Senator Dr. Richard Duckwitz	16.06.1944–end

Freien und Hansestadt Hamburg

Reichsstatthalter	
Gauleiter SS-Obergruppenführer Karl Kaufmann	16.05.1933–end
Allgemeine Vertreter und Präsident der Staatsverwaltungs	
SS-Gruppenführer, Hauptmann der Reserve Georg Ahrens	01.04.1938 – end
Leiter der Staats-und Gemeindeverwaltung	
Gauleiter, SS-Obergruppenführer Karl Kaufmann	16.05.1933 – 01.04.1938
Carl Vincent Krogmann	01.04.1938–end
Regierender Bürgermeister	
Carl Vincent Krogmann	1933 – end

Freien und Hansestadt Lübeck

The Hanseatic Harbour of Lübeck was independant until 1937 then became part of the prussian province of Schleswig Holstein.

Reichstatthalter	
Gauleiter, SS-Obergruppenführer Friedrich Hildebrandt	26.05.1933 – 1937
Regierender Bürgermeister	
Dr. Otto-Heinrich Drechsler	05.1933 – 01.1937

6.1.1 Stabsoffizier der Schutzpolizei (Staff Officer of the Schutzpolizei)

The Schutzpolizei des Reiches was the executive police branch in those larger towns and cities where a Staatliche Polizeiverwaltung (National Police Administration) had been established. Command was vested in a "Kommandeur der Schutzpolizei" who came under the relevant police president, police director etc. This structure meant that each Police Administration decided on police actions and exercised disciplinary powers. The Kommandeur was responsible for the tactical methods to be used in any actions ordered and for their operations. A separate command post was created to supervise and co-ordinate all activities of the uniformed police, by-passing the Police Administration. The post was titled "Befehlhaber der Ordnungspolizei".

To carry out liaison between the two commands, the BdO and the KDR der SCHUPO, a Stabsoffizier der SCHUPO was set up. The appointees were advisory members of the staff of the BdO accredited to each Regierungsbezirk. Relevant documents indicate that they were only appointed to the Regierungsbezirk in the state of Preussen plus one each accredited to the Reichsgau Sudetenland, Danzig-Westpreussen and Wartheland. One anomaly exists in that the Taschenbuch für Verwaltungsbeamte (Directory of Administration Officials) for 1943 issued by the Ministry of the Interior, shows a Stabsoffizier der SCHUPO appointed in the Reichsgau Steiermark in what had been österreich. No such post is shown in any other Austrian Reichsgau. The following list is taken from the Taschenbuch and the two Regierungsbezirk with no stabsoffizier listed, Schleswig-Holstein and Sigmaringen, were the sole Regierungsbezirk within their provinces and therefore such a post was not required. It will be noted that from a list of 38 officers only 6 held SS rank.

Stabsoffizier	**Regierungsbezirk**
Major der Schutzpolizei Siegmeier	Aachen/Rhein
Major der Schutzpolizei Bodenstadt	Allenstein/Ostpreussen
Oberstleutnant der Schutzpolizei Gottfried Saupe	Arnsberg/Westfalen
Major der Schutzpolizei Skischally	Aurich/Hannover
Major der Schutzpolizei Brau	Breslau/Niederschlesien
Major der Schutzpolizei Rieck	Düsseldorf/Rhein
Major der Schutzpolizei Schmidt-Hammerstein	Erfurt/Sachsen
Major der Schutzpolizei Fuchs	Frankfurt/Mark Brandenburg
Major der Schutzpolizei Faber	Gumbinnen/Ostpreussen
Major der Schutzpolizei Prange	Hannover/Hannover
Major der Schutzpolizei Robert Buchholz	Hildesheim/Hannover
Oberstleutnant der Schutzpolizei Karl Brockmann	Kattowitz/Oberschlesein
Major der Schutzpolizei Schimmel	Kassel/Hessen-Nassau
Oberst der Schutzpolizei Hans Günther Putz	Koblenz/Rhein
Oberstleutnant der Schutzpolizei Ludwig Buch	Köln/Rhein
Major der Schutzpolizei Kopka	Königsberg/Ostpreussen

Major der Schutzpolizei, SS-Sturmbannführer Erich Fischer	Köslin/Pommern
Major der Schutzpolizei, SS-Sturmbannführer Gustav Vogelsanger	Liegnitz/Niederschlesien
Major der Schutzpolizei Richard Harnisch	Lüneburg/Hannover
Major der Schutzpolizei Merck	Magdeburg/Sachsen
Major der Schutzpolizei, SS-Sturmbannführer Hermann Schröder	Minden/Westfalen
Major der Schutzpolizei, SS-Sturmbannführer Fritz Beck	Münster/Westfalen
Major der Schutzpolizei Karl Beer	Oppeln/Oberschlesien
Major der Schutzpolizei Wilhelm Apeldorn	Osnabrück/Hannover
Oberstleutnant der Schutzpolizei Theodor Westphal	Potsdam/Mark Brandenburg
Major der Schutzpolizei Hermann Labude	Schneidemühl/Pommern
Oberstleutnant der Schutzpolizei Bernhard Stockhofe	Stade/Hannover
Oberst der Schutzpolizei Porath	Stettin/Pommern
Major der Schutzpolizei Below	Trier/Rhein
Major der Schutzpolizei, SS-Sturmbannführer Arno Dettert	Wiesbaden/Hessen-Nassau
Major der Schutzpolizei Barth	Zichenau/Ostpreussen
Oberstleutnant der Schutzpolizei, SS-Obersturmbannführer Helmut Dunnebier	Reichsgau Sudetenland
Major der Schutzpolizei Filzeck	Reichsgau Danzig-Westpreussen
Oberstleutnant der Schutzpolizei Hans-August Damm	Reichsgau Wartheland
Oberstleutnant der Schutzpolizei Rudolf Belleville	Reichsgau Steiermark

6,2 Polizeiverwaltung (Police Administrations)

At the beginning of the 19th century police administrations were established in various towns in the states that later became the German nation. The first police presidency was set up in Braunschweig in 1807 and it was followed by one in Berlin in 1809 and Dresden in 1853. This process was accelerated and most towns had a Police Administration by the beginning of the Great War. In 1918 the police service set up Einwohnenwehren (Militarized self defence units) to combat the Bolshevik uprisings throughout Germany. State Police Administrations developed during the 1920's but before the Nazi takeover there was no Reich police, each province controlling its own Police Administration and there was no centralised control although there was co-operation between the individual forces. The Reich Minister of the Interior had relatively little police authority, not even having a bureau for the investigation of crime but the government did have some leverage. It defrayed part of each state's police budget with an annual subsidy, which served as a direct lever for Reich pressure. This subsidy justified federal legislation that required some degree of organisational uniformity among state forces, in an attempt to keep them free of partisan politics. As a result the Reich Ministry of the Interior could count on more than the goodwill of the states in implementing his guidelines, however the the threat of with drawing the subsidy had its limitations. State governments, generally suspicious of the federal government, jealously guarded their police powers and were reluctent to give any of these powers away to some centralised office. The Versailles treaty restricted the size of all these police forces. Article 162 limited increases in state a local police forces beyond their 1913 strength by tying such increases to populations changes. The Interallied military Commission set more precise details, originally decreeing a maximum of 92,000 men, but gradually raising it to 157,000. Of this total, the maximum was 105,000 for state police, of whom a limit of 35,000 could be housed in barracks. The final limit set by the Interallied Commission was a ratio of approximately one policeman to every four hundred inhabitants. Following the Nazi takeover in January 1933 a decree issued by the Reich and Prussian Interior Ministry dated 30 January 1934 transferred control from the individual provinces and states to the Reich being administered from Berlin. A further decree dated 17 June 1936 created the post of Chief of the German Police within the Interior Ministry and appointed the Reichsführer-SS, Heinrich Himmler to the post. It subordinated the country wide Police Administration to this office. When first established under centralised authority the average Staatliche Polizeiverwaltung (state Police Administration) was organised as follows:

Verwaltungspolizei (Administration Police)

Abteilung I	Politische Polizei (Political Police)
Abteilung II	Fremdenpolizei, Pass-und Meldewesen (Foreigners and passports)
Abteilung III	Verkehr, Feuerschutz (Traffic and Fireservice)
Abteilung IV	Gewerbepolizei (Trade police)
Abteilung V	Gesundheits-und Veterinär, Strafverfugungen, Rechtshilfefachen (Medical, Veterinary, Prosecutions, (Legal assistence)
Dienststelle P	Präsidialgeschäftsstelle (Chancellery)
Dienststelle Ka	Polizeikasse (Cashier)
Dienststelle Rv	Polizeirechnungsrevisor (Accountancy)
Dienststelle A	Leitender Polizeiarzt (Medical)
Dienststelle T	Leitender Polizeitierarzt (Veterinary)
Dienststelle W	Wirtschaftsabteilung (Economics)

Schutzpolizei (Protection Police)
Kommando der Schutzpolizei, Gruppen Abschnittskommandos, Reviere (Police commands, groups and sectors)
Kraftfahrdienst, Motor Strassenpolizei (Motorised Traffic Police)
Wasserschutzpolizei (Waterways Police)
Fernmelddienst (Registration Service)
Sanitätsdienst (Medical Service)
Polizeischulen (Training Schools)
Kriminalpolizei (Plain Clothes Detective Police)

Kriminaldirektion, Kriminalinspektion und Kriminalkommissariate

The organisation underwent a few minor changes throughout the war but it basically retained the main components, the SCHUPO and the KRIPO. The largest administrative departments were the traffic, price control and signals offices. From the above it will be noted that the Verwaltungspolizei was run by civil servants and the Schutzpolizei and Kriminalpolizei was under professional police officers. Each Police Administration had a standing deputy who held the rank of Oberregierungsrat and the heads of the administrative departments were Polizeirat, Polizeiamtmann or Polizei Oberinspekteur. The Schutzpolizei commanders held ranks from Major-General to Major depending on the size of the town. The Kriminalpolizei commanders held the ranks of Regierung und Kriminaldirektor to Regierung und Kriminalrat. As has been noted in the chapter on the Kriminalpolizei, the head of the Polizeiverwaltung (Police President, Police Director) was titled Chef der KRIPO, whilst the executive head responsible for the day to day running of the department was titled Leiter der KRIPO.

The arrival of the National Socialists in January 1933 occasioned a wave of changes in the post of Police Presidencies and Police Directorates, numerous holders were transferred or retired because of suspect loyalty to the Nazi manifesto. Those removed were initially replaced by SA leaders, however many of these did not remain after the purges of the SA in June 1934 being replaced by members of the newly independent SS. A sample of towns is shown below to indicate such changes:

Town	**1933**	**1945**
Breslau	SA-Ogruf. Edmund Heines	SS-Brigaf. Otto Ullmann
Dortmund	SA-Ogruf. Wilhelm Schepmann	SS-Brigaf. Georg Altner
Dresden	SA-Gruf. Georg von Detten	SS-Brigaf. Johannes Thiele
Gleiwitz	SA-Brigaf. Hans Ramshorn	SS-Oberf. Dr. HeinrichVitzdamm
Hannover	SA-Ogruf. Viktor Lutze	SS-Staf. Dr. Erich Deutschbein
Kassel	SA-Ogruf. Franz Pfeffer von Salomon	SS-Brigaf. Lucian Wysocki
Magdeburg	SA-Gruf. Konrad Schragmuller	SS-Brigaf. Andreas Bolek
Regensburg	SA-Ogruf. Hans Georg Hofmann	SS-Ostubaf. Fritz Popp

Only eight police administrations remained under an SA officer during the whole of the Nazi period, Duisburg, Frankfurt am Main, Königsberg, Koblenz, Krefeld, Recklinghausen, Waldenburg and Wuppertal.There was also a direct connection with the Gestapo. When the Gestapo was created on the 27 April 1933, a network of offices were set up in each district of Preussen and this spread to the remaining states. Initially each office was Abteilung I of the administration of the Police Presidency and at first, a number of police presidents and directors became head of their respective Gestapo offices. In November 1934 the following, mainly SA and SSofficers, combined the post of police president with that of head of the Gestapo as follows:

Town	**Holder**
Altona	SA-Gruppenführer Paul Hinkler
Breslau	SA-Obergruppenführer Edmund Heines
Kassel	SA-Obergruppenführer Franz Pfeffer von Salomon
Königsberg	SA-Obergruppenführer Adolf Kob
Minden	Regierungsrat Friedrich von Werder
Oppeln	SA-Brigadeführer Wilhelm Metz
Potsdam	SA-Obergruppenführer Wolf Graf von Helldorf
Schneidemühl	SS-Standartenführer Rudolf Loeffel
Stettin	SS-Brigadeführer Fritz Herrmann
Wesermünde	Landrat Dr. Franz zur Nieden

The Gestapo was under the control of Hermann Göring as Minister President of Preussen at this time but SS incusion was already underway. On the 20 April 1934, Heinrich Himmler had been appointed deputy head of the Gestapo and although, on paper, Göring's deputy, in practice he was in command. A decree dated the 20 November 1934 issued by Göring stated "Organizational reasons impel me to authorize the Reichsführer-SS to represent me in Gestapo matters hitherto dealt with through the Prussian State Ministry". The control was completed when Himmler was appointed Chief of the German Police on the 17 June 1936 and Abteilung I of the police presidency became a kind of liaison with the newly established Gestapo Leitstellen (leading offices) which were now run by professional civil servants from the SS as follows:

Town	**Holder**
Altona	SS-Gruppenführer Bruno Streckenbach (post combined with Hamburg)
Breslau	SS-Brigadeführer Anton Dunckern
Kassel	SS-Obersturmbannführer Günther Herrmann
Königsberg	SS-Oberführer Dr. Heinrich Vitzdamm
Minden (now under Bielefeld)	SS-Standartenführer Otto Bovensiepen
Oppeln	SS-Oberführer Dr. Emanuel Schäfer
Potsdam	SS-Brigadeführer Wilhelm Graf von Wedel
Schneidemühl	SS-Obersturmbannführer Dr. Walter Hammer
Stettin	SS-Brigadeführer Fritz Herrmann
Wesermünde	SS-Obersturmbannführer Dr. Oswald Schäfer

It will be noted that the head of the Gestapo in Stettin was still Fritz Herrmann who was still Police President. Two unique cases remained until the early 1940's. In Nürnberg Dr. Benno Martin was Police President and head of the Gestapo from the 5 July 1934 to the 17 December 1942 and Fritz Popp combined both posts in Regensburg from the 7 December 1940 until the 20 December 1941. Reinhard Heydrich also took a hand and a number of men brought up in the Party Security Service (SD) formed a nucleus of new Police Administrators. In 1933 Dr. Hermann Ramsperger was appointed to the Police Presidency in Mannheim and Dr. Wilhelm Harster became Police Director of Tübingen and by the end of the war 23 police administrations had been headed by former members of the SD. In comparison only 7 posts had been headed by senior officers of the Schutzpolizei. From the above it must be obvious that the police presidencies were never to be wholly under uniformed police control but were run by civil servants. The presidents task was one of administration rather than the prevention and detection of crime. It must also be obvious that Himmler intended, from the start, to bring each post under the direct control of the SS and although he did not succeed in placing SS-men in every post, he succeeded in over 75%. Police Administration came under the various "Höhere Polizeibehörden" (Higher Police Authorities). These were senior civil servants appointed by the various district departments as follows:

Higher Police Authority Administrative Areas

States Preussen, Bayern, Reichsgaue Sudetenland, Danzig-Westpreussen and Wartheland
Regierungspräsident (District President)
States Sachsen, Württemberg, Baden, Thüringen , Oldenburg, Braunschweig
Ministeries of the Interior
State Mecklenburg
Department of Internal Affairs in the State Ministery
States Hessen, Anhalt, Lippe
Reich Governor (Reichsstatthalter) acting through the State Government
State Schaumburg-Lippe
State Administration
Hanseatic Stadt Hamburg
Reich Governor acting through the city state administration
Hansatic Stadt Bremen
Governing Mayor (Regierende Bürgermeister)
Reichsgaue Westmark, Wien, Nieder-Donau, Ober-Donau, Salzburg, Steiermark, Kärnten and Tirol-Vorarlberg

The Kreispolizeibehörden (District Police Authority) were controlled by the appropriate Higher Police Authority. In a Landkreis (Rural District) the Landrat functioned as Kreispolizeibehörde, in a Stadtkreis (Urban District formed around a large town) the Oberbürgermeister had the task and in a district with a major Police Administration, the former Police Administrator. Kreispolizeibehörde in turn supervised Ortspolizeibehörde which were local police authorities under Bürgermeister of smaller towns and rural communities and Police Administrators in towns with State Police Administration. The police administrator was initially appointed by the individual Länder and from 1937 by the Reich Ministry of the Interior. Their ranks were based on the size of the Police District.

Police districts

Berlin

Had the title of Police President with the equivalent rank of Generalleutnant der Polizei

Hamburg, Wien and police districts with populations over 500 000

Had the title of Police President with the equivalent rank of Generalmajor der Polizei

Police districts with a population between 200 000 and 500 000

Had the title of Police President with the equivalent rank of Oberst der Polizei. This also applied to the deputy police presidents of Berlin and Wien but their title was Police Vice President

Police districts with populations from 100 000 to 200 000

Had the title of Police President with the equivalent rank of Oberstleutnant der Polizei

Police districts with populations from 40,000 to 100,000

Had the title of Police Director with the equivalent rank of Major der Polizei

Police Presidents or Directors who were not confirmed could be shown as:

Stellvertreter (stellv): deputy to the Police President or Director, often the Chief of the Protection Police.
Kommissarischer (kommis): probationary or temporary appointment. Mit der Wahrmehmung der Geschäfte beauftragt (mdWdG): in charge of in Vertretung (i.V): acting as Police President or Police Director. Police Administrators were "political" civil servants, they were appointed with regard to their loyalty to the Party and their leadership ability. They came from those with the following backgrounds; senior civil servants, administrative police officials, retired protection police of ficers, political police officers, SS, SA, NSKK or NSFK leaders, political leaders etc. From 1944, the Police President of the largest cities had the right to wear the uniform and rank badges of General, Generalleutnant or Generalmajor der Polizei (mit der Uniform eines General der Polizei or m.d.U.d.). This applied to all not only those in the SS. For instance, Wolf Graf von Helldorf, an SA General, wore police general's uniform.

6.2.1 Organisation of Police Administrations

Main Urban Police District were Polizeipräsidium (Police Presidency)
Middle size and Small Urban Police District were Polizeidirektion (Police Directorate)

Aachen situated in the Regierung Aachen in the Prussian Rheinprovinz. It had a population of 163 000 in 1944.

Landsgerichtsrat Karl Hermans	25.03.1933 -.08.1933 (kommis)
SS-Brigadeführer und Generalmajor der Waffen-SS Dr. Adolf Katz	08.1933–31.12.1936 (kommis until 18 October 1933)
SS-Brigadeführer und Generalmajor der Polizei Carl Zenner	01.01.1937–04.01.1943 (kommis until 9 April 1938)
SS-Oberführer August Flasche	04.01.1943–end (kommis until 6 November 1943)

Altenburg situated in the State of Thüringen, it had a population of 46 000 in 1944. Originally a subordinate Police Office (Polizeiamt) run by a junior official, it was granted independent status as a Police Directorate in March 1941.

SS-Sturmbannführer und Major der Schutzpolizei Karl Legner 07.1941–31.01.1942 (Stellv.)

Polizei Oberinspekteur (1) Albert Neuschwander 31.01.1942–05.1942 (Stellv.)

Amtsrat (2) Georg Hans Friedrich Vogel 05.1942–end (kommis until 5 April 1943)

Altona-Wandsbek situated in the Prussian Province of Schleswig-Holstein. This Police Presidency was abolished in 1937 and the two districts were put under Hamburg as Polizeiämter. Altona was under Dr. Zimmermann and Wandsbek was under Herr Boe.

Otto Eggerstedt 1929–01.1933

Regierungsdirektor Dr. Diefenbach 01.1933–20.03.1933

SA-Gruppenführer, Gauleiter a.D. Paul Georg Otto Hinkler 20.03.1933–08.03.1937

Augsburg situated in the Regierungsbezirk Augsburg (State of Bayern). It had a population of 185,891 in 1944. Originally a Police Directorate, it was upgraded to a Police Presidency in May 1938.

SS-Brigadeführer, Oberstleutnant der Reserve (3)
Rolf von Humann-Hainhofen 15.12.1933–16.03.1936

SS-Brigadeführer und Generalmajor der Polizei (m.d.U.d.) Wilhelm Starck 16.03.1936–end
(kommis until 1 December 1936)

Aussig situated in the Regierungsbezirk Aussig (Reichsgau Sudetenland). It had a population of 68,277 in 1944. It was returned to Czechoslovakia after the war and is now known as Usti-nad-Labem in the Czech Republic
SS-Standartenführer Dr. Gustav Nutzhorn 11.10.1939–08.05.1945 (kommis until 6 September 1940)

Baden-Baden situated in the Landskommissariat District Karlsruhe (State of Baden). It had a population of 34,000 in 1944.
Herr Dorner 1934–.04.1936

Regierungsrat Boffert 03.1937–11.1937 (kommis)

SS-Mann, Oberregierungsrat Dr. Herbold 11.1937 -01.1938 (kommis)

SA-Scharführer, Oberregierungsrat Dr. Ernst 01.1938–01.07.1940
(kommis until 1 June 1938)

SA-Sturmführer, Regierungsrat Mallebrein 01.07.1940–end (kommis until March 1942)

Berlin situated on the River Spree in the Prussian Province of Mark Brandenburg, it was the Reich (and Prussian) capital and was self governing. It had a population of 4,339,000 in 1944. The post of Police President here was unique because of its status as the countries capital city. The city administration had a double function: it was a Landesverwaltungsbezirk (State Administrative District) and a Selbstverwaltende Körperschaft (Autonomous Administrative Authority) ranked as a Regierungsbezirk. In the state of Preussen, Police Presidents were subordinate to the relevant Regierungspräsident (District President) but the Police President in Berlin was equal to a Regierungspräsident. Berlin ceased being the capital in 1945 when the country was divided but was appointed a new after the re-unification.

Dr. Kurt Melcher	07.1932–15.02.1933
Konteradmiral a.D. Magnus von Levetzow	15.02.1933–01.12.1935
SA-Obergruppenführer, General der Polizei (m.d.U.d.) Wolf Graf von Helldorf	01.12.1935–03.08.1944
SS-Gruppenführer und Generalleutnant der Polizei Kurt Göhrum	03.08.1944 – end

Polizeivizepräsident:

Rudolf Diels (kommis)	11.1933–04.1934
Heinrich Neubaur	04.1934–06.1934
Traugott Bredow	07.1934 – 1937
Paul Kanstein	1938–1940
Hans Scholtz	1940 -1945

Bialystok situated in Poland, it had formerly been part of White Russia. After the German invasion of Russia in June 1941 it was incorporated into the Prussian Province of Ostpreussen. It had a population of 103,000 in 1944. The Police Presidency was established in June 1944, before that date the uniformed police had been under the direct command of the BdO in Königsberg. The town was under the Higher SS and Police Leader for Russland Mitte und Weissruthenien and it had its own SS and Police Leader. It is not known why a Police President was created especially so late in the war. The town is now in Poland.

Ministerialrat (4) Heinrich Meinecke	06.1944–01.1945

Bielefeld situated in the Regierungsbezirk Minden in the Prussian Province of Westfalen. It had a population of 126,393 in 1944. The post of Police President was abolished during April 1934.

Regierungsrat Friedrich von Werder	25.03.1933–04.1934

Bitterfeld situated in the Regierungsbezirk Merseberg in the Prussian Province of Sachsen. It was put into the new Province of Halle-Merseberg in 1944. It had a population of 56,000 in 1944.

SS-Obersturmbannführer und Oberstleutnant der Schutzpolizei Paul Wilhelm Fydrich	04.1938 – 1939 (mdWdG)
Regierungsrat Melcher	1939–01.02.1940 (stellv)
SS-Sturmbannführer, Regierungsrat Kurt Mainz	01.02.1940–1943
SS-Scharführer Dr. Tschochner	1943–end (i.V.)

Bochum situated in the Regierungsbezirk Arnsberg in the Prussian Province of Westfalen. It had a population of 679,000 in 1944.

Stadtrat, Landrat a.D. Sarrazin — 15.02.1933–31.07.1933

SS-Obergruppenführer, Hauptdienstleiter der NSDAP (5)
Fritz Schlessmann 3 — 1.07.1933–04.08.1938
(kommis until 3 April 1934)

SS-Brigadeführer und Generalmajor der Polizei (m.d.U.d.)
Walter Oberhaidacher — 04.08.1938–23.03.1944
(kommis until 7 October 1939)

SS-Brigadeführer und Generalmajor der Polizei Georg Asmus — 23.03.1944–15.04.1945

Braunschweig situated in the state of Braunschweig. It had a population of 227 000 in 1944.

Kreisdirektor Johannes Lieff — 01.11.1931–01.1938
SS-Standartenführer Hermann Schmauser — 01.1938–end (kommis until 31 May 1939)

Bremen was an independent Hanseatic City State, it included the city of Bremen, the port of Bremerhaven and eleven small communities. It had a population of 442 000 in 1944. The head of the city police had the title of Polizeiherr until 1 October 1937.

Stadtrat Dr. Richard Market — 06.03.1933–1934
SS-Oberführer Theodor Laue — 1934–1936
Dr. Beuthien — 1936–01.10.1937
SS-Brigadeführer, SS-Hauptsturmführer der Reserve
(6) Curt Ludwig — 01.10.1937–20.11.1941
(kommis until 2 March 1939)

SS-Obergruppenführer und General der Waffen-SS und der Polizei

Luxemburg 1940: Left to right: Kreisleiter Müller, Baurat Vogel,Regeirungspräsident SS-Brigadeführer Heinz Siekmeier, Gauleiter Gustav Simon, Polizeipräsident SA-Brigadeführer August Willhelm Wetter, Oberbürgermeister Dr. Hengst

Carl-Albrecht Oberg	01.04.1941–15.04.1941 (kommis)
SS-Brigadeführer und Generalmajor der Polizei Johannes Schroers	20.11.1941–end (kommis until 1 March 1942)

Breslau situated in the Regierungsbezirk Breslau in the Prussian Province of Niederschlesien (Lower Schlesien). It had a population of 631 000 in 1944. The city is now in Poland and is known as Wroclaw.

Regierunsrat Joachim von Alt-Stutterheim	1931–25.03.1933
SA-Obergruppenführer Edmund Heines	25.03.1933–30.06.1934
SS-Brigadeführer, Hauptdienstleiter Albrecht Schmelt	05.07.1934–01.05.1941 (kommis until 18 October 1934)
SS-Obergruppenführer General der Waffen-SS Franz Breithaupt	01.05.1941–15.08.1942 (kommis until 7 May 1941)
Regierungsdirektor Hauke	29.06.1942–14.05.1943 (i.V.)
SS-Brigadeführer und Generalmajor der Polizei (m.d.U.d.) Otto Ullmann	14.05.1943–end (kommis until 27 October 1943)

Bromberg situated in the Regierungsbezirk Bromberg in the Reichsgau Danzig/Westpreussen. It had been part of Preussen until 1918 when it was given to Poland by the Versailles Treaty. It had a population of 131 181 in 1944. It was returned to Poland after the war and is now known as Bydgoszcz.

SS-Brigadeführer und Generalmajor der Polizei (m.d.U.d.) Max Henze	09.09.1939–02.10.1939
SS-Oberführer, Major a.D. (7) Otto von Proeck	02.10.1939–12.05.1942 (in charge of Police administration then kommis from 1 April 1940 until 10 July 1941)
Regierungsrat Dr. Kracke	12.05.1942–31.07.1942 (kommis)
SS-Standartenführer, Leutnant der Reserve Carl-Otto von Salisch	01.08.1942–07.02.1945 (kommis until 22 December 1942)
SS-Oberführer und Major a.D. Otto von Proeck	09.02.1945–.04.1945
SS-Brigadeführer und Generalmajor der Polizei (m.d.U.d.) Max Henze	04.1945–end

Brüx situated in the Regierungsbezirk Aussig in the Reichsgau Sudetenland. Prior to 1938 it had been part of Czechoslovakia and prior to 1918, it was in österreich. It had a population of 131,000 in 1944. After 1945 it was returned to

Czechoslovakia under the name Most. The town was evacuated in the 1970's and it was totally destroyed to make way for an extension in local brown coal mining.

SS-Standartenführer, Hauptmann der Schutzpolizei a.D.
Rudolf Loeffel — 25.10.1939–10.04.1942

SS-Standartenführer, Oberregierungsrat, Hauptsturmführer der Reserve
Nils-Otto Wiese — 10.04.1942–30.05.1944 (kommis until June 1943)

SS-Obersturmbannführer, Hauptmann der Reserve Kurt Herfurth — 30.05.1944–end

Brünn situated in Böhmen-Mähren in what had been part of Czechoslovakia, it became part of the Protectorate of Böhmen-Mähren and controlled eight political districts. The Protectorate retained its own police force under strict German control. A Police Directorate was established following the administrative reform decree of 23 May 1942 (8) The town was returned to Czechoslovakia after the war and is now in the Czech Republic known as Brno.

Polizeioberrat Dr. Jungwirth — 1942–1944

Regierungsdirektor Dr. Herrmann — 1944–end

Chemnitz situated in the Regierungsbezirk Chemnitz in the State of Sachsen. It had a population of 338,000 in 1944. After the war, it was part of the German Democratic Republic and was known as Karl-Marx-Stadt. Following the re-unification of Germany it was renamed Chemnitz in 1993.

Oberregierungsrat Ernst Schwarmkrug — 01.10.1922–31.12.1934

Herr Schübert — 31.12.1934–.06.1936

SS-Brigadeführer und Generalmajor der Polizei (m.d.U.d.)
Willy Weidermann — 06.1936–19.09.1942 (kommis until 31 July 1937)

SS-Oberführer, Oberführer der Waffen-SS (9) Erich Tschimpke — 19.09.1942 -07.1943 (i.V.)

SS-Standartenführer, Leutnant der Reserve Günther Sachsofsky — 12.03.1943–end

Cuxhaven situated in the Regierungsbezirk Stade in the Prussian Province of Hannover. It had a population of 34,000 in 1944. Originally a Polizeiamt, it was raised to the status of Police Directorate in 1938.

Major der Schutzpolizei Harri Hellwege-Emden — 1938–06.03.1939

SS-Standartenführer Karl d'Angelo — 06.03.1939–30.03.1943 (kommis until 18 April 1940)

SS-Obersturmbannführer, Obersturmbannführer der Waffen-SS
Emil Sator 01.04.1943–end (kommis)

Danzig This was the old international free port that had been under the political control of the Nazis since the 1930's. After the conquest of Poland in 1939 it became part of Germany and was situated in the Regierungsbezirk Danzig in the Reichsgau Danzig-Westpreussen. It had a population of 280,000 in 1944. A German Chief of Police known as "Polizeichef" was appointed on the 28 June 1939. From September 1939 a Police Administration was set up and a Police Presidency was officially established on the 1 April 1940, this included the harbour of Zoppot. After the war, the port was returned to Poland and it is now known as Gdansk.

SS-Brigadeführer, Obersturmführer der Reserve Johannes Schäfer
28.06.1939–19.09.1939 (Polizeichef)

SS-Brigadeführer und Generalmajor der Polizei (m.d.U.d.) Max Henze
19.09.1939–01.10 1941 (kommis 1 April 1940)

SS-Oberführer Walter Stein
01.10.1941–01.11.1944 (kommis until 10 February 1943)

SS-Standartenführer, Oberst der Schutzpolizei Erich Rottmann
01.11.1944–end (kommis)

Darmstadt situated in the Provinze of Starkenburg in the State of Hesse. It had a population of 116,000 in 1944. Originally a Police Directorate, it was upgraded to a Police Presidency on the 7 May 1940.

SA-Brigadeführer Daniel Hauer
09.1933–1934

Oberregierungsrat Dr. Pabst
1934–01.06.1937 (kommis)
Oberst der Schutzpolizei a.D. Karl Geppert
01.06.1937–end (Police Director until 7 May 1940)

Dessau situated in the State of Anhalt, it had a population of 120,000 in 1944.

NSKK-Oberführer Wilhelm Trippler
06.1936–30.06.1939 (kommis until 1 December 1937)

SS-Oberführer, Hauptsturmführer der Reserve Ernst Hildebrandt
30.06.1939–30.05.1944 (kommis until 6 July 1940)

SS-Standartenführer, Hauptsturmführer der Reserve Nils-Otto Wiese
30.05.1944–end (kommis)

Dortmund situated in the Regierungsbezirk Arnsberg in the Prussian Province of Westfalen. It had a population of 545,000 in 1944.

Stabschef der SA Wilhelm Schepmann
15.02.1933–12.1934

SA-Obergruppenführer Otto Schramme
12.1934–14.01.1942 (kommis until 1 July 1935)

SS-Brigadeführer und Generalmajor der Polizei (m.d.U.d.) George Altner
14.01.1942–10.04.1945

SS-Standartenführer und Oberst der Polizei Rudolf Batz
10.04.1945–end

Dresden situated in the Regierungsbezirk Dresden in the State of Sachsen. It had a population of 631,000 in 1944.

SA-Gruppenführer Georg von Detten
1933–.08.1933

SS-Brigadeführer und Generalmajor der Polizei Walter Hille
08.1933–11.01.1939 (kommis)

SS-Brigadeführer Fritz Herrmann
11.01.1939–08.11.1939

SS-Brigadeführer und Generalmajor der Polizei (m.d.U.d.) Karl Pflomm
08.11.1939–19.11.1944 (kommis until 5 June 1940)

SS-Brigadeführer und Generalmajor der Polizei (m.d.U.d.) Walter Oberhaidacher
19.11.1944–26.01.1945

SS-Brigadefuührer und Generalmajor der Polizei Johannes Thiele
26.01.1945–end

Duisburg situated in the Regierungsbezirk Düsseldorf in the Prussian Province of Rhein, it was known as Duisburg Hamborn until 30 March 1935. It had a population of 436,000 in 1944.

Herr Meyer
01.07.1926–01.03.1933

Regierungsdirektor (14) Heinrich Refardt
01.03.1933–11.09.1933

SA-Gruppenführer Heinrich Knickmann
11.09.1933–05.1937

SS-Obergruppenführer und General der Waffen-SS und der Polizei Karl Gutenberger
05.1937–11.1939 (kommis until 7 May 1938)

SS-Brigadeführer und Generalmajor der Polizei Lucian Wysocki
11.1939–08.1941

NSKK-Oberführer Willi Forster
08.1941–09.1943 (kommis)

SA-Gruppenführer Franz Bauer
09.1943–end (kommis)

Düsseldorf situated in the Regierungsbezirk Düsseldorf in the Prussian Rhein Province. It had a population of 542,000 in 1944.

Hans Langels
01.07.1926–29.04.1933

SS-Obergruppenführer Fritz Weitzel
01.05.1933–19.06.1940 (kommis until 1 November 1933)

SS-Brigadeführer und Generalmajor der Polizei (m.d.U.d.) August Korreng
19.06.1940–17.04.1945 (kommis until 25 January 1941)

Elbing situated in the Prussian Province of Ostpreussen, it was transferred to the Reichsgau Danzig-Westpreussen on the 1 April 1940. It had a population of 85,000 in 1944. After the war it was given to Poland and it is now known as Elblag.

SA-Brigadeführer Xavier Dorsch
10.1933–11.1942 (kommis until 28 December 1933)

Regierungsrat Blume
11.1942–30.11.1943 (kommis)

Regierungsrat Dr. Kohler
01.12.1943–end (kommis until August 1944)

Erfurt situated in the Regierungsbezirk Erfurt in the Prussian Province of Sachsen. It had a population of 106,000 in 1944.

SA-Obergruppenführer Werner von Fichte
06.1933–01.08.1934 (kommis until 22 September 1933)

Staatsrat Albert Stange
01.08.1934–11.1934 (i.V)

Oberregierungsrat Harte
11.1934–13.04.1937 (kommis until 1 February 1935)

SS-Brigadeführer und Generalmajor der Polizei (m.d.U.d.) Karl Pflomm
13.04.1937–08.11.1939

SS-Oberführer Alexander von Woedtke
08.11.1939–04.08.1941 (kommis until 1 March 1940)

SS-Oberführer Heinrich Wicke
04.08.1941–28.07.1944 (kommis until 12 June 1942)
unbesetzt (vacant) 28.07.1944–24.01.1945

SS-Brigadeführer und Generalmajor der Waffen-SS und der Polizei Otto Gieseke
24.01.1945–end

Essen situated in the Regierungsbezirk Düsseldorf in the Prussian Province of Rhein. It was the headquarters of the Krupp empire and had a population of 685,000 in 1944.

Dr. Kurt Melcher
1919–07.1932
unbesetzt .07.1932–24.06.1933

SS-Gruppenführer und Generalleutnant der Polizei Karl Zech
24.06.1933–01.10.1937 (kommis until 14th July 1933)

SS-Obergruppenführer, Hauptdienstleiter der NSDAP Fritz Schlessmann
01.10.1937–.11.1939

SS-Obergruppenführer und General der Waffen-SS und der Polizei Karl Gutenberger
11.1939–29.06.1941

SS-Brigadeführer und Generalmajor der Polizei (m.d.U.d.) Max Henze
29.06.1941–end (kommis until October 1942)

Esslingen situated on the River Neckar in the State of Württemberg. The Police Directorate was downgraded to a Polizeiamt on the 13 September 1938 and was upgraded to a Police Directorate again on the 1 May 1941. It had a population of 50,000 in 1944.

Polizeirat Josef Wilhelm
1923–01.06.1931

SA-Sturmhauptführer Ernst Hahn
01.06.1931–25.02.1935

Regierungsrat Dr. Gerhart Rooschüz
25.02.1935–01.05.1941 (He remained when the office was downgraded in September 1938)

SA-Obersturmbannführer, Polizeirat Otto Hoch
01.05.1941–25.09.1943 (kommis until 1 December 1941)

Polizeirat Dangel
25.09.1943–end (i.V.)

Flensburg situated in the Regierungsbezirk Schleswig in the Prussian Province of Schleswig-Holstein. It had a population of 66,865 in 1944 and it served as the seat of Government under Hitler's successor as Chancellor, Grand Admiral Karl Dönitz in May 1945.

Oberregierungsrat Hinckel
01.10.1929–31.05.1931

Regierungsdirektor Konrad Fulda
01.06.1931–.02.1937

Regierungsrat Dr. Heinrich Schulte (Kommissarischer)
02.1937–09.09.1937

SS-Brigadeführer und Generalmajor der Polizei Hinrich Möler
09.09.1937–01.08.1941 (kommis until 27 May 1938)

SS-Standartenführer, Oberstleutnant der Schutzpolizei a.D. Hans Hinsch
01.08.1941–end (kommis until October 1943)

Frankfurt am Main situated in the Regierungsbezirk Wiesbaden in the Prussian Province of **Hessen-Nassau.** It had a population of 556,000 in 1944. It was known as the 'Stadt des Deutschen Handwerks' (the city of German handicrafts).

Generalleuntant z.V. Reinhard von Westerem zum Gutacker
15.02.1933–.09.1933

SA-Obergruppenführer Adolf-Heinz Berckerle
09.1933–.06.1941 (kommis until 18 January 1934)

Regierungsdirektor Dr. Seiler
06.1941–23.12.1942 (He was the deputy Police President throughout the war)

SA-Brigadeführer Fritz Stollberg
23.12.1942–end

Frankfurt an der Oder situated in the Regierungsbezirk Frankfurt in the Prussian Province of Mark Brandenburg. It had a population of 84,000 in 1944.

Oberregierungsrat Dr. Gerhard Bode
1936–.04.1938 (i.V.)

SS-Brigadeführer, Rittmeister der Reserve Erasmus Freiherr von Malsen-Ponickau
04.1938–31.05.1940 (kommis until 11 March 1939)

SS-Obersturmbannführer, Obersturmführer der Reserve Walter Bachmann
09.10.1939–end (kommis until 12 August 1940. He took over in October 1939 because von Malsen had been posted to Posen and he held both posts until 31 May 1940).

Freiburg am Breisgau situated in the Landskommissariat Freiburg in the State of Baden. It had a population of 112,000 in 1944.

SS-Standartenführer, Leutnant der Reserve Günther Sacksofsky
01.08.1934–21.09.1940

SS-Obersturmbannführer Otto Henninger
21.09.1940–end (kommis. until 24 April 1942)

Friedrichshafen situated in Landskreis Friedrichshafen in the State of Württemberg. It had a population of 26,000 in 1944.

Landrat Eduard Quintenz
05.1923–24.02.1936

Regierungsrat Dr. Hermann Buttner
16.12.1937–04.10.1939 (kommis until 3 November 1938)

Regierungsrat Dr. Erhard Pfisterer
06.11.1939–11.02.1941 (kommis until the 17 December 1940)

SS-Untersturmführer, Regierungsrat Dr. Heinz Spiess
11.02.1941–1943 (kommis until 29 July 1942)

Landrat Knapp
1943–25.09.1943 (i.V.)

SA-Obersturmbannführer, Polizeirat Otto Hoch
25.09.1943–02.11.1944

SS-Obersturmbannführer Otto Gluck
02.11.1944–end (kommis)

Gera situated in the Landskreis Gera in the State of Thüringen. It had a population of 84,000 in 1944.

SS-Brigadeführer, Ministerialdirigent Hans Kehrl
07.1930–01.10.1932

SS-Obersturmbannführer, Oberregierungsrat Dr. Walter Rohde
01.10.1932–31.05.1940 (kommis until 3 April 1933)

Regierungsrat Dr. Kohler
31.05.1940–30.11.1943 (kommis until 27 July 1940)

Regierungsrat Blume
30.11.1943–end (kommis until August 1944)

Giessen situated in the Landskreis Giessen in the Province of Oberhessen in the State of Hesse. It had a population of 69,000 in 1944.

SS-Brigadeführer und Generalmajor der Polizei Heinz Jost
01.10.1933–15.07.1934 (kommis until 1 January 1934)

Herr Heine
15.07.1934 -1935 (kommis)

Herr Meusel
1935–01.04.1936 (kommis)

Major der Schutzpolizei Harri Hellwege-Emden
01.04.1936 -1938

SA-Oberführer Martin Lutter
1938–08.03.1943 end (kommis until 13 October 1940)

Gladbach-Rheydt see Mönchengladbach-Rheydt
Gleiwitz situated in the Regierungsbezirk Gleiwitz in the Prussian Province of Oberschlesien (Upper Schlesien). It had a population of 516,000 in 1944. After the war it became part of Poland and is now known as Gliwice.

Herr Wackerzapp
"-"–04.1933

SA-Brigadeführer, Hauptmann der Schutzpolizei a.D. Hans Ramshorn
04.1933–01.07.1934 (kommis until 30 October 1933)

Heinrich Neubaur
01.07.1934–30.11.1937

SS-Brigadeführer, Leutnant der Reserve Dr. Günther Palten
30.11.1937–26.11.1939 (kommis until 30 July 1938. His name was Patschowsky until late in 1938)

SS-Brigadeführer, Major der Reserve Dr. Hermann Ramsperger
12.04.1940–28.06.1943 (kommis until August 1940)

SS-Oberführer, Oberregierungsrat Dr. Heinrich Vitzdamm
28.06.1943–end

Gotenhafen situated in Poland until 1939 it was known as Gdynia. After the German occupation it became part of the Regierungsbezirk Danzig in the Reichsgau Danzig-Westpreussen and changed its name to Gotenhafen. It had a population of 70,000 in 1944. After the war it was returned to Poland and again became known as Gdynia.

SS-Brigadeführer und Generalmajor der Waffen-SS und der Polizei Christoph Diehm
01.03.1939–22.10.1941 unbesetzt (vacant) 22.10.1941–.07.1942

SS-Obersturmbannführer, Oberregierungsrat Dr. Helmut Müler
07.1942–24.01.1944 (kommis until 25 January 1943)

SS-Oberführer Maximilian Brand
24.01.1944–end (i.V.)

Gotha situated in the Landskreis Gotha in the State of Thüringen. It had a population of 55,000 in 1944.

SS-Obersturmbannführer, Hauptmann der Reserve Kurt Herfurth
01.08.1931–end

Graz situated in the Reichsgau Steiermark (Steiermark) in Österreich. It had a population of 211,000 in 1944.

SA-Obergruppenführer Gauleiter Siegfried Uiberreither
03.1938–23.05.1938

SS-Brigadeführer, Gauleiter a.D., Generalmajor der Polizei (m.d.U.d.) Andreas Bolek
22.05.1938–30.07.1938

SS-Oberführer Maximilian Brand
30.07.1938–24.01.1944 (kommis until 27 October 1939)

SS-Standartenführer Dr. Arnold Rust
24.01.1944–end

Graudenz situated in the Regierungsbezirk Marienwerder in the Reichsgau Danzig-Westpreussen. It had a population of 55,000 in 1944. It was a police directorate until 24 February 1943 when its status was elevated to police presidency. After the war it was handed to Poland and is now known as Grudzidz.

SS-Standartenführer, Leutnant der Reserve Fritz Meyer
28.07.1939–10.06.1944 (kommis until 25 September 1940)

SS-Sturmbannführer Heribert Kammer
03.1944–end (kommis until 14 December 1944)

Hagen situated in the Regierungsbezirk Arnsberg in the Prussian Province of Westfalen. It had a population of 154,827 in 1944. Originally a police presidency it was disbanded on 1934.

Regierungsdirektor Heinrich Refardt
11.1932–01.03.1933

SS-Brigadeführer, Major der Schutzpolizei a.D. Fritz Herrmann
16.03.1933–01.07.34

Halle an der Saale situated in the Regierungsbezirk Merseburg in the Prussian Province of Merseburg. It had a population of 290,000 in 1944

Oberst der Schutzpolizei a.D. Berend Roosen
17.02.1933 -12.2.1936

SA-Obergruppenführer Wilhelm Jahn
12.2.1936–11.1.1939 (kommis until 28 October 1936)

SA-Brigadeführer Friedrich Habenicht
11.1.1939–14.08.1940

SS-Oberführer, Oberregierungsrat (10) Dr. Heinrich Vitzdamm
18.10.1939–28.06.1943 (kommis until 14 August 1940)

SS-Brigadeführer, Rittmeister der Reserve Erasmus Freiherr von Malsen-Ponickau
28.06.1943–20.12.1943

Ministerialrat Maximilian Rheins
20.12.1943–end

Hamburg situated in northern Germany it was an independent Hanseatic City State, self administrating. From 1933, it was run like a Prussian province with a Reichstatthalter who also the local Party Gauleiter. On 1937, the former Prussian towns of Altona, Wandsbeck and Harburg-Wilhelmsburg became part of Hamburg. It had a population of 1,694,328 in 1944. The head of the city Police Administration had the title of Polizeiherr until the 1 January 1937 when it was changed to police president.

SA-Gruppenführer Alfred Richter
05.03.1933–15.03.1933

SS-Brigadeführer, Oberleutnant der Reserve Dr. Hans Nieland
15.03.1933–07.10.1933 (kommis)

SA-Standartenführer Wilhelm Boltz
07.10.1933–31.12.1936

SS-Brigadeführer, Ministerialdirigent (11) Hans Kehrl
01.01.1937–end (kommis until 25 July 1937)

Hamm situated in the Regierungsbezirk Arnsberg in the Prussian Province of Westfalen. It had a population of 60,000 in 1944.

Dr. Johann Wilhelm Sommer
02.04.1928–10.03.1933

SS-Brigadeführer und Generalmajor der Polizei Johannes Schoers
11.03.1933–14.03.1933 (i.V)

SA-Sturmführer, Major der Schutzpolizei Georg Mählich
15.03.1933–22.12.1938 (kommis until 20 September 1933)

Regierungsrat Heme
20.12.1938–16.09.1939 (i.V.)

Major der Schutzpolizei Stolzenberg
16.09.1939–18.02.1940 (i.V.)

SS-Standartenführer Arthur Friderici
19.02.1940–19.02.1941 (kommis until 28 August 1940)

Polizeirat August Georg Leise
10.02.1941–13.01.1942 (Kommis to 18.05.1941)

Regierungsrat Dr. Eberhard Rotmann
13.01.1942–06.04.1945 (kommis until 6 July 1942)

Hanau situated in the Regierungsbezirk Kassel in the Prussian Province of Hessen-Nassau. It had a population of 40,532 in 1944.

Kreisleiter Fritz Löser
1933–01.02.1942

Major der Schutzpolizei Josef Oberesch
01.02.1942–18.12.1942 (i.V.)

SS-Obersturmbannführer, Amtsrat, Hauptmann der Reserve Hermann Fehrle
18.12.1942–end

Hannover situated in the Regierungsbezirk Hannover in the Prussian Province of Hannover. It had a population of 472,527 in 1944.

Oberregierungsrat Johannes Habben
1931–15.02.1933

Stabschef der SA Viktor Lutze
15.02.1933–25.03.1933

Oberregierungsrat Johannes Habben
25.03.1933–08.12.1937

SA-Gruppenführer Waldemar Geyer
08.12.1937–14.10.1942

SS-Standartenführer, Hauptmann der Reserve Dr. Erich Deutschbein
14.10.1942–end (kommis until 27 July 1943)

Harburg-Wilhelmsburg this town, originally in the Regierungsbezirk Stade in the Prussian Province of Hannover, became a district in the Hanseatic City State of Hamburg in Octopber 1937. Originally a Police Presidency, it was downgraded to Police Directorate 1 April 1936 and then was demoted to a Polizeiamt under the control of the Hamburg Polizeipräsidium on 1 February 1937, the office being run by Polizeiamtsleiter Rohl.

Fregattenkapitän der Reserve (12) Carl Christiansen
18.12.1933–01.08.1934

Staatsrat Albert Stange
01.08.1934–.09.1935

SS-Standartenführer, Hauptmann der Schutzpolizei a.D.Rudolf Loeffel
31.12.1934–01.02.1937

Heidelberg situated in the Landskommissarbezirk Mannheim in the State of Baden. It had a population of 88,000 in 1944.

Regierungsrat Biermann
1934–01.07.1934

SS-Obersturmbannführer Otto Henninger
01.07.1934 – 09.1940

Regierungsrat Kärcher
1940 – end (kommis until February 1944)

Heilbronn situated in the Landskreis Heilbronn in the State of Württemberg. It had a population of 78,000 in 1944.

Polizeirat Josef Wilhelm
01.06.1931–10.1935

Landrat Dr. Heubach
10.1935–08.06.1938 (kommis)

SS-Oberführer Heinrich Wicke
08.06.1938–04.08.1941 (kommis until 14 April 1939)

Wilhelm Dambacher
04.08.1941–01.04.1943 (i.V in charge of daily duties when no incumbant had been appointed)

SS-Standartenführer Karl D'Angelo
01.04.1943–20.03.1945

Hof an der Saale situated in the Regierungsbezirk Ansbach in the State of Bayern. It had a population of 45,000 in 1944.

Oberregierungsrat Hasse
1933 -1935

Oberregierungsrat Wirsching
1935–10.08.1937

SS-Oberführer, Hauptmann der Reserve Ernst Hildebrandt
10.08.1937–01.10.1940 (kommis until 1938)

SS-Obersturmbannführer, Major der Schutzpolizei a.D. Emil Schmitt
01.10.1940–end (kommis until 30 September 1942)

Iglau head of the Oberlandsbezirk Iglau in the Protectorate of Böhmen-Mähren. It had been in the Province of Böhmen-Mähren in Czechoslovakia until 1939 (see the entry under Brünn for its status). After the war it was returned to Czechoslovakia and it is now in the Czech Republic and is known as Jihlava.

SS-Oberführer, Untersturmführer der Reserve Emanuel Sladek
15.03.1939–end (kommis until 1 August 1943)

Innsbruck situated in the Reichsgau Tirol in Österreich, it had a population of 100,000 in 1944. Originally a Police Directorate, it was upgraded to Police Presidency in November 1942.

SS-Gruppenführer und Generalleutnant der Polizei, Untersturmführer der Reserve Konstantin Kammerhofer
22.03.1938–03.1938

SS-Untersturmführer Dr. Adolf Franzelin
03.1938–25.04.1940 (kommis until January 1940)

Oberregierungsrat Dr. Bohme
25.04.1940–10.07.1941(i.V)

SS-Standartenführer, Oberregierungsrat Dr. Hans Dornauer
10.07.1941–end (kommis until 5 November 1942)

Jena situated in the Stadtkreis Jena in the State of Thüringen. It had a population of 73,000 in 1944

SS-Obersturmbannführer, Kriminaldirektor August Finke
1933–.12.1934

Regierungsrat (14) Dr. Ludwig
12.1934–04.1939 (kommis)

SS-Obersturmbannführer, Oberregierungsrat Walter Schmidt
04.1939–01.02.1943 (kommis until 19 September 1939)

SS-Obersturmbannführer, Polizeirat Hans Schulze
01.02.1943–end (kommis until 28 October 1943)

Kaiserslautern situated in the Regierungsbezirk Pfalz in the State of Bayern. It became a Landkreis in the Reichsgau Westmark during the war. It had a population of 71,000 in 1944.

Oberregierungsrat Karl Müller
1934–1935

Hauptmann der Schutzpolizei Freiherr von Hausen
1935–02.1938

SS-Obersturmbannführer, Oberleutnant der Reserve Dr. Werner Beuschlein
02.1938–end (kommis until 19 March 1939)

Landrat Karl Müller
1943–end (i.Vdeputised for Beuschlein who was absent on duty with the army).

Karlsbad situated in the Regierungsbezirk Eger in the Reichsgau Sudetenland. It had formerly been in Czechoslovakia. The post of Police Director was established on the 25 October 1939. The population was 64,000 in 1944. The town was returned to Czechoslovakia after the war and is now in the Czech Republic, known as Karlovy Vary.

SA-Sturmführer, Major der Schutzpolizei a.D. Georg Mählich
25.10.1939–04.09.1940

Bürgermeister Hans Krauss
04.09.1940–11.1942 (kommis)

SS-Hauptscharführer, Regierungsrat Dr. Karl Hanik
11.1942–end (kommis)

Karlsruhe situated in the Landskommissarbezirk Karlsruhe in the State of Baden. It had a population of 188,000 in 1944.

SA-Obergruppenführer Hanns Ludin
08.03.1933–1934 (kommis)

SA-Gruppenführer Richard Wagenbauer
1934–24.06.1934 (kommis)

SS-Hauptsturmführer Dr. Wilhelm Heim
24.06.1934–01.09.1937 (kommis)

SS-Oberführer Leutnant der Reserve Carl Engelhardt
01.09.1937–21.06.1940 (kommis until 1 July 1938)

SS-Oberführer Günther Claasen
21.06.1940–end (kommis until 28 May 1942)

Kassel situated in the Regierungsbezirk Kassel (Prussian Province of Hessen-Nassau). It had a population of 217,000 in 1944.

SA-Obergruppenführer, Gauleiter a.D. Franz Pfeffer von Salomon
22.06.1933–07.1936 (kommis until 1 July 1933)

SS-Brigadeführer und Generalmajor der Polizei (m.d.U.d) Max Henze
08.01.1937–01.10.1940 (kommis until 16 October 1937)

SS-Brigadeführer und Generalmajor der Polizei Dr. Herbert Böttcher
01.10.1940–12.05.1942 (kommis until 30 January 1942)

SS-Oberführer, Major a.D. Otto von Proeck
12.05.1942–13.03.1944

SS-Brigadeführer und Generalmajor der Polizei Lucian Wysocki
13.03.1944–end

Kattowitz situated in the Regierungsbezirk Kattowitz in the Prussian Province of Oberschlesien. It had a population of 695,000 in 1944. After the war, it was given to Poland and is now known as Katowice.

SA-Brigadeführer, Hauptmann der Schutzpolizei a.D. Wilhelm Metz
10.1939 – 1942

Regierungsdirektor Niewiesch
1942–28.06.1943 (i.V.)

SS-Brigadeführer, Major der Reserve Dr. Hermann Ramsperger
28.06.1943–end (kommis until 31 August 1943)

Kiel situated in the Regierungsbezirk Schleswig in the Prussian Province of Schleswig-Holstein. It was the Germany's premier naval base and in 1944 it had a population of 274,000.

SA-Gruppenführer Joachim Meyer-Quade
04.1934–31.12.1938 (kommis until September 1934)

SS-Brigadeführer und Generalmajor der Polizei Bruno Krumhaar
31.12.1938–01.12.1942 (kommis)

SS-Oberführer, Untersturmführer der Reserve Georg Langosch
01.12.1942–end (kommis until April 1944)

Klagenfurt situated in the Reichsgau Kärnten in Austria. It had a population of 85,000 in 1944.

Oberpolizeirat Dr. Weiss.
03.1938–23.04.1940

Regierungsrat Walter von Lichem
20.06.1940–end

Koblenz situated in the Regierungsbezirk Koblenz in the Prussian Province of Rhein. It had a population of 91,908 in 1944.

Dr. Ernst Biesten
12.1929–29.05.1933

SA-Brigadeführer August Wilhelm Wetter
29.05.1933–end (kommis until 10 June 1933)

Königsberg situated in the Regierungsbezirk Königsberg in the Prussian Province of Ostpreussen. It had a population of 373,000 in 1944. It was given to Russia after the war and became one of their premier naval bases. It is now known as Kaliningrad.

SA-Obergruppenführer Adolf Kob
03.11.1933–31.01.1934 (kommis)

SA-Obergruppenführer Heinrich Schoene
01.02.1934–15.02.1942 (kommis until 1 April 1935)

SA-Brigadeführer Eugen Dorsch
15.02.1942–end

Köln situated in the Regierungsbezirk Köln (Cologne) in the Prussian Province of the Rhein. It had a population of 770,466 in 1944.

Polizeikommandeur Walter Lingens
28.07.1932–01.09.1935 (kommis until 1 December 1932)

SA-Gruppenführer Walter Hoevel
30.07.1935–04.1945 (kommis until 1 July 1936)

Konstanz situated in the Landeskommissariert Konstanz in the Province of Baden. The Police Presidency was downgraded to a Staatlichen Ortspolizei under Dr. Kauffman with effect from 15 March 1941

SS-Oberführer Walter Stein
14.11.1938–15.3.1941

Krefeld-Urdingen situated in the Regierungsbezirk Düsseldorf in the Prussian Province of Rhein. It had a population of 174,876 in 1943. The Police Presidency was disbanded in April 1934 and the Police Administration was put under the Düsseldorf Police Presidency.

Herr Isenbarth
1932–06.1933

SA-Standartenführer Wilhelm Eberhard Gelberg
06.1933–04.1934 (kommis until November 1933)

Krakau situated in Poland (Cracow), it became the seat of the Generalgouvernment after the German invasion of 1939. It had a population of 242,000 in 1944. The Police Presidency was established on the 25 September 1939. A decree of 1 November 1939 disbanded the office and set up a Police Administration run by the Poles under the control of Germans. The post of SS and Police Leader was set up on the 24 November 1939 and went to the former Police President.

SS-Gruppenführer Karl Zech
27.09.1939–24.11.1939

Leipzig situated in the Regierungsbezirk Leipzig in the State of Sachsen. It was known as the Reichsmessestadt (National Congress Town) and had a population of 709,000 in 1944.

SS-Brigadeführer und Generalmajor der Polizei Oskar Knofe
14.03.1933–28.04.1937 (kommis until 1 June 1933)

SA-Brigadeführer Fritz Stollberg
28.04.1937–23.12.1942 (kommis until 22 June 1938)

SS-Brigadeführer und Generalmajor der Polizei Wilhelm von Grolmann
23.12.1942–end (kommis until May 1943)

Leoben situated in the Regierungsbezirk Graz in the Austrian Province of Steiermark. It had a population of 80,000 in 1944.

Landrat Dr. Wilhelm Kadletz (15)
12.1941–end

Leslau formerly in Poland it was incorporated into the Reich in September 1939 and was placed in the Regierungsbezirk Hohensalza in the Reichsgau Wartheland. It had a population of 52,000 in 1944. Originally a Polizeiamt, it was raised to the status of Police Directorate on the 1 April 1940. After the war it was returned to Poland and is now known as Leszno.

Polizeirat Kessler
02.1940–1941

SA-Oberführer, Amtsmann Walter Wolf (16)
1941–end (kommis until 28 February 1942)

Litzmannstadt formerly in Poland where it was known as Lodz. It was incorporated into the Reich in October 1939. Situated in the Regierungsbezirk Litzmannstadt in the Reichsgau Wartheland, it had a population of 2,094,125 in 1943. It was returned to Poland after the war and is again known as Lodz

SA-Obergruppenführer Adolf Beckerle
09.1939 – 02.10.1939

SS-Brigadeführer, Obersturmführer der Reserve Johannes Schäfer
02.10.1939–01.10.1940

Regierungsdirektor Karl Bartsch
01.10.1940–20.03.1941 (i.V.)

SS-Brigadeführer und Generalmajor der Polizei (m.d.U.d.) Dr. Wilhelm Albert
12.04.1941–11.08.1944

SS-Oberführer, Oberführer der Waffen-SS Otto Reich
04.1943–18.08.1943 (kommis)

SS-Oberführer Walter Stein
08.1944–end (kommis until 1 November 1944)

Linz situated in the Regierungsbezirk Oberdonau in the Austrian Province of Oberdonau, it had a population of 212,000 in 1944. Initially a Police Directorate, it was elevated to Police Presidency on the 25 July 1939.

SS-Oberführer Josef Plakolm
15.03.1938–end (kommis until November 1939)

Lübeck situated in the Regierungsbezirk Schleswig in the Prussian Province of Schleswig-Holstein. It had the status of an independent Hanseatic City State until 1937. The Police Administration was under a Polizeiherr until 1 April 1937. It had a population of 155,000 in 1944.

SS-Brigadeführer und Generalmajor der Polizei Walter Schröder
06.03.1933–end (kommis until May 1933)

SS-Standartenführer und Oberst der Schutzpolizei Joachim Petsch
01.06.1942–03.01.1945 (i.V. Schröder was absent serving as SS and Police Leader in Lithuania)

Ludwigsburg situated in the Landskreis Ludwigsburg in the State of Württemberg. It had a population of 44,600 in 1944. Originally a Polizeiamt, it was elevated to a Police Directorate in April 1941.

Polizeirat Schumacher
10.34–07.08.1937

SS-Obersturmbannführer, Hauptmann der Schutzpolizei Albert Memminger
07.08.1937–end

Ludwigshafen situated in the Regierungsbezirk Pfalz in the State of Bayern. It became part of the Reichsgau Westmark in the 1940's. It had a population of 145,000 in 1944. Originally a Police Directorate, it was elevated to a Police Presidency on the 25 July 1939.

SS-Brigadeführer, Hauptmann der Reserve Dr. Walter Stepp
12.04.1934–09.11.1934

Regierungsdirector Walther Antz
09.11.1934–end

Luxemburg was the capital of the independent Great Duchy of Luxemburg. It was incorporated into the Reich in June 1940 and became part of the Gau Koblenz-Trier which was changed to Reichsgau Moselland on the 29 August 1942. Until 1941 it was a Police Administration was and then it was upgraded to a Police Directorate. It had a population of 58,000 in 1944. After the war it returned to its independent status.

SA-Brigadeführer August Wilhelm Wetter
Summer 40 – Summer 41 (kommis)

SS-Standartenführer, Major der Schutzpolizei Ernst Neumeyer
Summer 1941–.02.1942 (kommis until 31 December 1941)

Polizeirat Fritz Albert Gerth (17)
02.1942–end (kommis until 25 January 1943)

Oberstleutnant der Schutzpolizei Kalden
08.1943–end (i.V.)

Magdeburg situated in the Regierungsbezirk Magdeburg in the Prussian Province of Sachsen. It had a population of 337,000 in 1944.

SA-Gruppenführer Konrad Schragmüler
23.05.1933–30.06.1934 (kommis until May 1934)

Fregattenkapitän der Reserve Carl Christiansen (12)
01.07.1934–08.09.1937

SS-Brigadeführer, Gauleiter a.D., Generalmajor der Polizei (m.d.U.d.) Andreas Bolek
01.12.1937–end (kommis until 23 November 1938)

Mährisch-Ostrau formerly in the Czechoslovakian Province of Böhmen-Mähren, it was the seat of the Oberlansbezirk Mährisch-Ostrau in the Protectorate of Böhmen-Mähren where after the reform of 1942 a Police Directorate was created. The Bezirk was the "Ruhrgebiet"(25) of the Protectorate It had a population of 230,000 in 1944. After the war ti was returned to Czechoslovakia and is now in the Czech Republic known as Ostrava.

Oberregierungsrat Dr. Merler
1942–1944

SS-Obersturmbannführer, Oberlandrat Dr. Gustav Jonak
1944–end

Mainz situated in the Province of Rheinhessen in the State of Hesse. It had a population of 159,000 in 1944. Originally a Police Directorate, it was elevated to a Police Preisdency in April 1940.

SS-Standartenführer, Sturmbannführer (Fachführer), Obersturmführer der Reserve Willi Herbert (18)
01.10.1933–01.04.1936 (kommis until April 1934)

Oberstleutnant der Schutzpolizei a.D. Meusel
01.04.1936–.04.1940 (kommis until April 1938)

Major der Landespolizei a.D. Max Reichardt
04.1940–end (kommis until 11 August 1941)

Mannheim situated in the Landskommissarbezirk Mannheim in the State of Baden. It had a population of 285,000 in 1944.

Ministerialdirektor Dr. Jakob Bader
06.1921–07.09.1933

SS-Brigadeführer, Major der Reserve Dr. Hermann Ramsperger
07.09.1933–12.04.1940 (kommis until 1 April 1937)

SA-Brigadeführer Friedrich Habenicht
12.04.1940–18.01.1944

SA-Gruppenführer, Gauleiter a.D. Paul Georg Otto Hinkler
18.01.1944–end

Marburg am Drau originally situated in Yugoslavia, it was incorporated into the Gau Kärnten in Österreich as the Zivilverwaltung (civil administration) Kärnten on the 15 November 1941 (19). It had a population of 72,000 in 1944. After the war it was returned to Yugoslavia as Maribor. It is now in the State of Slovenia.

SS-Obersturmbannführer, Regierungsrat Dr. Adolf Wallner
15.11.1941–end (kommis until 22 November 1941)

Memel was part of the German State of Preussen until 1918, then it became part of the independent State of Lithuania. It had always had a 60% predominance of Germans in its population and Hitler demanded its return on the 20 March 1939. This occurred on the 22 March 1939 and it became part of the Regierungsbezirk Gumbinnen in the Prussian Province of Ostpreussen. It had a population of 47,000 in 1944. After 1945 it returned to Lithuania and is now known as Klaipeda

SS-Brigadeführer und Generalmajor der Polizei Dr. Herbert Böttcher
22.03.1939–01.10.1940 (kommis until 27 March 1940)

SS-Oberführer, Kriminalrat, Untersturmführer der Reserve Bernhard Fischer-Schweder
01.10.1940–end (kommis until May 1941)

Regierungsdirektor Hauke
10.1942–end (i.V. vice Bernhard Fischer-Schweder on duty with the Waffen-SS.)

Metz situated in the French Province of Lorraine, it was incorporated into the Zivilverwaltung Lothringen (Civil Administration Lorraine) attached to the Reichsgau Westmark on July 1940. It had a population of 240,000 in 1944. Until January 1944, the Police President Saarbrücken was in charge of Police Presidency in Metz. In September 1944, the newly appointed Police President was also created SS and Police Leader. It was returned to France in November 1944.

SS-Gruppenführer und Generalleutnant der Polizei Willy Schmelcher
07.1940–08.01.1942

SS-Brigadeführer und Generalmajor der Waffen-SS und der Polizei Christoph Diehm
08.01.1942–25.01.1944

SS-Brigadeführer, Untersturmführer der Reserve Rudolf Weiss
25.01.1944–01.09.1944

SA-Standartenführer Jansen
02.09.1944–13.09.1944

SS-Brigadeführer und Generalmajor der Polizei Anton Dunckern
14.09.1944–18.11.1944.

Minden situated in the Regierungsbezirk Minden in the Prussian Province of Westfalen. It had a population of 30,544 in 1944 It was downgraded to Polizeiamt late in 1934.

Regierungsrat Friedrich von Werder
04.1934–.12.1934

Mönchengladbach-Rheydt also known as Gladbach-Rheydt, it was situated in the Regierungsbezirk Düsseldorf in the Prussian Province of Rhein. It had a population of 206,000 in 1944.

Herr Elfes
1932–20.03.1933

Regierungdirektor Dr. Diefenbach
20.03.1933–05.1933

SA-Standartenführer Richard Grunert
05.1933–31.12.1941 (kommis until 1 November 1933)

SS-Standartenführer Kurt Wehrle
01.01.1942–end (kommis until 12 January 1943)

Mülhausen originally known as Mulhouse, a town in the French Province of Alsace until June 1940 when it was incor porated in the Zivilverwaltung Elsass (Civil Administration Alsace) as part of the Reichsgau Baden. It had a population of 150,000 in 1944 and it was returned to France late in 1944.

SA-Oberführer Alfred Stapelmann
06.1940–10.07.1941

SS-Standartenführer, Leutnant der Reserve Günther Sacksofsky
10.07.1941–31.01.1943 (kommis until 25 July 1941)

SS-Standartenführer, Obersturmbannführer der Reserve Ulrich Weist
01.02.1943–.12.1944 (kommis until 9 September 1943)

München situated in the Regierungsbezirk München in the State of Bayern, it was known as the "Hauptstadt der Bewegung" (Capital City of the Movement). It had a population of 829,000 in 1944.

Julius Koch
1929–03.03.1933

Reichsführer-SS Heinrich Himmler
03.03.1933–04.07.1933 (kommis)

SA-Obergruppenführer August Schneidhüber
04.07.1933–30.06.1944

SS-Obergruppenführer, Reichsleiter Philipp Bouhler
30.06.1934–31.10.1934 (kommis)

SS-Gruppenführer und Generalleutnant der Polizei Otto von Oelhafen
30.06.34 – 01.04.1936 (vertretungweise Polizeipräsident= acting like Police President)

SS-Obergruppenführer und General der Waffen-SS und der Polizei Karl Friedrich Freiherr von Eberstein
01.04.1936–23.10.1941

SA-Brigadeführer Regierungsdirektor Franz Mayr
23.10.1941–07.04.1943

SS-Brigadeführer und Generalmajor der Polizei (m.d.U.d.) Hans Plesch
07.04.1943–end (kommis until 14 May 1943)

Münster situated in the Regierungsbezirk Münster in the Prussian Province of Westfalen. The Police Presidency was established in May 1937. The city had a population of 142,000 in 1944.

SS-Oberführer Günther Claasen
15.05.1937–08.09.1939 (kommis until 25 June 1938)

SS-Brigadeführer und Generalmajor der Polizei, Obersturmführer der Reserve Otto Heider
08.09.1939–01.02.1942 (kommis until 25 July 1940)

SS-Oberführer August Flasche
01.02.1942–29.05.1942 (kommis)

SS-Oberführer, Standartenführer der Waffen-SS a.D. Heinz Manger
29.05.1942–end (kommis until 12 August 1943)

Nürnberg-Fürth situated in the Regierungsbezirk Ansbach for Ober and Mittelfranken in the State of Bayern. An important city for the Nazis, second only to München, it was the base for the annual Party Rally held every September until the war. It had a population of 510,000 in 1944. Originally a Police Directorate it was elevated to a Police Presidency on the 20th November 1936. (20)

SS-Oberführer, Ministerialdirektor Heinrich Gareis
01.10.1923–03.04.1933

SS-Brigadeführer, Rittmeister der Reserve Erasmus Freiherr von Malsen-Ponickau
20.04.1933–15.08.1933

SA-Obergruppenführer, Oberstleutnant der Luftwaffe Hanns Günther von Obernitz
01.09.1933–05.07.1934 (kommis)

SS-Obergruppenführer und General der Waffen-SS und der Polizei Dr. Benno Martin
05.07.1934–17.12.1942 (kommis until 1 October 1934)

SS-Brigadeführer und Generalmajor der Polizei Otto Kuschow
17.12.1942–end (kommis until June 1943)

Oberhausen situated in the Regierungsbezirk Düsseldorf in the Prussian Province of Rhein. It had a population of 330,000 in 1944. The post was abolished on the 14 October 1942 and its duties were put under the Police Presidency in Hannover. The post was re-instated in April 1943.

Herr Weyer
1932–15.02.1933

SA-Gruppenführer Friedrich Karl Niederhoff
17.02.1933–.03.1936

SS-Brigadeführer und Generalmajor der Polizei Lucian Wysocki
03.1936–.11.1939 (kommis until 4 October 1938)

SA-Standartenführer Wilhelm Veller
11.1939–22.06.1941 (kommis until 31 August 1940)

SS-Standartenführer, Regierungsdirektor, Hauptmann der Reserve Dr. Erich Deutschbein
22.06.1941–14.10.1942 (kommis until 1 August 1942)
Closed 14.10.1942–.04.1943

SA-Brigadeführer Karl Veller
04.1943–end (kommis until January 1945)

Offenbach situated in the Province of Starkenburg in the State of Hesse. It had a population of 86,000 in 1944.

SA-Oberführer Hans Eichel
11.05.1934–.12.1934

Polizeirat Dr. Käss
12.1934–1935

Major der Landspolizei a.D. Max Reichardt
1935–05.1941 (kommis until 31 March 1936)

SA-Oberführer Hans Eichel
05.1941–end

Olmutz had been part of Czechoslovakia until March 1939. After the German takeover it was put into the Oberlandbezirk Mährisch-Ostrau in Böhmen-Mähren in the Protectorate of Böhmen-Mähren. It was returned to Czechosloakia after the war and is now known as Olomouc in the Czech Republic.

Oberregierungsrat Dr. Pohl
1942–end

Oppeln situated in the Regierungsbezirk Oppeln in the Prussian Province of Oberschlesien (Upper Schlesien). It had a population of 73,000 in 1944. Originally a Police Directorate, it was elevated to a Police Presidency in April 1939 and was demoted to a Police Directorate again in March 1943. After the war it was given to Poland and is now known as Opole.

SA-Brigadeführer, Hauptmann der Schutzpolizei a.D.Wilhelm Metz
04.1933–13.09.1939 (kommis until 1 November 1933)

SS-Brigadeführer, Generalmajor der Polizei (m.d.U.d.) Dr. Wilhelm Albert
13.09.1939–12.04.1940 (kommis)

Regierungsrat Dr. Erich Rotmann
12.04.1940–09.02.1941 (kommis)

NSKK-Obersturmführer, Oberregierungsrat Dr. Otto Heigl
09.02.1941–07.02.1945 (kommis until 1 March 1943)

Pforzheim situated in the Landskommissarbezirk Karlsruhe in the State of Baden. It had a population of 78,000 in 1944.

SS-Hauptsturmführer Dr. Wilhelm Heim
09.03.1933–26.06.1934

SS-Standartenführer Kurt Wehrle
26.06.1934–31.05.1942 (kommis until 19 July 1934)

Regierungsrat Dr. Schneider
31.05.1942–end

Pilsen had been in Czechoslovakia until March 1939. After the German takeover it was put into the Oberlandsbezirk Pilsen in Böhmen-Mähren in the Protectorate of Böhmen-Mähren. It was returned to Czechoslovakia after the war and is now known as Plzen in the Czech Republic.

Oberlandrat Dr. Eckholdt
01.10.1939–01.12.1942

Major der Schutzpolizei Paul Richard Schiefelbein
01.12.1942–05.1945.

Plauen in Vogtland situated in the Regierungsbezirk Zwickau in the State of Sachsen. It had a population of 112,000 in 1944.

SS-Brigadeführer und Generalmajor der Polizei Hermann Franz
08.03.1933–16.05.1938 (kommis until 1 June 1933)

SS-Brigadeführer und Generalmajor der Polizei (m.d.U.d.) Georg Altner
16.05.1938–12.06.1942 (kommis until 10 July 1939)

SS-Sturmbannführer Dr. Wilhelm Uhlig
12.06.1942–end (kommis until July 1942)

Posen was part of the Prussian Province of Westpreussen until 1918. It was then given to Poland and was taken back by Germany in September 1939. It became part of the Regierungsbezirk Posen in the Reichsgau Wartheland. It had a population of 280,000 in 1944. After the war it was returned to Poland and it is now known as Poznan.

SS-Brigadeführer, Rittmeister der Reserve Erasmus Freiherr von Malsen-Ponickau
10.1939–01.09.1943 (kommis until 31 May 1940)

SS-Brigadeführer und Generalmajor der Polizei Max Montua
01.09.1943–23.02.1945 (kommis until April 1944)

SS-Standartenführer, Oberregierungsrat Dr. Rudolf Lange
23.02.1945–end

Potsdam situated in the Regierungsbezirk Potsdam in the Prussian Province of Mark-Brandenberg. It had a population of 137,000 in 1944.

SA-Obergruppenführer, General der Polizei (m.d.U.d.) Wolf Graf von Helldorf
18.03.1933–06.12.1935

SS-Brigadeführer, Hauptmann der Reserve Wilhelm Ernst Graf von Wedel
06.12.1935–19.10.1939 (kommis until 1 May 1936)
unbesetzt 19.10.1939–20.04.1940

SS-Oberführer Heinrich von Dolega-Kozierowski
20.04.1940–end

Prag had been the capital of Czechoslovakia until the Germans takeover in March 1939. It was then put in the Oberlandsbezirk Prag (Prague) in the Protectorate of Böhmen-Mähren. It was returned to Czechoslovakia after the war and again became the capital city. It is now the capital city of the Czech Republic and is known as Praha.

Richard Biernet
1939–01.08.1942

SS-Brigadeführer und Generalmajor der Polizei (m.d.U.d.) Willy Weidermann
01.08.1942–end

SS-Standartenführer, Regierungs und Kriminaldirektor Friedrich Sowa
15.10.1943–end (i.V. deputised for Weidermann who was involved in the creation of the SS-Main District covering the Protectorate).

Recklinghausen situated in the Regierungsbezirk Münster in the Prussian Province of Westfalen. It had a population of 679,000 in 1944.

Regierungsrat Kurt Klemm
28.02.1933–.11.1934 (kommis until 9 May 1933)

SA-Gruppenführer, Rittmeister der Reserve Hans Vogel
11.1934–end (kommis until 1 January 1936)

Regensburg situated in the Regierungsbezirk Niederbayern und Oberpfalz in the State of Bayern. It had a population of 96,000 in 1944.

SA-Obergruppenführer, char. Generalmajor Hans Georg Hofmann
09.03.1933–04.04.1933 (kommis)

SS-Obersturmbannführer, Oberregierungsrat Fritz Popp
06.04.1933–end (kommis until 1 June 1933)

Reichenberg had been in the Sudetenland part of Czechoslovakia until October 1938. It was then situated in the Regierungsbezirk Aussig in the Reichsgau Sudetenland. It had a population of 117,000 in 1944. After the war it returned to Czechoslovaia and it is now known as Liberec in the Czech Republic.

SS-Oberführer, Oberleutnant der Reserve Paul Leffler
25.10.1939–24.05.1944 (kommis until 30 August 1940)

SS-Standartenführer Karl Jäger
24.05.1944–end

Reutlingen situated in the Landskreis Reutlingen in the State of Württemberg. It had a population of 38,000 in 1944. Originally a Police Directorate, it was demoted to a Polizeiamt on the 1 May 1941.

Regierungsrat Karl Sinn
26.05.1926–16.05.1934 (kommis until 17 October 1927)

SS-Obersturmbannführer, Hauptmann der Schutzpolizei Albert Memminger
16.05.1934–01.05.1941 (kommis until 1 August 1937)

Rostock situated in the Landskreis Rostock in the State of Mecklenburg. The Police Presidency was established in February 1938. The port had a population of 123,000 in 1944.

SS-Standartenführer, Polizeimedizinalrat a.D. Dr. Hans Sommer
02.02.1938–end (kommis until 1 October 1938)

Saarbrücken situated in the Landskreis Saarbrücken in the Saarland, it was under French occupation until 1935. After the return to Germany it became part of the Reichsgau Westmark and it had a population of 341,000 in 1944. The Police President of Saarbrücken was also the Police President of Metz until January 1944. It is now in the Province of Saar.

SS-Gruppenführer und Generalleutnant der Polizei Willy Schmelcher
01.03.1935–06.12.1941

SS-Brigadeführer und Generalmajor der Waffen-SS und der Polizei Christoph Diehm
06.12.1941–25.01.1944

SS-Brigadeführer, Untersturmführer der Reserve Rudolf Weiss
25.01.1944–03.04.1944

SS-Obersturmbannführer Dr. Fritz Dietrich
03.04.1944–end (komiss until 24 July 1944).

Salzburg situated in northwest Austria. It was part of the Reichsgau Salzburg. It had a population of 83,000 in 1944. The Police Directorate was created by the Austrian Republic in July 1922. (21)

SS-Obersturmbannführer, Hauptmann der Reserve Dr. Benno von Braitenberg-Zennenberg
03.1938–end (kommis until 23 April 1940)

Dr. Ambros Pitter
1943–end (i.V. deputised for the incumbant, absent on military duties)

Sankt Polten situated in the Reichsgau Niederdonau (Lower Danube) in Österreich. It had a population of 46,000 in 1944.

SS-Obersturmbannführer, Regierungsrat Dr. Leopold Wittmann
01.03.1938–end (kommis until 8 November 1939)

Schneidemühl situated in the Regierungsbezirk Schneidemühl in the Prussian Province of Pommern. Originally a Police Directorate, it was abolished in October 1939. It is now situated in Poland and is know as Pila.

SS-Standartenführer, Hauptmann der Schutzpolizei a.D. Rudolf Loeffel
27.03.1933–01.12.1934 (kommis until 8.August 1933)

Regierungsrat Dr. Paul Nicolas Cossmann
01.12.1934–.12.1935 (kommis)

SA-Oberführer Ulrich Schulz-Sembten
12.1935–10.1939 (kommis until 1 August 1937)

Sosnowitz formerly part of the Austro-Hungarian Province of Galicia, it was handed over to Poland in 1918. Captured by the Germans in September 1939, it became part of Regierungsbezirk Kattowitz in the Prussian Province of Oberschlesien (Upper Schlesien). It had a population of 306,000 in 1944. It was returned to Poland in 1945 and is now known as Sonowiec.

SS-Oberführer Alexander von Woedtke
31.10.1940–end (kommis until 16 July 1941)

Stettin situated in the Regierungsbezirk Stettin in the Prussian Province of Pommern, it had a population of 382,000 in 1944. After 1945 it was handed over to Poland and is now known as Szczecin.

Oberregierungsrat, Major der Schutzpolizei a.D. Elder Roman Borck
24.02.1933–26.09.1933

SS-Sturmbannführer, Sturmbannführer der Waffen-SS Fritz Karl Engel
19.10.1933–28.02.1934

SS-Brigadeführer Fritz Herrmann
28.02.1934–11.01.1939 (kommis until 1 October 1935)

SA-Obergruppenführer Wilhelm Jahn
11.01.1939–.07.1943

SA-Standartenführer, Oberregierungsrat Karl Grundey
07.1943–end (kommis until March 1944)

Strassburg was situated in the French Province of Alsace until June 1940 when it was made part of the Grossdeutschen Reich. It was situated in the Zivilverwaltung Elsass (Civil Administration Alsace) in the Reichsgau Baden until late 1944 when it was returned to France.

SS-Oberführer, Leutnant der Reserve Carl Engelhardt
21.06.1940–11.1944 (kommis until October 1941)

Stuttgart situated in the Landskreis Stuttgart in the State of Württemberg. It was known as the "Stadt der Auslanddeutschen" (Town of Germans living abroad). It had a population of 460,000 in 1944.

Oberregierungsrat Rudolf Klaiber
20.12.1922–31.05.1938

SA-Brigadeführer, char. Generalmajor der Polizei a.D. Karl Schweinle
27.06.1938 – 16.08.1944 (kommis until 29 November 1938)

SS-Oberführer Heinz Wicke
08.1944–end (kommis until 31 December 1944)

Suhl situated in the Regierungsbezirk Erfurt in the Prussian Province of Sachsen. It had a population of 24,000 in 1944.

Landrat Sethe
01.11.1933–end

Thorn formerly in the Prussian Province of Westpreussen, it was given to Poland in 1918. Captured in September 1939, it was put in the Regierungsbezirk Bromberg in the Reichsgau Danzig-Westpreussen. It had a population of 73,000 in 1944. It was returned to Poland in 1945 and is now known as Torun.

SS-Standartenführer Hans Weberstedt
10.1939–15.03.1941

SS-Oberführer Walter Stein
15.03.1941–05.06.1942 (kommis)

SS-Standartenführer Alfons Graf
05.06.1942–end (kommis until 26 June 1943)

Tilsit situated in the Regierungsbezirk Gumbinnen in the Prussian Province of Ostreussen. It had a population of 70,000 in 1944. It was given to Poland in 1945 and is now known as Tczew.

Hauptmann der Schutzpolizei Hoffmann
10.1933–.12.1933

SA-Obertruppführer Friedrich Bucher
21.11.1933–28.02.1934 (kommis)

SA-Oberführer Ludwig Denzler
28 02.1934 -..1935 (kommis)

Landrat Dr. Gerhard Brix
1935–19.10.1938 (kommis)

SS-Standartenführer Dr. Arnold Rust
30.09.1938–06.09.1940 (kommis until 6 September 1939)
unbesezt (vacant)
06.09.1940–27.09.1941

SS-Obersturmbannführer, Regierungsrat Heinz Thieler
27.09.1941–end (kommis until 30 March 1942)

Troppau was originally the capital city of Austrian Schlesien. After 1918 it was given to Czechoslovakia and from October 1938 it was taken into the Grossdeutschen Reich and was put in the Regierungsbezirk Aussig in the Reichsgau Sudetenland. It had a population of 84,000 in 1944. It was returned to Czechoslovakia in 1945 and is now known as Opava in the Czech Republic.

Oberst der Schutzpolizei Johann Bauer
25.10.1939–1940

Regierungsrat Dr. Lange
1940–12.1941 (kommis)

SS-Oberführer Richard Pruchtnow
.12.1941–22.06.1943 (kommis until 20 June 1943)

Oberregierungsrat Dr. Hübertus Schonberg
06.1943–end (i.V. until 1 July 1943)

Tübingen situated in the Landskreis Tübingen in the State of Württemberg. It had a population of 32,000 in 1944. The Police Directorate was downgraded to a Polizeiamt in October 1938.

Landrat Dr. Hermann Ebner 23.07.1928–12.04.1933

SS-Gruppenführer und Generalleutnant der Polizei Dr. Wilhelm Harster
15.01.1934–22.05.1934 (kommis)

Regierungsrat Dr. Erhard Pfisterer
22.05.1934–12.1934

Polizeirat Bucheler
12.1934–end (he remained in charge of the Police Office after October 1938)

Tschenstochau was a Polish city situated in the Distrikt Radom in the Generalgouvernment after the German takeover in September 1939. A Police Presidency was planned in October 1939 with SS-Brigadeführer Albrecht Schmelt, the Police President in Breslau, in charge. The plan was abandoned before it could be completed and the police were put under the Stadthauptmann Dr. Franke (22). The city is now in Poland and is known as Czestochowa.

Ulm an der Donau situated in the Landskreis Ulm in the State of Württemberg. It had a population of 76,000 in 1944.

Oberregierungsrat Emil Schmid
27.10.1924–30.06.1933

SS-Brigadeführer Wilhelm Dreher
01.07.1933–30.01.1942 (kommis until 23 January 1935)

Herr Richter
30.01.1942–17.02.1943 (kommis)

SA-Brigadeführer, Reichsbahnrat Erich Hagenmeyer
17.02.1943–24.04.1945 (kommis until 14 September 1943)

Regierungsrat Wilhelm Darmbacher
24.04.1945–end (kommis)

Waldenburg situated in the Regierungsbezirk Breslau in the Prussian Province of Niederschlesien (Lower Sachsen) It had a population of 93,000 in 1944. After the war it was given to Poland and is now known as Walbrzych.

NSFK-Gruppenführer Ferdinand von Hiddessen
20.02.1933–04.09.1940

SA-Standartenführer, Major der Schutzpolizei a.D. Georg Mählich
04.09.1940–end (kommis until 21 March 1941)

Warschau situated in Poland, it was the country's capital city until the German takeover in September 1939. It then became part of the Generalgouvernment, although not the capital city, that distinction passed to Cracow (Krakau).

A Police Presidency was established in September 1939 (23). The post was abolished by a decree dated 1 November 1939. In July 1943 a decree stated that the Police Administration was to be removed from the control of the Stadthauptmann and it was again to be called a Police Presidency. After 1945 it again became the capital of Poland.

SS-Oberführer Günther Claasen
25.09.1939–24.11.1939

SS-Gruppenführer und Generalleutnant der Waffen-SS und Polizei Jürgen Stroop
15.07.1943–13.09.1943

SS-Brigadeführer und Generalmajor der Polizei Franz Kutschera
08.09.1943–01.02.1944

SS-Oberführer Walter Stein
01.02.1944–31.03.1944

SS-Brigadeführer und Generalmajor der Polizei Paul Otto Geibel
31.03.1944–end

Weisenfels situated in the Regierungsbezirk Merseburg in the Prussian Province of Sachsen (from 1944 it was put in the new Province of Halle-Merseburg). It had a population of 86,000 in 1944.

Regierungsrat Heinrich Neubaur
04.1933–.06.1934 (kommis until April 1934)

Regierungsdirektor von Rappard
06.1934–01.01.1936 (kommis until 1 Febraury 1935)
unbesetzt 01.01.1936–27.10.1937

SS-Standartenführer, Hauptmann der Schutzpolizei a.D. Rudolf Loeffel
27.10.1937–25.06.1940 (kommis until 16 April 1938)

SA-Oberführer Hans Schulz-Sembten
25.06.1940–end

Wesermünde situated in the Regierungsbezirk Stade in the Prussian Province of Hannover. It had a population of 113,000 in 1944. Originally a Police Presidency, it was abolished on the 22 March 1934. It was re-established on the 5 February 1940.

Landrat Dr. Franz zur Nieden
1933–22.03.1934

Oberstleutnant der Schutzpolizei a.D. Meusel
05.02.1940–.12.1942 (kommis until July 1940)

SA-Gruppenführer Franz Bauer
12.1942–end (kommis until June 1944)

Weimar situated in the Landskreis Weimar in the State of Thüringen. Originally a Police Directorate it was upgraded to a Police Presidency on the 1 April 1933. It had a population of 66,000 in 1944.

SS-Obersturmbannführer, Oberregierungsrat Dr. Walter Rohde
01.08.1931–01.10.1932

SS-Brigadeführer, Staatssekretar Walter Ortlepp
01.10.1932–03.06.1936

SS-Brigadeführer und Generalmajor der Polizei (m.d.U.d.) Karl Pflomm
23.04.1936–13.04.1937 (kommis until 27 May 1936)

SS-Gruppenführer und Generalleutnant der Polizei Paul Hennicke
13.04.1937–01.10.1942 (kommis until 2 April 1938)

SS-Obersturmbannführer, Oberregierungsrat Walter Schmidt
01.10.1942–end (kommis until 1 February 1943)

Wien situated in Austria, it was that country's capital city until March 1938. After the Anschluss (German takeover) in March 1938 it became the capital of the Land Österreich then of Reichsgau Wien (Wien). It had a population of 1,925,000 in 1944 After 1945 it returned to its original status in Österreich.

SS-Oberführer Dr. Otto Steinhäusl
01.03.1938–20.06.1940 (kommis until January 1940)

SS-Brigadeführer Leo Gotzmann
20.06.1940–end (kommis until 24 January 1941)

Polizeivizepräsident:
Josef Fitzthum 03.1938 – 06.1940
Dr. Leo Gotzmann 06.1940 – 01.1941
Regierungsdirektor Hedrich 1941–end

Wiener-Neustadt situated in Austria, it was part of the Reichsgau Niederdonau (Lower Danube) after the Anschluss. It had a population of 41,000 in 1944.

Oberpolizeirat Dr. Ernst Merkel 12.1938–04.07.1939

SS-Obersturmbannführer Dr. Otto Kittel
04.07.1939–end (kommis until 19 February 1940)

Wiesbaden situated in the Regierungsbezirk Wiesbaden in the Prussian Province of Hessen-Nassau. It had a population of 171,000 in 1944. (24)

Oberregierungsrat Adolf Heinrich Freiherr von Gablenz
22.02.1933–08.1944 (kommis until 1 March 1933)

SS-Brigadeführer und Generalmajor der Polizei Anton Diermann
08.1944–end

Wilhelmshaven situated in the Stadtkreis Wilhelmshaven in the State of Oldenburg on the North Sea Coast. It had a population of 113,000 in 1944.

Major der Schutzpoplizei Hartmann
12.1934–1936 (kommis)

SS-Oberführer Heinrich von Dolega-Kozierowski
1936–20.04.1940 (stellvertreter until 24 November 1937)

SS-Standartenführer Dr. Arnold Rust
24.04.1940–08.03.1944 (kommis until 28 August 1940)

SS-Oberführer und Oberst der Schutzpolizei Ferdinand Heske
08.03.1944–end (kommis until late 1944)

Wittenberg situated in the Regierungsbezirk Merseburg in the Prussian State of Sachsen. It was put in the new Province of Halle-Merseberg in 1944. Originally a Polizeiamt it was elevated to a Police Directorate in December 1937. It had a population of 52,000 in 1944.

SS-Standartenführer, Oberstleutnant der Schutzpolizei Paul Krieg
02.12.1937–12.09.1941 (kommis until 28 September 1938)

SS-Obersturmbannführer, Hauptmann der Schutzpolizei a.D. Erwin Wickert
12.09.1941–end (kommis until 26 August 1942)

Worms situated in the Landkreis Worms in the Province of Rheinhessen in the State of Hesse. It had a population of 51,000 in 1944.

SS-Brigadeführer und Generalmajor der Polizei Heinz Jost
15.03.1933–01.10.1933

SA-Oberführer Hans Eichel
01.10.1933–27.09.1941 (kommis until 1 April 1934)

SS-Obersturmbannführer, Polizeirat Hanns Löw
27.09.1941–end (kommis until 24 February 1942)

Wuppertal situated in the Regierungsbezirk Düsseldorf in the Prussian Province of Rhein. It had a population of 703,000 in 1944.

Landrat, Oberkriegsverwaltungsrat Dr. Kessler (13)
05.1933–10.07.1933 (kommis)

SA-Standartenführer Wilhelm Veller
10.07.1933–30.03.1934

SA-Brigadeführer Friedrich Habenicht
01.04.1934–08.03.1939 (kommis until 1 December 1934)

SA-Gruppenführer, Gauleiter a.D. Paul Georg Otto Hinkler
08.03.1939–18.01.1944

SA-Brigadeführer Heinz Krahne
18.01.1944–end (kommis until January 1945).

Würzburg situated in the Regierungsbezirk Würzburg in the State of Bayern. It was elevated from Police Directo- rate to Police Presidency on the 24 January 1941. It had a population of 108,617.

Regierungsdirektor Eder (21)
1926–30.06.1936

SA-Standartenführer Karl Wicklmayr
30.06.1936–end (kommis until April 1937)

Znaim situated in southern Böhmen-Mähren in Czechoslovakia until March 1939. It was then placed in Reichsgau Niederdonau (Lower Danube) in Austria and had a population of 27,000 in 1944. It was returned to Czechoslovakia in 1945 and is now known as Znojmo in the Czech Republic.

Regierungsrat Dr. Kohler
25.10.1939–30.03.1940

SS-Sturmbannführer, Landrat Dr. Alfred Kottek
01.04.1940–end

Zwickau situated in the Regierungsbezirk Zwickau in the State of Sachsen. It was a Police Directorate until January 1939 when it was upgraded to Police Presidency. It had a population of 87,000 in 1944.

SS-Obersturmbannführer, Oberstleutnant der Schutzpolizei Helmut Dunnebier
.03.1933–20.09.1936 (kommis until May 1933)

SS-Brigadeführer, Rittmeister der Reserve Erasmus Freiherr von Malsen-Ponickau
20.09.1936–.04.1938

SS-Obergruppenführer und General der Waffen-SS und der Polizei Carl-Albrecht Oberg
06.01.1939–27.09.1941 (kommis until 4 October 1939)

SS-Standartenführer, Oberregierungsrat Jakob Beck
27.09.1941–end (kommis until 24 February 1943)

Notes;

(1) Polizei Oberinspektor: (field) administrative police rank equivalent to Hauptmann der Polizei

(2) Amtsrat: (staff) administrative police rank equivalent to Major der Polizei

(3) Oberstleutnant der Reserve: Lieutenant Colonel in the Reserve Officer Corps of the army. Police administrators could be mobilized into the Wehrmacht without leaving their current duties, their deputies taking care of daily tasks.

(4) Ministerialrat: civil service rank equivalent to Oberst der Polizei

(5) Hauptdienstleiter der NSDAP: senior executive of the National Socialist Party who held such position as deputy Gauleiter or head of Main Office in Direction of the NSDAP.

(6) SS-Hauptsturmführer der Reserve: Captain in the Reserve Officer Corps of the Waffen-SS. Police administrators who were members of the Allgemeine-SS (General SS) could be mobilised into field units or administrative offices of the armed SS. Their Waffen-SS rank is based upon their post and not on their original General SS rank.

(7) a.D. or ausser Dienst: retired officer in army, Police or Administration kept their rank with mention "a.D. "It is similar to the titles kept by some British and American officers who put the word 'retired' after their rank.

(8) The reform of Protectorat Administration of 1942 (Reichsauftragverwaltung) introduced German offices next to Czech ones to maintain tight control of the Czech administration. One Police Presidency was created in Prag and

4. Police Directorates were set up at Brünn, Pilsen, Mährisch-Ostrau and Olmütz. All these towns were seats of a German Oberlandrat (senior district administrator equivalent to a German District President).

(9) a few active officers of Waffen-SS were appointed Police administrators during the war for example Tschimpke and Sator.

(10) Oberregierungsrat: (staff) civil service rank equivalent to Oberstleutnant der Polizei .

(11) Ministerialdirigent: (staff) civil service rank equivalent to Generalmajor der Polizei.

(12) Fregattenkapitän: marine officer rank equivalent to Oberstleutnant.

(13) Oberkriegsverwaltungsrat: civil service rank in military Administration equivalent to Oberstleutnant.

(14) Regierungsrat: civil service rank equivalent to Major der Polizei.

(15) The Landrat was part time head of some smaller Police Directorates (Leoben, Suhl and Znaim).

(16) Polizei Amtmann: (staff) administrative police rank equivalent to Hauptmann der Polizei.

(17) Polizeirat: (field) administrative police rank equivalent to Hauptmann der Polizei.

(18) Fachführer (specialist officers) were reserve officers of Waffen-SS equivalent to Sonderführer in the army. They were mainly involved in the areas of recruitment, economics, resettlement or security matters.

(19) Befehlsblatt des Chefs der Sicherheitspolizei und des SD Nr 49 of 13 December 1941.

(20) Bayerisches Gesetz-und Verordnungsblatt Nr 36 of November 1936.

(21) Regierungsdirektor: (staff) civil service rank equivalent to Oberstleutnant der Polizei.

(22) Decrees issued by Hauptamt ORPO 25 September, 27 October and 1 November 1939.

(23) Decrees from the Chief of the ORPO dated 25 September and 27 October 1939

(24) A letter dated 31 July 1933 (Tagebuch Nr 136) stated that the Reichsführer-SS approved the appointment of SS-Oberführer (later Obergruppenführer) Wilhelm Rediess as Police President in Wiesbaden. However there was no evidence that this appointment took place and Rediess remained in command of SS Abschnitt (District) XI in Koblenz.

(25) Ruhrgebiet this was the term used to cover a heavy industrialised region, it actually stands for the Ruhr area in Western Germany.

6.2.2 Biographies Of The Police Administrators

ALTNER Ernst Georg

Born 4 December 1901 in Waldheim (Sachsen).

Worked as a mechanical engineer in the gas industry. Joined the SA 10 April 1926 and transferred to the SS 10 May 1929. Served as a full time Allgemeine-SS officer until 1938 when he transferred to Police Administration. He remained in this field until the end of the war. Rose to the rank of Brigadeführer with effect from 1 January 1942. Killed in action in Dortmund 12 April 1945.

d'ANGELO Karl

Born 9 September 1890 in Osthofen (Rhine Hessen).

Trained as a printer and served in the army from October 1912 to November 1918. Returned to the printing trade and worked in his fathers business until 1934. Politically active, he was in constant trouble with the French occupying troops in the Rhineland from 1921 to 1924. Joined the SS 1 October 1929 and rose to the rank of Standartenführer with effect from 15 September 1935. He served in a concentration camp and then in the frontier police forces before joining the Police Administration in March 1939.

ANTZ

A former Bayern civil servant, he served in Police Administration in the area that later became Reichsgau Westmark.

ASMUS Georg Friedrich Robert

Born 7 October 1888 in Gross-Grabe bei Mullhausen (Thüringen).

Joined the army 1901 and served in the Great War until September 1918 when he was captured by the British. Remained a prisoner until November 1919. Joined the Schutzpolizei 3 July 1920 as Hauptmann and rose to the rank of Generalmajor with effect from 10 March 1944. He commanded police units in Germany and Russia during this period. He was placed in retirement from the Police 1 May 1944 but he had already transferred to Police Administration by this time and he remained in this field until the end of the war. He joined the SS as Standartenführer 30 January 1939 and rose to the rank of Brigadeführer with effect from 10 March 1944.

BACHMANN Walter

Born 12 March 1900 in Dresden (Sachsen).

Served in the Great War and then went into business. Served in the Allgemeine-SS and rose to the rank of Obersturm_ bannführer with effect from 9 November 1940. He was active in the Security Service of the SS (SD) from 1935 until he joined Police Administration in 1940. He received army training and was commissioned Leutnant 1 February 1940 Served in the Totenkopf-Division as a Zugführer 10 Kompanie der Totenkopf-Infanterie-Regiment 3 to 26 March 1941 when he transferred to the Polizei-Division. Promoted Oberleutnant der Schutzpolizei 1 October 1941. He was wounded by a grenade on the River Luga in Northern Russia 3 August 1941 and left military service 8 November 1941. He transferred to the Waffen-SS as Obersturmführer der Reserve August 1944 with senority from 1 October 1941.

BADER Dr. Jakob

Born 30 July 1883 in Lahr (Baden).

Studied law and economics and graduated as a lawyer being awarded a Doctorate in 1911. Worked in the Chamber of Commerce in Kreis Offenburg until July 1912 and then in the secretariat of the Baden Ministry of the Interior. Served in the artillery during the Great War as Hauptmann der Reserve. In 1919 he returned to the Interior Ministry, in Police

Administration. After leaving the post in Mannheim in 1933, he returned to the Interior Ministry as Ministerialdirektor. He died in February 1939.

BARTSCH Karl

He was a civil servant who was appointed to his first post on 24 March 1911. He left Police Administration and was appointed Regierungsdirektor in Allenstein 1 April 1937.

BATZ Rudolf Christoph

Born 10 November 1903 in Langensalza.

His father died in the great influenza epidemic of 1919 and as a result he had to give up his education and start work to provide for his family. He later returned to his studies at the University of Göttingen, studying law. Graduated and worked as a legal official in district courts. Joined the Gestapo in July 1935 and headed the Gestapo offices in Linz and Hannover before transferring to the SS and Police action units operating behind the front in Russia killing Jews and political commissars. He commanded the Security Police and SD in Krakau and then in Arnsberg and ended the war in Dortmund. Joined the SS on 22 December 1935 and rose to the rank of Standartenführer with effect from 30 January 1945. He was appointed in Police Administration in last months of the war. He hanged himself in prison in Wuppertal 8 February 1961 whilst awaiting trial for war crimes.

BAUER Franz Bernhard August

Born 24 February 1894 in Neuenburg.

Served as a Non Commissioned Officer in the Great War and then served in a Freikorps units. Joined the Sicherheitspolizei in Marienwerder as Hauptwachmeister in 1919. Left the police and worked in agriculture 1922. Member of the Party from 1925, he lost his job in 1929 due to his political activities. Joined the SA and was promoted Standartenführer 9 September 1932. Führer SA-Standarte 98 from September 1932. He later rose to the rank of SA-Gruppenführer with effect from 9 November 1942. Führer z.V. SA-Gruppe Oberrhein 1944. Served in the army as Leutnant 1939. Promoted Oberleutnant and served in the French campaign. Wounded in action in Russia September 1941, he was released from military service September 1942 and underwent police training from October to December 1942. He then served in Police Administration until the end of the war.

BAUER Johann

Born 30 March 1888.

Served in the Great War and then joined the Schutzpolizei. Promoted Oberstleutnant 20 April 1939 and later Oberst. Joined the Party 1 May 1933 Served as Commander of the Schutzpolizei in Troppau in 1939. He retired from active service then joined Police Administration.

BECK Jakob

Born 14 August 1889 in Eichelberg.

Studied legal jurisprudence at the University of München. Served in the Royal Bayern army during the Great War and after the war he served as a civil servant in Regensburg and Grafenau. Joined the Police Administration in München August 1930 as Regierungsrat. From March 1933 until October 1939 he served in Bayern Political Police and then the Gestapo until October 1939 being promoted Oberregierungsrat. Joined the SS 20 August 1933 and rose to the rank of Standartenführer with effect from 20 April 1941. He served as temporary Inspector of the Security Police and SD in München from August 1940 to August 1941 (deputizing for Gustav-Adolf Scheel who was absent serving as Reichsstudentführer) and then he transferred to Police Administration Zwickau in succession to Carl Oberg.

BECKERLE Adolf-Heinz

Born 4 February 1902 in Frankfurt am Main.

Studied law, political economics and philosophy and achieved a diploma in political economy. Worked in North and South America in banking and industry and served briefly in the Schutzpolizei. Joined the SA and rose to the rank of Obergruppenführer with effect from 9 November 1937. He commanded the SA-Gruppe Hessen from February 1933 to June 1941. He headed a Police Administration until he was appointed German Ambassador to Bulgaria in June 1941. He was head of the Reichsluftschutzbund for Hessen from 1933 to 1 November 1938. Surviving the war, he was arrested in 1960.

BEUSCHLEIN Dr. Werner

Born 29 August 1908 at Kaerlstadt.

He studied law and was graduated as a Doctor of Law. He then served as a legal civil servant. Appointed Regierungs-sessor in 1933 and was promoted Regierungsrat in 1934. Member of Party from 1930, he joined SS in 1932 and rose to the rank of Obersturmbannführer on 10 September 1939. He joined Police Administration in 1938. He was mobilized into the army as 2nd Lieutenant in 1943 and his police post in Kaiserslautern was run by the local Landrat Karl Müller.

BIERMANN

He was a civil servant who rose to the rank of Regierungsrat on the 13 December 1928. He served in Police Administration in 1934 and then returned to civil administration. During the war, he served in the city administration in Strassburg in occupied Alsace.

BLUME

He attended university where he studied law and in 1936 he served as a Gerichtsassessor in the Police Administration in Königsberg. Promoted Regierungsassessor in 1936 and Regierungsrat in 1939, he served in the District Administration in Liegnitz. He moved to the Police Administration in Frankfurt an der Oder in 1939 and to the staff of the Police Administration in Posen in 1942. This was purely a paper transfer as he actually served on the staff of the Commander of the Ordnungspolizei in Rowno. Posted back to Germany in November 1942, he took over the post in Elbing and remained as a Police Director until the end of the war.

BODE Dr. Gerhard

Born 1 January 1897 in Görlitz.

He studied law and was appointed Assessor on 13 June 1922. He was appointed Leiter Dezernat 2c (international communism, communist youth associations) in Abteilung Ia (Political Police) in the Berlin Police Presidium in the 1930's. Promoted Regierungsrat in Königsberg 1931. On the 14 December 1933, he was promoted Oberregierungsrat and was appointed Leiter Hauptabteilung I (Organisation and Administration) in the Gestapoamt by Reinhard Heydrich Considered politically weak, he was removed in 1938 and transferred to Police Administration. Soon after transferred to the Regierungspräsidium in Frankfurt an der Oder as head of General Abteilung I. In 1940 he moved to the Oberpräsidium in Stettin.

BOHME Dr.

Served as a civil servant and rose to the rank of Oberregierungsrat. He ran the post in Innsbruck until a permanent replacement could be found.

BOLEK Andreas

Born 3 May 1894 in Weinbergen in the district of Lemberg (Poland) in what is now the Ukraine.

Served in the Austrian army during the Great War and then worked in the electrical business as an administrator. Served in the Austrian branch of the Party as Gauleiter for Oberösterreich and then as deputy Landesleiter for the whole of Österreich. He escaped to Germany to avoid arrest in 1933. He obtained German citizenship on august 1934. Member of Reichstag since 1936. Involved in police duties since 1935, he joined Police Administration in November 1937. He served in the SS and rose to the rank of Brigadeführer with effect from 9 November 1937 given the honourary rank of Generalmajor der Polizei on 19 February 1944. He was killed in the defense of Magdeburg May 1945.

BOLTZ Wilhelm

Born 26 September 1896 in Weissenfels.

He was a prominent Hamburg businessman and worked as a Director of Hafendampfschiffahrts AG. A member of the SA, he rose to the rank of Standartenführer. In 1931, he founded the SA Naval Section in the city. He was appointed to the Police Administration in 1933. He was reported to have been on good terms with both Himmler and Heydrich. He died in Hamburg 22nd October 1939.

BORCK Edler C. Roman

Born 16 April 1888 in Stettin (Pommern).

Joined the army 1906 and served until 1919 in the artillery. After the war he joined the Schutzpolizei as Hauptmann. Promoted Major 1921. Left the police 1 April 1923. Studied economics and law and then worked in private industry. He was a Member of the Prussian Landtag from 1924 to 1933 and was deputy Leader of the Stahlhelm for Pommern. He headed a Police Administration on 1933 then served as Oberregierungsrat in Regierung Stettin.

BÖTTCHER Dr. Herbert

Born 24 April 1907 in Prökels (Memelland).

Studied law and graduated as a Doctor of Law in 1931. Joined the civil service as a legal official and spent two years in rison for political crimes from January 1934. After release, he served as President of the Memel High Court where he remained until he joined the Police Administration in 1939. A member of the SS since 1939, he rose to the rank of Brigadeführer in November 1944. Transferred to the SS and Police in 1942, he served in Radom. He was badly wounded during an anti partisan action in July 44. He was given the rank of Generalmajor der Polizei on 11 November 1944. He was executed by the Poles in Warsaw 12 June 1950.

BOUHLER Philip

Born 11 September 1899 in München (Bayern).

Served in the artillery during the Great War and was badly wounded August 1917. As a result he was invalided out of the army. Studied at the University of München and joined the Party in 1921. He worked as a newspaper editor and as businessmanager for the Party until 1934 and then he was appointed Reichsleiter and head of the Führer Chancellery which was an Party office used for the execution of secret decrees. He was responsible for overseeing the euthanasia program of killing the incurably sick. A member of the SS since 1933, he rose to honorary rank of Obergruppenführer with effect from 30 January 1936. He held temporary command in Police Administration after the purge of SA in 1934. He committed suicide 10 May 1945.

BRAITENBERG-ZENNENBERG von Dr. Benno

Born 29 August 1896 in Bozen in the Südtirol (Österreich).

Served in the Austrian army during the Great War and then in the Freikorps units Oberland until 1921. A university graduate in law, he joined the Austrian Police Administration and rose to the rank of Oberpolizeirat with effect from 18 May 1938. As member of the German Police Administration, he was promoted Oberregierungsrat 1 August 1939. Mobilized in September 1939 in the army, he was given the rank of Hauptmann in March 1940 and Major in September 1941. A member of the Austrian SS from June 1934, he rose to the rank of Obersturmbannführer with effect from April 1940.

BRAND Maximilian

Born 4 April 1888 in München (Bayern).

He served in the army during the Great War and then in a Freikorps units. He was arrested in Passau in 1920. He moved to Österreich and was arrested again in 1921. He moved back to Germany and worked as an agricultural merchant. An active member of the Allgemeine-SS, he rose to the rank of Oberführer with effect from 10 September 1939. He served in the Security Service of the SS (SD) between 1932 and 1935. He joined the Police Administration after the Anschluss in 1938. He died 2 November 1954.

BREIHAUPT Franz

Born 8 December 1880 in Berlin.

He joined the army in 1891 and served until 1921 when he left with the rank of Major. An active member of the SS- since December 1932, he served as SS-Standortführer (Garrison commander) for Berlin from 1934 to January 1942. He joined the Police Administration in 1941 and he was appointed head of the SS-Legal Office in August 1942. Promoted Obergruppenführer on 20 April 1944. Shot by his side 20 April 1945.

BRIX Dr. Gerhard

Graduate in law, he was appointed Regierungsassessor 19 December 1925. Served in the Präsidialabteilung of the Regierung Gumbinnen on 1931. Appointed Landrat for Tilsit 21 May 1933, he took over the Gestapo office in Tilsit in 1934. Then in 1936 he held temporary command in local Police Administration. Moved to the Civil Administration in Bialystok from 1942.

BUCHER Friedrich

Born 9 July 1880 in Passau.

Educated in München and passed his arbitur. Joined the Bayern army 6 July 1901. Commissioned Leutnant 9 March 1902 and was promoted Oberleutnant 3 March 1911 and Hauptmann 15 December 1914. Represented the Bayern Government on the Armistice Commision in Spa 28 August 1919 to 1 July 1920. Wehrkreiskommissar for Niederbayern until 1922. Left active service in the army 31 March 1920. Promoted brevet Major 29 June 1920. Worked in the timber industry in München, Hamburg and Bremen. Joined the Party 1 February 1929. Schulungsleiter in Gau Hamburg 1 February 1929 to 10 March 1933 He served as the first chief of the Gestapo office in Tilsit during which time he headed Police Administration. After leaving the Police Administration he served as a courier for the Foreign Office and he joined the SA. Promoted SA Obertruppführer 20 April 1938. Promoted Major der Reserve in the army 1 December 1938. He underwent military service 19 August 1939 to 16 May 1940 and then returned to the Foreign Office in the Poltical Culture department. He died in Passau 12 April 1959.

BUTTNER Dr. Hermann

Born 3 October 1901 in Stuttgart (Württemberg).

A graduate as a Doctor of Law he joined the Württemberg civil service. Headed the Agricultural High School in Hohenheim from March 1934. In 1937, he was appointed to the Police Administration. He served for twelve months in occupied Poland and then returned to Germany as Landrat for Freudenstadt. An honorary member of the SA, he was a Party member from 1 May 1933.

CHRISTIANSEN Carl

Born 24 February 1884 in Wyk on the North Friesland Island of Fohr.

His brother was the General der Flieger Friedrich Christiansen, Wehrmacht Commander in Holland during the war. Served in the Imperial Navy and then in the merchant service as a ships master. In the Police Administration since 1933, he moved from Bremen to the post in Harburg on 16 February 1933 and moved to Magdeburg on 1 August 1934. He retired from state service in September 1937. Recalled to the navy as Fregattenkäpitan der Reserve on June 1940. Served on his brother's staff in Holland then as Reichskommissar for the See and Inland shipping in Holland and Belgium. Later as Generalinspekteur beim Reichskommissar für Seeschiffahrt, he was under orders of the Gauleiter of Hamburg Karl Kaufmann. He was briefly imprisoned after the war but was released in 1947. He was awarded the Knight´s Cross of the War Service Cross with Swords 19 November 1944.

CLAASSEN Günther

Born 1 December 1888 in Warsaw (Poland).

He served in the flying service during the Great War and then worked in agriculture. An active member of the SS since 1932, he rose to the rank of Oberführer with effect from 12 September 1937. He left Allgemeine-SS service on May 1937 for Policeadministration duties. He died in an internment camp at Zuffenhausen 22 July 1946.

COSSMANN Dr. Paul Nicolas

He was trained as a lawyer and was awarded a Doctorate. He served as a legal official in the civil service with the rank of Regierungsrat. He headed Abteilung I Verwaltung Polizei in the Flensburg Police Administration. He was also chief of the Gestapo office at Schneidemühl in 1935. He died in December 1935.

DAMBACHER Wilhelm

Born 11 June 1905.

A graduate in law, he became a civil servant in Land Württemberg. Promoted Regierungsassessor 18 May 1936 and Regierungsrat 1 November 1938. From 1938, he held several leading posts in Württemberg Police Administration.

DENZLER Ludwig

Born 9 February 1906.

An active member of the SA, he was promoted SA-Sturmbannführer 1 July 1932. Stabsführer SA-Untergruppe Danzig in SA-Gruppe Ostland 1 July 1932–1 September 1933. Promoted SA-Standartenführer 1 January 1933. Führer SAStandarte 43 1 September 1933–1 March 1934. Führer SA-Standarte 41 1 March 1934–28 February 1935. Führer beim SA-Gruppe Pommern 28 February 1935–1 November 1936. Führer SA-Standarte 54 1 November 1936–30 June 1939. Führer z.vV SA-Gruppe Pommern 1 July 1939–1945. While serving in Police Administration in 1934/1935, he was

Duisburg. Left to right, NSKK Oberstleutnant der Polizei Willi Forster, Ministeraldirektor Werner Bracht, Oberleutnant der Schutzpolizei Hermann Fuchs, Unknown

also head of the Gestapo office in Tilsit. Promoted SA-Oberführer 30 January 1942. Kreiseleiter des Kreises Schlochau 1941. Sentenced to 10 years in prison by the Poles 21 February 1948. Released 7 October 1955.

DETTEN von Georg

Born 9 September 1887 in Hagen.

He joined the army and served until 1919 rising to the rank of Rittmeister. Worked in agriculture and then in banking. Joined the SA 1929. Stabsführer SA-Gruppe Mitte 16 January 1932. Mit der Führung (entrusted with the leadship of) SA-Gruppe Mitte 16 February 1932 then Führer SA-Gruppe Sachsen from 23 February 1932. He rose to the rank of SA-Gruppenführer. Appointed Sonderkommissar der Obersten SA-Führung in Preussen in 1932. He served in Police Administration in 1933. Member of the Reichstag since 1933. He was arrested in the wake of the Röhm putsch of 30 June 1934 and was shot at Berlin-Lichtefelde by a firing squad from the Leibstandarte SS 1 July 1934.

DEUTSCHBEIN Dr. Erich

Born 14 July 1892 in Eisenberg (Thüringen).

Studied law at University and achieved a Doctorate 1914. Served in the artillery during the Great War and then in a Freikorps units. After the war he served as a legal official in local administration in the State of Thüringen. Led the Gestapo office in Stettin for two months in 1933 and then joined the Police Administration. He remained in this field until the end of the war. Joined the SS 10 August 1939 and rose to the rank of Standartenführer with effect from 30 January 1945.

DIEFENBACH Dr.

He was a civil servant who was appointed to his first post on the 8 January 1921. He served as Regierungsrat in Abteilung I of the District Presidency in Minden in 1931. Posted to Police Administration in 1933 and then served as Referent in Abteilung IV Kommunalverwaltung in the Reich Ministry of the Interior. Later he was appointed as Regierungsdirektor in the District of Koslin.

DIEHM Christoph

Born 1 March 1892 in Rottenacker (Württemberg) Served in the army from October 1912 to October 1924 when he left with the rank of Oberfeldwebel. Worked as a farmer and engine fitter. Joined the SA in March 1928 and transfer red to the active service in SS as Oberführer 22 March 1932. He rose to the rank of Brigadeführer with effect from 21 March 1934. He joined Police Administration 1 March 1939. Posted to the Ukraine on 23 April 1943 for training in SS and Police duties, he remained in this field until August 1944 and at the same time retained his Police Administra-

Strassbourg 1940, Gauleiter Robert Wagner speaks to Leo Götzmann Polizeipräsident Wien

tion post. He was given the rank of Generalmajor der Polizei on 1 August 1944 and Generalmajor der Waffen-SS on 9 November 1944. Died in Rottenacker 21st February 1960.

DIERMANN Anton

Born 25 February 1889 in Husten in the Prussian district of Arnsberg.

Served in the army during the Great War and was commissioned Leutnant 18 May 1918. Joined the Schutzpolizei in March 1920 as Leutnant. He was promoted Oberleutnant 21 July 1921 and Hauptmann 23 September 1923. He transferred to the Gendarmerie 12 May 1927 and was promoted Major 1 April 1930. He was promoted Oberstleutnant der Gendarmerie 1 November 1937. He served in Poland, France, Russia and Czechoslovakia and finally at Police Headquarters in Berlin and was promoted Oberst 1 January 1942. He was promoted Generalmajor der Polizei. In January 1944. Joined the SS 1 September 1942 and appointed to the rank of Brigadeführer with effect from 30 January 1944. After leaving his post in Berlin he was without assignment until he took over Police Administration duties. He retired 1 March 1945. He was a married man with two children. Died in Ettlingen 22 July 1982.

DIETRICH Dr. Fritz

Born 6 August 1898 in Lafraun in Tirol (Österreich).

Served in the Austrian army from 1915 to 1919 and then studied philosophy and graduated with a Doctorate. Worked in the chemical industry. Joined the Security Service of the SS (SD) on 7 May 1936. He rose to the rank of Obersturmbannführer with effect from 1 September 1941. He was appointed as Chief of Staff to the SD-Oberabschnitt South from November 1936. From 1941, he served as SS und Polizei Standortführer for Libau (Baltic area). In 1944 he returned to Germany and was appointed to Police Administration duties. On the 26 December 1944, he was made Kampfkommandant for Saarbrücken.

DOLEGA-KOZIEROWSKI Heinrich Georg von

Born 18 December 1889 in St. Georgsberg bei Ratzeberg (Schleswig).

Served in the army during the Great War and then worked as an administration official in the agricultural industry. Joined the SS on April 1934 and rose to the rank of Oberführer with effect from 9 November 1944. After a career in a Party publication house, he served in Police Administration from 1936. Died in Hamburg 15 April 1967.

Potsdam 1941. A unit by the Japanese Foreign Minister Yasuke Matsuoka to the "Sans soucis" palace, SS-Oberführer Heinrich von Dolega-Kozierowski, the police president is on the left followed by SS-Oberführer Georg-Jakob Sieber, Dr. Otto Meissner is on the right in diplomats uniform

DORNAUER Dr. Hans

Born 7 May 1892 in Wartberg an der Krems (Österreich).

Served in the Austrian army during the Great War. Studied law after the war and was awarded a Doctorate in November 1921. He joined the Austrian Police Administration in April 1922, he served in Wien and then, in April 1937, he was transferred to Innsbruck. After the Anschluss, he was posted to the Security Police (SIPO). In 1941, he returned to Police Administration duties in Innsbruck. Joined the SS 1 March 1934 and rose to the rank of Standartenführer with effect from 20 April 1943. Died in Graz 9 December 1954.

DORSCH Eugen

Born 31 July 1896 in Auer.

Served in the Great War and then became active in the Party. An active member of the SA, he was promoted Standartenführer on 1 July 1932 whilst commanding SA-Standarte 3. He rose to the rank of Brigadeführer with effect from 30 January 1938. He was posted to Police Administration from 1933. SA leader at disposal of SA-Gruppe Tannenbergon 1944.

DREHER Wilhelm

Born 10 January 1892 in Ay (Schwabia).

He was trained as a machinist and mechanic then from 1910, he served in the Imperial Navy. Released from navy after the Great War, he joined the State railways as an engine Driver. Left the railways and worked as a locksmith. Joined the SS 27 August 1931 and rose to the rank of Brigadeführer with effect from 30 January 1936. Served in Police Administration from July 1933 and moved to the post of Regierungspräsident (District President) of Sigmaringen in September 1942. He died in Weissenheim 19 November 1969.

DUNCKERN Anton

Born 29 June 1905 in München (Bayern)

He was a legal graduate in from the University of München. Served as a legal official in the Bayern Political Police from the late 1920's. He joined the SS 1 October 1930 and rose to the rank of Brigadeführer with effect from 9 November 1942. He served in the Security Service of the SS (SD) from 1934. He commanded various Gestapo offices until February 1939 when he took over the Security Police and SD in Braunschweig. Remained in the Security Police until the end of the war. During the last months of the fighting in Lorraine, in autumn 44, he took over the Police Administration in Metz alongside his SIPO/SD duties. Captured by US troops in Metz 18 November 1944. Sentenced to 20 years in prison by a French court 1947. Released 1954 and moved back to München where he practiced as a lawyer.

DUNNEBIER Helmut

Born 9 October 1898 at Zwickau (Sachsen).

He served in the Great War then joined the Schutzpolizei. From 1933, he moved to Sachsen Police Administration. Whilst in the post at Zwickau, he held the rank of Major and later rose to the rank of Lieutenant-Colonel. Joined the SS 10 September 1939 with the rank of Obersturmbannführer. During the war, he served as SS and Polizeistandortführer for Voroschilovsk under the SS and Police Leader for North Caucasus, SS-Oberführer Karl-Heinz Burger, from 1942 to July 1943. Then, he served as Staff officer of the Schutzpolizei on the staff of the Civil Authority in Reichsgau Sudetenland.

EBERSTEIN Friedrich Karl Freiherr von

Born 14 January 1894 in Halle an der Saale.

Served in the Great War then in a Freikorps units. Worked in banking and manufacturing and ran his own company until 1929. An active member of the SS from 1929, he was posted to SA from July 1930 where he rose to the rank of Gruppenführer with effect from 1 September 1932. He commanded SA-Gruppe Hochland from 1 September 1932 to 20 February 1933. He returned to SS-duties in February 1933 and rose to the rank of Obergruppenführer with effect from 30 January 1936. He served as Leader of the SS-Main District South from 1 April 1936. Appointed Higher SS and Police Leader for Wehrkreis VII from 12 March 1938. He was head of the Police Department IV in the Bayern Interior Ministry from 15 December 1937. He was dismissed from all his posts 20 April 1945 by order of Martin Bormann for defeatism. He was godfather to Reinhard Heydrich. He died in Tergensee Bayern 10 February 1979.

EBNER Dr. Hermann

Born 24 February 1896 in Ludwigshafen.

Served in the infantry during the Great War. He was badly wounded in 1917 and was invalided out of the army. Graduated and was awarded a Doctorate in Law from the University of Tübingen in 1923. In December 1923, he was appointed Regierungsassessor in Oberamt Leonburg and on 13 May 1927 as Amtsmann to Oberamt Tübingen. He served in Police Administration from July 1927 until 12 April 1933 when he was dismissed from his Police Director post following differences with local Party leaders. He returned to Civil service duties in Oberamt Herrenburg and then was promoted Landrat in Marbach on the 15 September 1933. He moved to Heidenheim on the 1 October 1938. After feuding with the local Kreisleiter he was conscripted into the army where he remained until the end of the war.

ECKOLDT Dr.

He was a lawyer who entered the civil service on the 18 July 1931. Alongside his Administrative Police duties, he was appointed to the post of Oberlandrat for the District of Pilsen, which included the communities of Pilsen, Kralowitz, Pilsek, Taus, Schuttenhosen and Strakonitz on 1 October 1939.

EDER

He was a Bayern civil servant who was appointed to his first post in 1907. He joined Police Administration in 1926. After leaving his post in Würzburg in 1936, he returned to the civil administration in Augsburg. Ranked Regierungsdirektor in 1939 he moved to München in 1940. He later returned to Augsburg as Director of the Administrative Court.

EGGERSTEDT Otto

He was a social democratic politician who served in the Police Administration. Involved in the 'Bloody Sunday' riots in Altona on 25 July 1932, he was accused of being an 'agent provocateur' for the von Papen government. He was removed because of his political affiliations in January 1933.

EICHEL Hans

He joined Party on 1931 and became active member of the SA. Promoted SA-Standartenführer 1 April 1933, serving in SA-Gruppe West. Promoted SA-Oberführer 30 January 1938 serving in SA-Gruppe Kurpflaz. From 1933, he served in Police Administration with the rank of Polizeirat, and was appointed Polizeidirektor in May 1934. He was tried for the killing of two US pilots, was sentenced to death and was executed on 3 December 1948.

ENGEL Fritz Karl

Born 3 March 1898 in Strelowhagen.

He worked in car industry, heading a sales office in Essen from 1927 to 1931. A member of the SA from 1925 to 1929 he then joined the newly created SS in Ruhr area. He became an active SS member from 1931 and served as Stabs-führer to SS-Gruppe West from 1931 until June 1933 and to SS-Gruppe East until December 1933. He rose to the rank of Oberführer with effect from 15 September 1933. He was the first head of the Gestapo office in Stettin alongside his Police Administration duties. Investigations into a temporary concentration camp in the Stettin shipy- ards led to charges being brought against him. He was dismissed from the SS on March 1934. He rejoined the SS as Sturmbannführer on 9 November 1942 and served in the 4. SS-Polizei Panzergrenadier Division.

ENGELHARDT Carl

Born 29 March 1901 in Aglasterhausen near Mannheim.

He works in the chemical industry from 1925 to 1934 under Wilhelm Keppler (later Economic Advisor to Hitler). He joined the Party and the SA in 1926 and rose to the rank of Oberführer on 30 January 1940. He was a Party official from 1934 to 1937 then he was appointed to Police Administration. He was transferred to SS with the rank of Oberführer on 21 June 1941. During the war he was involved in Police Administration in Alsace.

ERNST Dr.

A graduate in Law he served as a Regierungsassessor in the Baden Interior Ministry and rose to the rank of Oberre-gierungsrat in September 1940. He joined the Party 1 July 1932. He was posted in Police Administration in 1938. In February 1940, he moved to the Interior Ministry in Berlin. He ended the war as Landrat for Waldshut. He held the rank of Scharf-ührer in the SA.

FEHRLE Hermann-Georg

Born 30 August 1899 in Esslingen in Württemberg.

Served in the army from July 1917 and then, in 1921, he became member of Police Administration in Württemberg. He moved to Hauptamt ORPO in 1937. He joined the SS 9 November 1938 and rose to the rank of Obersturm- bannführer with effect from 9 November 1943. He was attached to the staff of IdO Wien from 1938 to 1939 then returned to Berlin. Promoted Amtsrat in November 1940, he returned to Police Administration duties in February 1942.

FICHTE Werner von

Served in the Great War and then in the Ehrhardt Brigade, a Freikorps unit. He later joined the Party and became active in the SA. He rose to the rank of Gruppenführer. He led the SA-Gruppe Westfalen from 1932 to 1 Novem-ber 1932 and again from 1933 to July 1933. He served on the staff of SA High Command (OSAF) from July 1933. He was arrested during the purge of the SA Leadership 30 June 1934 and was dismissed from all posts.

FINKE August

Born 12 August 1906.

He served in Police Administration in 1934/1935 then he joined in the Criminal Police rising to the rank of Krimi-nal-direktor and during the war he headed the Criminal police office in Gleiwitz. He joined the SS in April 1935 and rose to the rank of Obersturmbannführer with effect from 9 November 1943.

FISCHER-SCHWEDER Bernhard

Born 12 January 1904 in Berlin-Spandau.

He studied mechanical engineering and joined the SA in 1925 rising to the rank of Oberführer in 1935. He was arrested on the 30 June 1934 as a result of the purge of the SA Leadership. He had served under Edmund Heines who was executed. No evidence was produced against him and he was released 21 September 1934. He joined Berlin police force in 1933 and then served in the Gestapo in Sachsen. Transferred to the SS as Oberführer on November 1941. He joined Police Administration in 1940 and then served in SS and Police duties in Russia until he was charged with drunkenness in March 1943 as a result of which he was posted to the Waffen-SS. After the war he spent 10 years in prison for war crimes. He died 28 November 1960.

FÖRSTER Wilhelm Karl "Willi"

Born in Frankfurt am Main 26 September 1890.

After schooling he trained as a businessmann. Served in the artillery during the Great War and then returned to business in Cologne. Ran his own business 1929 to December 1931. Joined the Motor SA 1 May 1932. Joined the Party 1 February 1933. Transferred to the Party Motor Corps and served as Führer SA Motorstandarte Köln and the Motorstandarte Bonn 1933–30.09.1936. Promoted NSKK-Sturmhauptführer 30 January 1935. Transferred to the NSKK active list. Führer der NSKK Motorstandarte 73 01.10.1936–20.04.1938. Promoted NSKK-Oberstaffelführer 01.10.1936.and NSKK-Standartenführer 20 April 1938. Beim NSKK Motorgruppe Niederrhein 20.04.1938–1945. Promoted NSKK-Oberführer 20 April 1940. In 1941, he was posted to Police Administration duties and then on 16 February 1944 he returned to NSKK duties. Luftschutzleiter des Luftschutzortes Duisburg-Hamborn 16.02.1944. Died in Duisburg 29 October 1954.

FLASCHE August

Born 15 February 1902 in Münster.

Served in the Great War and then worked as a cashier and bookeeper. He joined SS in 1931 and was active in the Allgemeine-SS rising to the rank of Oberführer with effect from 10 September 1944. He was posted to Police Administration in 1942. He fled from Aachen before the US army arrived and Himmler believed he had been too hasty. It was intended that he be brought before an SS-Honour Court on a charge of cowardice but the war ended before such a court could be convened. Tried in 1946 for war crimes, he served a 10 year prison sentence. He was released in 1951.

FRANZ Friedrich Hermann

Born 16 August 1891 in Leipzig-Stötteritz (Sachsen).

Served in the army during the Great War and then joined the Schutzpolizei. From 1933 to 1938, he served in the Police Administration of Sachsen. He then returned to SCHUPO duties. He achieved the rank of Generalmajor with effect from 14 September 1944. During the war, he served in Russia and then achieved the status of Higher SS and Police Leader in Greece on a temporary basis. He joined the Hitlerjugend as an instructor and served from 1933 until August 1940 rising to the rank of Oberbannführer. Transferred to the SS as Obersturmbannführer on 1 August 1940, he rose to the rank of Brigadeführer with effect from 14 September 1944. He died 18 February 1960.

FRANZELIN Dr. Adolf

Born 8 August 1902 in Innsbruck (Österreich).

Graduate in Law. He was a leading Austrian politician who worked for Anschluss with Germany. He served first in the Gestapo Office in Innsbruck then he was appointed to Police Administration duties. He joined the SS as Untersturmführer in November 1938 and rose to the rank of Obersturmführer. Died 25 April 1940 from tuberkulosis.

FRIDERICI Arthur

Born 27 May 1900 in Osnabrück.

Served in the Great War from March 1917 and in a Freikorps units. Became active in anti French sabotage in the Ruhr from May 1924. He joined the SA in September 1924 and rose to the rank of Sturmbannführer with effect from 31 December 1930. Transferred to the SS 1 April 1931 he rose to the rank of Standartenführer with effect from 20

December 1934. Served as a full time paid SS leader until 1 January 1935. Went into Police Administration in February 1940. He was involved in an air raid on Hamm on 28 September 1940 and suffered depression as a result. He shot himself in his office 9 February 1941.

FULDA Konrad

Born 23 April 1878.

He was a civil servant who had served as deputy Police President in Magdeburg and Cologne and then he served as Regierungsdirektor in Schleswig, Stade and Arnsberg. He was appointed to the Police Administration in Flensburg in succession to Herr Hinckel who had died suddenly. He retired February 1937.

FYDRICH Paul Wilhelm

Born 24 January 1893 in Willudden (Ostpreussen).

He served in the Great War when he was wounded quite severly. After the war he joined the Schutzpolizei and rose to the rank of Oberstleutnant. He served as Kommandeur der Schutzpolizei in Bitterfeld from April 1938. In 1938/39, he held temporary command post in Administrative Police. Later in 1943, he moved to Weissenfels as Kommandeur der SCHUPO. He joined the SS on the 1 July 1939 with the rank of Sturmbannführer and was promoted Obersturmbannführer with effect from 18 November 1943.

GABLENZ Adolf Heinrich Anton Franz Freiherr von

Born in Soest 12 August 1882.

He was the son of Generalleutnant Heinrich Freiherr von Gablenz. He was a graduate in law. He served in the Great War achieving the rank of Hauptman der Reserve. After the war he became a civil servant and was a Regierungsrat in Merseberg until 1921 when he moved to Schiedemühl. Promoted Oberregierungsrat 1922. Moved to Stettin 1926 and to Wiesbaden where he took up the police post 22nd February 1933. He died in Wiesbaden 18 August 1944.

GAREIS Heinrich

Born 1878 in Burgebach (Oberfranken).

Studied legal jurisprudence and entered the Bayern state service as a legal official in Kulmbach 1905. He did not serve in the military during the Great War but was decorated for his government service. Appointed Staatskommissar in Nürnberg in 1920. Joined the Police Administration October 1923 and served until April 1933. He was responsible for keeping law and order in Nürnberg during the period of the Hitler München putsch of November 1923. Although attracted to the ideas of Hitler, he was careful never to step into overt opposition to the State. Joined the SS 10 July 1938 and rose to the rank of Oberführer with effect from 21 June 1939 He served as a Bayern District President until June 1943 when he was placed in retirement.

GEIBEL Paul Otto

Born 1898 in Dortmund (Ruhr).

Served in the Imperial Navy during the Great War and then worked in a Insurance Company. Member of the SA from December 1931 until April 1935 rising to the rank of Sturmbannführer. Transferred to the SS in December 1938, he rose to the rank of Brigadeführer with effect from 26 October 1944. Joined the Gendarmerie 1 April 1935 with the rank of Major. He served at Police headquarters in Berlin until March 1944 when he was appointed SS and Police Leader in Warsaw. Promoted Oberstleutnant 1 April 1939 and Oberst der Gendarmerie 14 July 1942. During Polish assignment, he also performed Police Administration duties. He was promoted Generalmajor der Polizei 1 September 1944. He was transferred to Prague 1 February 1945 as Commander of the Ordnungspolizei. Sentenced to imprisonment by the Poles, he committed suicide in prison at Varsovia 12 November 1966.

GELBERG Wilhelm Eberhard

Born in 7 December 1894 in Forde bei Grevenbrück (Westfalen).

Served in the 4 Thüringischen Infanterie-Regiment Nr. 72 as Stosstruppführer and then as a company officer 1914 to February 1917. Commissioned Leutnant der Reserve. Captured by the British February 1917. Released November 1919. Went into business November 1919 and worked in various firms until 25 May 193. Joined the Party 1921 left in the wake of the München Putsch of November 1923 and rejoined 1931. He joined the SA. Führer SA-Sturmbann III/97 30 January 1933–15 August 1933. He served in Police Administration from 1933 to April 1934. Führer SA-Stan- darte 257 15 August 1933–19 April 1936. Promoted SA-Obersturmbannführer 9 November 1933. After leaving the post in Krefeld, he became Oberbürgermeister of Neussin Rheinprovinz 1 April 1934 to 21 January1938. Promoted SA-Standartenführer 9 November 1934. Führer SA Reservestandarte 40 20 April 1936–31 March 1937. Führer SA-Standarte 257 1 April 1937–30 April 1938. Oberbürgermeister Wuppertal 1 April 1937–14 January 1938. Oberbürger-meister Oberhausen 19 January 1938–5 June 1940 SA-Führer z.V. der SA-Brigade 73 1 May 1938–5 June 1940. He served in the army as Hauptmann der Reserve and Company commander. Killed in action on the Oisen-Asisne Canal 5 June 1940.

GEPPERT Karl

Born 25 December 1879.

Served in the Great War and then joined the Schutzpolizei where he rose to the rank of Oberst. Retiring from active service, he served in Police Administration from 1937 until the end of the war.

GERTH Fritz Albert

Born in 15 April 1900 in Brückenkopf (Posnania).

He served in Schutzpolizei from 1920 to 1924, then he worked in a printing house. He joined Party and SA in 1930. He was reactived in the Police Administration in 1934 and rose to the rank of Polizeirat May 1941. He served in Weis-senfels 1934 to 1936 and then at Police headquarters in Berlin. Moved to Koblenz as head of Abteilung IV (Gewer-bepolizei) in 1937 then to Wittenberg. Transferred to Klagenfurt in Österreich 1939, he was moved to Luxemburg in November 1940 as Polizeioberinspekteur. He took over the Police Administration in 1941 which he ran until August 1943. Put on trial before the SS and Police Court in Metz for having an illicit affair with a Luxemburg woman, he was sentenced to six weeks house arrest and then two months in prison. He retained the title of Police Director but the office was run by the SCHUPO commander Oberstleutnant Kalden. The General State Prosecutor of Luxemburg declared there were no charges to be brought against him in September 1947.

GEYER Waldemar

Born 14 March 1882 in Breslau (Schlesien).

Graduated as an architect. He was active member of the SA from 1923. Gausturmführer und 1 Standartenführer der Berlin-Brandenburg SA 1927. Promoted SA-Standartenführer 10 May 1931. In Stab Obersten SA-Führung in Mün-chen und Kommandiert of the SA-Gruppe Berlin-Brandenburg 1 September 1932. Leader of the SA-Brigade 27 from 1933 to 1936. Ranked Gruppenführer with effect from 14 March 1932. He was Member of the Reichstag since 1933. In 1933, he was transferred to Police Administration duties. He left Police duties in 1943 to become Landesführer der Technische Nothilfe for Schlesien He was given the right to wear the uniform of a Generalmajor der Polizei. As SA-Leader he was at disposal of SA-Gruppe Schlesien. He died 5 September 1947.

GIESEKE Otto

Born 24 March 1891 in Hohenhameln (Hannover).

Qualified as a junior school teacher in 1914 but joined the army before he could take up a post. Served in the Great

War being commissioned Leutnant 17 December 1915. Joined the Schutzpolizei and was promoted Oberleutnant 1 ne 1920. He was promoted Hauptmann der SCHUPO 1 June 1926 and Major 1 April 1935. He served in the Police Division as a regimental commander until May 1943 and was then transferred to command the guard unit protecting the military highway construction to Southern Russia (Durchgangstrasse IV). He was promoted Oberstleutnant der SCHUPO 1 August 1940 and Oberst 1 April 1942.

In March 1944, he took over command of the Ordnungspolizei in the Baltic States. He remained there until January 1945 when he was transferred to the Police Administration. Promoted Generalmajor der Polizei 1 May 1944. He joined the SS 1 June 1940 and rose to the rank of Brigadeführer with effect from 10 June 1944. He was awarded the Knight ´s Cross of the Iron Cross 6 October 1942 for his bravery in action in Northern Russia. Died of a heart attack in Hannover 21 July 1958.

GLÜCK Otto

Born 7 May 1900 in Bettenhausen.

After schooling, he worked for his father in forestry. He served in the Great War from 1916 and was wounded in November 1918 ending the war in a field hospital in Liège (Belgium). He served in the Württemberg Police until 1925 nd then worked as a photographer. He was member of the SA from 1 May 1930 to 1 October 1931 then he transferred to the SS. He rose to the rank of Obersturmbannführer with effect from 11 September 1938. He was active member of the Security Service of the SS (SD) from 1933 to 1935. He served as Security Director for Daimler-Benz until he joined the Police Administration in 1944.

GÖHRUM Kurt

Born 27 March 1891 in Aalen (Württemberg).

Trained as a professional officer he was commissioned Leutnant 18 August 1911and was promoted Oberleutnant 5 October 1916, he left army after the Great War. He joined the Police in Württemberg in 1919 and was promoted Hauptmann 30 January 1920. He was promoted Major der SCHUPO 1 May 1932, Oberstleutnant 1 September 1934 and Oberst 1 January 1939. He was further promoted Generalmajor der Polizei 1 August 1943 and Generalleutnant 1 April 1944. A member of the SS since 1943, he was ranked Gruppenführer. He was given the title of Higher Police Leader for Berlin, a unique post for the capital which gave him authoity over all police units in the Berlin area. After dismissal of Graf von Helldorf involved in Putsch against Hitler, he took over the position of Police President Berlin and served in both posts at the same time. He was arrested by the Russians and died in captivity 11 April 1953.

GÖTZMANN Leo

Born 14 July 1893 in Olmütz (now Olomouc) (Böhmen-Mähren).

He graduated in law from the University of Wien. Served in the Austrian army during the Great War. Member of the Police Administration in Wien from 1920 to 1924 and then transferred to the Austrian State security service. He was ismissed for being sympathetic to the Nazis 14 August 1933. Arrested 25 July 1934, he was sentenced to life in prison 23 March 1935 and remained in prison until the Anschluss of March 1938. Appointed as deputy Police President of Wien from June 1940. Joined the SS as Standartenführer 20 April 1941 and rose to the rank of Brigadeführer witheffect from 9 November 1942. He died in the American internment camp at Zuffenhausen 6 December 1946.

GRAF Alfons

Born 12 December 1899 in Kunrafshofen (Bayern).

Conscripted into the army in 1915, he served until February 1920. He joined the Schutzpolizei in 1920 but left aftera brief period to work as a telegraphist. Member of the SS since 27 January 1931, he was a full time commander of field units of Allgemeine-SS. He achieved the rank of Standartenführer with effect from 13 September 1936. He was appointed to Police Administration in March 1942 and remained there until the end of the war.

GROLMANN von Wilhelm

Born 16 July 1894 in Schweidnitz.

He served in the Great War and then joined the Schutzpolizei. He was dismissed in the wake of the München Putsch of November 1923. He was Party and SS member since 1930. He became active member of the SA from 1931 to 1935 and rose to the rank of Brigadeführer with effect from 1 September 1933. He rejoined the Schutzpolizei on April 1935 and rose to the rank of Major-General with effect from 26 March 1942. Transferred to the SS 1 January 1939 as Oberführer, he rose to the rank of Brigadeführer with effect from 26 March 1942. He had served as personal adjutant to the Interior Minister Wilhelm Frick and then as head of the personnel office at Police Headquarters. In 1942, he was transferred to Police Administration. He died in Seefeld/Hechendorf 20 June 1985.

GRUNDEY Karl

He was trained civil servant who served as Amtsrat in Abteilung II Polizei in the Prussian Ministry of the Interior until 1934 when he was promoted Regierungsrat and transferred to the Police Administration in Weissenfels. Dezernat in Präsidialabteilung Police Adninistration Berlin 1939. Promoted Oberregierungsrat June 1939. Leiter der Präsidial Geschäftsstelle in the Police Administration in Berlin From June 1939. He took over Police Administration in Stettin in 1943. Joined the SA and was promoted SA-Sturmbannführer in SA-Gruppe Berlin/Brandenburg 30 January 1942. Promoted SA-Obersturmbannführer 20 April 1943 and SA-Standartenführer 20 April 1944. Transferred to SA-Gruppe Pommern in 1944.

GRUNERT Richard

Born 5 November 1890 in Eisleben.

Served in the Great War as an infantry officer. After the war he entered the banking profession working for the Deutsche Bank in Berlin and Düsseldorf. In 1924, he moved to the post of senior clerk in the banking firm of B.Simons and Company. A member of the SA, he rose to the rank of Standartenführer. He was transferred to Police Administration from 1933. Retaining his police post, he was mobilized to the army in 1939. He was killed in action in 1941.

GUTENBERGER Karl

Born 18 April 1905 in Essen (Ruhr).

Worked in banking and then as a financial official in the steel industry. Member of the SA since 1923, he became active member in 1932 and rose to the rank of Brigadeführer by 1939. Member of the Reichstag from 1932. He served in Police Administration from May 1937 to June 1941. Transferred to the SS as Brigadeführer 1 June 1940, he rose to the rank of Obergruppenführer with effect from 1 August 1944. From June 1941 he served as Leader of SS-Main District West and Higher SS and Police Leader for Wehrkreis VI. He was appointed Inspector for 'Passiven Widerstand und Spezialabwehr West', the "Werewolf" guerilla organization that was supposed to attack the allied in areas that had been captured. Died in Essen 8th July 1961.

HABBEN Johannes

Born 9 February 1875 in Bagband Kreis Aurich in Ostfriesland.

Attended the universities of Göttingen, Heidelberg and München and graduated as a lawyer. He made his career in the Police Administration in Hannover, rising from Referendar to Oberregierungsrat rank, he was head of the Criminal Police during the Great War. He was appointed Deputy Police President of Hannover March 1933 and was made Police President 25 March 1933. He remained until retirement in October 1936. He died in Hannover 12 February 1958.

HABENICHT Friedrich

Born 6 June 1896 in Heilingenbruch.

Served in the Great War. He became active in the party in the 1920's. A member of the SA he was promoted Stanartenführer in September 1932 and leader of the SA-Standarte 213 in Niedersachsen. He rose to the rank of Brigadeführer with effect from 20 April 1933. He was transferred to Police Administration in 1934 remaining until the end of the war. During this period he was Führer z.V SA-Gruppe Oberrhein.

HAGENMEYER Erich

Born 21 August 1892 in Deggingen (Württemberg).

Joined the Württemberg State Railways as a middle rank civil servant in August 1908. Served in the army during the Great War and then returned to the railways. Promoted Reichsbahnoberinspektor in February 1934, Reichsbahn- amstmann on 30 March 1939 and finally Reichsbahnrat on 17 February 1943. Joined the Nazi Party from August 1920 until it was banned in 1923. Rejoined Party on 27 July 1927. Member of the SA from 1 September 1929, he rose to the rank of Brigadeführer with effect from 20 April 1936 He headed the SA-Brigade 56 throughout the war. Mobilized into the army as Hauptmann der Reserve from September 1939 to February 1942. Member of the Reichstag since 1939.

HAHN Ernst

Born 6 January 1888.

He served in the Great War. Graduating as a lawyer he entered the civil service in 1920. He was transferred to Police Administration in 1923 and remained until 1936. Promoted Oberregierungsrat, he returned to Württemberg Administration until 1939. Then he returned to Police Administration in Stuttgart holding senior posts, ranked as Regierungsdirektor on February 1944. He was member of the Party from May 33 and joined the mounted SA as Hauptsturmführer.

HANIK Dr. Karl

Born 2 October 1904.

A graduate in law, he was a civil servant who achieved the rank of Regierungsrat from 20 April 1941. He served in the Police Administration in Danzig from the 31 August 1938. He was a honorary collaborator with the SD in Danzig since 12 May 1939 and joined the SS as Hauptscharführer 1 February 1943. Erwin Schulz, head of the SIPO/SD Personnel department wrote to Maximilian von Herff of the SS-Personnel Office on the 12 June 1943 asking that Dr. Hanik be given the rank of Sturmbannführer in the SS. The request was passed to Himmler who replied on 24 June 1943 stating that Dr. Hanik must go on an SS Leadership course first and nothing further happened. He was posted in Sudetenland from 1942 until the end of the war.

HARSTER Dr. Wilhelm

Born 21 July 1904 in Kelheim (Niederbayern).

Attended the University of München where he studied legal jurisprudence. Awarded a Doctorate in Law in 1927. He served in the Police Administration in Stuttgart from October 1929 to January 1934 in the criminal then the political police departments. He joined the SS 1 November 1933 and rose to the rank of Gruppenführer with effect from 9 November 1944. Member of the SD from 29 October 1935. He left the Police Administration in Tübingen for Gestapo Office in Berlin before taking over as head the Gestapo office in Innsbruck. From 30 November 1939, he was Inspector of the Security Police and the SD for Kassel and on the 15 July 1940 he moved to Holland as BdS. He was transferred to Karl Wolff's staff in Italy 29 August 1943 where he performed the same function.

He was ranked Generalleutnant der Polizei on 9 November 1944. He was sentenced to 12 years in prison in The Hague June 1945 and was released in 1953. He joined the Bayern Interior Ministry with the rank of Oberregierungsrat in 1953, retiring in 1963. He was re-arrested in January 1966 as a result of investigations into Karl Wolff's activities in Italy. Tried in Bonn he was sentenced to 15 years in prison but was immediately released due to his age. Died in München 25 December 1991.

HARTE

He was a civil servant who rose to the rank of Oberregierungsrat. He was appointed Landrat for Quedlingburg in January 1934. He moved to the Police Administration in November 1934 and remained until he retired on 1 October 1936.

HAUER Daniel

Born 17 February 1879 in Bad Durkheim (Rheinpfalz).

He worked in the family wholesale company and then on the Railways. He served in the Great War. Member of the SA from 1 October 1927, he rose to the rank of Brigadeführer with effect from 1 July 1933. In 1931 he was appointed Führer SA-Brigade 50 (Darmstadt) then in February 1934 he became Leader of SA and SS Garrison in Stuttgart. He took over Police Administration duties from 1933 to 1934. He was President of the Investigations Commitee of Sondergerichts der Oberste SA-Führung for the SA-Gruppe Süd West from 16 August 1934 to 30 April 1936. Then he was put at disposal of SA-Gruppe Hessen until wars end. He was a Member of the Reichstag from 1933.

HAUSEN Dr. Freiherr von

He served in the Schutzpolizei rising to the rank of Hauptmann. He joined the Police Administration in 1935. In 1938, he became a courts administrator and was given the rank of Oberverwaltungsgerichtsrat. He achieved a Doctorate in Law. In 1942, he was promoted Reichsrichter in the Reichsverwaltungsgerichtsrat.

HEIDER Otto

Born 26 May 1896 in Bremerhaven.

Served in the Great War. He studied electrotechnics then worked as an electrical engineer. Became a Party worker and official in the free Hanseatic city of Bremen. Appointed Senator for Labour and Technical matters in Bremen May 1933 and served as Regierender Bürgermeister of the city during 1936 and 1937. Joined the SS as Obersturmbannführer 9 November 1935 and rose to the rank of Brigadeführer with effect from 30 January 1942. Appointed to Police Administration duties from 1937 to August 1943. He headed the Family Office in the SS-Race and Settlement Main Office until the end of the war. He died 13 May 1960.

HEIGL Dr. Otto

Born in 1905 in Nürnberg (Franken).

He was a trained lawyer who joined the Police Administration in Nürnberg in 1931. He graduated with a Doctorate in Philosophy in 1927. He served as a legal official in local administration in Ansbach from 1932 and then in Munchberg 1933. Promoted Landrat for Rehau in 1933. In 1934, he returned to the Police Administration in Braunschweig being responsible for the protection of Herman Göring factories. He remained there until his posting to Oppeln. He was mprisoned after the war due to his status as a civil servant, no charges were brought against him and he was released. He returned to civil service in Bayern and rose to the rank of Oberregirungsrat in 1959, serving in the Niederbayern administration. He retired in October 1967.

HEIM Dr. Wilhelm

Born 25 May 1900 in Mannheim.

He served in the Great War from 1917 and then returned to his legal studies. Achieved a Doctorate of Law in 1922. Member of the staff of the Police Administration in Karlsruhe from 1925. In 1927, he moved to Mannheim as transport referent. He led the Police Administration in Baden from 1933. He joined the SS in 1935 and rose to the rank of Hauptsturmführer with effect from 9 November 1936. He was dismissed from the SS and the Party by the Gau Court in Baden for violation of Party rules. Documents show that the real reason was that he was friendly with a number of prominent Jews. He joined the army and was killed in action 15 August 1942 as Leutnant. On the 25 September 1942, he was posthumously re-admitted into the SS with his old number and rank.

HEINES Edmund

Born 21 July 1897 in München (Bayern).

Served in the Great War. Joined the SA in 1922 and became the senior SA Leader in Schlesien. Rose to the rank of Obergruppenführer. Leader of SA-Gruppe Schlesien from June 1931 then SA-Obergruppe III in 1934. Member of Reichstag since 1932. He was appointed to Police Administration from March 1933. He was arrested in Bad Wiessee 30 June 1934 and was shot on Hitlers order on the 1 July 1934.

HELLDORF Wolf Graf von

Born 14 October 1896 in Merseburg.

Served in the Great War and then in the Freikorps units. Member of the SA, he rose to the rank of Obergruppenführer with effect from March 1933. He was head of the SA-Gruppe Berlin-Brandenburg from 21 July 1930 then Führer of SA-Obergruppe I from 1 September 1932 to 20 February 1933. From 1933, he served in Police Administration. From November 1938, he served as liaison officer for the SA with the Police and was later appointed Higher Police Leader for Berlin. He was awarded the Knight ´s Cross of the War Service Cross with Swords 10 February 1944. Arrested in the wake of the attempt on Hitler's life on 20 July 1944. He was hanged 15 August 1944.

HELLWEGE-EMDEN Harri

Born 21 October 1889.

He served in the Great War and then joined the Schutzpolizei, being promoted Major 20 April 1937. He was appointed to Police Administration duties in 1938/1939 and then returned to the SCHUPO. He moved to Giessen and was promoted Oberstleutnant in 1942.

HENNICKE Paul

Born 31 January 1883 in Erfurt (Thüringen).

Worked as a railway engineer and locksmith. Served in the Great War and then returned to the railways as an official. Member of the Allgemeine-SS from 1929, he rose to the rank of Gruppenführer with effect form 30 January 1938. From 1937, he was appointed to Police Administration duties. He was posted to Russia as an SS and Police Leader and was given the rank of Generalleutnant der Polizei 16 September 1942. In 1944, he was in charge of the Volksturm organisation in Middle Germany. Involved in the fight around Regensburg in April 1945. He died in Braunschweig 25 July 1967.

HENNINGER Otto

Born 21 August 1884 in Kürnbach.

He studied law at the Universities of Heidelberg, Freiburg and Berlin. Served in the Great War. He joined the civil service as a lawyer. Member of the SS from 1 June 1936, he rose to the rank of Obersturmbannführer with effect from 30 January 1939. He was appointed to Police Administration duties from 1934 serving until the end of the war.

HENZE Max

Born 23 September 1899 in Koythen (Anhalt).

Served in the Great War from 1917. He worked as a shopkeeper. A member of the SS from 1927 he rose to the rank of Brigadeführer with effect from 15 December 1933. In 1933, he led the SS-Rollkommando attached to Gestapo Headquarters. He was member of Reichstag since 1936. Transferred to the Police Administration from October 1937. He was allowed to wear Uniform of Generalmajor der Polizei from 1944. Hanged in Poland 10 March 1951.

HERBERT Willi

Born 28 May 1904 in Frankfurt am Main.

Trained as a teacher, he gave that up and became a hairdresser, running his own business until 1931. Member of the SS since 1927, he rose to the rank of Standartenführer effective 29 July 1932. From 1933 to 1934, he took over leading duties in Police Administration. He was member of the Reichstag from 1933. He left Allgemeine-SS service to serve as a nationality specialist officer in the SS-Volksdeutsche Mittelstelle headquarters during the war.

HERBOLD Dr.

Trained as a lawyer, he served in the Party as head of the office for senior administrators in Gau Baden. He was also a civil servant. In 1937/1938, he served in Police Administration. He rose to the rank of Oberregierungsrat. He was member of the SS from October 1935 with the rank of SS-Mann.

HERFURTH Kurt

Born 7 August 1890 in Kahla (Thüringen).

He studied the law. Served in the Great War then returned to the civil service. He joined the Police Administration in 1931 in Gotha. Member of the SS from 1933, he rose to the rank of Obersturmbannführer with effect from 30 January 1939. Mobilized into the army in August 1939 he served until the 30 November 1943 with the rank of Hauptmann. Then he served in Police Administration in Sudetenland.

HERMANNS Karl

Born 9 April 1894 in Höddelbusch

Attended the University of Heidelburg, Berlin and Bonn studying political economics. Served as a military administrator in Belgium during the Great War. After the war he worked in banking and in 1924 moved to Aachen as a legal official. He was a State Court Official with the rank of Landsgerichtrat. Appointed to a temporary post in Police Administration in March 1933, he remained until August 1933 and then served as Landsgerichtpräsident for Aachen. After the war he worked as a lawyer. Died in Gmünd 1 August 1975.

HERRMANN Fritz

Born 15 June 1885 in Magdeburg.

He served in the Great War at the front then as a staff officer. Served in the Schutzpolizei from 1920 to 1922 when he was forced out for political reasons. Worked as a newspaper editor from 1929. Appointed to Police Administration duties and chief of the local Gestapo office from March 1933 until 1938 and was then appointed. District President in Danzig then Lüneburg. Member of the SS from April 1934, he rose to the rank of Brigadeführer with effect from 21 June 1944. He died in Lüneburg on 21 November 1970.

HERRMANN Karl

Born 27 October 1891 in Grube Ilse Nord Lausitz (Brandenburg).

He joined the army in 1913 as Leutnant with senority from 5 May 1912 Promoted Oberstleutnant der SCHUPO 18 December 1917. Left the army 1920 and joined the Schutzpolizei with the rank of Oberleutnant. He was promo- ted Hauptmann der SCHUPO 13 July 1921 and Major 1 October 1932. His service was varied encompassing the SCH-UPO in the field and at the Headquarters in Berlin. Promoted Oberstleutnant der SHUPO 1 October 1934, Oberst 1 November 1938 and Generalmajor der Polizei with effect from 21 June 1943, he was actually promoted 20 April 1944. He joined the SS in January 1939 and rose to the rank of Brigadeführer with effect from 21 June 1943. His initial service was with an SS-Totenkopf-Standarte. During 1939, he was posted to Police Administration. From August 1940, he served in the Waffen-SS as a regiment and brigade commander and then as commander of the Waffen-SS for Böhmen-Mähren. Died in Salzuflen on 8 October 1960.

HESKE Ferdinand

Born 28 August 1892 in Lyck (Ostpreussen).

Trained as a machinist in the Paper industry. Served in the Imperial Navy during the Great War. Founder member of the German Volksbund in Königsberg on 1921. He worked as a commercial traveller. He joined the Party on 1 March 1926. Member of the SA from April 1931, he rose to the rank of Standartenführer. On November 1933 he took over as head of the SA-Feldjäger-Abteilung in Königsberg then he transferred to the Schutzpolizei on 1 April 1936 with the rank of Major. He was promoted Oberstleutnant 20 April 1937 and Oberst 1 April 1941. Transferred to the SS 1 March 1939, he rose to the rank of Oberführer with effect from 30 January 1943. During the war he was appointed as commander of a Polizei-Regiment in Poland. Then on 1944, he was appointed into Police Administration until the end of the war. Died in Lindau Bodensee on 19 June 1958.

HIDDESSEN Ferdinand von

Born 17 December 1887 in Minden (Westfalen).

Joined the army and served in the Great War in the Flying Service. He was the first pilot to fly over Paris on 30 August 1914. He was shot down over Verdun in 1915 and remained a French prisoner until 1919. Member of the Kreistag Schweidnitz on 1929. Member of the Reichstag from 1933. Served in the NSFK (National Socialist Flying Corps) rising to the rank of Gruppenführer. He served as Führer of the NSFK-Standarte 31. He was posted to Police Administration duties in 1933 and served until 1940 then he took over the NSFK-Gruppe 16 in occupied Alsace. Died 24 January 1971 in Neustadt an der Saale.

HILDEBRANDT Ernst Albrecht

Born 31 May 1895 in Offstein (Rhine Hessen).

He was one of four brothers. Three of them were members of the SS: Richard as Obergruppenführer and Fritz as a Standartenführer. He served in the Great War when he was a prisoner of the British from 4 February 1917. After his return to Germany, he studied social and economic sciences and then worked in a bank and for an automobile company. Member of the SS from February 1932, he rose to the rank of Oberführer with effect from 20 April 1944. From 1934 to 1937, he served into Security Service (SD) of the SS in Southern Germany. Then in August 1937, he was transferred to Police Administration duties were he remained until the end of the war. However the post was run by a deputies from 1942 as he served in the Waffen-SS and then undertook SS and Police duties in Russia and Italy. Died in Nürnberg 28 March 1970.

HILLE Walter

Born 24 May 1894 in Bischofswerda (Sachsen).

Studied political science and law. He served in the army during the Great Warbeing commissioned Leutnant 17 January 1916. Joined the Schutzpolizei on 1 August 1920 with the rank of Oberleutnant. Promoted Hauptmann 1 December 1927, Major 1 June 1933 Oberstleutnant 1 December 1933 and Oberst 1 April 1939. He was promoted brevet Generalmajor der Polizei 20 April 1942 and was confirmed in that rank with effect from 1 January 1944. Appointed to Police Administration from 1933 to January 1939, he then returnded to active service in the Schutzpolizei serving in Hamburg, München, Posen and Wiesbaden until the end of the war. He joined the Party 1 May 1937 and the SS 20 April 1943 as Brigadeführer. He committed suicide in an U.S.camp at Bischofswerda 6 May 1945.

HIMMLER Heinrich

Born 7 October 1900 in München.

Trained as an agriculture engineer. He served in the Bayern army from 1917 to 1918. Joined the Party in August 1923 and took part in the München Putsch of November 1923. Rejoined the Party in 1925 and became Deputy Gauleiter for Oberbayern until January 1929. Appointed Reichsführer-SS on 6 January 1929, it was subordinated to the SA until 30 June 1934. He temporarily led the Police Administration München in 1933 and then became Political Police Commander of all the German Länder. He was appointed Chief of the German Police on 17 June 1936, and at the outbreak of the war Reichskommissar for the Strengthening of Germandom. Appointed Reichsminister for the Interior in 1943, he was also General Plenipotentiary for Administration. After the attempt against Hitler in July 1944, he became Commander in Chief of the Replacement army. In the last months of the war he commanded army Groups for short periods. Committed suicide at Lüneburg 22 May 1945 whilst in British captivity.

HINKLER Paul

Born 25 June 1892 in Berlin.

Trained as a teacher. Served in the Great War and suffered a nervous breakdown following hard fighting near Soissons in France on September 1918. He left education in 1925. He joined Party in 1922 and was Gauleiter for Halle Merseburg 1926 to 1931. A member of the SA, he rose to the rank of SA-Gruppenführer with effect from 8 March 1939. From March 1933, he was appointed to Police Administration duties. He led the Gestapo Office in Schlewig in the 1930's. He was also temporary head of the Gestapo in November 1933. He was Member of Reichstag since 1936. From 1940, he was conscripted for frontline service in the army. Placed in retirement from Police service on 18 August 1943, he was put at disposal of the Stab OSAF. He died in Freiburg in May 1945.

HINSCH Hans

Born 21 March 1901.

From 1925 to 1929 he was member of the Schutzpolizei in Hamburg. A member of the SS from 1930, he rose to the rank of Standartenführer with effect from 22 July 1932. He headed SS-Standarte (Regiment) 28 in Hamburg in 1932–1933. Recalled into the Landespolizei in 1933, he transferred to the Schutzpolizei in 1934. He rose to the rank of Oberstleutnant by 1942. He was appointed to the Police Administration in 1941. He was retired from active police duties in July 1943 but remained in Police Administration until the end of the war.

HOCH Otto

Born 13 January 1891 in Bubenois.

Served in the Great War as Leutnant der Reserve. After the war, he joined the Administrative Police. Promoted Polizeioberinspektor in the Police Administration in Stuttgart in 1923. Promoted Polizeirat in July 1932, he served in various police posts in Württemberg. From May 1941, he held a leading post in the Police Administration. Member of the Party from December 1931, he also served in the SA, rising to the rank of Obersturmbannführer. He was a member of the Party Court for Württemberg from 1 November 1938.

HOEVEL Walter

Born 20 August 1894 in Wesel.

He served in the Great War in the artillery. After the war he worked in the family business. A member of the SA he rose to the rank of Gruppenführer with effect from 30 January 1942. He served as chief of staff to SA-Gruppe Niederrhein until July 1933 and then commanded SA-Brigade 71 in Cologne until the end of the war. He served in Police Administration from 1935 to 1944.

HOFMANN Hans Georg

Born 27 September 1873 in Hof.

He joined the army and served until January 1926 rising to the rank of brevet Colonel. He commanded the military Fortress in Ingolstadt from 1 April 1923. He was later given the brevet rank of Major-General. He joined the SA in 1933 and rose to the rank of Obergruppenführer. He headed all the SA in Bayern until 1933 and then was Inspector for the SA in Bayern and Sachsen. He served in Police Administration from 1933 and soon after he was appointed to the post of District President for Ober und Mittelfranken. From June 1934, he served as State Secretary to the Reichsstatthalter for Bayern. Member of the Reichstag from 1932. Died on 30 January 1942 in München.

HUMANN-HAINHOFEN Rolf Egbert von

Born 15 June 1885 in Hannover.

Served in the Great War. An active member in the Allgemeine-SS, he rose to the rank of Brigadeführer with effect from 12 September 1937. In June 1933 he was appointed to Police Administration duties and remained until October 1934. In 1937, he left active SS service to become Chief of Staff to Dienststelle Ribbentrop (Foreign Political Advisor of Hitler) then he held senior posts in various international relationship associations and was Vice-President of the United Committee for Old Fighters Associations. He was mobilized in 1940 as Major (then Oberstleutnant) in the army and was captured in the West of France in 1944. Died on 24 November 1961.

JÄGER Karl

Born 20 September 1888 in Schaffhausen (Switzerland).

Worked in the music industry and then joined the army. He served in the Great War in the artillery. Returned to the music industry after the war. A member of the SS since April 1933, he rose to the rank of Standartenführer with effect from 1 September 1940. A fully paid SS member since 1936, he joined Security Service of the SS (SD) in 1938. From July 1941 to September 1943, he commanded Einsatzkommando 3 in Einsatzgruppe A which operated in the Baltic States. He was also commander of the Security Police and the SD for Lithuania. He was transferred to Police Administration duties in May 1944. Arrested for war crimes in April 1959, he hanged himself in his cell in Heidelberg 22 June 1959.

JAHN Wilhelm

Born 2 February 1891 in Soest.

He served in the Great War. A member of the SA, he rose to the rank of Obergruppenführer with effect from 9 November 1937. He commanded the SA-Gruppe Nordsee in 1932. From 1935 until 1943 he served in the Police Administration. Retiring in 1943 he was put at disposal to SA-Gruppe Elbe.

JONAK Dr. Gustav

Born 23 May 1903 in Sudetenland.

Trained as a Lawyer, he the German civil service in 1938. He was promoted Oberregierungsrat on 1 February 1942. He served as Oberlandrat for Mährisch-Ostrau in the Reichprotektorat Böhmen-Mähren during the war. He joined the SS in 1940 and rose to the rank of Obersturmbannführer with effect from 20 April 1942. On 1944, he took over Police Administration duties without leaving his civil service post.

JOST Heinz

Born 9 July 1904 in Holzhausen near Frankfurt am Main.

Studied law at the Universities of Giessen and München and passed his state exams 1930. Practiced as a solicitor and served in the SA from March 1929 to July 1934. He was given his first Police Administration post as a result of patronage by Dr. Rudolf Werner Best and he was dismissed from his second post in Giessen due to a quarrel between the group led by the Gauleiter Jakob Sprenger and that led by Dr. Heinrich Müller and Dr. Rudolf Werner Best. He joined the SS from 28 July 1934 and rose to the rank of Brigadeführer with effect from 20 April 1939. An active member of the Security Service of the SS (SD), he served at SD Headquarters in Berlin and became the first head of the Amt VI (Foreign Intelligence) in the newly created RSHA from August 1939. He commanded Einsatzgruppe A of the SIPO and SD, operating in the Baltic States, from March to September 1942 and he was also Kommandeur der SIPO und SD in Riga. Then he was posted to Rosenberg's East Ministry as a Representative with an army Group. After months of illness he was pensioned in January 1945. Sentenced to life in prison 10 April 1948, the sentence was commuted to 10 years. He was released December 1951 and died 12 November 1964.

JUNGWIRTH Dr.

He studied law and graduated with a doctorate in law. He served as a State official in the administration of the Protectorate Böhmen-Mähren. He was appointed to Protectorate Police Administration from 1942 until 1944 with the rank of Polizeioberrat.

KADLETZ Dr. Wilhelm

He was a trained lawyer and joined the civil service on 6 July 1921. He served as Landrat for Leoben. From 8 September 1941, he was also in charge of Police Administration duties of his administrative District.

KALDEN

An officer in the Schutzpolizei, he was promoted Major in 1942. He served the staff of the Schutzpolizei in Danzig then on 1942 he was transferred to Luxemburg as Commander of the Schutzpolizei. He was promoted Oberstleutnant and was appointed as standing deputy Police Director following the disgrace of the incumbant Fritz Gerth. He remained there until the end of the war.

KAMMER Heribert

Born 4 September 1900 in Danzig.

He served in the Great War and entered the Police in Danzig on November 1921. He joined the Party in April 1931. A member of the SS from June 1933, he rose to the rank of Sturmbannführer with effect from 1 January 1940. When Danzig was unified with the Reich in 1939, he joined the Police Administration. He was ranked Polizeirat. He took over the Police Administration in Gaudenz in March 1944 as standing deputy for the incumbant Fritz Meyer. He was officially appointed to the post on 2 January 1945.

KAMMERHOFER Konstantin

Born 23 January 1899 in Turnau in Steiermark (Österreich).

He served in the Great War. Then he worked as a procurist. From 1921 to 1924 he was a member of the Austrian National Socialist Party. He was leader of the SA in Steiermark from November 1933. He left Österreich 1934 to avoid arrest. Transferred to the SS in February 1935, he rose to the rank of Gruppenführer with effect from 1 July 1943. In 1938, he was trained in Police duties in Essen but two months after the appointment to Police Administration in Innsbruck, he left to concentrate on his command of the SS-District in Wien. In 1941, he was involved in the creation of Flemish SS and he rose to the rank of Untersturmführer der Reserve on 1 June 1942. From May 1942, he was transferred to SS and Police duties, first in South Russia then as Higher SS and Police Leader for Croatia in March 1943. He died in Oberstdorf (Hannover) on 29 September 1958.

KÄRCHER Heribert

He joined Civil Service in Baden. In the 1930's he held various post in District and Police Administration with the rank of Regierungsrat. He took over the senior post in Police Administration in 1944 as Polizeidirektor serving until the end of the war.

KATZ Dr. Adolf

Born 9 March 1899 in Hannover.

He served in the Great War, then in a Freikorpsunit. He graduated from university as a Doctor in Law. He worked in Insurance Companies until 1933. Joined the SS in September 1930. He was appointed to Police Administration duties in 1933 and remained until 1936 when he took over full time Allgemeine-SS duties. He was a Member of the Reichstag since 1936. He joined the Waffen-SS and ended the war as chief of Office II of the SS-Personal Main Office. Rose to the rank of Brigadeführer and Generalmajor der Waffen-SS with effect from 30 January 1944. Died in Rhondorf on 7 May 1980.

KEHRL Hans Julius

Born 6 August 1892 in Jüterbog.

He served in the Great War where he was wounded in the stomach and lungs in August 1914. He returned to duty 1916. After the war he joined the Schutzpolizei. He was transferred to the Landespolizei in Thüringen in 1924 and was transferred to Police Administration duties in 1930. He served in the Thüringen Ministry of the Interior at the request of Wilhelm Frick in 1932. In 1934, he followed his chief to Reich Ministery of the Interior. He retired as Ministerialdirigeant in 1937 to take over the Police Administration in Hamburg were he remained until the end of the war. He was member of the SS from January 1937 and rose to the rank of Brigadeführer with effect from 1 January 1942. During the war, he was part of one of the most efficient administrations of any German city and was responsible for most of the air-raid precautions taken in the city. He was rewarded by award of the Knight's Cross of the War Service Cross with Swords on 24 September 1944. He died in Hamburg on 22 April 1961.

KESSLER Dr.

He was a civil servant who was appointed to his first post 2 November 1929. He held the rank of Regierungsrat whilst serving in Police Administration in Wuppertal and was appointed Landrat for Mährisch-Schonberg in Regierung Troppau 1 September 1935. He served in military administration duties during the war with the rank of Oberkriegsverwaltungsrat.

KITTEL Dr. Otto

Born 29 December 1897 in Friedersdorf (Österreich).

He served in the army from 1916 and then attended university from where he graduated with a Doctorate in Law in 1926. He worked as a legal officer in Police Administration in Wien from March 1928. He was promoted Polizeikommissar Sixth Class on 1 January 1935. He was member of the SS since April 1934 and rose to the rank of Obersturmbannführer with effect from 9 November 1940. After the Anschluss, he joined Gestapo Office in Wien and was ranked Regierungsrat from 1939. In July 1939, he returned to the Police Administration serving until the end of the war.

KLAIBER Rudolf

Born 30 May 1873 in Kunzelsau.

He graduated in Law and Economics from the University of Berlin and Tübingen. Served in the army for one year and then joined the civil service in Heilbronn and then Wangen in Württemberg. In August 1910 he was appointed Regierungsassessor in the Stuttgart city administration then in 1911 Polizeireferent for Stuttgart. In 1914 he was appointed Chairman of the newly created Landespolizeizentralstelle Württemberg and whilst in this post he developed the criminal police for the State. He served in the Great War as Leiter der Militär Zentralpolizeistelle Württemberg, being promoted Hauptmann der Reserve in 1917. In December 1920, he became Chairman of the Polizeipräsidium in Stuttgart. He was also appointed Chairman of the Landeskriminalpolizeiamt for Württemberg. From 1925 he was member of the International Criminal Police Commission. After the Nazis came to power, he feuded with Party leaders but was supported by the civil service because of his outstanding abilities. He retired on 31 May 1938 and was appointed honorary District leader of the German Red Cross in Stuttgart. He died on 8 June 1957.

KLEMM Kurt

Born 19 January 1894 in Mulhausen (Thüringen).

Graduated as a solicitor in 1915. Served in the Great War as an infantry officer. He entered the Civil Service in 1919 and rose to the rank of Regierungsrat in 1928 in the administration in Recklinghausen. He was a member of the German Peoples Party before joining the Nazi Party in 1931. From 1933 to 1935, he served in the Police Administration. After leaving his post in Recklinghausen he was appointed Regierungspräsident in Münster. In 1942, he was appointed Generalkommissar Zitomir in Reichskommissariat Ukraine.

KNICKMANN Heinrich August

Born 25 September 1894 in Horstermark.

He served in the Great War where he was wounded twice. Left the army as Leutnant. Trained in community welfare, he worked in the town administration in Buer. A member of the SA from 1923, he rose to the rank of Gruppenführer. He commanded the SA-Gruppe in Niederrhein from July 1934 to August 1941. He served in Police Administration from 1933 to 1937. He was Member of the Reichstag in 1932 and 1933. He served in the army during the war and was killed in action 5 August 1941.

KNOFE Oskar

Born 14 May 1888 in Pirna (Elbe).

Trained as an Officer. He served in the flying service as a pilot during the Great War. He left army in 1920 and joined the Landespolizei. In 1933, he joined the Police Administration serving until 1937 when transferred to the Schutzpolizei where he served throughout the war. He rose to the rank of Generalmajor with effect from 1 December 1941. He was member of the SS from April 1939 rising to the rank of Brigadeführer with effect from 9 November 1941.
Died in Percha on 3 November 1978.

KOB Adolf

Born 7 June 1885 in Prague.

He joined the Royal Saxon army in 1906 and served in the Great War as a staff officer and artillery commander. Left the army as Major and joined the Sächsische Landspolizei serving until 1923. Then he worked in industry. Member of the Party from 1930, he joined the SA the following year and rose to the rank of Obergruppenführer with effect from 9 November 1937.He commanded the SA-Obergruppe IV from 20 February 1933 to July 1933 and then he led the SA-Obergruppe I until 30 January 1934. He also led the SA-Gruppe Ostland from the 15 September 1933 to 30 January 1934. He was Member of the Reichstag from 1933. He joined the Police Administration in November 1933 and served until January 1934. Then he served as Inspecteur East in OSAF. On July 1934, he moved to the head of SA-Gruppe Mitte and later SA-Gruppe Neckar. In 1944, he took over the post of Inspecteur der SA-Kavallerie.

KOHLER Dr. Johannes

He was trained civil servant. He served in the Police Administration in Österreich in 1938/39 and then in 1940 he moved to Germany. Formerly a Polizeirat in 1938, he rose to the status of Police President in 1944.

KORRENG August

Born 1 May 1878 in Trier (Rhine Palatinate).

He studied criminal law. In 1907, he entered in Police Administration. He served in the army during the Great War. Then he returned to Police duties. He was arrested by the French and spent two years in prison from 1923 to 1925 for political crimes. He was dismissed in 1930 for political reasons. He joined the Party in 1931. A member of the SS from November 1931, he rose to the rank of Brigadeführer with effect from 1 January 1942. In 1933, he returned to the Police Administration, remaining until the end of the war. During 1938/1939, he led the Gestapo Office in Düsseldorf. He was awarded the Knight's Cross of the War Service Cross 25 February 1945 for his service to the city of Düsseldorf. He committed suicide in Plettenberg on 7 June 1945.

KOTTEK Dr. Alfred

Born 23 March 1906 in Znaim (Österreich).

He attended university where he studied law and graduated as a Doctor in Law. He was an active member of the Sudetendeutsche Partei which campaigned for the incorporation of the Sudenteland into the German Reich. He served as a Kreisleiter from 1934 until 1938. He worked as a Lawyer in Iglau and then in 1936 moved to Znaim. After the German takeover, he was appointed Landrat for the Znaim district. From April 1940, he ran that post concurrently with the local Police Administration post, remaining until the end of the war. He was member of Reichstag from 1938. He became member of the SS on January 1939 with the rank of Sturmbannführer.

KRAHNE Heinz

Served in the Great War. Joined the SA and rose to the rank of Brigadeführer. Posted to Police Administration on 18 January 1944 and he remained in this field until the end of the war.

KRAUSS Hans

He was a trained civil servant. In 1937, he was appointed to Police Administration duties. He returned to town administration duties as Mayor of Karlsbad. Then in 1940 he took over a Police Administration in Sudetenland, serving until 1942.

KRIEG Paul

Born 29 July 1901 in Berlin-Charlottenburg.

After service in a Freikorps units unit which fought against the Spartakists, he worked as a motor-car salesman. He served in Frontbann Nord under Kurt Daluege orders 1924 to 1926. He was member of the SA from 1926 to 1931 then transferred to the SS 1 September 1931. After service in Allgemeine-SS motor units, he joined the Police Administration March 1935 being appointed Polizeikommissar for Wittenberg on 1 December 1935. He remained in that post when it was elevated from Communal Police to Reich Police with status of a Police Director. He was promoted Hauptmann der SCHUPO on 20 April 1937 and rose to the rank of Oberstleutnant with effect from 1 September 1942. He rose to the SS-rank of Standartenführer with effect from 30 January 1942. He served as SS and Polizeistandortführer in Vilna (Lithuania) from 1941 until 18 April 1944 and then returned to Wittenberg.

KRUMHAAR Bruno

Born 21 August 1885 in Neubrück on the River Spree.

He joined the Imperial Navy and served in the Great War. After the war he joined the Schutzpolizei where he rose to the rank of Generalmajor with effect from 1 July 1942. He was member of the SS from 20 April 1939 and rose to the rank of Brigadeführer with effect from 9 November 1942. He took over Police Administration duties from 1939 to 1943. Then he served as Inspector of the Waterways Police. Died as a Russian prisoner on 27 September 1945.

KUSCHOW Otto

Born 31 December 1880 in Zwenzow (Mecklenburg).

He served in the Great War. In 1920 he joined the Landespolizei in Thüringen and then the Schutzpolizei. He rose to the rank of Generalmajor with effect from 21 June 1944. He was the first deputy Inspector of the Ordnungspolizei in Kassel and commanded the Schutzpolizei in Nürnberg from December 1938. He was member of the SS from July 1942 rising to the rank of Brigadeführer with effect from 21 June 1944. He joined the Police Administration in June 1943 serving until the end of the war. He was killed leading a Kampfgruppe in Nürnberg 20 April 1945.

KUTSCHERA Franz

Born 22 February 1904 in Oberwaltersdorf in Wien (Österreich).

He served briefly in the Austrian Navy in 1918 and then worked as a gardener. He was member of the SS in Österreich from 1 November 1931 and he was active in the movement to return Österreich to the Reich which led to terms of imprisonment. He served first as Deputy Gauleiter for Kärnten from March 1936 to February 1938 and then took over the Gauleiter post. After one month he was reduced to the deputy again and served until November 1941. He succeeded the Gauleiter who had died in February 1939 and ran the two posts concurrently until he was dismissed for scheming with the Higher SS and Police leader Alfred Rodenbücher to cause the break up of Gau Salzburg. He took up full time SS and Police duties in Russia and served as SS and Police leader in Mogilew and then in Warsaw. He was promoted SS-Brigadeführer on 9 November 1940. He was killed by Polish Partisans at 9.10 am on 1 February 1944 whilst driving to his office.

LANGE Dr. Rudolf Erwin

Born 18 April 1910 in Weisswasser Kreis Rothenberg.

He was trained as a lawyer and served in the Gestapo. He was member of the SS from 30 September 1937 and rose to the rank of Standartenführer with effect from 30 January 1945. He headed the Gestapo office in Stuttgart to July 1939, in Weimar until early 1940 and in Erfurt to July 1940. He commanded a section in Einsatzgruppe A, serving in the Baltic States, from June to December 1941 and then he commanded Einsatzkommando 2 in Einsatzgruppe A until

April 1943. He commanded the Security Police and SD in Latvia from December 1941 to January 1945. He represented the Inspector of Security Police and SD for the Baltic States Dr. Walter Stahlecker at the Gross-Wannsee Conference in Berlin 20 January 1942 which decided the ultimate fate of the Jews. He took over Administrative Police duties in the last months of the war.

LANGE Dr.

He should not be confused with Dr. Rudolf Lange who served in Latvia. This man studied law at university and graduated with a Doctorate. He was appointed Rechtsanwalt (attorney) in May 1940 serving in Troppau. He took over the Police Administration post follwing Johann Baur and stayed until the next permanent candidate could be found.

LANGOSCH Georg Robert Heinrich

Born 29 July 1902 in Rostock.

Trained as a lawyer he worked in Kiel, Flensburg and Altona. He joined the civil service in the Hanseatic state of Hamburg in 1936 and rose to Regierungsdirektor rank in January 1943. He was member of the SS from 25 June 1933 and rose to the rank of Oberführer with effect from 30 January 1944. In 1941, he served as a specialist in the Waffen-SS. He transferred to the Police Administration in November 1943 until the end of the war.

LAUE Theodor Louis Heinrich

Born 1 March 1893 in Bremen.

Served in the Great War and then went into business. From 1934, he became member of the Senate of the Hanseatic state of Bremen. He served in the SA from 1 July 1931 to November 1933. He was appointed as head of Police Administration for the city of Bremen from 1934 to 1936. Then he returned to the businessworld. He was member of the SS from June 1935 and rose to the rank of Oberführer with effect from 9 November 1943. During the war he served in the army.

LEFFLER Paul

Born 1 December 1890 in Braunschweig.

He served in the Imperial Navy from April 1910. During the Great War he served as an observer in a Naval flying detachment. Graduated as an engineer in hydraulics, he worked in that field until 1932. Member of the SS since November 1931 he rose to the rank of Oberführer with effect from 20 April 1939. He served in the Party Security Service from 1932 as Heydrich's Adjutant. In 1935 he became an active member of the Allgemeine-SS. He was appointed to the Police Administration from September 1939 and remained in that field until the end of the war. He was dismissed from the post in Reichenberg after he feuded with Konrad Henlein, however according to Ernst Hitzegrad, Leffler was found drunk during an air raid on Reichenberg and that is why he was dismissed. He was then transferred to staff of HSSPF West. He served as town councillor in Wolfsburg after the war.

LEGNER Karl

Born 3 October 1894.

Former officer in SCHUPO staff in Dresden, he was ranked Major in 1940. He was member of the Allgemeine-SS and rose to the rank of Sturmbannführer with effect from 1 September 1940. In 1940, he was appointed to Police Administration and served until the end on the war. In 1941, his office was upgraded to Police Direction status.

LEVETZOW Magnus von

Born 8 January 1871 in Flensburg.

Trained as a navy cadet. He served in the Imperial Navy, during the Great War, he was a senior staff officer. He retired with rank of Rear Admiral. He was member of the Reichstag from 1932. In 1933 he was appointed Police President of Berlin until April 1936. He died in Berlin 13 March 1939.

LICHEM Dr. Walter von

Graduated from university as a Doctor in law. He was an Austrian civil servant in the Police Administration holding the rank of Oberpolizeirat. After the Anschluss, he moved to German Police Administration and was promoted Regierungsrat. He took over a Police Administration in June 1940 until the end of the war.

LEISE August Georg

Born 28 November 1876 in Soest.

After schooling he became a civil servant in the district office in Soest. Served in the army 1 October 1894 to 1920 as a military clerk. Transferred to the Police service in Hamm 1 February 1907 as Polizeisekretär Commissioned Leutnant der Landwehr 11 February 1916. After leaving the army he returned to Hamm as Stadtobersekretär in May 1920. Appointed Instructer in the Administration Officials School in Hamm March 1926. He remained in the Police service in Hamm until the end of the war. He was a member of the SA and was a sponsoring member of the SS.
Captured by the Americans he died in hospital in Villers-Helon near Soissons in France 21 July 1945.

LIEFF Johannes

Born in 9 May 1879 in Braunschweig.

Studied law and practiced as a lawyer. He joined civil service in 1901 and was ranked Regierungsrat from 1916. He served in the Braunschweig Interior Ministry from 1924 until 1927. In April 1934, he was appointed Kreisdirektor (District director). From November 1931, he was appointed to Police Administration. After leaving the Police Presidency in 1938, he was appointed President of the Braunschweig Administrative Court.

LINGENS Walter

Born 4 March 1882 in Aachen.

Attended the Kriegsschule in Hannover and served in the army until 1920. As an artillery officer he rose to the rank of Major. He joined the customs service in July 1920 and in April 1921 was transferred to the SCHUPO. As Major der Schutzpolizei he served in the Oberpräsidium in Hannover and was then appointed Führer der Bereitschaftabteilung Aachen and finally Kommandeur der SCHUPO in Aachen. He was then transferred to the Prussian Ministry of the Interior as Organisation Referent for the SCHUPO. Promoted Oberstleutnant, Oberst and finally Polizeikommandeur (the equivalent of Major-General). On July 1936, he was appointed to Police Administration. After leaving the post in Cologne on 1936, he moved to the Reichsluftschutzbund as Führer der Landesgruppe XIII Rheinland-Westfalen.
Died on 3 March 1940.

LOEFFEL Rudolf Albert

Born 6 July 1887 in Mannheim.

Joined the army October 1908 as a cadet and served until September 1919. He joined the Schutzpolizei in 1919 and served in Stettin until 1924 when he retired. Studied criminal law and Police Administration and joined the Prussian Administration Police in March 1933. He was member of the SA from on March 1930 and rose to the rank of Sturmbannführer. He headed the Gestapo office in Lüneburg until his move to Harburg in September 1935. He was transferred to Weisenfels on 1 February 1937. Transferred to the SS as Sturmbannführer on 15 March 1935 and rose to the rank of Standartenführer with effect from 1 August 1940. Due to conflict with HSSPF Dresden, he retired in April 1942.

LÖSER Fritz

Born 23 January 1893 in Gross-Auheim.

Served in the Great War in the Infantry as Gefreiter der Reserve. He was a prisoner of war June 1917 to October 1919. Worked in industry for the Dunlop company in Hanau from 1919. Joined the Party on 1 December 1930. Kreisleiter des Kreis Hanau June 1932 to 1 September 1937. Landrat des Kreises Hanau 15 June 1933 to May 1945. Died in Hanau 3 May 1973.

LÖW Hans

Born 6 January 1883 in Nürnberg (Franken).

A graduate in civil administration matters, he became a civil servant in 1902. He served in the Royal Bayern army during the Great War. He returned to the civil service and moved to Police Administration in Fürth. Ranked Polizeirat in 1939. He was member of the SS from 1 July 1933 and rose to the rank of Obersturmbannführer with effect from 1 September 1942.

LUDIN Hanns

Born 10 June 1905 in Freiburg (Bade).

Served in the artillery from 1924 to 1930 when he resigned with the rank of Oberleutnant following a trial for political offences at which Hitler appeared as a witness. He was sentenced to eighteen months fortress-imprisonment. He joined the Party and the SA and rose to the rank of Obergruppenführer with effect from 9 November 1937. He served as Leader of SA-Gruppe South West until January 1941 when he was appointed Ambassador to Slovakia. He was hanged in Prague 9 December 1947.

LUDWIG Curt

Born 28 March 1902 in Aschara in Gotha.

Studied at an Agricultural college and then worked in farming. Served as an agricultural official in Gau Thüringen. He was member of the SS from 1 April 1929 and rose to the rank of Brigadeführer with effect from 20 April 1945. From 1935 to 1943 he took over command of Allgemeine-SS districts in Kassel then Bremen. He served in Police Administration from 1938 until 20 November 1941 when he was dismissed from the post in Bremen for excessive drinking. He served for the remainder of the war in the Waffen-SS achieving the rank of Hauptsturmführer der Reserve with effect from 30 January 1945. He died in Bremen 2 April 1989.

LUDWIG

He was a trained civil servant of the Land Thüringen. He held rank Regierungsrat when he was appointed to Police Administration in 1934. He was promoted Oberregierungsrat in April 1939 and was transferred to the Interior Ministry in Thüringen. From November 1939 he moved in the Protectorate of Böhmen-Mähren as Oberlandrat at Budweis.

LUTTER Martin

Born 1885.

He was a Prussian civil servant who served as Regierungsrat in the Police Administration in Bad Nauheim. He served in the SA being promoted SA-Standartenführer on 9 November 1934. Führer SA-Standarte 116. Promoted SA-Oberführer on 30 January 1940. He took over the post Giessen in 1940. This post covered the Police posts in Bad Nauheim and Friedberg. He was killed in action as Hauptmann and Engineer Battalions Commander on 8 March 1943.

LUTZE Viktor

Born 28 December 1890 in Bevergen near Münster.

He worked for the postal service until 1914 when he joined the army and served through the Great War. He was active member of the SA from 1923. He commanded the SA-Gruppe Nordsee in 1932 in succession to Wilhelm Jahn. He commanded the SA-Obergruppe II from 1 September 1932 and the SA-Obergruppe VI from 20 February 1933. He was in this post when Hitler picked him to succeed the disgraced Ernst Röhm as Stabschef der SA on 1 July 1934. He died in a car crash 1 July 1943.

MÄHLICH Georg

Born 27 June 1880 in Steinau.

He was the son of Regierungsrat Ernst Mählich. Attended a Gymnasium in Fraustadt and then studied law. Joined the army 1905 as a one year volunteer. Served in 2 Silesien Grenadier Regiment "King Friedrich III" Nr 11, 1905 to 1906. Commissioned Leutnant der Reserve 1908. Joined the Police in Berlin as Polizei-Offizier-Anwärter 1 February 1909. Commissioned Leutnant der Schutzpolizei 1 October 1910. He left the army as Hauptmann der Reserve a.D. 1911. Recalled to the army in the Infanterie-Regiment Nr 141 2 August 1914 He was wounded and was captured by the Russians 20 August 1914. He was released 23 April 1921. Awarded the Iron Cross 1 and 2nd Class and the Wound Badge in Black. Returned to the Schutzpolizei 1921 beim Polizei-Luftüberwachungsabteilung Holstenau Promoted Major der SCHUPO 20 June 1921. Schutzpolizei Abschnittskommandeur in Kiel anmd then in Schleswig. Posted to the Osnabrück district 15 January 1925, Kommmandeur der Schutzplizei Osnabrück 1 April 1929–31 March 1931. Inspektions-Kommandeur in Dortmund 1 April 1931–14 March 1933 mit der Führung der Polizeidirektion Hamm 15 March 1933–25 March 1933 Kommissarischer der Verwaltung der Polizeidirektorenstelle in Hamm 25 March 1933–20 September 1934. Polizeidirektor hamm 20 April 1934–3 December 1938 MWGB der Orts- und Kreispolizei in Karlsbad 3 December 1938–21 March 1941. Polizeipräsident Waldenburg und Leiter der Staatsliche Kriminalpolizei Abteilung Waldenburg 21 March 1941–1945. He was member of the SA and rose to the rank of Standartenführer.

MAINZ Kurt

Born 9 March 1908 in Rotenburg/Fulda.

He studied law. He was member of the Party and Hitler Youth from 1932 then moved into SA in 1933. In 1937, he joined the SS and the Security Service (SD) rising to the rank of Sturmbannführer with effect from 20 April 1940. He was a civil servant in the Police Administration from 1930's. He was promoted Regierungsrat in 1939 then took over the Police Directorate duties from 1939. He served in the army as Leutnant der Reserve.

MALLEBREIN

Born 29 November 1907.

He was a trained civil servant in Land Baden. He rose to the rank of Regierungsrat in January 1938. In 1942, he was appointed to Police Administration duties. He was also member of the SA and held the rank of Sturmführer.

MALSEN-PONICKAU Johann-Erasmus Freiherr von

Born 5 June 1895 in München (Bayern).

He came from a military family and joined the army. He served until 1919 and then ran the family estate in Schwaben. He was an active member of the Allgemeine-SS from November 1930 rising to the rank of Brigadeführer with effect from 15 August 1933. He led SS-Districts in München and Stuttgart. He was appointed to Police Administration duties from April 1933 and ended the war as SS and Police leader on the Adriatic Coast. A snob who tried to avoid the 'vulgar' company of his comrades, his career is peppered with complaints and reprimands from Himmler. Died on 12 June 1956.

MANGER Heinz

Born 18 August 1897 in Kassel.

He served in the army airship corps during the Great War. Then he worked as an electrical engineer. He was member of the SS from March 1933 and rose to the rank of Oberführer with effect from 30 January 1943. He served in the SS-communications sector. In 1940 he joined the Signal Corps of the Waffen-SS. Then in April 1942, he was transferred to the Police Administration. He died in Hammersbach 21 July 1977.

MARKET Dr. Richard

He was a local politician and was Mayor of Bremen at this time.

MARTIN Dr. Benno

Born 12 February 1893 in Kaiserslautern (Palatinate).

He served in the Bayern army during the Great War. Then he joined the Landespolizei serving from 1920 to 1923. He also achieved a doctorate in law from the University of Erlangen. He wrote the standard police training manual which was used in Bayern police training schools. He was appointed to Police Administration duties from 1923 in Nürnberg and took over as its head in 1933 remaining until December 1942. He was member of the SS from 10 April 1934 and rose to the rank of Obergruppenführer with effect from 1 August 1944. From December 1942 he served as Higher SS and Police leader for Sudetengau, Thüringen and Württemberg in Wehrkreis XIII. He was a very able man who was able to manoeuvre his way through the intricate Party politics in Nürnberg and he remained a power in the city until the end of the war. Tried five times after the war he was found not guilty in every case. Died on 2 July 1975.

MAYR Franz

Born 28 September 1890 in Burgheim.

He served in the Great War. Gradudated as a Doctor in Law, he worked as an attorney. He was member of the SA and rose to the rank of Brigadeführer with effect from 30 January 1942. He joined the Police Administration in 1936 with rank of Regierungsrat. He rose to the rank of Regierungsdirektor in August 1941. He took over Police Administration in München in 1941. From 1943, he became District President of München serving until the end of the war.

MEINECKE Heinrich

He was a state civil servant. He served in the Prussian then the Reich Ministery of Interior. From 1936, he served in the Police Headquarters (Hauptamt ORPO). He was promoted Regierungsrat in 1935, Oberregierungsrat in 1937 then Ministerialrat in 1940. He had been head of Group I in the Hauptbüro of Hauptamt Ordnungspolizei from June 1936 to November 1943. Then he was transferred to Police Administration duties.

MELCHER Dr. Kurt

Born 8 July 1881 in Dortmund.

He graduated as a Doctorate in Law. He was a Prussian civil servant. He served as Police President from 1919 in Essen then Berlin. After leaving the Police Presidency in Berlin he was appointed Oberpräsident in Magdeburg then retired in 1934.

MEMMINGER Albert

Born 24 March 1888 at Wildberg.

He served in the Great War. He joined the Schutzpolizei in 1918. Became a supporter of the Party although he did not join until the late 1930's. Early in 1934 he was responsible for raising the Nazi flag over the Police barracks at Reutlingen and, as a result he was dismissed by the Police Director Karl Sinn. He was member of the SS from 1933 and rose to the of Obersturmbannführer 9 November 1942. He was reinstated in the Police Administration from 1934 and remained until the end of the war.

MERLER Dr.

He was a Sudeten German. He graduated with a Doctorate in Law. He was a trained civil servant in Austrian Police Administration and rose to the rank of Oberpolizeirat. Appointed to the Protectorate Böhmen-Mähren, he served in the staff of the Oberlandrat for Mährisch-Ostrau. He was promoted Oberregierungsrat in February 1940 and was given the Police Administration post in succession to a Dr. Bucher who was not a supporter of the German administration. Merler was posted to a Ministry in Prague in 1944. He was put on trial in at the end of the war. He was sentenced to death and hanged in Prague in 1946.

METZ Wilhelm

Born in Gleiwitz 29 October 1893.

Served in the Great War and then in the Froniter force in Oberschlesien.

He joined SCHUPO in 1920 and served in Abstimmungspolizei and then he served in Gleiwitz. Retired as Haupt mann der Schutzpolizei. Joined the Party and the SA in 1930. Promoted SA-Standartenführer 20 January 1932. Führer SA-Standarte 22 20 January 1932–14 September 1933. Mit der Kommissarischer Verwaltung der Polizeidirektorenstelle in Oppeln 25 March 1933–1 April 1933. Polizeipräsident von Oppeln 1 April 1933–November 1933. SA Führer z.b.V. der SA-Brigade 17 "Oberschlesien" 15 September 1933–1 May 1935. MdF SA-Brigade 17 1934–1 May 1935. Promoted SA-Oberführer 9 November 1934. Returned to Police Administration duties 1 May 1935. Polizeverwalter in Troppau October 1938–1939. Mit der Aufbau der Polizei in Oberschlesien und in Dombrauer Kohlengebiet 1939. Polizeipräsident Kattowitz from 1940. Promoted SA-Brigadeführer 9 November 1942 with senority from 30 January 1942. Died in Kattowitz 31 March 1943.

MEUSEL

He joined Schutzpolizei and rose to the rank of Oberstleutnant. He was appointed to Police Administration duties in 1935. After leaving the Police Administration in 1942, he became the city Mayor.

MEYER Fritz

Born 26 April 1900 in Gitter Kreis Goslar.

Trained as a tobacco importer. He served in the army for six months in 1918. Returned to tobacco importing from 1919 until 1931. He was member of the SS from 1 July 1930 and rose to the rank of Standartenführer with effect from 20 April 1934. He was a full time paid leader in Allgemeine-SS until 1939 then he joined the Police Administration and reverted to honourary status in the Allgemeine-SS. He was brought before a Peoples Court late in 1943 for uttering defeatist talk. Sentenced to three years in prison the sentence was suspended providing he served in the Waffen-SS. He was demoted to the rank of SS-Mann.

MEYER-QUADE Joachim

Born 22 November 1897 in Düsseldorf. (Rhein).

He served in the Great War where he was captured by the French on the Somme in 1915. He returned home in February 1920. He worked in agriculture then the agricultural press from 1920 to 1930. He was member of the SA from 1927 rising to the rank of Obergruppenführer. He was member of the Reichstag from 1930 to 1932 then from 1933 till the end. He commanded the SA-Gruppe Nordmark from 31 January 1934. In 1933, he was Landrat in Schleswig. He was appointed to Police Administration duties from 1934 remaining until 1938. He also served as Chief of the Gestapo Office in Kiel. He served in the army and was killed in action 12 September 1939.

MÖLLER Hinrich

Born 20 April 1906 in Grevenkop.

He had various jobs after leaving school, he also served in the army for two months in 1924. He served in the Schutzpolizei from 1930 to 1934. Active member of the SS from October 1930, he rose to the rank of Brigadeführer with effect from 30 January 1944. He was appointed to Police Administration in 1937. During 1940, he joined the Recruiting Office of the Waffen-SS. After leaving Police Administration in 1941, he joined the SS and Police service in East. He remained in that field until the end of the war. He died in Kiel in 1974.

MONTUA Max

Born 18 May 1886 in Prust Kreis Schwetz (Westpreussen).

Trained as an agriculturalist. He served in the army during the Great War. After the war, he joined the Schutzpolizei in 1919 and rose to the rank of Generalmajor with effect from 1 September 1943. During the war, he served in occupied Poland and the Protectorate of Böhmen-Mähren. Retired from the Schutzpolizei mid 1944 and served in the Police Administration until the end of the war. He joined the Party 4 May 1933 and the SS 9 November 1941 achieving the rank of Brigadeführer on 27 September 1943. He committed suicide in Dahme on 20 April 1945.

MÜLLER Dr. Helmut

Born 18 December 1906 in Danzig.

Graduated as a Doctorate in Law. He served as a legal official in the Oberlandgericht in Kassel from 1930. Moved to the Police Administration in Danzig July 1934. He was member of the SS from 1 October 1934 and rose to the rank of Obersturmbannführer with effect from 30 January 1940. He was mobilized in the flak arm of the Waffen-SS in 1940/1941 then took over duties in Police Administration. Returned to Waffen-SS in 1944.

MÜLLER Karl

Born 18 December 1906.

He was a Bayern civil servant who rose to the rank of Oberregierungsrat. He served as Landrat for the District of Kaiserslautern from 1 March 1920. In 1934, he undertook temporary duties in Police Administration. He ran the Police Directorate again in 1943 on behalf of the incumbant who was on duty with the Wehrmacht.

NEUBAUR Heinrich

Born 30 April 1889.

He was a law graduate. During the Great War, he served in the Flying Service. Then he worked as a Prussian civil servant. In 1925, as Regierungsrat he served in Departments 1 and 3 in the district Police Administration in Koblenz. An early member of the Party, he was active in Gau Koblenz Trier. After 1933, he took over as head of various Police Administrations. From 1937, he moved to the Münster District Administration.

NEUMEYER Ernst

Born 4 May 1901.

He was an early member of the SA and rose to the rank of Standartenführer. He was appointed temporary Polizeikommissar of the Gemeindepolizei in Cleve on the 1 June 1934 and was confirmed in that post on the 1 December 1934. He joined Schutzpolizei and rose to the rank of Major. He was appointed Commander of the Schutzpolizei in Luxemburg in 1940 and became temporary Police Director in 1941. After leaving the Police Administration, he returned to Schutzpolizei duties and commanded a Motorized Gendarmerie company in Potsdam. He later commanded Police Battalion 9 under the KdO in Esseg. He was transferred to the SS and rose to the rank of Standartenführer on 1 July 1940.

NEUSCHWANDER Albert

He served in the Great War and after leaving the army he joined the Schutzpolizei rising to the rank of Oberinspekteur. He served as temporary head of the Police Administration in Altenburg in 1942.

ZUR NIEDEN Dr. Franz

Trained as a lawyer, he worked as a Prussian civil servant. Landrat for Seestemunde, he took over Police Administration of Wesermünde in 1931. In 1933/34, he also headed the Gestapo Office in Wesermünde. After Police Administration was disbanded he was reinstated as Landrat for Wesermünde on the 22 March 1934. He retired in 1938.

NIEDERHOFF Friedrich Carl

Born 27 August 1884 in Mülheim (Ruhr).

Passed his Abitur and joined the army 1904. He served in the Great War in the infantry rising to the rank of Hauptmann. Served in Freikorps units after the war and from 1921 to 1925 he fought against the French occupation of the Ruhr. A member of the Stahlhelm, he later became a Landesführer. He joined the SA and commanded the SA-Gruppe Niederrhein. He rose to the rank of Gruppenführer. In 1933, he was appointed to Police Administration duties. He retired in 1937.

NIELAND Dr. Hans Heinrich

Born 3 October 1900 in Hagen (Westfalen).

Served in the artillery in 1918 and then studied political science. Graduated as a Doctor in Law 1922. He passed his legal exams in 1928 then worked as a legal official in Hamburg. He joined the Party in 1926 and held a number of senior posts in the Gau Party organization. From 1931 to 1933, he headed the Foreign Department of the Party in Berlin. Then he returned to Hamburg and took up the Police Administration. From 1934 he served as Senator for Finance in the Hamburg Hanseatic State government. He was elected to the Reichstag from 1930 to 1933. He joined the SS on 15 January 1934 and rose to the rank of Brigadeführer with effect from 30 January 1939. He served as Mayor of Dresden from 1940. Died in Reinbeck 29 August 1973.

NUTZHORN Dr. Gustav

Born 8 August 1886 in Oldenburg.

Achieved a Doctorate in Philosophy in 1912. He served in the Great War, then he worked in education. From 1933, he headed town administration of Rüstringen and reached the status of Oberbürgermeister. In 1933, he was also chief of the Gestapo office in Rüstringen. In 1939, he joined the Police Administration in Sudetenland. He was member of the Allgemeine-SS from 1935 and rose to the rank of Standartenführer with effect from 1 April 1941. Died in Bad Zwischenahn 29 June 1981.

OBERG Carl Albrecht

Born 27 January 1887 in Hamburg.

He served in the artillery during the Great War. Then he worked in the Banana import industry. He was member of the SS from 7 April 1932 and the Security Service of the SS (SD) from 15 May 1933. He left the SD on the 1 October 1935 after differences with Heydrich and served in the Allgemeine-SS. He was posted to Police Administration duties in 1938. In 1941, he was transferred to SS and Police duties in Poland and in May 1942 he was selected to become the Higher SS and Police leader in Paris. He was promoted Obergruppenführer 1 August 1944. He spent nine years in a French prison from 1954 to 1965. He died in Flensburg on 3 June 1965.

OBERHAIDACHER Walther

Born 22 September 1896 in Bozen (Südtirol).

He served in the Austrian army during the Great War. He worked in engineering in Graz. Member of the Party from 10 September 1926, he rose to the post of Gauleiter for Steiermark. He was imprisoned for political crimes and escaped to Germany in 1934. Member of the Reichstag from 1936. He was appointed to Police Administration duties from 1938 and in this capacity was given the honorary rank of Generalmajor der Polizei in 1944. He joined the SS from 30 January 1938 rising to the rank of Brigadeführer with effect from 9 November 1938. He was killed in action in Dresden 30 April 1945.

OBERNITZ Hanns-Günther von

Born 5 May 1899 in Düsseldorf (Ruhr)

He served in the Great War and then he studied agriculture and passed his agricultural exams. He worked as a landowner running an estate. He was member of the SA from 5 August 1929 and rose to the rank of Obergruppenführer with effect from 9 November 1937. He led SA in München then Schlesien and from March 1933 commanded SA-Gruppe Franken. He joined the Luftwaffe during the war and was killed in action January 1944 as commander of the Luftwaffe-Jäger-Regiment 24.

OLDENBURG Helmut

Born 5 November 1892.

He served in the Great war and later joined the National Socialist Motor Corps (NSKK) rising to the rank of Gruppenführer. He commanded the NSKK Motor Gruppe Hochland during the war.

ORTLEPP Walter

Born 9 July 1900 in Gotha (Thüringen).

He served in the army from June to November 1918 and then he studied law at the Universities of Jena and Güttingen. Graduated in 1922. He worked in the Land Court of Weimar until June 1930. He was member of the Party from 1923 and became Aide de Camp of Gausturm Thüringen in 1929. In 1930, the Nazi Minister of Interior Dr. Wilhelm Frick, appointed him as Chief of the Criminal Police of the Police in Weimar. He took over Police Administration duties in 1932. He was member of the Reichstag from 1933. After leaving the police post in 1936, he was appointed head of the Thüringen Interior Ministry and was given the rank of State Secretary by Hitler personally. He joined the SS on 4 September 1931 and rose to the rank of Brigadeführer with effect from 20 April 1937. He also served as Landesführer for the German Red Cross in Thüringen. He died in Aschaffenburg 23 October 1971.

PALTEN Dr. Günther

Born 3 March 1903 in Schnellewalde (Obershlesien).

His family name was Patschowsky until 1938. Graduated as a Doctorate in Law on March 1925. He worked as a lawyer in Breslau until 1937. He was member of the SS from 4 April 1932 and joined the SD on 15 September 1932. He rose to the rank of Brigadeführer with effect from 21 June 1944. He was member of the Gestapo from 1933 and became a senior official in the Gestapo Headquarters in Berlin until December 1937. Transferred to Police Administration in December 1937. He was promoted District President in Bromberg in November 1939. He moved to Linz in February 1940 and remained there until the end of the war. Died as a Polish prisoner 17 May 1945.

PETSCH Joachim

Born 14 February 1891 in Berlin.

He served in the Great War and was commissioned Leutnant 2 September 1915. He joined the Schutzpolizei in 1920 and was promoted Oberleutnant 13 July 192. He was promoted Hauptmann 1 April 1926, Major 1 April 1935, Oberstleutnant 1 August 1940 and Oberst 1 February 1944 with effect from 20 April 1944. He commanded the Schutzpolizei in Kassel in 1936 then Lübeck from August 1938. During the war he commanded Polizei-Regiments in Poland. He was member of the SS from 20 April 1941 and rose to the rank of Standartenführer with effect from 20 April 1944. When the Police President was posted to SS and Police duties, Petsch took over the Police Administration in Lübeck until Walter Schroeder returned at the end of 1944. He joined the Party 1 May 1933.

PFEFFER von SALOMON Franz

Born 19 February 1888 in Düsseldorf (Ruhr).

He studied law briefly then became a professional soldier. He served in the Great War in combat and staff positions ending the war with the rank of Hauptmann. He then formed a Freikorps unit, units which served in the Ruhr, Baden and in the Baltic states. He became a Gau leader in the Völkisch Social Block and led this Gau into the NSDAP in 1925. He was appointed Oberste SA-Führer 1 November 1926 and resigned in 1930. He remained in the SA as Chief of Staff of the General Inspector of the SA and SS until April 1933. He was then transferred to the 'at disposal' list. Member of the Reichstag from 1932. He took over the Police Administration duties in 1933 and also headed the local Gestapo office. In 1936, he was promoted District President in Wiesbaden. He fell from favour in 1941 and in November of that year was expelled from the Party and the SA and he was twice arested. Later released, he ended the war as commander of a Volksturm Division. Died on 12 April 1968 at München.

PFISTERER Dr. Erhard

Born 16 December 1906 in Stuttgart (Württemberg).

Graduated as a lawyer in 1929. Served in the Police Administration from 1934 until 1938 and then in the Land Administration of Württemberg. He served in civil administration in Poland from 1939. Then he took over Police Administration in Friedrichshafen. He served in the army until he was wounded in October 1941. In 1943, he was transferred to the civil administration in Rottweil. Member of the Party from 1 May 1937. He was in the SA from 1933 to 1936 then he transferred into the NSKK.

PFLOMM Karl

Born 31 July 1886 in Reutlingen (Württemberg).

He attended school in Pittsburg USA for two years and then trained as a glass and ceramics cutter and polisher. He served in the Great War then returned to his trade. Member of the SS from 17 August 1930, he rose to the rank of Brigadeführer with effect from 20 April 1936. He undertook active SS duties from 1933 to 1936. He was appointed to Police Administration duties in April 1936 and remained in that field until the end of the war. He suffered serious head injuries in a car crash in November 1931. Whilst in Dresden he fought against incursions by the security police under Georg Klein, which he claimed were eroding his own authority. He lost the battle and was retired in November 1944. He committed suicide in Dresden 15 February 1945.

PLAKOLM Dr. Josef

Born 22 July 1889 in Gallneukirchen (Oberösterreich).

He served in the Austrian army during the Great War. He graduated as a Doctor in Law and served in the legal department of the Linz City Administration from 1923. From 1934 he provided legal advice for Party members. He was member of the SS from July 1936 and rose to the rank of Brigadeführer with effect from 9 November 1944. He transferred to Police Administration from March 1938. He died in Salzburg 24 December 1956.

PLESCH Hans

Born 26 February 1905 in Wilhelmshaven.

He attended university and graduated as a solicitor. He worked for the court in Oldenburg in 1933. He was member of the SS from 1 December 1930 and rose to the rank of Brigadeführer with effect from 30 January 1944. He gave up full time service in the SS to work in the motor industry in May 1937. He joined the army in February 1940 and was commissioned Leutnant der Reserve. He commanded a company in Infantry Regiment 6 until February 1943. Wounded April 1942, he was invalided out in February 1943. He was awarded the Knight's Cross of the Iron Cross 8 April 1942 for bravery in action. Appointed to Police Administration duties from April 1943. He died in Oldenburg 17 May 1985.

POHL Dr.

Graduated as a Doctor in Law on 29 April 1919. He was a trained civil servant. He was promoted Oberregierungsrat on the 1 October 1939 and served in the District of Troppau (Sudetenland). He was appointed to Police Administration in Olmütz whilst on the staff of the Oberlandrat. He moved to the staff of the District in Zichenau late in 1943 whilst remaining titular Police Director in Olmütz.

POPP Fritz

Born 30 June 1882 in Nürnberg (Franken).

He studied law in München and Erlangen, then served in civil administration at Nürnberg and Ansbach. Served in the Bayern army from August 1914 to December 1918. Left the army as Rittmeister der Reserve. He returned to the administration in Ansbach. He was member of the SA from 1933 to 1940. He joined the Party in 1935. He served in Police Administration duties from 1933 and was the first head of the Gestapo office in Regensburg in 1936. He transferred to the SS on 1 January 1940 as Obersturmbannführer. Died on 26 March 1955 at Würzburg.

PROECK Otto von

Born 12 August 1886 in Arys (Ostpreussen).

Served in the army from 1905. Transferred to the colonial forces in September 1912 and served in the Cameroons where he was arrested by the Spanish in March 1916. He was interned until November 1919. Served in the Schutzpolizei until 1923 as Major. Then went into business. He was a member of the staff of the Kyffhäuserbund, a veterans organisation from 1933 to 1939. He was member of the SS from 22 January 1935 and rose to the rank of Oberführer with effect from 20 April 1937. He was appointed to Police Administration from September 1939. He was court-martialed before an SS and Police Court in Kassel December 1943 charged with being absent from duty during an air raid on Kassel in the night of 22/23 October 1943. Matters were put into abeyance until after the war by order of the Reichsführer-SS 2 April 1944.

PRUCHTNOW Richard

Born 8 April 1892 in Berlin.

Served in the Great War and then worked in banking as a cashier and bookeeper. In August 1931 he joined the Finance Department of the city administration in Berlin. He was member of the SS from November 1931 and rose to the rank of Oberführer with effect from 30 January 1943. He also served in the SD as staff officer. He was conscripted in 1940. From 1941 to 1943, he served as Administrator of the Gestapo Headquarters in Berlin then transferred to Police Administration in Sudetenland in 1943. Died after a short illness on 22 June 1943.

QUINTENZ Eduard

Born 21 January 1888 in Gmünd.

Graduated as a lawyer. Joined the army but did not serve in the Great War due to illness. Served in the Württemberg Civil Administration. He served in Police Administration from 1923. He joined the Party 1 May 1933. He left the Police Direction Friedrichshafen in 1936 after a feud with the local Kreisleiter. He was appointed Landrat for Oberndorf then Tüttlingen (Württemberg) in 1938.

RAMSHORN Hans

Born 17 March 1892 in Mittenwalde-Nabelschwerdt.

He joined the Prussian army cadet corps in 1902 and was commissioned Leutnant in 1910. He served in the Great War. After the war served in a Freikorps unit. In 1920, he joined Sicherheitspolizei and rose to the rank of Hauptmann. Member of the Party and the SA, he rose to the rank of Brigadeführer by 1933. Führer SA-Untergruppe Oberschlesien from October 1932 to 1933 then Führer SA-Brigade Oberschlesien. Member of the Reichstag from 1932. In March 1933, he was appointed to Police Administration duties. He was arrested in the wake of the Röhm Purge of 30 June 1934 and was shot at Deutsch-Lissa 1 July 1934.

RAMSPERGER Dr. Hermann

Born 3 December 1892 in Konstanz (Württemberg).

He served in the infantry and the flying service during the Great War. Graduated as a Doctor in Law in 1924. Joined the Criminal police as a legal official in 1929. He commanded the Political Police in Baden from March 1933 until he was transferred to Police Administration in September 1933. He remained in this field until the end of the war. He served in occupied Poland from 1943. Member of the SS from 13 March 1933, he rose to the rank of Brigadeführer with effect from 1 January 1942. He died in Merseburg 17 January 1986.

RAPPARD Dr. von

He was a civil servant from 13 April 1917. As Regierungsrat he served in the Präsidialabteilung in the Schleswig District from 1931 until 1934. In 1934, he was appointed to Police Administration duties. He was promoted Regierungsdirektor 1 February 1935. After leaving the post in Weisenfels in 1936, he was transferred to the Oppeln District and then served as Verwaltungsreferent in the Wasserbaudirektion Kurmark. During the war, he served as Regierungsdirektor in the District Administration in Breslau.

REFARDT Heinrich

Born 10 February in Bachstedt (Thüringen).

Graduated as a lawyer August 1914. He served in the Great War then returned to civil administration duties after the war. He was appointed head of the traffic division of the Police Presidency in Düsseldorf in 1927. After leaving Duisburg. He was appointed temporary District President in Aurich and then, in 1937, District President of Frankfurt an der Oder.

REICH Otto

Born 5 December 1891 in Waldhausen (Ostpreussen).

He served in the Great War and joined the SS in 1931 rising to the rank of Oberführer with effect from 1 September 1941. One of the founder members of the Leibstandarte SS, he had a varied career in the Death Head units and the Waffen-SS. He had suffered a head wound during the Great War and this caused him personality problems which meant that he felt slighted and was quick to take offence throughout his career. In 1943 he took over Police Administration duties and then served in Ordnungspolizei until the end of the war. He died in Düsseldorf 20 September 1955.

REICHARDT Max

Born 30 May 1887.

He served in the Great War then he joined the Landespolizei. He rose to the rank of Major. In 1936, he was transferred to the Police Administration duties were he remained until the end of the war. He also held the rank of Oberleutnant der Reserve in the army.

RHEINS Maximilian

Born 14 April 1888 in Neuss (Rhineland).

Trained as an administrative jurist, he was appointed Gerichtsreferendar in March 1910. He rose through the civil service ranks reaching the rank of Regierungsdirektor with effect from 10 October 1928. Joined the Prussian Ministry of the Interior in December 1932. He was promoted Ministerialrat on 1 August 1933. Joined the ORPO Main Office in June 1936 as a department head and remained there until the reorganization of 1943. He was transferred to Police Administration duties in December 1943.

RICHTER Alfred

Born in Wismar 12 July 1895.

He served in the Great War ending as a company commander with the rank of Leutnant on the Reserve. In 1919 he became a founder member of the Minenwerfer-Sturmabteilung in Heuschkel and then served in the Garde-Kavellerie-Schützen-Korps a Freiwilligen unit. Left the Reichswehr 1 July 1920. Joined the SCHUPO in Hamburg 1 July 1920 and served until 30 September 1930. He was dismissed as Oberstleutnant on the 30 September 1930 for his political activities. He was a member of the Deutsche Schutz-und Trutzbund a right wing para military group. He was a member of the Landsmannschaft 'Hammonia' in the German Landsmannschaft. Joined the Party and the SA 1 September 1930. Promoted SA-Sturmbannführer 15 July 1931.

Member of the Hamburg Burgerschaft 27 Septmeber 1931–1933. Führer SA-Standarte 76 1 January 1932–31 May 1933. Promoted SA-Standartenführer 2 August 1932 with senority from 1 July 1932. On 5 March 1933, he was appointed the first Nazi Polizeiherr. He was instrumental in removing anti Nazi elements from the police in Hamburg. On the 11 March 1933 he became Senator for Inner Administration in Hamburg remaining in that post until 1937. SA-Führer z.V. SA-Gruppe Hansa 1 June 1933–30 June 1933. Promoted SA-Oberführer 20 April 1935. Gruppenreitersführers der SA-Gruppe Hansa 1 July 1936–1945. Promoted SA-Brigadeführer 9 November 1937. Appointed Generalluftschutzführer for Hamburg July 1939. Führer des Sportsgaus Hamburg 1 March 1942. Promoted SA-Gruppenführer 20 April 1943. After the war he was de-nazified in Oldenburg and joined the West German civil service as Regierungsrat. Member of the German Party. Member of the City council in Oldenburg 1952 to 1961. Member of the Lower Saxon Parliament 1958. Died in Oldenburg 12 November 1981.

ROHDE Dr. Walter

Born 9 March 1893 in Kahla (Thüringen).

Studied national economics at the universities of Jena and Berlin from 1912 to 1914. Then, he served in the army. Graduated as a Doctor in Law in 1919. He joined the civil service in the Thüringen Ministry of the Interior with the rank of Regierungsassessor. Promoted Regierungsrat in 1923. In June 1930 he established the Police Administration in Gotha and remained in Police Administration duties until the end of the war. He was Führer der Flieger Untergruppe Thüringen Ost in the Deutsche Luftsport Verband. He was member of the SS from 1935 and rose to the rank of Obersturmbannführer with effect from 30 January 1939.

ROOSCHÜZ Gerhart

Born 3 June 1906 in Sindelfingen.

Graduated as a lawyer. He served in the civil service in Oberndorf (Württemberg). He was member of the Party from May 1933 and was member of the SA. He joined the Police Administration 14 June 1934 and remained in various posts until April 1940. Served in the army from 1940 until the end of the war.

ROOSEN Berend

Born 17 February in Hamburg.

He served in the army from 1891 to 1920 rising to the rank of Oberstleutnant. He joined the SCHUPO as Oberst 1 July 1923 and commanded the SCHUPO in Sauerland (Ruhr) until November 1923 and then in Königsberg. He was transferred to Police Administration duties from February 1932. He retired in December 1935.

ROTMANN Eberhard Dr.

Born 30 December 1906 in Burgsteinfurt.

He was a legal graduate. He joined the Prussian civil service as a legal official and was promoted Regierungsrat in 1936. Joined the Party 1 May 1933. In 1937, he was appointed to Police Administration duties. He took over as head of a Police Administration in 1941 and remained there until the end of the war. He was a member of the last SS Groups to leave the area in advance of the US forces. Died in Horstmar 9 December 1987.

ROTTMANN Erich

Born 8 November 1892 in Königsberg (Ostpreussen).

He joined the army and was commissioned Leutnant 28 April 1914. He served in the Great War and was a prisoner of war from November 1918 until February 1920. Then he joined Schutzpolizei in Schleswig Holstein being promoted Oberleutnant on 13 July 1921. He held various post in Prussian SCHUPO and was promoted Hauptmann on 1 January 1936. He joined Party on 1 March 1932. From November 1935 to September 1936, he was Commander of the Feld-Jäger-Abteilung Berlin. Promoted Major der SCHUPO on 1 January 1935. He served in Preussen Minister of Interior from 1936 to 1939 then returned to SCHUPO duties. Promoted Oberstleutnant on 1 September 1939 and Oberst 1 April 1944. He took over SS and Police duties in Eastern Europe in 1942. He returned to Danzig and in 1944 took over as head of the Police Administration. He was member of the SS from November 1938 and rose to the rank of Standartenführer on 1 May 1944.

RUST Dr. Arnold

Born 3 May 1889 in Biskupin (Posnania in Poland).

He served in the Imperial Navy from 1909 and graduated as a Doctor in Law in March 1922. He served in the Technical Emergency Services organization (TENO) until 1929. He left due to budget cuts and worked as an consulting engineer and lawyer. He was member of the SS from 14 August 1934 and rose to the rank of Standartenführer with effect from 30 January 1941. He was active member of the SD from 1934 to 1938. He was appointed to Police Administration duties from March 1939 serving until the end of the war.

SACKSOFSKY Günther

Born 24 September 1901 in Mannheim (Bade).

He studied the law at the University of Heidelberg and passed his Assessor exam in the 1920's. He joined the Party in May 1933. He was member of the SS from 1934 and rose to the rank of Standartenführer with effect from 1 January 1942. He served in civil service in Baden and was ranked Regierungsrat. He was transferred to Police Administration duties in 1934 and remained until the end of the war. He served in Alsace from 1940 to 1942.

SALISCH Carl Otto von

Born 28 November 1902 in Glogau (Schlesien).

He served in Freikorps units Orgesch in 1920/1921 and was a member of the SA from 1933 serving in the Training Staff (Ausbildungswesen). He transferred to the SS on 20 April 1936 and rose to the rank of Standartenführer 9 November 1944. He was active in the Security Service of the SS until 1942 and took part in the Venlo operation that resulted in the capture of two British MI6 agents on the Dutch border in 1940. He was appointed to Police Administration duties in September 1942. He was tried before a Party court in Bromberg February 1945 for defeatism, was sentenced to death and was shot 7 February 1945.

SATOR Emil Adolf

Born 26 July 1905 in Würzburg (Franken).

He studied the law and served in the Schutzpolizei from 1 April 1924 to 15 February 1931. He joined the Party in August 1931. He joined the SS on 1 December 1932 and rose to the rank of Obersturmbannführer with effect from 9 November 1941. He served in the Leibstandarte, the Death Head units, and the SS-VT. During the war he was conscripted into the Waffen-SS serving until 1943. He was appointed to Police Administration duties in January 1943, and trained in Wilhelmshaven under Dr. Arnold Rust. He remained until the end of the war.

SCHÄFER Johannes

Born 14 December 1903 in Leipzig (Sachsen).

He worked in commerce until 1930. He was member of the SS from 13 January 1927. Transferred to the SA on 1 February 1929, he rose to the rank of Oberführer in 1933. He served in the SA Training Organisation (SA-Ausbildungswesen). He returned to the SS as Standartenführer on 7 July 1935 and rose to the rank of Brigadeführer with effect from 1 September 1939. Took part in active service in Danzig in the late 1930's. He was transferred to Police Administration duties in June 1939. Posted to occupied Poland he served there until October 1940. He joined the Waffen-SS in January 1942 and served until the end of the war rising to the rank of Obersturmführer der Reserve with effect from 20 April 1944. He died in Bielefeld 28 April 1993.

SCHEPMANN Wilhelm

Born 17 June 1894 in Hattingen (Ruhr).

He served in the Great War where he was wounded three times and joined state service after the war. He joined the Party in 1921. A member of the SA from 1930 he rose to the rank and status of Stabschef der SA 17 August 1943 in succession to the deceased Viktor Lutze. He commanded the SA-Gruppe in Westphalen from November 1932 to 1933 then the SA-Obergruppe Westfalen Niederrhine and finally the SA-Obergruppe in Sachsen from July 1934 to August 1943. Member of the Reichstag from 1933. He was appointed to Police Administration duties from 1933 to 1936 then promoted Kreishauptmann (District Leader) In Dresden. He died 26 July 1970.

SCHLESSMANN Fritz

Born 11 March 1899 in Essen (Ruhr).

He served in the Imperial Navy during the Great War and then he worked for the Krupps Industrial Group as an engineer. He joined the Party and the SA in 1922. He rejoined the Party on 17 December 1925 and transferred from the SA to the SS 5 May 1930. Member of the Reichstag from 1933. He served as a full time Allgemeine-SS officer until 1 February 1939, as SS-District Leader in Bochum then Essen. He ended the war as Obergruppenführer with effect from 9 November 1944. He was transferred to Police Administration duties from 1933 to 1939 and then he was involved in Party duties as Deputy Gauleiter for Essen. He ran the Gau from 1940 when the Gauleiter, Josef Terboven, was posted to Norway as Reichskommissar. He died in Essen 31 March 1964.

SCHMAUSER Hermann

Born 15 August 1893 in Hof (Bayern).

He was the younger brother of SS-Obergruppenführer Heinrich Schmauser. He served in the Great War and was wounded four times. He worked in banking then in industry. He joined the Party in August 1931. He was member of the SA from 1931 and was promoted SA-Standartenführer on 1 July 1932. Transferred to the SS on 20 February 1936 with the rank of Standartenführer. He joined the Police Administration in August 1937 and remained in that field until October 1944. He retired due to illness at the end of 1944 and was put at disposal of the staff of Höhere SS und Polizeiführer West.

SCHMELCHER Willy

Born 25 October 1894 in Eppingen (Bade).

He served in the Great War and then was trained and worked as a construction engineer. Member of the SS from 1931, he rose to the rank of Gruppenführer with effect from 9 November 1943. Member of the Reichstag from 1933. He was full time SS-leader from 1933 to 1935 and then he was transferred to Police Administration duties in March 1935. After leaving the Police duties in Metz and Saarbrücken (held both posts concurrently), he was posted to Russia as an SS and Police leader in 1941. He served as head of the Technical Emergency Service (TENO) from October 1943 fol lowing the disgrace of the incumbant Hans Weinrich and was appointed temporary Höhere SS und Polizeiführer for the Wartheland in December 1944. He achieved the rank of Lieutenant-General in the Police with effect from 9 November 1943. He died in Saarbrücken 15 February 1974.

SCHMELT Albrecht

Born 19 August 1899 in Breslau (Schlesien).

He served in the Great War from 1917 and was badly wounded, being shot in the lung. After the war he joined the German Postal Service in the telegraph department. He joined the Intelligence office of the Party in 1929. Member of the SA from 1929, he rose to the rank of Standartenführer by 1936. Transferred to the SS as Oberführer on 24 January 1940 and rose to the rank of Brigadeführer with effect from 9 November 1942. Member of the Reichstag from 1933. He was appointed to Police Administration duties from 1934 to 1941. After leaving Police Administration, he served as a District President for Oppeln until March 1944. As special representative of the Reichsführer-SS in his duties of Reichskommisar for the Strengthening of Germandom (RKFDV), he ran the 'Organisation Schmelt' in Gau Niederschlesien which was used for labour impressment in Schlesien for work in war industries. He died in Bad Warmbrunn 8 May 1945.

SCHMID Emil

Born 10 March 1873 in Friedrichsthal (Saarland).

He studied Law at the Universities of Tübingen and Berlin from 1892 and graduated in 1898. In December 1902 he was appointed Police Commissioner in the City Police Administration in Stuttgart. Moved to the post of deputy Amtsmann in the city 1904 and then served as Chairman of the Oberamt in Schorndorf. He was transferred to Police Administration in 1924 and remained until he left the post in Ulm at the request of the local Kreisleiter in June 1933. He then moved to the Ministry of the Interior with the rank of Oberregierungsrat. Appointed President of the Civil Servant Pension Fund Council, he retired in March 1938.

SCHMIDT Walter

Born 30 April 1906 in Gotha (Thüringen).

He was a trained civil servant and served in the Thüringen n Ministry of the Interior from June 1931. He joined the Party in 1929. He joined the SS in October 1932 and rose to the rank of Standartenführer with effect from 27 February

1943. He transferred to Police Administration duties in 1936 as Polizeirat and remained in that field throughout the war. He was also leader of the local SD office.

SCHMITT Emil

Born 22 February 1891 in Nürnberg (Franken).

He served in the army during the Great War as a paymaster. He served in the Bayern Landespolizei from the 1 December 1920 to 30 June 1936 rising to the rank of Major. He joined the Party in 1933. He was member of the SS from July 1936 rising to the rank of Obersturmbannführer with effect from 30 January 1941. He served as an administration officer in the SS-Verfügungstruppen. He transferred to Police Administration duties in October 1940 and remained until the end of the war.

SCHNEIDER Dr.

Graduated with a Doctorate in Law on 22 December 1923. He became a civil servant in Württemberg state service. Ranked Regierungsrat on 1 July 1935 in the Bezirkamt Lorrach. He transferred to the Police Administration in Heidelberg in August 1936. He stayed there until his appointment to the post in Pforzheim in March 1942.

SCHNEIDHUBER August

Born 8 May 1887 in Traunstein (Bayern).

He was a Bayern army cadet until March 1907 then he was commissioned Leutnant. He served in the Great War rising to the rank of Major. Worked in agriculture after the war. He was member of the SA from 1928 rising to the rank of Obergruppenführer by 1934. Führer SA-Gruppe Süd from 1928 to 1931, Führer SA-Gruppe West from 1931 to 1934 and Führer SA-Obergruppe III from 1932 to 1934. Member of the Reichstag from 1932. He was appointed to Police Administrtion duties from April 1934. He was arrested personally by Hitler at München airport 30 June 1934 and was shot at the Stadelheim Prison on the same day.

SCHÖNBERG Dr. Hübertus

He was a trained lawyer and worked as a Prussian civil servant from the 2 November 1929. As Regierungsassessor, he served as Department Chief in the Police Prasidency in Königsberg in 1934. He then served in the Police Presidency Berlin in 1935. Promoted Oberregierungsrat in 1939, he led Department IV (Economics Affairs) in the Police Presidency of Berlin. He was appointed temporary District Vice President in Bromberg in 1940 then moved to Troppau in 1941. He took over Police Administration duties in Sudetenland on 1943.

SCHOENE Heinrich

Born 25 November 1889 in Berlin.

He served in the Great War where he was wounded twice. He joined the Party and the SA in 1925. From May 1928 he was founder and organizer of the SA-Gausturm Nordmark. Promoted Gruppenführer in June 1932 and Obergrup penführer on 20 April 1934. He led the SA-Gruppe in Nordmark from 15 February 1932 until 31 January 1934 then the SA-Gruppe Ostland (later Tannenberg) until April 1943. Member of the Reichstag from 1933. He also served as Landesgruppenführer der Reichsluftschutzbund for Ostpreussen until March 1939. He served in Police Administration from February 1934 until September 1941 and was then appointed Generalkommissar for Volhynia in the Reichskommissariat Ukraine. In April 1943, he was appointed Inspector of the Naval SA. He was killed in Königsberg on 9 April 1945.

SCHRAGMULLER Konrad

Born 11 March 1895 in Ostrich (Ruhr)

He was a Prussian army cadet until 1914 and then he was commissioned Leutnant and served in the Great War. He worked in agriculture and ran an estate. He joined the Party and the SA and rose to the rank of Gruppenführer by 1933. He served as SA Special Commissar for Sachsen in 1934. He was a Member of the Reichstag from 1932. He was appointed to Police Administration duties in 1933. He was arrested 30 June 1934 and was shot at Berlin-Lichterfelde on 1 July 1934.

SCHRAMME Otto

Born 1 October 1898 in Berlin.

He served in the Great War from 1917 to 1918 being badly wounded. He left the army in 1919 as Unteroffizier. He then worked as an official in the Reich Finance Ministery. He joined the SA and rose to the rank of Obergruppenführer with effect from November 1944. He commanded the SA-Gruppe in Westfalen from July 1933. He was a Member of the Reichstag from 1933. He was appointed to Police Administration from 1934 until 1942. He died on 25 May 1941.

SCHROEDER Walther

Born 26 November 1902 in Lübeck.

He studied mechanical engineering and worked as a senior engineer in the dockyard in Hamburg then Lübeck. Member of the SA from 1925 to 1930. He joined the Party in 1925 and served as a senior Party leader until 1936. Joined the NSKK from September 1936 as Standartenführer. Promoted Oberführer 30 January 1938. He was transferred to the SS as Oberführer on 20 April 1938. Promoted Brigadeführer 27 September 1941. He ran the Police Administration in Lübeck from 1933 until the end of the war with periods of absence as SS and Police Leader in Latvia. He was involved in a major scandal over the disappearence of large amounts of food and clothing following an air raid on Lübeck 29 March 1942. As a result of the investigation, SS-Standartenführer Wilhelm Janowsky was executed and Schroeder was considered to have been an unwitting accomplice. He died in Lübeck on 3 November 1973.

SCHROERS Johannes

Born 7 January 1885 in Langenberg (Rhineland).

He served in the army during the Great War and then he served in the Prussian Landespolizei from 1918 until 1934 He transferred to the Schutzpolizei with the rank of Major in 1934. He rose to the rank of Generalmajor with effect from 9 December 1941. He was appointed to Police Administration duties from November 1941 remaining until the end of the war. He was member of the SS from 30 January 1940 rising to the rank of Brigadeführer with effect from 18 August 1942. Died in Bremen on 18 June 1960.

SCHULZE Hans

Born 31 July 1903 in Weimar (Thüringen).

He studied agriculture and worked in that field until 1922. He joined the Thüringen State service in the Finance Department in September 1928 and later moved into Reich Finance Administration. He joined the Party in 1930. He was member of the Hitler Youth from 1931 until 1939. He came back to Thüringen State Service in 1933 as Stadtsrat in Rudolstadt then Reichsamtsmann on the staff of the Landrat in Rudolfstadt. He joined the Police Administration in 1939 as Polizeirat then took over the post in Jena in 1943. He was member of the SS from 20 April 1939 and rose to the rank of Obersturmbannführer with effect from 20 April 1941. He was also leader of the local SD office.

SCHULZ-SEMBTEN Hans

He served in the Great War. A member of the SA, he rose to the rank of Oberführer. He served as Führer V Sturmbann in the SA-Standarte 12 in September 1932. He was appointed to Police Administration duties in 1935 and remained until the end of the war.

SCHWARMKRUG Ernst

Born 2 February 1870 in Schneeburg (Schlesien).

Graduated as a lawyer in 1894. He served in the Chemnitz Police from 1899 to 1901 and then moved to the Justice Administation. He served in the army in the Great War. He was appointed Police Director for Chemnitz in May 1919 and remained until he retired in 1934.

SCHWEINLE Karl

Born 16 September 1885 in Tutzing (Oberbayern).

He joined the army in 1906 and served in the Great War where he was awarded the Iron Cross 1. and 2. Class. In April 1920 he joined the Bayern Landespolizei as Hauptmann. He was involved in the München Putsch of 9 November 1923 and as a result was expelled from the police in February 1924. He rejoined the Bayern Landespolizei as Major 1 April 1933. Promoted Oberstleutnant 1 October 1933. Appointed Kommandeur der SCHUPO for Nürnberg-Fürth on 1 April 1934 and Kommandeur der Schutzpolizei for Württemberg on the 1 April 1935. Promoted Oberst der SCHUPO 1 October 1934. He took over the new post of IdO for Wehrkreis XIII with its headquarters in Nürnberg on the 1 October 1937. He retired with the rank of brevet Major-General of Police 30 April 1938. As a result of a meeting between Himmler and the Bayern Minister of the Interior Dr. Schmid, Schweinle was given the Police President post in Stuttgart. He finally retired in December 1944. He joined the Party in May 1929 and was member of the SA from February 1932. He rose to the rank of Brigadeführer with effect from 30 January 1942. He died 10 October 1954.

SETHE

He was a civil servant in State Thüringen from January 1927. He was promoted Regierungsrat in 1933 whilst on the staff of the Landrat in Suhl. He was appointed Landrat from 1 November 1933 and was unpaid (nebenamtlich) Police Director for Suhl until the end of the war.

SINN Karl

Born 10 August 1890.

Graduated in Law in 1918. He served as an apprentice attorney and then an apprentice judge in the Landsgericht Tübingen until January 1922. Appointed deputy chairman of the Police Office in Tübingen (Vorstand Polizeiamt). Appointed chairman of the Police Direction in Reutlingen 22 May 1926 with the rank of Regierungsrat. As a result of the dismissal of Memminger from the SCHUPO, he was himself dismissed and was posted to Balingen (Württemberg) as Landrat.

SLADEK Emanuel

Born 16 August 1902 in Iglau (Sudetenland).

He served in the Czech army from 1922 to 1924. Then, he worked in the textile industry. As a Volksdeutsch he took part in espionage activities in aid of the German army in 1938 and was arrested. He was released when the Germans occupied the bulk of Böhmen-Mähren in March 1939. He joined Police Administration in Sudetenland. He was active member of the SS from April 1939 and rose to the rank of Oberführer with effect from 30 January 1945. He led the SS-District in the Protectorat and became the last Leader of SS-Oberabschnitt Böhmen-Mähren in February 1945. He was sentenced to death by the Czechs and was hanged in Prague 1947.

SOMMER Dr. Hans-Eugen

Born 13 December 1901 in Rostock (Pommern)

He served in a Freikorps units and graduated as Doctor in Medecine in 1925. A member of the SA from 4 May 1925, he rose to the rank of Standartenführer. Transferred to the SS with the same rank 20 April 1939. He joined the Mecklenburg Landespolizei as Stabsarzt on 1 April 1933. He was appointed Polizeimedizinalrat 1 November 1934. On 1 October 1938, he transferred to Police Administration. As friend of Gauleiter Friedrich Hildebrandt, he served as Gaugerichtsbeisitzer for Gau Mecklenburg-Lübeck.

SOWA Friedrich

Born 12 September 1896 in Hohendorf.

He studied law and theology at the University of Königsberg and served in the infantry during the Great War. He joined the Criminal Police after the war and served in Berlin until June 1939. He then headed the KRIPO office in Stettin until April 1941. Joined the SS as Oberscharführer 15 January 1938 and rose to the rank of Standartenführer with effect from 21 June 1943. He headed the military Police in Paris from 1940 to April 1941 and was then posted to Prague were he took over the KRIPO office. He deputized for the incumbant Police President Willy Weidermann who was often absent helping to organize the new SS-Main District for Böhmen-Mähren.

STANGE Albert

Born 17 January 1899 in Plauen (Thüringen).

He served in the Great War and then in a Freikorps unit. He was a founder member of the Party in Erfurt serving as propaganda leader until 1929. Member of the Prussian Landstag from 1929. Prussian State Coucillor from 1933. He was appointed State Commissar for Economy in Erfurt in July 1933. From 1933 until 1935 he served in Police Administration and then he returned to civil administration.

STARCK Wilhelm

Born 20 May 1891 in Gemersheim am Rhein (Rhine).

He joined the army in 1910 and served in the Great War. He was an instructor to Heinrich Himmler in Bayern Infanterie-Regiment 22. He left army and joined the Bayern Landespolizei in 1920. He was involved in the Putsch of München and left the Police in December 1923. He worked in the post office then in a printing house until 1932. He was member of the SS from 1929 and was active in the Allgemeine-SS. He rose to the rank of Brigadeführer with effect from 20 April 1934. He was transferred to Police Administration duties in 1936 and briefly headed the local Gestapo Office. He was considered to be a lazy and insolent man who put his state position before his Party duties. He tried, without sucess, to curb the excesses of the Gestapo in Augsburg. Died 21 November 1968.

STEIN Walter

Born 6 November 1896 in Schwelm (Westfalen).

Trained as a locksmith. He served in the army in the Great War. He had to give up his trade because of a wound which left his right elbow too stiff for him to work in his trade. He worked as a long distance coach driver until 1933. He was an active member of the SS from 1 November 1930 and rose to the rank of Oberführer with effect from 1 January 1936. Served as honorary judge in the German Labour Front from 1933 to 1936. He was transferred to Police Administration duties from 1941 in occupied Poland. He served as SS and Police Leader Warsaw in 1944 and ended the war as Korpsintendant of the XII. SS-Armee-Korps. He died in Garmisch-Partkirchen on 11 August 1985.

STEINHAUSL Dr. Otto

Born 10 March 1879 in Budweis (Böhmen-Mähren).

He studied law and joined the Police Administration in Wien in December 1907 serving until 1922. During the Great War he was made responsible for all internal and external espionage for the Austrian General Staff. He created the Police Administration in Salzburg in 1922 then moved back to Wien in 1931. Arrested in the wake of the assassination of the Chancellor Dollfuss, he was sentenced to seven years in prison in December 1935. Released in July 1936, he moved to Bayern. He returned to Wien after the Anschluss. He was appointed as Police President of Wien. On 1940 he became President of the International Kriminal-Polizei Kommission. He was member of the SS from 20 April 1938 and rose to the rank of Oberführer. He died after a short illness in Wien on 25 June 1940.

STOLLBERG Fritz

Born 25 February 1888 in Cologne Mülheim (Rhein).

Attended a Higher Mechanical Engineering School in Cologne and then worked in the Deutz Motor Works in Cologne and Aschaffenburg. He remained in the motor industry until 1933. He was member of the SA from 15 March 1933. Served as Führer SA-Jäger-Standarte J 2 from July 1933. Took over command of SA-Brigade 35 (Leipzig) in November 1935. Promoted SA-Brigadeführer with effect from 30 January 1937. Later served at the disposal of SA-Gruppe Hessen. Member of the Reichstag from 1936. He served in Police Administration from 1937 until 1942.

STROOP Jügen

Born 26 September 1895 in Detmold (Lippe).

He served in the Great War, then worked in the Land registry in Detmold until March 1933. He was member of the SS from July 1932 and rose to the rank of Gruppenführer with effect from 9 November 1943. After service as a Standarte and District commander in the Allgemeine-SS, he joined the SS and Police and served as Inspector of Security for the military motorway (DG IV) which linked Lemberg in Poland to Stalino in Southern Russia. In February 1943 he served on the staff of the SS and as a Police Leader for Lemberg and then took over the post in Warsaw. During this period he led Police Administration in Warsaw. Whilst here he undertook the infamous destruction of the Warsaw Ghetto. In September 1943 he took over the post of Höhere SS und Polizeiführer for Greece and in November 1943 he transferred to the HSSPF post covering Wehrkreis XII in the Rhineland, Luxemburg and Lorraine. He was sentenced to death by a Polish Court 23 July 1952 and was hanged in Warsaw on the site of the former Ghetto 6 March 1952.

THIELE Johannes

Born 22 March 1890 in Dresden (Sachsen).

He joined the army April 1909 and served until January 1920. He left army and joined the Schutzpolizei in 1920. Transferred to the Criminal Police April 1928 as Kriminalrat. He remained in this field until the end of the war rising to the rank of Generalmajor der Polizei with effect from 21 June 1944. He served at Security Police Headquarters in Berlin until 1939 and then transferred to Hamburg as head of the criminal police and finally as Inspector of the Security Police and SD. He was transferred to Police Administration in Dresden in January 1945. He was member of the SS from 30 November 1936 and rose to the rank of Brigadeführer with effect from 21 June 1944. Sentenced to death, the sentence was commuted to 15 years in prison. Died in Werl prison 22 September 1951.

THIELER Heinz

Born 17 September 1909 in Kuckerneese (Ostpreussen).

He studied law and political science at the University of Königsberg and passed his Assessor exam in December 1935.

He joined the Party in 1931. In 1936 he became a civil servant. From September 1937 he served in the Police Administration in Suhl, in Oppeln, in the Wasserstrassendirektion (waterways direction) in Kiel and then in Poland at Litzmannstadt. He took over the post in Tilsit in 1941 and remained there until the end of the war. A member of the SS from 16 May 1933, he rose to the rank of Obersturmbannführer with effect from 1 January 1942.

TRIPPLER Wilhelm

Born 30 August 1897 in Nienburg (Weser).

Studied businessadministration in 1912. He served in the army during the Great War from 1915 to 1918. Left the army as Gefreiter having been wounded three times in the left arm and shoulder blade. He worked in the family business as manager from 1920 to 1926 then in industry. He lost his job due to his National Socialist activites in 1931. Served in the Party as head of the social department in Gau Magdeburg-Anhalt. He was Gebietsinspekteur der NSDAP for Central Germany from 1 January 1935. He served in Police Administration from June 1936 to June 1939 and then returned to Party duties as Propaganda leader in Gau Magdeburg-Anhalt. Joined the NSKK as Oberführer from 30 January 1937. He was a Member of the Reichstag from 1934.

TSCHIMPKE Erich

Born 11 March 1898 in Breslau (Schlesien).

He served in the infantry and the flying service in the Great War. After which, he drifted from job to job mainly in farming. He was member of the SS from 30 July 1932 and rose to the rank of Oberführer with effect from 19 September 1942. He served in Police Administration, in September 1942, as a stop gap whilst a successor was being found for the incumbant. His speciality was transport and he showed something of a flair for organization and the solving of supply and logistical problems in the Waffen-SS. From March 1943, he served into Eastern Administration in Russia. From April 1944, he was assigned to HSSPF Italian as liaison officer next to Militia Armata. He died in Heppenheim on 3 July 1970.

TSCHOCHNER Dr.

Trained as a lawyer he served as a civil servant with the rank of Regierungsrat on the staff of the Landrat in Peine in 1940. He served in Police Administration in Halle then he took over as standing deputy Police Director in the Police Administration in Bitterfeld. It is presumed that a permanent candidate was to have been found but the critical war situation prevented this. He held the rank of Scharführer in the SS.

UHLIG Dr. Albert-Wilhelm

Born 9 September 1891 in Dresden (Sachsen).

He studied law at the University of Leipzig until 9 November 1914. He joined the Royal Saxon army and served on the Western front until he was captured by the French 8 August 1918. Returned home 14 February 1920. Then returned to his legal studies and graduated as a doctor in law in 1921. He served in the Saxon Interior Ministry and then in the city administration in Chemnitz and Arnsberg. Promoted Regierungsrat, he was posted to the civil administration in Dresden 1 September 1925. Returned to the Saxon Interior Ministry on August 1933. He served under the SS-Brigadeführer Dr. Karl Fritsch. In the Spring of 1935, he moved to the Police department in the Ministry. He served in the Police Administration from 1937 until the end of the war. Member of the SS from March 1935, he rose to the rank of Sturmbannführer with effect from 9 November 1941.

UIBERREITHER Dr. Sigfried

Born 29 March 1908 in Salzburg (Österreich).

He studied legal science and then worked as a secretary for the Steiermark health insurance. Graduated as a doctor in law in Graz 22 July 1933. He was member of the SA from 1931 and was promoted SA-Brigadeführer 12 March 1938, Gruppenführer 9 November 1938 and Obergruppenführer 9 November 1943. He held temporary Police Administration post in March 1938 remaining until he was appointed Gauleiter for Steiermark 22 May 1938. He became Reichsstatthalter for Steiermark on 15 March 1940. After being interned in Dachau and Nürnberg, he fled to South America. He later returned to Germany where he died in 1980.

ULLMANN Otto

Born 21 September 1899 in Homburg (Saarland).

Served in the Great War and then studied electrical engineering graduating with a diploma. He was then involved in the erection of transformer stations. Served as a minor Party leader until the 1 July 1936 when he joined the SS. He rose to the rank of Brigadeführer with effect from 15 May 1943. Served as chief of staff to Heinrich Himmler until May 1943 when he transferred to Police Administration duties. Died as a Russian prisoner of war 29 September 1955.

VELLER Wilhelm

Born 9 October 1896 in Witten (Ruhr).

Served in the Great War and then studied philosophy at the University of Bonn. He was involved in right wing politics and was imprisoned for political agitation in the 1920's. Joined the SA and rose to the rank of Oberführer with effect from the 1 January 1931. Führer SA-Untergruppe Düsseldorf in January 1931.He was dismissed from the Wuppertal post because of illegal activities inside the concentration camp at Kemna. As a result he was demoted to SA-Standartenführer and was posted to the SA-Gruppe in Dresden March 1934. He was recalled to Police Administration duties in November 1939. He enlisted in the army in 1941 and was killed in action on the Eastern front 22 July 1941.

VETTER Karl

Born 15 April 1895 in Todtnau (Baden).

He was a farmer and served as an official in the Party Farming Organisation in Kurhessen until September 1934. From June 1935 he served as General Inspector in the Food Estate Office. From February 1937 he served as a special representative in the Reichs Food and Agricultural Ministry. He joined the SS April 1934 and rose to the rank of Standartenführer with effect from 14 May 1936.

VITZDAMM Dr. Heinrich

Born 29 February 1892 in Stralsund.

Attended university where he studied national economics and was awarded a doctorate in philosophy in 1914. Served in the Great War then continued his studies in England. Joined the civil service in 1922 and the Gestapo in 1933. Transferred to Police Administration duties in October 1939 where he remained until the end of the war. Joined the SS 1 January 1935 and rose to the rank of Oberführer with effect from 21 June 1944. He died 23 February 1975.

VOGEL Hans

Born 9 June 1887 in Borlinghausen.

Worked as a primary school teacher in Posen 1906 to 1914, served in the Great War and then in the Grenzschutz Ost. Joined the SCHUPO as Oberleutnant 1 March 1920. Left the Police 1 April 1924. Served in the SA rising to the rank of Gruppenführer with effect from 9 November 1944 and commanded SA-Brigade 70 in Detmold from January 1935 and then z.V. Führer SA-Gruppe Westfalen. He was a Member of the Reichstag and held the rank of Polizeirat in the Police Administration.

WAGENBAUER Richard

Born 30 June 1896 in Gemersheim in Rheinpfalz.

Joined the Royal Bayern Army Cadet Corps and served in the Great War in the artillery and with Airships used for spotting for the artillery. Served in the Freikorps units von Epp and Detachment Hierl until 1928. Joined the SA 1 October 1932 and rose to the rank of Gruppenführer. He briefly served in Police Administration in June 1934. He commanded the SA-Gruppe Bayerwald from 15 May 1937 until 1944 and served as Trustee for Labour for Baden.

WALLNER Dr. Adolf

Born 17 May 1889 in Strassgang bei Graz in Österreich.

Studied law and was awarded a doctorate. Served in the Austrian army during the Great War, he was captured by the Russians in 1915 and remained a prisoner until 1919. On his return home he served in the Police Administration in Graz from July 1919. Joined the SS 22 December 1939 and rose to the rank of Obersturmbannführer with effect from 9 November 1942. Served as Regierungsrat in the Gestapo in Graz until moving to Marburg.

WEBERSTEDT Hans

Born 17 March 1875.

He served in the Great War and then joined the Schutzpolizei rising to the rank of Major. Served as a Party press-officer in 1933 and gave evidence against the defendents in the Reichstag Fire trial. Joined the SS and rose to the rank of Standartenführer by 1941. He was President of the Reichsbundes fr Deutsche Sicherheit in Volksbund für das Deutschtum Ausland from the summer of 1933. He was dismissed form all posts and from the SS 15 October 1941.

WEDEL Wilhelm Ernst Graf von

Born 18 November 1891 in Berlin.

Joined the army 1911 and served until February 1919.Worked in banking and industry and from 1923 went into farming. Served in the SA from 28 February 1932 rising to the rank of Oberführer with effect from 1 May 1933. Transferred to the SS as Oberführer 4 May 1935. Rose to the rank of Brigadeführer with effect from 20 April 1938. Served in Police Administration from March 1935. He died after a short illness 19 October 1939.

WEHRLE Kurt

Born 16 January 1905 in Staufen.

Studied law at the Universities of Heidelberg and Freiberg and graduated as a lawyer 1932. He worked as secretary to the Baden Interior Minister Karl Pflaumer from 1 October 1932. Joined the Police Administration June 1934. Joined the SS 20 January 1933 and rose to the rank of Standartenführer with effect from 9 November 1942.

WEIDERMANN Willy

Born 25 November 1898 in Ziegenruck an der Saale.

Served in the Great War and then worked in banking until 1934. Founded an SS unit in Zwickau March 1926 and joined the SS 24 March 1926. Rose to the rank of Brigadef ührer with effect from 1 September 1944. Transferred to Police Administration June 1936, he served in Prague from March 1943 until the end of the war. He died at Eitorg 28 February 1985.

WEINREICH Hans

Born on 5 September 1896 in Merseburg an der Saale.

He served in the army during the Great War and was a British prisoner of war from October 1917. After his return to

Germany he joined the police in Berlin. Leaving in the wake of the Kapp Putsch of July 1920 he worked in agriculture and then in industry. He served in the SA from 1922 until December 1936 rising to the rank of Gruppenführer. From December 1936 he served as a Gruppenführer in the SS. He was given the rank of Generalmajor der Polizei in the Police 1 January 1941 and was promoted Generalleutnant on the 1 June 1942. He served in the TENO from 24 April 1934. He left the service in disgrace. He was a married man with one daughter and he had been openly consorting with a prostitute. He caught veneral disease and then promised to marry the girl. As a result of the disgrace his wife and daughter committed suicide on the 15 November 1942. He was brought before an SS-Honour Court was found guilty of conduct prejudicing the good order and discipline of the SS, was demoted to SS-Mann and was dismissed from all his posts with effect from 25 November 1943 (Reichsführer-SS Tagebuch Nr III 10/43g). He survived the war and died in Düsseldorf on the 23 December 1963.

WEIS Dr.

He was an Austrian civil servant with the rank of Hofrat. He was the first Police Direktor in Klagenfurt after the Anschluss and from March 1940 he served as a Regierungsreferender in Reichsgau Niederdonau.

WEISS-Rudolf August Vincent

Born 31 May 1899 in Berlin-Zehlendorf.

He served in the Great War and then worked for the German postal service in the telegraph department Transferred to the Interior Ministry as a junior official in the Police department. Joined the SS 1 May 1930 and rose to the rank of Brigadeführer 30 January 1939. Served as Landsgruppen leader in the Air Raid protection organisation for Hessen und Rheinland-Süd from November 1938. Served on SS and Police duties in Russia from October 1943 and transferred to Police Administration January 1944. He fled from Metz in September 1944 and as a result he was accused of cowardice. He was posted to the Dirlwanger Brigade as Untersturmführer der Reserve as a punishment and was killed in action at Lieberose 22 February 1945.

WEIST Ulrich

Born 16 December 1898 in Sommerfeld.

Served in the Great War from 1915 to 1919. He studied law at University but did not get a degree.Went into business and joined the SS 25June 1933, he rose to the rank of Standartenführer with effect from 9 November 1943.He served in the Allgemeine-SS, in the Selbstschutz during the take over of Poland and then in the Waffenn SS. Transferred to the Police Administration January 1943 and served in that field until the end of 1944 when he moved back to the Waffen-SS on the staff of the XIV. SS-Armee-Korps.

WEITZEL Fritz

Born 27 April 1904 in Frankfurt am Main.

He was trained as a locksmith and worked in that trade until 1929 when he took up full time work for the Party. Joined the SS 18 November 1926. He became the senior SS-leader in the western half of Germany and rose to the rank of Obergruppenführer with effect from 9 September 1934. He was posted to Norway in April 1940 as the first Höhere SS und Polizeiführer. Whilst on leave in Düsseldorf he was involved in an air raid during the early morning of 19 July 1940 and he was killed by bomb fragments.

WERDER Friedrich von

Born 4 January 1891 in Neu Buckow in Pommern.

Served in the Great War and then studied law. Joined the Police Administration in Berlin in 1930. In 1932 he moved to Bielefeld and remained there until the post was disolved. He then served as District President in Stettin and then in Potsdam.

WESTREM ZUM GUTACKER Reinhard von

Born 12 April 1879 in Haus Hulgrath in the Rheinland.

Served in the army from 8 December 1895 to 30 September 1930 when he retired with rank of Generalmajor. Served in the Police Administration February 1933 to September 1939 when he was recalled to the army with his old rank. Promoted Generalleutnant on the 'at disposal' list 1 April 1942. He was Commander of Prisoners of War in the Wehrkreis XII from the 1 October 1940 to 30 April 1943. Retired 30 April 1943. Died in Wiesbaden in 1956.

WETTER August Wilhelm

Born 25 September 1890 in Forsthaus Giebelhardt near Wissen an der Sieg.

Studied agriculture and forestry. Member of the Prussian Landstag and then Member of the Reichstag. Joined the SA and rose to the rank of Brigadeführer with effect from 1 July 1933. He commanded the SA-Untergruppe Koblenz-Trier from 1 January 1932. Served in Police Administration from May 1933 until the end of the war. Gaujägermeister for Jagdgau Rheinland-Süd. Führer z.V. SA-Gruppe Mittelrhein in 1944.

WICKE Heinrich

Born 20 June 1886 in Kassel.

Trained as a pharmacist 1903. Served in the Great War and then set up and ran his own pharmacy business until 1938. Joined the Party 1 September 1930 and the SS 17 April 1931 and rose to the rank of Oberführer with effect from 30 January 1945. Served in Police Administration from June 1938.

WICKERT Erwin

Born 18 March 1884 in Dolzig in Königsberg.

Served in the Great War and then joined the Schutzpolizei July 1921 as Hauptmann. Served as a department head in the Party leadership from 1932 until 22 September 1939 and then returned to the Schutzpolizei. Transferred to the Police Administration 1 December 1941. Joined the SS 1 June 1940 as Sturmbannführer and rose to the rank of Obersturmbannführer with effect from 20 April 1943.

WICKLMAYR Karl

Born 31 March 1904 in Gumpersdorf-am-Inn in Oberbayern.

Studied law and became a Rechtsanwalt. Took part in the München Putsch of November 1923. Joined the Party 1929 and the SA 1932. Promoted SA-Sturmbannführer June 1936. He was appointed Regierungspräsident (District President) for Schneidemühl in Westpreussen in July 1944, the police post in Würzburg being run by his deputy Regierungsrat Endros.

WIESE Nils-Otto

Born 15 August 1898 in Georgsmarienhutte Kreis Osnabrück.

Served in the Great War and joined the SS in the early thirties. Rose to the rank of Standartenführer with effect from 10 September 1939. Served in the Saxon Interior Ministry as Adjutant to the Minister, Dr. Karl Fritsch, in 1935. Served in the Leibstandarte SS as Hauptsturmführer der Reserve with effect from 1 August 1940 and then served as Adjutant to the Reichswirtschaftminister Walter Funk. He was transferred to the Police Administration in 1943.

WILHELM Josef Georg

Born in Tuttlingen 29 August 1897

Trained as a police official and served in the KRIPO in Stuttgart from 1910. Served in the Great War and then returned to Police Administration duties. He was believed to be an opponent of the Nazi Party and as a result the senior local

SA leader Obergruppenführer Dietrich von Jagow wanted him removed. The local Police President Rudolf Klaiber supported him and as a result an Unterkommissar was appointed from the SA, SA-Standartenführer Dr. Sommer,to supervise his actions. He was finally removed in October 1935 and was posted to the traffic division in Stuttgart. He served in the traffic division of the Oberpräsidents office for Rheinprovinz from 7 October 1942.

WIRSCHING

Joined the civil service 11 December 1908. He served as Bezirks Oberamtmann in Hof in Bayern and was promoted Oberregierungsrat 1 December 1937. He served in Police Administration from 1935 until August 1937.

WITTMANN Dr. Leopold

Born 27 July 897 in Angern in Österreich.

Served in the Austrian army in the Great War. Studied law and achieved a diploma. Joined the Police Administration in Wien in 1923 and served there until 1933 when he took up various other legal posts. Returned to Police Administration in St. Polten from 1 March 1938. He joined the SS as Staffelmann in February 1942 and rose to the rank of Obersturmbannführer with effect from 9 November 1942.

WOEDTKE Alexander von

Born 2 September 1889 in Berlin.

Served in the army from 1900 to 1920 and then ran the family estate until 1930. Joined the SS 28 February 1931 and rose to the rank of Oberführer with effect from 20 April 1943. Served in the establishment of SS and Police in Poland in 1939 and then transferred to Police Administration where he remained until the end of the war.

WOLF Walter

Born 17 February 1902.

He served in the SA and rose to the rank of Oberführer. He served in Dresden until appointed in Police Administration with rank fo Polizeiamtmann. He spent the war in his Warthegau post.

WYSOCKI Lucian

Born 18 January 1899 in Gentomie Kreis Stargard in Westpreussen.

Served in the Great War and then worked as a miner and quarryman. Joined the SA in 1 February 1929 and rose to the rank of Brigadeführer with effect from 30 January 1939. Left the SA at his own request and joined the SS as Brigadeführer with effect from 21 June 1940. Served in Police Administration from March 1936. Appointed SS and Police Leader (SSPF) for Lithuania from August 1941. He died in Rheinhausen 13 December 1964.

ZECH Karl

Born 6 February 1892 in Schwinemünde.

Served in the army from 1911 until 1919 and then worked as a miner and a mine official. Joined the SS 13 January 1931 and rose to the rank of Gruppenführer with effect from 30 January 1938. He served at SS-Hauptamt as a department head. Commanded an SD main district which duties were interspersed with periods in Police Administration. Appointed as SS and Police Leader for Krakau in 1939. He was removed for disobeying orders in October 1940. He worked in industry until 1944 when he was brought before an SS-Court on charges to do with his period in industry. Found guilty, he was dismissed from the SS 14 March 1944 and as a result he committed suicide in April 1944.

ZENNER Carl

Born in Oberlimburg 11 June 1899.

Served in the Great War then in a Freikorps units. Achieved a Diploma in Businessstudies. A member of the SA, he rose to the rank of Standartenführer in 1929. Transferred to the SS on 2 April 1930, he served as a paid full time member of the Allgemeine-SS. He was posted to Police Administration in 1937. Appointed as SSPF for Minsk from 1941 until 1942, he then returned to SS-Hauptamt. Achieved the rank of Brigadeführer with effect from 21 June 1941. He died 16 June 1969.

6.3 Organisation of the Inspectors of Ordnungspolizei

This position was created by an order from the Reich and Prussian Ministry of the Interior dated 1 September 1936. The intention was to create a position that avoided the chain of command that went through the police presidencies, police directorates, etc. to the Ministry of the Interior. Himmler's intention was to create a chain of command that was wholly under SS-control and this position was the senior uniformed police command in the Reich. The initial establishment set up Inspectorates in Königsberg, Stettin, Berlin, Breslau, Magdeburg, Hannover, Münster, Kassel, Kiel and Koblenz. The first Inspectors were appointed to take effect from 15 September 1936. From this date the chain of command for the Schutzpolizei and the Gendarmerie would be as follows:

Operational

KDR Schutzpolizei and Gendarmerie => Inspekteur der Ordnungspolizei => HSSPF => Reichsführer-SS

Administrative

KDR Schutzpolizei and Gendarmerie => Polizeipräsident => Regierungspräsident => Minister der Innern

As the Germans incorporated new territories to the Old Reich (Altreich) in the 30's to form the Great Reich (Gross-Deutsche Reich), new posts were established and these will be explained under the relevant heading. The original title of this post was
INSPEKTEUR der ORDNUNGSPOLIZEI and was shortened to IdO in many documents. This title was changed to Befehlhaber der ORDNUNGSPOLIZEI effective 15 December 1943, shortened to BdO.

Organisation of the Inspectors (IdO)

Berlin: Established on 1 September 1936 to cover the Prussian Province of Brandenburg. The command came under the Höhere SS und Polizeiführer "Ost" (from 1 November 1939 "Spree") allocated to the army Wehrkreis III. It did not include the city of Berlin that remained under an independent Kommandeur der Schutzpolizei.

Inspekteure

Generalmajor der Polizei Dr. Kurt Münchau	15.09.1936 – 09.1936
Oberst der Schutzpolizei Eduard Bier	09.1936–01.08.1937
SS-Gruppenführer und Generalleutnant der Polizei Otto Klinger	01.8.1937–10.06.1939
SS-Gruppenführer und Generalleutnant der Polizei Georg Schreyer	10.06.1939–01.04.1940
SS-Gruppenführer und Generalleutnant der Polizei Ernst Hitzegrad	01.04.1940–16.02.1942
Generalmajor der Polizei Curt Kowalski 1	6.02.1942–01.10.1942
Generalmajor der Polizei Dr. Friedrich Wolfstieg	01.10.1942 – 03.1945
Oberst der Schutzpolizei Bodo von Schweinichen	03.1945–02.05.1945

Berlin: This position was the original Schutzpolizei command for the city of Berlin and remained independent of any IdO. The post was under the control of the Hühere SS und Polizeiführer "Ost" (from 1 November 1939 "Spree") and was allocated to army Wehrkreis III.

Kommandeure

Generalmajor der Polizei Dr. Kurt Münchau	01.04.1936–16.04.1937
SS-Gruppenführer und Generalleutnant der Polizei Jürgen von Kamptz	06.04.1937–12.06.1939
SS-Gruppenführer und Generalleutnant der Polizei Otto Klinge	12.06.1939–08.08.1944
SS-Brigadeführer und Generalmajor der Polizei Erik von Heimburg	08.08.1944–02.05.1945

Bremen: Established on 1 September 1936 to cover the cities of Hamburg and Bremen and the state of Oldenburg. It was under the control of the Höhere SS und Polizeiführer "Nordwest" and was allocated to the army Wehrkreis X. The headquarters moved to Hamburg on 1 April 1937.

Inspekteur

SS-Gruppenführer und Generalleutnant Dr. Heinrich Lankenau	15.09.1936–01.04.1937

Breslau: Established on 1 September 1936 to cover the Prussian Provinces of Ober und Niederschlesien. On 21 September 1939 a new post was established in Breslau "BdO beim Militärbereich Ost Oberschlesien" to cover that part of occupied Poland incorporated into the Reich in Gau Schlesien. Its commander the same officer serving as the IdO Breslau. The post was abolished on 25 October when the two posts were combined. It was under the control of the Höhere SS und Polizeiführer "Südost" and was allocated to army Wehrkreis VIII.

Inspekteure

SS-Gruppenführer und Generalleutnant der Polizei Paul Riege	15.09.1936–20.04.1940
SS-Brigadeführer und Generalmajor der Polizei Oskar Grussendorf	20.04.1940–01.09.1943
SS-Gruppenführer und Generalleutnant der Polizei Rainer Liessem	01.09.1943–01.08.1944
Oberst der Schutzpolizei Hans Müller	01.08.1944 – end

Darmstadt: Established 1 October 1936 for the state of Hesse. It was under the control of the Höhere SS und Polizeiführer "Fulda Werra" and was allocated to the army Wehrkreis IX. The post was downgraded to Kommandeur der Gendarmerie status on 31 December 1938 reporting to the IdO in Kassel.

Inspekteure

SS-Brigadeführer und Generalmajor der Polizei Rudolf Müller-Bonigk	26.10.1936–06.1938
SS-Brigadeführer und Generalmajor der Polizei Fritz Schüberth	06.1938–31.12.1938

Dessau: Established on 1 September 1936 for the state of Anhalt. It came under the control of the Höhere SS und Polizeiführer "Mitte" and was allocated to the army Wehrkreis XI. The post was abolished on 1 July 1937 and the state of Anhalt was put under the IdO in Magdeburg

Inspekteur

Oberst der Schutzpolizei Walter Keuck	01.09.1936–01.07.1937

Dresden: Established on 1 September 1936 for the state of Sachsen. It came under control of the Höhere SS und Polizeiführer "Elbe" and was allocated to the army Wehrkreis IV. It took over the Prussian Province of Sachsen on 12 August 1939 when the command in Magdeburg was abolished.

Inspekteure

Oberst der Schutzpolizei Wolfgang Thierig	15.9.1936–01.11.1937
SS-Gruppenführer und Generalleutnant der Polizei Otto von Oelhafen	01.11.1937–16.12.1939
SS-Gruppenführer und Generalleutnant der Polizei Emil Höring	16.12.1939–23.02.1942
SS-Gruppenführer und Generalleutnant der Polizei Ernst Hitzegrad	23.02.1942–01.09.1943
SS-Brigadeführer und Generalmajor der Polizei Dr. Walter Gudewill	01.09.1943–03.1944
Generalmajor der Polizei Hans Podzun	03.1944–01.02.1945
SS-Brigadeführer und Generalmajor der Polizei (m.d.U.d.) Walter Oberhaidacher	01.02.1945 – end

Egerland: Established on 1 October 1938 to cover Regierung Karlsbad in the Reichsgau Sudetenland. It came under the control of Höhere SS und Polizeiführer "Südost" and was allocated to army Wehrkreis VIII. It was absorbed into the BdO in Reichenberg on 20 December 1938.

Inspekteur

SS-Beweber und Generalmajor der Polizei Josef Albert	01.10.1938–20.12.1938

Erfurt: Established in Kassel on 1 September 1936, it moved to Erfurt on 3 August 1944 and covered the states of Thüringen and Hesse. It was under the control of the Höhere SS und Polizeiführer "Fulda-Werra" and was allocated to the army Wehrkreis IX.

Befehlhaber

Generalmajor der Polizei August Matt	03.08.1944–09.08.1944
SS-Brigadeführer der Generalmajor der Polizei Rudolf Müller-Bonigk	09.08.1944–end.

Hamburg: Established on 1 September 1936 in Bremen it moved to Hamburg on 1 April 1937. It covered the cities of Hamburg and Bremen and on 1 July 1937 it took over the state of Oldenburg. On 31 December 1938 it took over the Prussian Province of Schleswig-Holstein from the abolished command in Kiel. It was under the control of the Höhere SS und Polizeiführer "Nordwest" (from 24 May 1940 "Nordsee") and was allocated to the army Wehrkreis X

Inspekteure

SS-Obergruppenführer General der Polizei
Rudolf Querner 01.04.1937–31.10.1940
SS-Gruppenführer und Generalleutnant der Polizei
Herbert Becker 31.10.1940–21.04.1942
SS-Gruppenführer und Generalleutnant der Polizei
Rainer Liessem 21.04.1942–01.09.1943
SS-Gruppenführer und Generalleutnant der Polizei
Dr. Carl Retzlaff 01.09.1943–01.01.1945
SS-Brigadeführer und Generalmajor der Polizei
Walter Abraham 01.01.1945 – end

Hannover: Established on 1 September 1936 to cover the Prussian Province of Hannover and the state of Schaumburg-Lippe. It took over the Land Braunschweig from 1 July 1937 and the state of Anhalt on 12 August 1939 when the post in Magdeburg was disolved. Hannover came under the control of the Höhere SS und Polizeiführer "Mitte" and was allocated to the army Wehrkreis XI.

Inspekteure

SS-Brigadeführer und Generalmajor der Polizei
Helmut Mascus 15.9.1936–12.6.1939
SS-Standartenführer und Oberst der Gendarmerie
Dr. Oscar Lossen 12.6.1939–7.2.1941
Generalmajor der Polizei
Walter Basset 07.02.1941–11.5.1943
Oberst der Schutzpolizei
Walter Keuck 11.5.1943–end.

Kassel: Established on 1 September 1936 to cover the Prussian Province of Hessen-Nassau. It took over the state of Thüringen on 1 July 1937. Kassel also took over the state of Hesse on 31 December 1938 when the command in Darmstadt was downgraded to Kommandeur der Gendarmerie. It came under the control of the Höhere SS und Polizeiführer "Fulda-Werra" and was allocated to the army Wehrkreis IX. The headquarters moved to Erfurt on 3 August 1944 and it lost the Province of Hessen-Nassau that went to the BdO in Wiesbaden.

Inspekteure

SS-Brigadeführer und Generalmajor der Polizei
Karl Hoffmann 15.09.1936–01.08.1937
SS-Gruppenführer und Generalleutnant der Polizei
Georg Schreyer 01.08.1937–10.06.1939
SS-Gruppenführer und Generalleutnant der Polizei
August Edler von Meyszner 10.06.1939–07.09.1940
SS-Brigadeführer und Generalmajor der Polizei
Karl Hoffmann 07.09.1940–16.01.1944
Generalmajor der Polizei August Matt 16.01.1944–03.08.1944

Kiel: Established on 1 September 1936 to cover the Prussian Province of Schleswig-Holstein. It was under the control of the Höhere SS und Polizeiführer "Nordwest" and was allocated to army Wehrkreis X. Kiel was downgraded to Kommandeur der Gendarmerie status on 31 December 1938, reporting to the IdO in Hamburg.

Inspekteur

SS-Brigadeführer und Generalmajor der Polizei	
Bruno Krumhaar	15.09.1936–31.12.1938

Koblenz: Established on 1 September 1936 to cover the Prussian Rhein Province. It took over the Saarland on 1 July 1937. It came under the control of the Höhere SS und Polizeiführer "Rhein" and was allocated to the army Wehrkreis XII. During the winter of 1939/1940 the headquarters moved to Wiesbaden.

Inspekteur

SS-Gruppenführer und Generalleutnant der Polizei	
Georg Jedicke	01.10.1936–winter 1939/1940

Königsberg: Established in September 1936 to cover the Prussian Province of Ostpreussen. On 21 September 1939 a command titled "BdO beim Militärbereich Südost Preussen" was established to cover that part formely in Poland which was being attached to the Gau Ostpreussen. The two commands were combined on 25 October 1939. It was under the control of the Höhere SS und Polizeiführer "Nordost" and was allocated to the army Wehrkreis I.

Befehlhaber

Generalmajor der Polizei Curt Kowalski	15.09.1936–05.04.193
SS-Brigadeführer und Generalmajor der Polizei	
Curt Pohlmeyer	05.04.1939–01.01.1940
SS-Gruppenführer und Generalleutnant der Polizei	
Otto von Oelhafen	01.01.1940–01.05.1941
SS-Gruppenführer und Generalleutnant der Polizei	
Georg Jedicke	01.5.1941–15.07.1941
Generalmajor der Polizei	
Karl Franz	15.07.1941–01.03.1942
SS-Brigadeführer und Generalmajor der Polizei	
Rudolf Müller-Bonigk	01.03.1942–05.08.1944
SS-Brigadeführer und Generalmajor der Polizei	
Fritz Schüberth	05.08.1944–End

Linz: Established in March 1938 to cover the Reichsgau Oberdonau in Österreich. It came under the control of the Höhere SS und Polizeiführer "Donau" and was allocated to the army Wehrkreis XVII. The post was abolished on 26 April 1938 and command was vested in the IdO in Wien.

Inspekteur

SS-Brigadeführer und Generalmajor der Polizei	
Johannes Schroers	11.03.1938–26.04.1938

Magdeburg: Established on 1 September 1936 to cover the Prussian Province of Sachsen. It took over the state of Analt on 1 July 1937 when the post in Dessau was abolished. The post came under the Höhere SS und Polizeiführer "Mitte" and was allocated to the army Wehrkreis XI. It was abolished on 12 August 1939 and the Province of Sachsen was put under the IdO in Dresden. The state of Anhalt was put under the IdO in Hannover.

Inspekteure

\SS-Brigadeführer und Generalmajor der Polizei Leo von Falkowski	15.09.1936–04.05.1938
SS-Brigadeführer und Generalmajor der Polizei Curt Pohlmeyer	04.05.1938–05.04.1939
SS-Standartenführer und Oberst der Gendarmeie Dr. Oscar Lossen	05.04.1939–10.06.1939
SS-Brigadeführer und Generalmajor der Polizei Oskar Knofe	10.06.1939–12.08.1939

Note: Oberst der Schutzpolizei Martin Valtin served as the representive for the IdO Hannover from August 1939.

München: Established on 1 September 1936 to cover the state of Bayern. It was under the control of the Höhere SS und Polizeiführer "Süd" and was allocated to the army Wehrkreis VII. On 1 October 1937 the area covering North Bayern was removed and was placed under a new post set up in Nürnberg. On 8 April 1940 the district of Pfalz was removed and was put under a new post set up in Saarbrücken.

Inspekteure

Generalmajor der Polizei Karl Schweinle	01.10.1936–15.08.1937
SS-Brigadeführer und Generalmajor der Polizei Karl Hoffmann	15.08.1937–07.09.1940
SS-Gruppenführer und Generalleutnant der Polizei Otto von Oelhafen	07.09.1940–01.05.1941
SS-Brigadeführer und Generalmajor der Polizei Walter Hille	01.05.1941–30.06.1942
Oberst der Schutzpolizei Kurt Wolter i.V.	30.06.1942–01.10.1942
SS-Gruppenführer und Generalleutnant der Polizei Otto von Oelhafen	01.10.1942–01.02.1944
Generalmajor der Polizei Ludwig Mühe	01.02.1944 – end

Münster: Established on 1 September 1936 to cover the Prussian Province of Westfalen and the state of Lippe. It was under the control of the Höhere SS und Polizeiführer "West" and was allocated to the army Wehrkreis VI.

Inspekteure

SS-Gruppenführer und Generalleutnant der Polizei Herbert Becker	15.09.1936–15.06.1939
SS-Standartenführer und Oberst der Gendarmerie Dr. Oscar Lossen i.V.	15.04.1938–01.04.1939
SS-Gruppenführer und Generalleutnant der Polizei Dr. Heinrich Lankenau mit der Wahrnehmung der Geschäfte	01.04.193 – 15.06.1939

	15.06.1939–01.12.1942
SS-Gruppenführer und Generalleutnant der Polizei	
Otto Schumann	01.12.1942–01.9.1943
SS-Gruppenführer und Generalleutnant der Polizei	
Kurt Göhrum	01.09.1943–01.08.1944
Oberst der Schutzpolizei Heinrich Kruse i.V.	01.08.1944–15.09.1944
SS-Gruppenführer und Generalleutnant der Polizei	
Rainer Liessem	15.09.1944 – end

Nord-Böhmen: Established on 1 October 1938 to cover the district of Aussig in the Reichsgau Sudetenland. It came under the control of the Höhere SS und Polizeiführer "Südost" and was allocated to the army Wehrkreis VIII. It was abolished and the area was absorbed into the BdO in Reichenberg on 20 December 1938.

Inspekteur

SS-Gruppenführer und Generalleutnant der Polizei	
Otto von Oelhafen	01.10.1938–20.12.1938

Nord-Mähren: Established on 1 October 1938 to cover the district of Troppau in the Reichsgau Sudetenland. It came under the control of the Höhere SS und Polizeiführer "Südost" and was allocated to the army Wehrkreis VIII. It was abolished and the area was absorbed into the BdO in Reichenberg on 20 December 1938.

Inspekteur

SS-Gruppenführer und Generalleutnant der Polizei	
Paul Riege	01.10.1938–20.12.1938

Nürnberg: Established on 1 October 1937 to cover the area of Northern Bayern that had been removed from the IdO in München. It came under the control of the Höhere SS und Polizeiführer "Main" and was allocated to the army Wehrkreis XIII.

Inspekteure

Generalmajor der Polizei Karl Schweinle	01.10.1937–25.04.1938
SS-Brigadeführer und Generalmajor der Polizei	
Paul Will	25.04.1938–22.03.1943
SS-Gruppenführer und Generalleutnant der Polizei	
Kurt Göhrum	22.03.1943–10.09.1943
SS-Brigadeführer und Generalmajor der Polizei	
Walter Griphan	10.09.1943 – end

Reichenberg: Established on 1 October 1938 to supervise the three commands set up in Aussig, Troppau and Karlsbad in the Reichsgau Sudetenland. It took over direct control when those three subordinate commands were abolished on 20 December 1938. It came under the control of the Höhere SS und Polizeiführer "Südost" and was allocated to army Wehrkreis VIII. The post was abolished on 30 September 1939 command being vested in the BdO in Prague. A Stabsoffizier der Ordnungspolizei, Oberstleutnant der Schutzpolizei Helmut Dunnebier, was appointed to represent this particular area.

Inspekteure

SS-Obergruppenführer und General der Polizei	
Karl Pfeffer-Wildenbruch	10.10.1938–21.12.1938
SS-Gruppenführer und Generalleutnant der Polizei	
Emil Hüring	21.12.1938–30.09.1939

Salzburg: Established on 1 June 1939 to cover the Reichsgau Salzburg, Kärnten, Steiermark and Tirol-Voralberg. It took over these Reichsgaue, which covered the whole of Southern Österreich, from the BdO in Wien. It came under the control of the Höhere SS und Polizeiführer "Alpenland" and was allocated to army Wehrkreis XVIII. In December 1943 the Reichsgau Tirol-Voralberg was put under the BdO in San Martino in Northern Italy. This command was responsible for anti-partisan duties for the independent country of Slovakia from 29 January 1942. It was not responsible for any other police duties in Slovakia (see Pressburg).

Inspekteure

SS-Brigadeführer und Generalmajor der Polizei	
Helmut Mascus	15.06.1939–06.02.1942
SS-Gruppenführer und Generalleutnant der Polizei	
Karl Brenner	06.02.1942–01.07.1942
SS-Brigadeführer und Generalmajor der Polizei	
Oskar Knofe	01.07.1942–07.03.1943
SS-Gruppenführer und Generalleutnant der Polizei	
Karl Brenner	07.03.1943–01.10.1943
Oberst der Schutzpolizei Walter Griep	01.10.1943–01.10.1944
Oberst der Schutzpolizei Kurt Wolter	01.10.1944–04.05.1945

Saarbrücken: Established in June 1940 to cover the Pfalz district in Bayern and to cover the Saarland. During the summer of 1940 it took over the French province of Lorraine. It came under the control of the Höhere SS und Polizeiführer Westmark in Saarbrücken 21 May 1943 and then it came under the Höhere SS und Polizeiführer "Rhein-Westmark" in Wiesbaden. It was allocated to the army Wehrkreis XII. The post was abolished on 31 December 1943 and the command was put under the BdO in Wiesbaden.

Inspekteure

SS-Gruppenführer und Generalleutnant der Polizei	
Paul Scheer	15.08.1940–15.05.1941
SS-Oberführer und Oberst der Schutzpolizei	
Hans Müller-Brunckhorst	15.05.1941–01.12.1941
Generalmajor der Polizei	
Maximilian Ritter von Zottmann	01.12.1941–31.12.1943

Stettin: Established on 1 September 1936 to cover the Prussian Province of Pommern and the state of Mecklenburg. It came under the control of the Höhere SS und Polizeiführer "Nord" (from 20 April 1940 "Ostsee") and was alocated to the army Wehrkreis II.

Inspekteure

SS-Brigadeführer und Generalmajor der Polizei	
Wilhelm Roettig	15.09.1936 -01.08.1937
SS-Gruppenführer und Generalleutnant der Polizei	
Otto Schumann	01.08.1937–01.08.1938
Generalmajor der Polizei	
Walter Basset	01.08.1938–01.11.1938
SS-Gruppenführer und Generalleutnant der Polizei	
Otto Schumann	01.11.1938–30.05.1940
SS-Brigadeführer und Generalmajor der Polizei	
Erik von Heimburg	30.05.1940–20.02.1942
SS-Brigadeführer und Generalmajor der Polizei	
Konrad Ritzer	20.02.1942 – end

Stuttgart: Established on 1 September 1936 to cover the states of Württemberg and Baden. The Prussian Independent District of Sigmaringen was included from 1 July 1937 and the French Province of Alsace from the summer of 1940. It came under the control of the Höhere SS und Polizeiführer "Südwest" and it was allocated to the army Wehrkreis V.

Inspekteure

Generalmajor der Polizei	
Karl Schweinle	01.09.1936 – 01.04.1937
Generalmajor der Polizei	
Curt Ruoff	01.04.1937–01.04.1939
SS-Gruppenführer und Generalleutnant der Polizei	
Gerhard Winkler	01.04.1939–15.08.1941
Generalmajor der Polizei	
Georg Wieder i.V.	05.08.1941–23.02.1942
SS-Brigadeführer und Generalmajor der Polizei	
Helmut Mascus	23.02.1942–01.05.1942
SS-Gruppenführer und Generalleutnant der	
Polizei Gerhard Winkler	01.05.1942–01.01.1944
Generalmajor der Polizei Kurt Petersdorff	01.01.1944 – end

Wien: Established in March 1938 to cover the Reichskommissariat Österreich except for the Oberdonau area. This area with its headquarters in Linz was abolished on 26 April 1938 and the area was included in the Viennese command. From the beginning the post was known as Befehlhaber der Ordnungspolizei beim Staatssekretär für das Sicherheitswesen und Höhere SS und Polizeiführer in Wien. This long and complicated title was dropped in the summer of 1939 and the command adopted a title in line with all other commands. It covered the whole of Österreich from 26 April 1938 until 1 June 1939 when a new command was set up in Salzburg to cover the whole of Southern Österreich. The post in Wien covered Reichsgaue Ober and Niederdonau and Wien. It came under the control of the Höhere SS und Polizeiführer "Donau" and was allocated to the army Wehrkreis XVII.

Inspekteure

SS-Gruppenführer und Generalleutnant der Polizei	
August Edler von Meyszner	15.03.1938–12.06.1939
SS-Gruppenführer und Generalleutnant der Polizei	
Herbert Becker	12.06.1939–29.11.1939
SS-Gruppenführer und Generalleutnant der Polizei	
Dr. Carl Retzlaff	29.11.1939–01.09.1943
SS-Brigadeführer und Generalmajor der Polizei	
Dr. Kurt Bader	01.09.1943–27.02.1944
SS-Gruppenführer und Generalleutnant der Polizei	
Otto Schumann	27.02.1944–01.10.1944
SS-Brigadeführer und Generalmajor der Polizei	
Dr. Kurt Bader	01.10.1944–13.04.1945

Wiesbaden: Established on 1 September 1936 in Koblenz to cover the Prussian Province of Rhineland, it moved its headquarters to Wiesbaden in the winter of 1939/1940. The Principality of Luxemburg was included from October 1940 and it took over the area formerly covered by the post in Saarbrücken from 31 December 1943. It came under the control of the Höhere SS und Polizeiführer "Rhein" (from 21 May 1943 "Rhein-Westmark") and was allocated to the army Wehrkreis XII.

Inspekteure

SS-Gruppenführer und Generalleutnant der Polizei	
Georg Jedicke	01.10.1936–15.05.1941
SS-Gruppenführer und Generalleutnant der Polizei	
Paul Scheer	15.05.1941–01.03.1942
Generalmajor der Polizei Karl Franz	01.03.1942–16.07.1942
SS-Brigadeführer und Generalmajor der Polizei	
Fritz Schüberth i.V.	16.07.1942–28.08.1942
SS-Brigadeführer und Generalmajor der Polizei	
Helmut Mascus	28.08.1942–15.12.1943
SS-Brigadeführer und Generalmajor der Polizei	
Walter Hille	04.01.1944–9.10.1944
Oberst der Gendarmerie Günther Niemann	09.10.1944 – end

The territorial conquests of the Third Reich meant senior members of the Uniformed Police, being responsible for public order, had to develop new forms of organisation to suit the new territories. The guidelines were based upon the status of the occupied country, the size of the territory and the level of security required. From 1938, the Ordnungspolizei were involved in operations in the rear area of the armed forces inÖsterreich, the Sudetenland and Czechoslovakia. They were used mainly to maintain order among the local population, for communications and for safeguarding industry and commerce. Therefore, the two levels of organisation set up were:

Staff organisation in occupied area to control the life of the country

Field units to fight against partisans

Field Organisation of the Ordnungspolizei in Occupied Countries

7.1 Staff Organisation

Befehlhaber der Ordnungspolizei (BdO)

The Befehlhaber der Ordnungspolizei was the senior Ordnungspolizei officer in an occupied country. He was under direct command of the HSSPF. In a notice dated 5 October 1939 dealing with appointment of Generalmajor Herbert Becker as BdO in Militärbezirk Lodz, Himmler listed the responsiblities that went with such an appointment: He had authority over local Ordnungspolizei battalions and over the relevant commanders of the Schutzpolizei and Gendarmerie. Later Befehlhaber der Ordnungspolizei became responsible for all Ordnungspolizei forces in an occupied area. (See "Organisation of Commander der Ordnungspolizei"). The staff of a Commander of Ordnungspolizei was organised as followed:

Chart of Befehlhaber der Ordnungspolizei Oslo (1943)

Befehlhaber (commander)	Generalleutnant Jürgen von Kamptz
Adjudant (aide-de-camp)	Hauptmann der Schutzpolizei Semm

Chef des Stabes (chief of staff)

Oberstleutnant der Schutzpolizei Gerhard Grosse	
I a (organisation)	Major der Schutzpolizei Scharf
I b(supply)	Hauptmann der Schutzpolizei Kunst
II a/b (personnel)	Major der Schutzpolizei Semm
II c (intelligence and relations) with Norwegian police	Oberleutnant der Schutzpolizei Hunold
Nachrichtenführer (Signals)	Major der Schutzpolizei Plath
Kraftfahrsachverständiger (Transport)	Major der Schutzpolizei Julius Vomberg
I/Luftschutz (Air Raid Protection)	Major der Schutzpolizei Adalbert Graf von Kottulinsky
I/FP (Fire Protection Police)	Oberstleutnant der Feuer.Schutzpolizei Schneider
I/Sp (sport)	Hauptmann der Schutzpolizei Beuge
Sanitäts. (Medical)	Oberfeldarzt der Polizei Dr Hauer
Weltan Eziehung (ideological training)	Oberleutnant der Schutzpolizei Friebel
TENO(Technical Emergency)	Bereitschaftsführer Dr Schmitz
Amt Verwaltung und Recht (Administration and Law)	Oberregierungsrat Grothe
Polizei-Regiment 27 (Oslo)	Oberstleutnant der Schutzpolizei Walter Endler

Kommandeur der Ordnungspolizei (KdO)

The KdO was the main Ordnungspolizei officer in the administrative district or military rear areas of an occupied country. He was under direct command of the relevant BdO for matters of organization, pay, discipline and tactically came under the control of the relevant SS and Police Leader (SSPF). He supervised two deputies, a Commander of Schutzpolizei (in many case the KdO himself) and a Commander of Gendarmerie. KdO were appointed in countries with major partisan activities. Depending on the size of the district, the rank of the KdO went from Generalmajor rank (KdO Kiew) to Major (KdO Tirana). In the last months of the war KdO were set up in the operational area of Schlesien.

Generalgouvernement (Poland)	
Krakau (Distrikt Krakau)	Oberst der Schutzpolizei Dr. Günther Merk
Radom (Distrikt Radom)	Oberstleutnant der Schutzpolizei von Bredow
Lublin (Distrikt Lublin)	Oberst der Schutzpolizei Hermann Kintrup
Warschau (Distrikt Warschau)	Oberstleutnant der Schutzpolizei Joachim Petsch
Lemberg (Distrikt Galizien)	Oberstleutnant der Schutzpolizei Walter Soosten
Reichskommissariat Ostland (Baltic countries)	
Riga (Generalkommissariat Lettland)	Oberst der Schutzpolizei Karl Knecht
Kauen (Generalkommissariat Lithauen)	unknown
Reval (Generalkommissariat Estland)	Oberstleutnant der Schutzpolizei Schallert
Minsk (Generalkom. Weissruthenien)	Generalmajor der Polizei Eberhard Herf (after 1943 independant of R.K.U. Ostland)
Reichkommissariat Ukraine (Ukraine)	
Kiew	Generalmajor Paul Scheer
Nikolajew	Oberst der Schutzpolizei Weiberg
Dnjepropetrowsk	Oberst der Schutzpolizei Wilhelm Weinbrenner
Tschernigow	Oberst der Schutzpolizei Georg Asmus Charkow Generalmajor Erik von Heimburg
Luzk (GK Wolhynien)	Oberstleutnant der Schutzpolizei Helmut Ribstein

Wien 1939: SS-Gruf.Dr. Ernst Kaltenbrunner welcomes the new ORPO commander Oberst Dr. Carl Retzlaff. Behind Kaltenbrunner is Polizei Präsident SS-Oberführer Otto Steinhäusl.

Shitomir	unknown
Simferopol (Krim)	Oberst der Gendarmerie Konrad Hitschler
Stalino	unknown
Rostow	Oberst der Schutzpolizei Herman Crux
Kaukasus	
Astrachan (Kalmuckien)	Oberst der Gendarmerie Felix Bauer
Ordschonikidse (Bergvölker)	Oberst der Gendarmerie Alois Menschik
Griechenland (Greece)	
Athen (Südost Griechenland)	Oberstleutnant der Schutzpolizei Gottlieb Nagel
Saloniki (Nord Griechenland)	Oberstleutnant der Schutzpolizei Dr. Johann Stut
Larissa (Mitte Griechenland)	Major der Schutzpolizei Gustav Jonuscheit
Peloponnes (Süd Griechenland)	Major der Schutzpolizei Gustav Vogelsanger
Arta (West Griechenland)	Major der Schutzpolizei Willi Hawranek
Albanien (Albania)	
Tirana	Major der Schutzpolizei Reinhard Trepkow
Italien (Italia)	
Bologna (Oberitalien Mitte)	Oberstleutnant der Schutzpolizei Otto Severt
Operationzone Alpenvorland (South Tirol)	
Bozen	Oberst der Gendarmerie Josef Albert
Ungarn	
Szeged	Hauptmann der Gendarmerie August Hopfner
Deutsches Reich	
Oberschlesien	
Niederschlesien	
Liegnitz	

Croat military C in C Slavo Kvaternik inspects Berlin Traffic Police June 1941

Left to right: (1)Walter Abraham, (2)in white coat: Slavo Kvaternik, (5) Otto Klinger

SS und Polizeistandortführer (SSPStOF)

A decree dated 2 August 1941 created, in the largest towns of occupied Russia, an SS und Polizeistandortführer (SS and Police Garrison Leader). He was responsible to the Stadtkommissar (Mayor). He had similar powers to a Police Administrator in Germany. In the largest towns the relevant SS and Police Leader undertook the duties. In medium sized towns, it was intended that such duties would also be undertaken by the SS and Police, however in the event only two SS-officers were appointed: Dr. Fritz Dietrich a former SD Leader and Paul Krieg a former Gemeindepolizei administrator. Depending on the size of the town the SS und Polizeistandortführer would have a Kommando der Schutzpolizei (company size) or a Schutzpolizei Dienstabteilung (platoon size) to enable him to maintain order.

Order of battle of SS und Polizeistandortführer (1942)

Ostland	
Dorpat	Major der Schutzpolizei Anton Perger
Libau	SS-Sturmbannführer Dr. Fritz Dietrich
Dünaburg	Major der Schutzpolizei Josef Vogt
Wilna	SS-Obersturmbannführer Paul Krieg
Baranowitschi	Major der Gend. Rudolf Schröder
Smolensk	Major der Schutzpolizei Ernst Seyffert
Witebsk	Major der Schutzpolizei Ulrich Freiherr von Hutten zum Stolzenberg
Mogilew	Major der Schutzpolizei Hübert Kölblinger
Pleskau	Hauptmann der Schutzpolizei Hermann
Warnholz	
Ukraine	
Krivoi-Rog	Major der Schutzpolizei Adolf Haan
Brest	Major der Schutzpolizei Rohde
Berditschew	Oberstleutnant der Schutzpolizei Hermann Kölle
Winniza	Major der Schutzpolizei Kurt Pomme
Gomel	Major der Schutzpolizei Kurt Feukert-Emden
Sumy	Major der Schutzpolizei Anton Perger
Kirowograd	Major der Schutzpolizei Heinrich Schultz
Krementschug	Major der Schutzpolizei Gustav Florian
Cherson	Oberst der Schutzpolizei Heinrich Hannibal
Poltawa	Major der Schutzpolizei Hermann Möller
Dnjepropetrowsk	Oberstleutnant der Schutzpolizei Willy Nickel
Nikopol	Major der Schutzpolizei Walter Bennewitz
Saporohje	Major der Schutzpolizei Gustav Schübert
Melitopol	Unknown

Similar posts were set up under the SS and Police leaders in Charkow, Stalino, Bergvölker and under the SS and Polizei leader in Nordkaukasien. All these posts were disbanded in October 1943.

Charkow	
Brjansk	Unknown
Kursk	Unknown

Orel	Unknown
Gaytzin	Major der Schutzpolizei Hermann Messer
Stalino	Major der Schutzpolizei Paul Amthor
Makejewka	Unknown
Mariapol	Unknown
Simferopol	Unknown
Bergvölker	
Grossnij	Unknown
Nordkaukasien	
Woroschilowsk	Oberstleutnant der Schutzpolizei Helmut
Dunnebier	
Pjatigorsk	Major der Schutzpolizei Friedrich Nagele

SS und Polizeigebietsführer

The SS and Police District Leader (SS und Polizeigebietsführer) post appears only in Reichskommissariat Ostland. They exercised authority over German gendarms and locally recruited auxilliary police forces (Schutzmannschaft) in the rural areas of a Gebietskommissariat (equivalent to a Landkreis). He was under orders of the Gebietskommissar and he led a Gendarmeriezug (platoon). Rural police organisation in Generalkommissariat Lettland:

SS und Polizeigebietsführer Riga Land
SS und Polizeigebietsführer Mitau
SS und Polizeigebietsführer Wolmar
SS und Polizeigebietsführer Libau

Polizeigebietsführer

Serbia and Montenegro

When Serbia came under German military administration and it was divided into four military Feldkommandantur. In each military garrison a Polizei Gebietskommandantur was set up:

Polizei Gebietskommandantur I in Nisch with four Polizei Kreis Stellen (Police District Offices)
Polizei Gebietskommandantur II in Belgrad with three Polizei Kreis Stellen
Polizei Gebietskommandantur III in Kraljewo with three Polizei Kreis Stellen
Polizei Gebietskommandantur IV in Sabac with one Polizei Kreis Stelle
In 1944, a new Polizei Gebietskommandantur "B" was created in the Banat where an important Volksdeutsche community resided. In Montenegro, two Police commands were created:
Polizei Gebietskommandantur S (Sjenica)
Polizei Gebietskommandantur Pdg (Podgorica)

Kroatien

Croatia declared itself independent on 10 April 1941 and its leader, Ante Pavelic, signed the "Pact of Rome" with Benito Mussolini. This meant that it was in the Italien sphere of influence although it did supply troops to help the Germans.

Following the Italien surrender the Germans took over direct control and established five Polizeigebietsführer under the control of the Höhere SS und Polizeiführer "Kroatien." The men appointed to these posts were SS-orientated rather than from the Ordnungspolizei sphere. They are mentioned here because they did perform similar duties to others with the same title.

Agram

SS-Brigadeführer und Generalmajor der	
Polizei Willi Brandner	10.07.1943–29.12.1944
SS-Oberführer Otto Reich	29.12.1944–06.01.1945
Aufgelost (disbanded) 6 January 1945	
Banja-Luca	
SS-Standartenführer und Oberst der Polizei Paul Dahm	15.07.1943–20.04.1945

Esseg

SS-Brigadeführer und Generalmajor der Polizei	
Dr. Ferdinand von Sammern-Frankenegg	15.07.1943–20.09.1944
SS-Standartenführer und Oberst der Polizei	
Paul Dahm	20.09.1944–20.04.1945

Knin

SS-Oberführer und Oberst der Polizei Richard Kaaserer	27.07.1943–20.05.1944
Disbanded 20 May 1944	

Sarajewo

SS-Oberführer und Oberst der Polizei Werner Fromm	01.01.1943- 26.04.1944

It will be seen that all these officers except Otto Reich held police rank. This was not Ordnungspolizei rank but came from their service in the SIPO.

General der Polizei, Jürgen von Kamptz

Dänemark

In 1944, two Polizeigebietsführer were created:

Nord Jütland

Süd Jütland (Copenhagen)

Major der Schutzpolizei Jakob Grobben	1944–1945

7.2 Field organisation of the Ordnungspolizei

7.2.1 Actions of the Ordnungspolizei prewar 1938 – 1939

Österreich (March and April 1938)

The Anschluss was the first occasion in which the Ordnungspolizei provided units for service alongside the army. 20,000 men were used, organized into five Marschgruppen (task groups). Based in Bayern (Dachau, Regensburg, Rottenburg, Deggendorf and München) the Marschgruppen were organized as follows:

Marschgruppe I	Oberst August Edler von Meyszner
Marschgruppe II	Oberst Rudolf Querner
Marschgruppe III (Graz)	Oberst Herbert Becker, then Oberst Arthur Mülverstedt
Marschgruppe IV (Wien)	Oberst Herbert Becker
Marschgruppe V	Oberst Karl Pfeffer-Wildenbruch

Each Marschgruppe included several Gruppen formed in various Länder. Gruppe 4 (Nordmark) consisted of seven Hundertschaft from the Schutzpolizei in Hamburg and one Hundertschaft from the Schutzpolizei in Bremen and Wilhelmshaven. Headed by Oberst Erik von Heimburg, the group was organised into three Abteilungen consisting of 42 officers, 976 Policemen and 43 civilians. It served in area of Niederösterreich (Wiener Neustadt, Wien and Eisenstadt). Following the end of the action, temporary IdO posts which had been created from former Gruppen were disbanded: Otto von Oelhafen leader of Group for Steiermark, Kärnten and Osttirol in Graz and Dr. Heinrich Lankenau leader of the group for Tirol Voralberg at Innsbruck. A parade of the Ordnungspolizei troops in Wien conducted by Rudolf Querner was followed by the return of the last 6,000 policemen to the Reich. Oberst Meyszner remained as IdO Wien and Becker as Kommandeur der Schutzpolizei Wien.

Sudetenland (1938) and Czechoslovakia (1939)

Five Police Districts (Abschnitte) were organized for the occupation of the Sudetenland:

Abschnitt I	Oberst August Edler von Meyszner
Abschnitt II	Oberst Paul Will
Abschnitt III	Generalmajor Arthur Mülverstedt
Abschnitt IV	Generalmajor Karl Pfeffer Wildenbruch
Abschnitt V	Generalmajor Wilhelm Roettig

Seven Batallions with 31 companies were used in the action. Three BdO Egerland (Karlsbad), Nord-Böhmen (Aussig) with two bataillons, and Nord-Mähren (Troppau), were appointed in October 1938. In December 1938 the posts were replaced by the BdO Reichenberg covering the Sudetenland. (See "IdO/BdO ")

In March 1939, Polizeieinsatzgruppen were involved in the occupation of Böhmen-Mähren under the command of Rudolf Querner. They remained until the creation of two Polizei-Regiments in and Böhmen-Mähren (see Polizei-Regiments)

7.2.2 Field Units of the Ordnungspolizei in WW II

Polizei-Bataillone 1939 – 1945

Police Battalions were created in September 1939. The basic organisation of a Police battalion in 1939:

Staff:

Commander
Aide-de-camp
Transport officer
Medical officer
Signal officer
Administrative officer

Units:

One company of 145 men each
One light armoured car section
One motorcycle section
One machine gun section
Support units (signals, medical, and transport)

At the outbreak of the war the German police force consisted of 475 officers and 15,328 men used in the creation of the Polizei-Division. 26,000 German policemen were used in the former territory of Poland and 6,000 Volksdeutsche (ethnic Germans) were selected to join the police.

Polizeigruppen Poland 1939 (see "General Government of Poland")

In the first days of the Polish Campaign, six Police groups formed with 13 Police bataillons headed by a BdO were attached to each army. The BdO wore a "Deutsche Wehrmacht" armband. Polizeigruppen were disbanded at the end of September 1939.

Polizei-Bataillons during western campaign 1940

During the campaign in Scandinavia in April 1940, six police battalions were sent to Norway. Police battalions 2, 3, 9, 91,105 and 312 served in the rear areas of the German army in the West. Two battalions (67 and 68) served in Holland. For the operation in France, police battalions were concentrated in the east alongside the Maginot Line for the occupation of newly annexed territories. Three battalions serving in the French province of Lorraine and Great Duchy of Luxemburg (121, 122 and 123) and three in the French province of Alsace (54, 55 and 74).

Order of battle of the Police Battalions (August 1940)

Protectorate Böhmen-Mähren	10 Police Battalions
General Government Poland	13 Police Battalions
	One Mounted Battalion
	One Signals Battalion
Eastern occupied territories (Westpreussen, Wartheland	
Oberschlesien	Seven Police Battalions

Norway	Three Auxilliary Police Battalions
Holland	Four Police Battalions
Reich	21 Police Battalions
26,000	new recruits 38 Police Training Battalions

They were divided into:
60 Police Battalions and Reserve Police Battalions
Three Auxilliary Battalions
38 Police Training Battalions

The strength of these Police Battalions was 1,376 officers and 57,800 men. New battalions were created in 1941 and 1942 for use in Balkans and Eastern territories. By a decree of the Reichsführer-SS dated 9 July 1942, all the Reserve Police Battalions and Police Battalions became part of Polizei-Regiments. They lost their former numbers, taking the number of their regiment. For example, Police Battalion created in Wien in 1939 served as Police Battalion III of Police Group 1 with 14. Armee in Poland. Later numbered Police Battalion 171, in 1942 it became the II./Polizei-Regiment 19 and served in the Balkans.

7.3 Polizei-Regiments 1939-1945

Polizei-Regiments were created on 4 November 1939 in the Generalgovernment of Poland to coordinate the uniformed police forces in each district. They initially had the name of the district: Polizei-Regimenter Krakau, Warschau, Lublin and Radom. In 1941, the police battalions stationed in Norway were organised into Polizei-Regiments "Nord-Norwegen" and "Süd-Norwegen." For Operation Barbarossa, a Polizei-Regiment was attached to each Higher SS and Police Leader appointed to the rear areas of the German army. They initially had the names "Middle," "North," "South" and "z.b.V" (at special disposal).

Order of Battle of the Polizei Regiments in Russia (beginning 1942)

Reichskommissariat Ostland

Polizei-Regiment "Nord" in Opotschka (Estonia)	Oberstleutnant der Schutzpolizei Hermann Keuper
Reserve Polizei-Bataillon 53 in Beshanizy	Hauptmann der Schutzpolizei Fechner
Polizei-Bataillon 319 in Peshariwizi	Major der Schutzpolizei Emmo Geissler
Polizei-Bataillon 321 in Dorpat	Major der Schutzpolizei Lothar Petersen
Reserve Polizei-Bataillon 2 in Rossitten	Major der Schutzpolizei Richard Röhrborn
Reserve Polizei-Bataillon 65 in Bjelaja	Major der Schutzpolizei Barkhold
Reserve Polizei-Bataillon 105 in Riga	Major der Schutzpolizei Hans Helwes
Reserve Polizei-Bataillon 11 in Kaunas	Major der Schutzpolizei Franz Lechthaler
Reserve Polizei-Bataillon 12 in Mitau	Major der Schutzpolizei Sternagel

Reserve Polizei-Bataillon 69 in Wilna	Major der Schutzpolizei Richard Sonnenberg
Reserve Polizei-Bataillon 32 in Minsk	Major der Schutzpolizei Leo von Braunschweig

Russland-Mitte

Polizei-Regiment "Mitte" in Mogilew	Oberst der Schutzpolizei Max Montua
Polizei-Bataillon 307 in Tschetschewitsch	Major der Schutzpolizei Stahr
Polizei-Bataillon 316 in Mogilew	Major der Schutzpolizei Behr
Polizei-Bataillon 322 in Gniesdorog	Major der Schutzpolizei Detlef Ohrt
Reserve Polizei-Bataillon 131 in Toporez	Major der Schutzpolizei Detlef Ohrt
Polizei-Bataillon 309 in Orel	Major der Schutzpolizei Ernst Weis
Polizei-Bataillon 317 in Beruschewsk	Oberstleutnant der Schutzpolizei Erwin Gresser

Reichskommissariat Ukraine

Polizei-Regiment "Süd" in Perejaslau	Oberstleutnant der Rene Rosenbauer
Polizei-Bataillon 314 in Krementschug	Major der Schutzpolizei Otto Severt
Polizei-Bataillon 303 in Kiew	unknown
Reserve Polizei-Bataillon 45 in Poltawa	Major der Schutzpolizei Martin Besser
Reserve Polizei-Bataillon 82 in Orel	Major der Schutzpolizei Rudolf Ebert
Polizei-Bataillon 311 in Pjatischatka	Major der Gendarmerie Walter Danz
Polizei-Bataillon 318 in Krementschug	Major der Schutzpolizei Walter Seltz

Verbände z.b.V (Kaukasus)

Polizei-Regiment "z.b.V." in Rowno	Oberstleutnant der Schutzpolizei Hans Griep
Polizei-Bataillon 304 in Kiew	Major der Schutzpolizei Karl Deckert
Polizei-Bataillon 315 in Shitomir	Hauptmann der Schutzpolizei Klaus
Polizei-Bataillon 320 in Rowno	Hauptmann der Schutzpolizei Dall
Polizei-Reiter-Abteilung I in Rowno	Major der Schutzpolizei Adolf Hahn
Reserve Polizei-Bataillon 9 (location unknown)	unknown

Following the decree of 9 July 1942, all Police Battalions were unified into motorized Polizei-Regiments numbered from 1 to 28. From 24 February 1943, all became "SS" Polizei-Regimenter. This assimilation into the SS was only at unit level. Individual police members didn't automatically become members of the SS. They had to apply to join the SS. Senior officer records show even at the end of the war, racial and other criteria were still followed and a number of requests for entry were refused.

Polizei-Regiments numbered 31 and above were renamed "SS-Polizei-Schützen-Regiment" by decree of 29 March 1943 because of their mixed staff. The first battalion was German. The second and third were foreign volunteers, mainly Ukrainians. They served in anti-partisan duties in the east. In some cases, Polizei Regiments were given special names instead of numbers. Those named after their commander:

Polizei-Regiment "Nagel" in Greece
Polizei-Regiment "von Braunschweig" in Russia

Polizei-Regiment "Griese" (Polizei-Regiment 14 renamed for a special action in Southern France during 1943)
Those named after the area in which they served:
SS-Polizei-Regiment "Alpenvorland"
SS-Polizei-Regiment "Sandschak"

The Polizei-Regiments force in occupied countries

The Schutzpolizei, component of the Ordnungspolizei, had always had a military element in its make up. Initially the function of militerized police units was to deal with civil unrest in the country, to provide guards for major festive occasions and to provide a force to maintain order after any major catastrophe or disturbance. In these duties they worked closely with Party para-military organisations especially the SS. From the end of the Great War until re-armament in March 1935, such duties were covered by the Landespolizei which were taken into the army. After re-armament, replacement units were created and this was done by the use of police reservists being called up to form police battalions. The gradual organisation of these units into regiments followed their increasing adaptation to carrying out purely military functions. During the occupation of Österreich in March 1938 and the Sudetenland in October 1938 approximately 120 to 150 motorised barrack police units called "Hundertschaften" (sentries) were mobilised for action. These companies were combined into "Marschgruppen" of approximately regiment size and took part in the occupation of Österreich and the Sudetenland, fully equipped for field service alongside the Wehrmacht.

With the attack on Poland in September 1939 the need for fully militerized units became more acute and this need increased as additional territory was occupied and police functions extended. The duties of these newly created units included the guarding of lines of communications, the patrolling and safe-guarding of guerrilla infested areas, task force operations against partisans alongside the army and the general maintenance of law and order in co-operation with the army and the SS. They also took an active part in the rounding up of Jews in occupied territories. Before the formation of the majority of the Polizei-Regiments in 1942, police battalions served in the east as independent units. They took part in the killing of Jews as a matter of course. The first two regiments were created in Danzig to co-operate with army "Gruppe Eberhard," a unit formed from the Landespolizei in Danzig that was under the command of Major-General Friedrich-Georg Eberhard. It became the 60. Infanterie-Division on 15 October 1939. Two more regiments were created in September 1939 in Kattowitz and Kielce. By the beginning of 1940 these four regiments had been disbanded.

Two seperate regiments were formed in occupied Czechoslovakia in May 1939 and these were the first to remain in existence until the end of the war. The bulk of the regiments were created in 1941/1942 and by 1945 there were a total of 39. In addition to these, there were a number of regiments formed without numbers. These were usually given the name of the commanding officer. Finally, there were a number of regiments formed in occupied territories under German command but with locally recruited manpower. In addition to these regular Polizei-Regiments there were regiments that formed part of the Waffen-SS controlled police divisions and mobile fire service regiments.The officers and men wore regular police uniforms and police ranks were used. On 24 February 1943 all regiments except the Polizei-Schützen-Regimenter (Numbers 31 to 38) were re-titled SS-Polizei-Regiments. This was done on the orders of Himmler to emphasise the merging of the police with the SS and from that date SS-ranks should have been used in conjunction the police ranks. In effect in the majority of cases this did not occur and the old police uniforms and ranks were retained. Those officers and men who were also members of the SS were distinguished by the wearing of an SS runes badge on the left breast pocket of their police uniforms. It must be emphasised that these regiments were not part of the Waffen-SS and remained under the control of the Kommandoamt of the Hauptamt Ordnungspolizei. Each regiment contained three battalions and all were motorised. The regiment staff also included a signals company, an armoured personnel carrier company, an anti-tank company and an engineering platoon. Some regiment numbers existed twice when a formation was disbanded and a later unit received the regimental designation.

Polizei-Regiment 1 was created on 1 September 1939 using men from the former Landespolizei in Danzig. It was transferred to the army on 18 October 1939 and became Infanterie-Regiment 243, under Oberst Emil Zellner, in the newly formed 60. Infanterie-Division. The regiment was later used to form Schützen-Regiment 114. Its II and III battalions formed parts of Schützen-Regimenter 304 and 394.

Kommandeur

"-"

Polizei-Regiment 1 was reformed in July 1942 in Berlin, consisting of Police Battalions 2, 3 and 10. Initially its I battalion served in northern Russia, the II battalion with the Security Police in the East and the III battalion in Oberkrain (Upper Kärnten). The I battalion served alongside SS-Brigade "Schudt" in December 1942 then, from 1943, it became part of the SS-Police Division. The I and III battalions served with Polizei-Regiment "Griese" in Marseille and became the I and III battalions of Polizei-Regiment 14 in March 1943. The regiment was reorganised in August 1944 in Hungary with the I battalion coming from Hamburg, the II battalion from Prague and the III battalion came from the III./ Polizei-Regiment 21 in Hungary. The Regiment saw action alongside the 8. SS-Kavallerie Division (SS-Oberführer Joachim Rumohr) in December 44/ January 45 and it retreated through Schlesien and East Germany with the 9. army (General der Infanterie Theodor Busse) later the 4 Panzer army (General der Panzertruppen Fritz-Hübert Grässer). It was disbanded on 12 March 1945 and remnants went to 35. SS-Panzer-Grenadier-Division (SS-Standartenführer Rüdiger Pipkorn).

Kommandeur

Oberstleutnant der Schutzpolizei Hans Helwes	-"--20.10.1944
SS-Obersturmbannführer Fritz Grandke	20.10.1944–12.03.1945

Polizei-Regiment 2 was created on 1 September 1939 using men from the former Landespolizei Danzig. It was transferred to the army on 18 October 1939, becoming Infanterie-Regiment 244 under Oberst Karl von Groddeck in the newly formed 60. Infanterie-Division. In 1940 it became Infanterie-Regiment 120.

Kommandeur

SS-Brigadeführer und Generalmajor der Polizei Paul Worm	01.09.1939–18.10.1939

Polizei-Regiment 2 was reformed in July 1942 in Tilsit. It then consisted of Police Battalions 11, 13 and 22. It served in central Russia taking part in operations "Adler" in July 1942, "Wisent" in November 1942 and "Hermann" in August 1943 against partisans. From november 43 to july 44 it served in Bielorussia with Polizei-Kampfgruppe "von Gottberg" (The regiment served at the front in the Polozk area in March 1944). It suffered heavy losses during the Russian summer offensive 44 serving under the 4. army. It moved to the Western Front during December 1944. It returned to Eastern Germany with army Group Center (Generalfeldmarshall Ferdinand Schörner) in last months of the war.

Kommandeur

Oberstleutnant der Schutzpolizei Hans Griep	07.1942–19.03.1943
SS-Gruppenführer und Generalleutnant der Polizei Jakob Sporrenberg	19.03.1943–30.06.1943
SS-Standartenführer Günther Anhalt	01.09.1943–15.07.1944
Oberst der Schutzpolizei Rudolf Haring	15.07.1944–.10.1944

SS-Standartenführer und Oberst der Schutzpolizei	
Richard Paust	10.1944–20.10.1944
Major der Schutzpolizei Johann Heinacker	20.10.1944- 23.11.1944
SS-Obersturmbannführer und Oberstleutnant	
der Gendarmerie Walter Gieseke	22.11.1944–02.12.1944
Hauptmann der Schutzpolizei Konrad Jansen	02.12.1944–end

Polizei-Regiment 3 was created on 8 September 1939 in Kattowitz. It was disbanded in January 1940.

Kommandeur

SS-Gruppenführer und Generalleutnant der Polizei Paul Scheer	08.09.1939–.01.1940

Polizei-Regiment 3 was reformed in July 1942 in Holland. It consisted of Police Battalions 66, 68 and 105 (from Poli-zei- Regiment 12). The Regiment staff and the I battalion were based in Tilburg, the II battalion in Amsterdam and the III battalion in Den Haag. It was involved in security tasks under the 88. Army Corps (General der Infanterie Hans- Wolfgang Reinhard) and under 59. Infanterie-Division (Generalleutnant Walter Poppe) at the end of 1944. It remained in Holland until the end of the war.

Kommandeur

Oberst der Schutzpolizei Hans Böhmer	09.07.1942–20.10.19
Unknown	20.10.1944–end

Polizei-Regiment 4 was created on 16 September 1939 in Kielce and disbanded in January 1940.

Kommandeur

Generalmajor der Polizei Dr. Friedrich Wolfstieg	16.09.1939–.01.1940

Polizei-Regiment 4 was reformed in July 1942 in France by order of the Befehlhaber der Ordnungspolizei in Paris, Bodo von Schweinichen. It consisted of Police Battalions 316 and 323 and its III battalion came from Organisation Todt Battalion 62. It moved to the Generalgouvernment in June 1943 where it was involved in anti-partisans operations against the Polish Home army and Polish Communist groups in the Zamosc area and Carpathian mountains. At the beginning of 1944, parts of the regiment were involved in several actions in Biabla Gora, Chelmno, Krasnik, Bilgoraj, Radzyn. In December 1944 became part of the Kampfgruppe "Hannibal" on the East Prussian borders in Wehrkreis I.

Kommandeur

Oberst der Schutzpolizei Bodo von Schweinichen	09.07.1942–06.01.1943
SS-Obersturmbannführer und Oberstleutnant	
der Schutzpolizei Erich Skowronnek	16.04.1943–18.08.1943
SS-Oberführer Otto Reich	18.08.1943–06.03.1944
SS-Obersturmbannführer	
und Oberstleutnant der Schutzpolizei Walter Danz	06.03.1944–01.1945
SS-Brigadeführer und Generalmajor	
der Polizei Heinrich Hannibal	01.1945–end

Polizei-Regiment 5 was created in July 1942 in Serbia by the Befehlhaber der Ordnungspolizei in Belgrade, Andreas May. It consisted of Police Battalions 64 and 322 plus its III battalion from the Colonial Police in Oranienburg. At the end of 1944, it was attached to the 91. Army Corps (Generalleutnant Werner von Erdmansdorff) then fight with Kampfgruppe "Lindenblatt". It served in Serbia until March 1945. In January 1943 members of the Regiment were used as instructors in the Polizei-Ausbildungs-Regiment in Oranienburg.

Kommandeur

Generalmajor der Polizei Andreas May	09.07.1942–1942
Major der Schutzpolizei Detlef Ohrt	1942–.05.1944
Oberstleutnant der Schutzpolizei Franz Lechthale	05.1944–04.07.1944
Oberstleutnant der Schutzpolizei Wilhelm Schwertschlager	04.07.1944–25.10.1944
Major der Schutzpolizei Wolfgang Hoffmann	25.10.1944–end

Polizei-Regiment 6 was created in July 1942 in Southern Russia for security duties with the army. It consisted of Police Battalions 82, 311 and 318. After service in Southern Russia with Security Divisions 454 (Generalleutnant Hellmuth Koch), 444 (Generalleutnant Adalbert Mikulicz) and 213 (Generalleutnant Alexander Goeschen), it was destroyed during the post Stalingrad fighting in January 1943. The remains were used by Polizei-Regiment 24. The Regiment was reformed in Hungary in October 1944, serving there until its destruction in Budapest on 11 February 1945.

Kommandeur

SS-Brigadeführer und Generalmajor der Polizei	
Dr. Günther Merk	15.09.1942–06.01.194
Oberstleutnant der Schutzpolizei Martin Valtin	06.01.1943–21.04.1943
SS-Obersturmbannführer und Oberstleutnant	
der Schutzpolizei Walter Soosten	21.04.1943–04.194
(The above two officers commanded the remnants of the Regiment	
staff at Aldershof)	
SS-Sturmbannführer und Oberstleutnant	
der Schutzpolizei Richard Maiwald	20.10.1944–12.1944
SS-Oberführer Helmut Dörner	12.1944–11.02.1945

(The last commander also commanded a Kampfgruppe in the IX. Waffen-Gebirgskorps der SS (Kroatische)

Polizei-Regiment 7 was created in July 1942 in Wehrkreis VI in Münster. It consisted of Police Battalions 309, 317 and 123. In January 1943 it moved to Norway where it stayed for the remainder of the war. One of its battalions was involved in protection of heavy water plant at Rjukan.

Kommandeur

Oberstleutnant der Schutzpolizei Schaber	09.07.1942–03.01.1944
SS-Standartenführer und	
Oberst der Schutzpolizei Gerhard Hoppe	03.01.1944–end

Polizei-Regiment 8 was created in July 1942 in central Russia for security duties with the army. It consisted of Police Battalions 91, 111 and 134 and saw action in southern Russia with Security Divisions 221 (Generalleutnant Johann Pfugbeil), 403 (Generalleutnant Wilhelm Russwurm), 286 (Generalleutnant Johann Richert) and 201 (Generalleutnant Alfred Jacobi) Destroyed in the Stalingrad battles of February 1943, its remnants were used in Polizei-Schützen-Regiment 36.

The regiment was reformed in the Protectorate of Böhmen-Mähren in November 1944 and one battalion served in Hungary alongside the 271. Volksgrenadier-Division (Generalmajor Martin Bieber) until March 1945 when it moved to Stettin.

Kommandeur	
Major der Schutzpolizei Paulus Meier	07.42 – 10.44
Oberstleutnant der Schutzpolizei Ernst Weis	11.1944–03.1945

Polizei-Regiment 9 was created in July 1942 in northern Russia for security duties with the army. It consisted of Police Battalions 6, 112 and 132 which were split up between 207 (Generalleutnant Karl von Tiedemann), 281 (Generalmajor Wilhelm von Stockhausen) and 287 security divisions. From december 1943, the regiment saw action alongside the Polizei-Gruppe Jeckeln in the Baltic states and it remained in the area until July 1944 when it was destroyed. Its remnants became part of III./Polizei-Regiment 16. The regiment was reformed around Polizei-Regiment "Alpenvorland" on 29 January 1945 in Northen Slovenia.

Polizei-Regiment 10 was created in June 1941 as Polizei-Regiment "Süd" for security duties in southern Russia. It became Polizei-Regiment 10 in July 1942 and consisted of Police Battalions 45, 303 and 314. Served under HSSPF Russland-Süd then as part of front Kampfgruppe "Prützmann" in Ukraine. Moved to Galicia in the spring of 1944, it was based in Kostopol in April and in Stanislawczik during May as part of 4. Panzer army. In July 1944 it moved to Slovenia under the control of Höhere SS und Polizeiführer Adriatic Coast Odilo Globocnik. Its headquarters were based in Görz with its I Battalion in Prestane, II Battalion in Idria and the III Battalion in Aidussena. It remained there until the end of the war.

Kommandeur	
Oberst der Schutzpolizei René Rosenbauer	06.1941–09.07.1942
SS-Oberführer und Oberst der Schutzpolizei	
Hermann Kintrup	03.07.1942–15.12.1943
Oberst der Gendarmerie Hans Köllner	15.12.1943–15.07.1944
Oberst der Schutzpolizei Richard Stahn	15.07.1944–20.10.1944
Oberstleutnant der Schutzpolizei Fritz Auscher	20.10.1944–end

Polizei-Regiment 11 was created late in 1941 as Polizei-Regiment "z.b.V." under the control of the Höhere SS und Polizeiführer "z.b.V.," Gerret Korsemann, in southern Russia. It became Polizei-Regiment 11 in July 1942 and consisted of Police Battalions 304, 315 and 320. It served in southern Russia until April 1944 when it moved to Galicia under Höchster SS und Polizeiführer Ukraine as part of Kampfgruppe "Prützmann" From July to September 1944 the unit served under the command of LVI. Panzer-Korps (General der Infanterie Johannes Block) in Galicia then in Vistula river area (Poland). In December 1944, remnants of the regiment moved to Sachsen.

Kommandeur	
Oberst der Schutzpolizei Walter Griep	12.41 – 07.42
Oberst der Schutzpolizei Erwin Gresser	07.42–16.03.1944
Oberst der Schutzpolizei Hermann Stührmann	16.03.1944–08.06.1944
SS-Sturmbannführer und Major der Schutzpolizei	
Hans Gewehr	08.06.1944–end

Polizei-Regiment 12 was created in July 1942 in Hamburg under the control of the Inspector of the Ordnungspolizei Rainer Liessem. It consisted of Police Battalions 103, 104 and 105. The latter battalion soon went to Holland to become part of Polizei-Regiment 3. The staff remained in Hamburg until 11 April 1944. The I Battalion became part of Polizei- Schützen-Regiment 31 in April 1943. II battalion went to Hungary in April 1944 and became the I./Polizei-Regiment 1 in August 1944. The III battalion went to Italy in October 1943 and served in Polizei-Regiment 15 in Verona from February to December 1944, ending the war in Campiglia. This regiment seems to have been a holding regiment used to supply battalions as needed.

Kommandeur

SS-Standartenführer, Oberst der Schutzpolizei	
Wilhelm Machtan	07.1942–end

Polizei-Regiment 13 was created in June 1941 as Polizei-Regiment "Mitte" under the control of the Höhere SS und Polizeiführer "Russland-Mitte," Erich von dem Bach. In the summer of 1942 it became Polizei-Regiment 13. Consisting of Police Battalions 6, 85 and 301, it served in central Russia with 286 then 203 Security Division (Generalleutnant Rudolf Pilz) later with Kampfgruppe " von Gottberg". In August 1944 it moved to Laibach in Slovenia to combat partisans.

Kommandeur

SS-Brigadeführer und Generalmajor der	
Polizei Max Montua	06.1941–12.01.1942
SS-Gruppenführer und Generalleutnant der Polizei	
Walter Schimana	12.01.1942–21.07.1942
SS-Brigadeführer und Generalmajor der Polizei	
Paul Worm	25.06.1942–27.01.1943
SS-Sturmbannführer und Major der Schutzpolizei	
Fritz Schill	27.01.1943–06.02.1943
SS-Standartenführer und Oberst der Schutzpolizei	
Willy Nickel	06.02.1943–15.11.1943
SS-Obersturmbannführer und Oberstleutnant	
der Schutzpolizei Hans Fleckner	15.11.1943–20.10.1944
Unknown	20.10.1944–end

Polizei-Regiment 14 was created on 7 July 1942 in central Russia under the control of Höhere SS und Polizeiführer Erich von dem Bach. It was known as Polizei-Regiment 38 until 9 July 1942. Consisting of Police Battalions 51, 122 and 313, it served in southern Russia with 286. Security Division and then with german divisions of the 8. Italian army until its destruction in Kharkov in January 1943. It was reformed in southern France from Polizei-Regiment "Griese" on 29 March 1943 and was involved in the destruction of the Port of Marseille. In the spring of 1944 it was transferred to Upper Krajina and Slovenia. In March 1945, I and II Battalions moved to the Oder front. Then in April 1945 the regiment staff, I and II battalions were used to form SS-Polizei-Grenadier-Regiment 3 in the 35. SS-Polizei-Grenadier- Division. The remainder of the regiment was disolved. On 6 April 1945 the regiment became SS-Polizei-Grenadier- Regiment 81 under Waffen-SS control.

Kommandeur

SS-Standartenführer und Oberst der Schutzpolizei	
Albert Buchmann	07.07.1942–31.12.19
Oberstleutnant der Schutzpolizei Bleher	31.12.1942–01.1943
SS-Obersturmbannführer und	
Oberstleutnant der Polizei Otto Peter	.01.1943–29.03.1943
SS-Standartenführer und Oberst der Schutzpolizei	
Bernhard Griese	29.03.1943–06.03.1944
SS-Standartenführer und Oberst der Schutzpolizei	
Willy Nickel	06.03.1944–.01.1945
SS-Standartenführer und Oberst der Schutzpolizei	
Bernhard Griese	01.1945–.04.1945

Polizei-Regiment 15 was created in July 1942 in northern Russia from part of Polizei-Regiment "Nord." It was under the control of Höhere SS und Polizeiführer Friedrich Jeckeln and consisted of Police Battalions 306 and 310. It served in southern Russia, minus a I battalion, from late 1942 until January 1943 as part of Kampfgruppe "Prützmann" when it was destroyed in the Stalingrad battles. It was reformed in Milowitz in February 1943 using SS-Polizei-Regiment "von Braunschweig" plus Polizei-Bataillon 305 from Polizei-Regiment 16 that became its I battalion. It moved to Norway in June 1943 where the regiment staff and I battalion were based in Sarpsborg, the II battalion in Mysen and III battalion in Bergen. It was transferred to Italy in the autumn of 1943. The regiment staff based in Vercelli, the I battalion in Turin, the II battalion in Mailand and the III battalion in Triest. Involved in actions against Italian partisans, it remained in this area until the end of the war.

Kommandeur

SS-Standartenführer und Oberst der Schutzpolizei	
Walter Endler	07.1942–09.10.194
Oberst der Schutzpolizei Emil Kursk	09.10.1942–15.03.1943
Oberst der Schutzpolizei Leo von Braunschweig	15.03.1943–15.07.1944
Oberst der Schutzpolizei Ludwig Buch	15.07.1944–20.10.1944
Unknown	20.10.1944–end

Polizei-Regiment 16 was created in July 1942 in northern Russia from part of Polizei-Regiment "Nord" under the control of Höhere SS und Polizeiführer Friedrich Jeckeln. It consisted of Police Battalions 56, 102 and 121. From November 1942 until July 1943, the regiment served in northern Russia next to 2. SS-Brigade (which later became the Latvian SS-Brigade) and the SS-Polizei-Division. Initially Police Battalion 305 was part of the regiment but this became the I./Polizei-Regiment 15 when it was reformed in February 1943. Its I battalion became a training battalion in Tilsit until 5 February 1943 and a new I battalion was created from the I./Polizei-Regiment 3 in July 1944. Part of Kampfgruppe "Jeckeln" from October 1943 to January 1944 serving in the Baltic States Its II battalion was reformed from Polizei-Regiment 9 in July 1944. The regiment was dissolved in December 1944.

Kommandeur

Oberst der Schutzpolizei Hermann Keuper	13.08.1942–10.1942
Oberst der Schutzpolizei Emil Kursk	15.03.1943–01.09.1943

SS-Brigadeführer und Generalmajor der Polizei Otto Gieseke	01.09.1943–23.11.1943
SS-Obersturmbannführer und Oberstleutnant der Schutzpolizei Walter Titel	23.11.1943–20.10.1944
Oberstleutnant der Schutzpolizei Walter Gieseke	20.10.1944–.12.1944

Polizei-Regiment 17 was created in northern Russia in July 1942 from part of Polizei-Regiment "Nord" under the control of Höhere SS und Polizeiführer Friedrich Jeckeln. It consisted of Police Battalions 42, 74 and 69. From September 1942 to March 1944 served with 16. Armee (Generaloberst Ernst Busch then General der Kavallerie Christian Hansen) in Northern area. Its III battalion became II battalion of the Polizei-Regiment 28 "Todt" and a new battalion was formed from the Polizei-Regiment "von Braunschweig" in Milowitz bei Lissa, it in turn became the I./Polizei-Schützen-Regiment 32 and another III battalion was formed in the spring of 1944. The regiment was served in northern Russia until the spring of 1944 when it moved to southern Russia. In June 1944 it moved to Warschau and took part with Polizei-Gruppe "von den Bach" in the fighting against the Polish Home army in the city in October 1944. It then served in the defence of the town until December 1944.

Kommandeur

Oberstleutnant der Schutzpolizei Richard Stahn	09.07.1942–12.1942
Oberst der Schutzpolizei Friedrich Wilhelm Bock	12.1942–1943
SS-Obersturmbannführer und Oberstleutnant der Schutzpolizei Wilhelm Hertlein	1943–04.07.1944
Oberstleutnant der Schutzpolizei Franz Lechthaler	04.07.1944–end

Polizei-Gebirgsjäger-Regiment 18 was created in July 1942 as Polizei-Regiment 18 in Garmisch-Partenkirchen under the control of the Commander of the Ordnungspolizei Kurt Wolter. It was re-designated as Polizei-Gebirgsjäger-Regiment 18 (Police Mountain Rifle Regiment) on 23 May 1943. It consisted of Police Battalions 302, 312 and 325. It served in Upper Krajina and Slovenia until March 1943 when it moved to Finland. The regiment fought in Northern Finland next to 18. Moutain Corps (General der Infanterie Franz Böhme). In October 1943 it moved to Greece and was engaged against partisans. It retreated with german army through Yugoslavia from October 1944. In December 1944 it was repatriated to Regensburg from the Balkans.

Kommandeur

SS-Brigadeführer und Generalmajor der Polizei Hermann Franz	09.07.1942–08.1943
Oberstleutnant der Schutzpolizei Hans Hösl	08.1943–02.10.1944
Major der Schutzpolizei Otto Mann	02.10.1944–.10.1944
Major der Schutzpolizei Johann Poys	10.1944–end

Polizei-Regiment 19 was created in July 1942 in Veldes for duty in the Alpenvorland. It consisted of Police Battalions 72, 171 and 181 and served in Lower Steiermark and Upper Kärnten until June 1944. It then moved to France under the control of the Befehlhaber der Ordnungspolizei, Paul Scheer. Stationed in Alps, the regiment moved to eastern of France. It fought alongside 16. Volksgrenadier-Division (Generalleutnant Ernst Haeckel) in Alsace at the end of 1944. Ended the war in Kärnten and Slovenia areas.

Kommandeur

SS-Standartenführer und Oberst der Schutzpolizei Bernhard Griese	09.07.1942–04.1943

Oberstleutnant der Schutzpolizei Hübert Kölblinger	04.1943–15.07.1944
Major der Schutzpolizei Bartscht	15.07.1944–end

Polizei-Regiment 20 was created in May 1939 as Polizei-Regiment " Böhmen". It consisted of Police Battalions Prag (later 319), Klattau (later 32), Tabor (later 316), Jung-Bunzlau (later 320) and Pardubitz (later 317). It became Polizei-Regiment 20 in July 1942 with Police Battalions 32, 317 and 319. Police Battalion 316 moved to central Russia in July 1941 and Police Battalion 320 to southern Russia in July 1942. The regiment served in Böhmen-Mähren and the I battalion became I./Polizei-Schützen-Regiment 33 in April 1943. A new I battalion was formed from the Police Training Battalion in Klagenfurt and in October 1943 it became an independent battalion in Rome. The regiment moved to West Emilia in Italy early in 1944 and in September 1944 it moved to Biella. Its II battalion moved to Hungary in March 1944 and became the I./Polizei-Regiment 1.

Kommandeur

SS-Gruppenführer und Generalleutnant der Polizei Reiner Liessem	05.1939–31.08.1940
SS-Brigadeführer und Generalmajor der Polizei Eberhard Herf	31.08.1940–06.1941
Oberst der Schutzpolizei Leo von Braunschweig	06.1941–03.1942
SS-Standartenführer und Oberst der Schutzpolizei Paul Baehren	03.1942–12.08.1942
SS-Brigadeführer und Generalmajor der Polizei Anton Diermann	12.08.1942–06.09.1943
Oberst der Schutzpolizei Hans-Georg Hirschfeld	2.09.1943–end

Polizei-Regiment 21 was created in May 1939 as Polizei-Regiment "Mähren." It consisted of Police Battalions Brünn (later 315), Iglau (later 318) and Holleschau (later 84). It became Polizei-Regiment 21 in July 1942 with Police Battalion 32 in Brünn, individual companies in Iglau and a new battalion formed in Prague. The regiment served in Mähren, its I battalion became the I./Polizei-Schützen-Regiment 34 in April 1943 and a new I battalion was formed. The III battalion moved to Hungary in March 1944 and in August 1944 it became the II./Polizei-Regiment 1. The regimental staff and the battalions became mobile without a fixed base in April 1945 to escape the advancing Russians.

Kommandeur

SS-Brigadeführer und Generalmajor der Polizei Paul Worm	15.05.1939–13.02.1940
SS-Brigadeführer und Generalmajor der Polizei Alfred Karrasch	13.02.1940–01.10.1941
SS-Standartenführer und Oberst der Gendarmerie Georg Attenberger	18.07.1942–15.02.1945
SS-Obersturmbannführer und Oberstleutnant der Schutzpolizei Walter Danz	15.02.1945–29.03.1945
SS-Standartenführer und Oberst der Gendarmerie Georg Attenberger	29.03.1945–end

Polizei-Regiment 22 was created on 4 November 1939 as Polizei-Regiment "Warschau," it consisted of three battalions that later became Police Battalions 301, 304 and 307. It became Polizei-Regiment 22 in 1942 and it then consisted of Police Battalions 41 and 53 plus individual companies from Zamosz, Lublin and Krakau that became the II battalion on

23 January 1943. It served in the Generalgouvernment with the regimental staff and the II and II battalions in Warschau and the I battalion in Lublin. It moved the central Russia in July 1944 as part of Polizei-Gruppe "von Gottberg" and it was destroyed in the general collapse of army Group "Centre" in that month. A winding up staff was abolished in Danzig on the 21 December 1944.

Kommandeur

SS-Gruppenführer und Generalleutnant der Waffen-SS und der Polizei Karl-Heinrich Brenner	04.11.1939–12.03.1940
SS-Brigadeführer und Generalmajor der Polizei Max Montua	12.03.1940–06.1941
SS-Standartenführer und Oberst derSchutzpolizei Joachim Petsch	06.1941–04.1943
Oberst der Schutzpolizei Rudolf Haring	04.1943–15.07.1944

Note: The regiment commander also held the post of Kommandeur der Ordnungspolizei for Warschau until June 1941

Polizei-Regiment 23 was created on 4 November 1939 as Polizei-Regiment "Krakau." It consisted of two battalions in Krakau that later became Police Battalions 311 and 321, a battalion in Jaslo that became Police Battalion 303 and one in Rzeszow that became Police Battalion 314. The regiment became Polizei-Regiment 23 in 1942 and consisted of Police Battalion 307. II and III battalions were formed on 23 January 1943 from individual companies from Krakau, Rzeszow, Lemberg, Radom, Tschenstochau and Kielce. The III battalion became III./Polizei-Regiment 24 early in 1943 and a new III Battalion was formed. The III battalion served against partisans in the Krakau district and the rest of the regiment served as a Kampfgruppe in Oberschlesien from August 1944. The II battalion was disbanded in November 1944 and the remainder of the regiment in March 1945.

Kommandeur

SS-Gruppenführer und Generalleutnant der Polizei Emil Höring	04.11.1939–01.1940
Oberst der Schutzpolizei Hermann Keuper	01.1940–12.1941
Oberstleutnant der Schutzpolizei Richard Gassler	12.1941–13.08.1942
Oberst der Gendarmerie Werner Bardua	13.08.1942–09.12.1943
Oberst der Schutzpolizei Felix Bauer	09.12.1943–.03.1945

Note: The regiment commander was also Kommandeur der Ordnungspolizei for Krakau until December 1941.

Polizei-Regiment 24 was created on 13 November 1939 as Polizei-Regiment "Radom." It consisted of a battalion in Radom (later Police Battalion 309), one in Tschenstochau (later Police Battalion 310) and one in Kielce (later Police Battalion 305). The regiment became Polizei-Regiment 24 in July 1942 with its headquarters in Lemberg, consisting of Police Battalions 83 and 153 from Lemberg and 93 from Upper Kärnten. It absorbed the remnants of Polizei-Regiment 6 after that regiment had been destroyed in the Stalingrad battles. The regiment served in Galicia with its III battalion still in Upper Kärnten. This battalion became part of the Polizei-Regiment "Griese" in France in January 1943 and a new III battalion was created from the III./Polizei-Regiment 23. The regiment served under the command of the Höhere SS und Polizeiführer "Russland-Mitte" in Mogilew from May 1943. It was part of Polizei-Gruppe "von Gottberg" from November 1943 until January 1944 and served in the area of 16. army in Bielorussia Following the collapse of army Group "Center" in November 1944 it was reformed in the area of Kattowitz-Hindenburg in Schlesien where it remained until the end of the war.

Kommandeur

SS-Oberführer und Oberst der Schutzpolizei	
Ferdinand Heske	13.11.1939–14.11.1940
SS-Brigadeführer und Generalmajor der Polizei	
Paul Worm	25.10.1940–24.06.1942
SS-Obersturmbannführer und	
Oberstleutnant der Schutzpolizei Walter Soosten	09.07.1942–21.04.1943
SS-Standartenführer und Oberst der Schutzpolizei	
Hans Egon Russel	21.04.1943–1944
SS-Obersturmbannführer und Oberstleutnant der Schutzpolizei	
Erich Treuke	1944–31.10.1944
Oberst der Schutzpolizei Borgsen	01.11.1944–03.12.1944
SS-Standartenführer und Oberst der Schutzpolizei	
Richard Paust	03.12.1944–01.1945
Oberst der Gendarmerie Werner Meltzer	01.1945–end

Note: The regiment commander also held the post of Kommandeur der Ordnungspolizei for Radom until 1942

Polizei-Regiment 25 was created in January 1940 as the Polizei-Regiment "Lublin" with battalions in Lublin, Zamosc and Biala Podlaska (they later became Police Battalions 306, 308 and 313). It became Polizei-Regiment 25 in July 1942 and consisted of Police Battalions 65, 67 and 101. The latter battalion has been the subject of quite extensive research into its activities in killing Jews in the Lublin area. The regiment served for the whole of its career in Poland against partisans While II and III Bataillon remained in West Poland, the first one "Cholm" fought in Upper Krajina on April 45.

Kommandeur

SS-Gruppenführer und Generalleutnant der Polizei	
Gerret Korsemann	01.03.1940–01.02.1941
SS-Brigadeführer und Generalmajor der Polizei	
Walter Griphan	01.02.1941–05.12.1941
SS-Oberführer und Oberst der Schutzpolizei	
Hermann Kintrup	05.12.1941–03.07.1942 (M.F.b. until 22.05.1942)
Oberst der Schutzpolizei August Preyssl	03.07.1942–15.07.1944
Oberstleutnant der Schutzpolizei Konrad Rheindorf	15.07.1944–30.10.1944
SS-Obersturmbannführer und Oberstleutnant	
der Schutzpolizei Erich Treuke	30.10.1944–.12.1944
Oberst der Schutzpolizei Rudolf Haring	12.1944–21.02.1945

Polizei-Regiment 26 was created in 1941 as Polizei-Regiment "Nord-Norwegen" under the control of the Höhere SS und Polizeiführer for Norway, Wilhelm Rediess. It became Polizei-Regiment 26 in July 1942 and was based in Drontheim. It consisted of Police Battalions 251, 255 and 256 and it served in Norway until May 1943 when it moved to Germany. Its I battalion was sent to Schneidemühl, II battalion to Aldershorst and the III battalion went to Thorn. In June

1943 it was sent to Baranowitschi in central Russia, moved to the Carpathians in September 1943 and to Kiev in October 1943. Served with Polizei-Kampfgruppe "Jeckeln" in December 1943 and was attached to 16. army up to the end of March 1944. Part of the regiment served with Polizei-Kampfgruppe "von Gottberg" from April 44 until it was destroyed in July 1944 in Bielorussia. The remnants of the regiments were disolved in November 1944.

Kommandeur

Oberstleutnant der Schutzpolizei Georg Weissig	1941–09.07.1942
SS-Standartenführer und Oberst der Schutzpolizei Walter Strehlow	09.07.1942–01.03 1944
Oberstleutnant der Schutzpolizei Georg Weissig	01.03.1944–.09.1944
Hauptmann der Schutzpolizei Hermann Zinner	09.1944–06.10.1944
SS-Obersturmbannführer und Oberstleutnant der Schutzpolizei Ernst Korn	06.10.1944–.11.1944

Polizei-Regiment 27 was created in 1941 as Polizei-Regiment "Süd-Norwegen" under the control of Höhere SS und Polizeiführer Wilhelm Rediess. It became Polizei-Regiment 27 in July 1942 and was based in Oslo, it consisted of police battalions 9, 44, 319 and 321. Its four battalions were situated in Kongsvinger, Oslo, Bergen and Halden. In June 1943 its I battalion became the I./Polizei-Regiment 15 and its IV battalion became the new I Battalion. It stayed in Norway until the end of the war.

Kommandeur

Unknown	1941–09.10.1942
SS-Standartenführer und Oberst der Schutzpolizei Walter Endler	09.10.1942–01.08.1944
SS-Oberführer und Oberst der Schutzpolizei Hans Müller-Brunckhorst	01.08.1944–end

Polizei-Regiment 28 "Todt" was created in July 1942 in Norway, it consisted of Police Battalions 252 and 253 in Norway and 313 in Wismar. The I battalion became the III./Polizei-Regiment 17, the II battalion became the I./Polizei-Regiment 15 and the III battalion became the III./Polizei-Regiment 14. In November 1942 the regiment was reformed as Polizei-Regiment 28 "Todt" for use in security duties in connection with building work in occupied territories and it consisted of police battalions 62 and 69 and a III battalion formed from various sources. Initially the I battalion was based in Brest (France), the II battalion in Riga and the III Battalion in Poltava. In August 1943 the whole regiment was concentrated in France to provide security for coastal defense construction. The regiment moved to Upper Krajina in February 1944 in area of Höhere SS und Polizeiführer Alpenland and saw action in Kärnten in June 1944. Later in 1945 it was located in Slovenia.

Kommandeur

Oberstleutnant der Schutzpolizei Fritz Helmut Kosterbeck	18.08.1942–20.10.1944
Major der Schutzpolizei Johann Heinacker	20.10.1944–end

Polizei-Regiment 29 was created on 16 March 1945 as Polizei-Regiment "z.b.V. 1" for use by SS-Polizei-Brigade "Wirth." It became Polizei-Regiment 29 in March 1945 and SS-Polizei-Grenadier-Regiment 89 on 6 April 1945 under Waffen-SS control.

Kommandeur
SS-Standartenführer und Oberst der Schutzpolizei
Friedrich Korff 16.03.1945–end

Polizei-Regiment 30 was created on 16 March 1945 as Polizei-Regiment "z.b.V. 2" for use by SS-Polizei-Brigade "Wirth." It became Polizei-Regiment 30 in March 1945 and SS-Polizei-Grenadier-Regiment 90 on 6 April 1945 under Waffen-SS control.

Kommandeur
Oberstleutnant der Schutzpolizei Fritz Auscher 16.03.1945–.04.1945
SS-Sturmbannführer und Oberstleutnant der Schutzpolizei
Helmut Diehl 04.1945–end.

Polizei-Schützen-Regiment 31 was created on 21 April 1943 using the I./Polizei-Regiment 12. The II and III battalions were formed on 14 May 1943. It served in central Russia as part of 4. army (Generaloberst Gotthard Heinrici) and was destroyed on the 30 August 1944. Its remnants became Einsatzgruppe "Vogt" of Polizeigruppe "Hannibal" in December 1944.

Kommandeur
SS-Brigadeführer und Generalmajor der Polizei
Heinrich Hannibal 21.04.1943–30.08.1944
SS-Sturmbannführer und Major der Schutzpolizei
Willy Vogt 30.08.1944–10.04.1945

Polizei-Schützen-Regiment 32 was created on 21 April 1943 and its I battalion had been the III./Polizei-Regiment 17. The II and III battalions were formed 16 May 1943. The I battalion later became the I./Galician SS-Freiwilligen-Regiment 5 and fought against partisans in the Lublin area. The rest of the regiment became Schutzmannschaft (Schuma) Battalion 206 on the 16 August 1943.

Kommandeur
Oberstleutnant der Schutzpolizei Franz Lechthaler

Polizei-Schützen-Regiment 33 was created on 21 April 1943 and its I battalion had been the I./Polizei-Regiment 20. The II and III battalions were formed on 14 May 1943. The regiment saw service in the Ukraine with 2 army (Generaloberst Walter Weiss) and then with 4. Panzer army. In March/April 44 served into Polizei-Kampfgruppe "Prützmann" then with Kampfgruppe "Brenner". It was disbanded on 25 March 1944 and its remnants were sent to Polizei-Regiment 10.

Kommandeur
Oberst der Gendarmerie Hans Köllner 21.04.1943–15.12.1943
SS-Standartenführer und Oberst der Schutzpolizei
Ernst Köhler 15.12.1943–25.03.1944

Polizei-Schützen-Regiment 34 was created on 21 April 1943, its I battalion had been the I./Polizei-Regiment 21. The II and III battalions were formed on 14 May 1943. The regiment saw service in anti-partisan warfare in the Bialystok district and then in Ostpreussen. From October to December 1944 it took part in the fighting in Warschau against the Polish Home army with 9. army It was disbanded on 5 February 1945 and its remnants became Grenadier-Regiment "Becker" in Division "Raegener" (Generalleutnant Adolf Raegener) in Oder area.

Kommandeur

Oberstleutnant der Schutzpolizei Martin Diez	21.04.1943–07.1944
Oberstleutnant der Schutzpolizei Franz Wichman	07.1944–05.02.1945

Polizei-Schützen-Regiment 35 was created on 21 April 1943, its I battalion had been the III./Polizei-Regiment 24. The II and III battalions were formed on 14 May 1943 and the regiment served in the Ukraine under 4. Panzer army until it was disbanded on 25 March 1944. Its remnants were absorbed by Polizei-Regiment 10.

Kommandeur

Oberstleutnant der Schutzpolizei Martin Valtin

Polizei-Schützen-Regiment 36 was created on 24 June 1943, its I battalion had been the II./Polizei-Regiment 1. The II and III battalions were formed in June 1943 from locally raised Schutzmannschaft Battalions and the regiment served in central and White Russia alongside the 4. army. It was disbanded on 30 August 1944.

Kommandeur

Oberstleutnant der Schutzpolizei Martin Valtin	09.07.1943–30.08.1944

Polizei-Schützen-Regiment 37 was created on 23 November 1943 from Police Security Detachment Southern Russia for Durchgangstrasse IV. The first company was made up of German policemen while the second, third and fourth companies were comprised of Cossacks. These companies were enlarged until the regiment had three battalions. It served in the Ukraine under the command of the Befehlhaber der Ordnungspolizei for Rowno, Karl-Heinrich Brenner in the area of 4. Panzer Army. The regiment was disbanded in April 1944 and remnants absorbed by Polizei-Regiment 11.

Kommandeur

SS-Brigadeführer und Generalmajor der Polizei Otto Gieseke	23.11.1943–25.03.1944

Polizei-Regiment 38 was created on 7 July 1942 for service in central Russia. It became Polizei-Regiment 14 on 9 July 1942.

Kommandeur

SS-Standartenführer und Oberst der Schutzpolizei Albert Buchmann	07.07.1942–09.07.1942

Polizei-Schützen-Regiment 38 was created on 15 August 1944 under the control of the Befehlhaber der Ordnungspolizei Schwarzes Meer (Black Sea), Werner Meltzer. It had three battalions and was disbanded in November 1944.

Kommandeur

Oberstleutnant der Schutzpolizei Ernst Weis	15.07.1944–20.10.1944

Polizei-Regiment 50 created in April 1945 using the I./Polizei-Regiment 21 as a basis. It is shown with three battalions but it is thought that it was never brought up to full strength. It is not known where it served.

Kommandeur

SS-Sturmbannführer und Major der Schutzpolizei Richard Dröge

The above is the complete list of numbered Polizei-Regiments excluding those that formed the two police divisions that served in the Waffen-SS. There were other Polizei-Regiments. Those that had names instead of numbers that were mainly formed as front line units near the end of the war, secondly those that were formed for use in specific occupied territories and consisted of locally recruited manpower and finally the number regiments in the fire service.

Polizei-Regiment "Beck" was created in March 1945 with two battalions and was also known as Polizei-Regiments Gruppe "Beck." Its formation and service details are unknown.

Kommandeur

SS-Obersturmbannführer und Oberstleutnant der Schutzpolizei
Fritz Bec 03.1945–end

Polizei-Regiment "Biesenthal" was created on 2 February 1945 with three battalions from Einsatzgruppen "A" and "B" of the Hauptamt Ordnungspolizei in the temporary camps called "Paula" and "Hindenberg" in Biesenthal.

Kommandeur

Unknown

Polizei-Regiment "von Braunschweig" was created at the training ground of Milowitz bei Lissa from the remnants of the destroyed Polizei-Regiment 15 in January 1943. It consisted of the I./Polizei-Regiment 15, a II battalion from the II./Polizei-Regiment 17 and a III battalion from the III./Polizei-Regiment 5. It became the new Polizei-Regiment 15 in February 1943.

Kommandeur

Oberst der Schutzpolizei Leo von Braunschweig 01.1943–.02.1943

Polizei-Regiment "Griese" was created in February 1943 for service in southern France with three battalions. The I battalion came from III./Polizei-Regiment 1, the II battalion from the II./Polizei-Regiment 4 and the III battalion from the III./Polizei-Regiment 24. It was specifically used for a special operation to destroy the old port of Marseilles, which was used by black marketeers, smugglers etc. Walter Schimana was brought in to head the operation. The regiment became the new Polizei-Regiment 14 on 29 March 1943

Kommandeur

SS-Standartenführer und Oberst der Schutzpolizei
Bernhard Griese 02.1943–29.03.1

Polizei-Regiment "Kreuzhofen" was created on 14 March 1945 in Neisse between Breslau and Kattowitz. Details are as yet unknown about this regiment.

Kommandeur
Unknown

Polizei-Regiment "Nagel" was created in the Balkans in March 1945 from the Freiwilligen-Polizei-Battalion "Montenegro" and two volunteer battalions from the Kommandeur der Ordnungspolizei in Athens, Dr. Johann Stut.

Kommandeur

SS-Obersturmbannführer und Oberstleutnant der Schutzpolizei Gottlieb Nage	03.1945–end

Polizei-Ausbildungs-Regiment "Oranienburg" was created on 15 January 1943 in Oranienburg for the training of 5,000 recruits taken from the Wehrmacht. The instructors came from the Colonial Police School in Oranienburg and from the III./Polizei-Regiment 5. The regiment consisted of seven battalions, each with four companies. The I, II and III battalions were based in Saaralben, the IV battalion in Zabern, the V battalion in Bergzabern, the VI battalion in Vollmersweiler and the VII battalion in Heidenheim in annexed French Alsace. The III battalion was disolved in April 1943 and in March 1943 the IV and V battalions moved to Thiers and Cannes in France. The regiment was disolved on 26 July 1943. Only the IV battalion remained and it was transferred to Riga under the control of the Befehlhaber der Ordnungspolizei for Ostland, Georg Jedicke. It was dissolved in July 1944.

Kommandeur

SS-Obersturmbannführer und Oberstleutnant der Schutzpolizei Rudolf Kaufmann	15.01.1943–03.1943
SS-Sturmbannführer und Oberstleutnant der Schutzpolizei Richard Graf	03.1943–05.1943
SS-Gruppenführer und Generalleutnant der Polizei Konrad Hitschler	05.1943–06.1943
SS-Sturmbannführer und Oberstleutnant der Schutzpolizei Richard Graf	06.1943–26.07.1943

The following named regiments were used to form numbered regiments and details will be found under the relevant number:

Polizei-Regiment "Süd"	Polizei-Regiment 10
Polizei-Regiment "z.b.V."	Polizei-Regiment 11
Polizei-Regiment "Mitte"	Polizei-Regiment 13
Polizei-Regiment "Nord"	Polizei-Regimenter 15, 16 and 17
Polizei-Regiment "Böhmen"	Polizei-Regiment 20
Polizei-Regiment "Mähren"	Polizei-Regiment 21
Polizei-Regiment "Warschau"	Polizei-Regiment 22
Polizei-Regiment "Krakau"	Polizei-Regiment 23
Polizei-Regiment "Radom"	Polizei-Regiment 24
Polizei-Regiment "Lublin"	Polizei-Regiment 25
Polizei-Regiment "Todt"	Polizei-Regiment 28
Polizei-Regiment "Nord-Norwegen"	Polizei-Regiment 26
Polizei-Regiment "Süd-Norwegen"	Polizei-Regiment 27

The following regiments were formed in occupied territories with mainly German commanders and local manpower. In the case of the Latvian Polizei-Regiments command was vested in well tried Latvians and they as non-Germanic were only allowed to join the Waffen-SS and not the Allgemeine-SS and as such they were given their own rank structure.

Galizische SS-Freiwilligen-Regiment 4 (Polizei) During 1943 three volunteer regiments were formed in Galicia in eastern Poland. Numbered 1 to 3 they were used to form the 14. Waffen-Grenadier-Division der SS (galizische Nr.1) in the Waffen-SS. Regiments 4 to 7 were raised for police duties. Number 4 was formed in July 1943 in Zabern. It had three battalions based in Zabern, Saaralben and Ferschweiler bei Trier. The III battalion moved to Holland in February 1944 and the rest of the regiment was destroyed at the Battle of Brody on 18 May 1944. The survivors were posted to the 14. Waffen-Grenadier-Division der SS (galizische Nr.1) (SS-Brigadeführer Fritz Freitag).

Kommandeur

Oberstleutnant der Schutzpolizei Siegfried Binz	22.07.1943–20.05.1944

Galizische SS-Freiwilligen-Regiment 5 (Polizei) formed in July 1943, its I battalion was from the I./Polizei-Schützen-Regiment 32. It served in anti-partisan warfare in Lublin-Hrubieszow and Cholm. It was disolved in July 1944 with its manpower going to the 14.Waffen-Grenadier-Division der SS (galizische Nr.1).

Kommandeur

Oberstleutnant der Schutzpolizei Franz Lechthaler	07.1943–.07.1944

Galizische SS-Freiwilligen-Regiment 6 (Polizei) formed on 6 August 1943 in the Lemberg district from the second batch of volunteers. Its formation staff came from the disolved Polizei-Schützen-Regiment 32 and was based in Fichtenwalde bei Gumbinnen. It had three battalions based in Südauen, Fichtenwalde bei Gumbinnen and Grajewo. In November 1943 the regiment was put under the control of the 1. Armee (Generaloberst Johannes Blaskowitz) in western France. It was disolved on 31 January 1944 and its manpower went to the 14. Waffen-Grenadier-Division der SS (galizische Nr.1) at the SS-Training ground at Heidelager.

Kommandeur

Oberst der Schutzpolizei Werner Kühn	06.08.1943–31.01.1944

Galizisches SS-Freiwilligen-Regiment 7 (Polizei) was formed on 29 September 1943 by the Befehlhaber der Ordnungspolizei in Paris, Paul Scheer. The staff and the I and III battalions were based in Salies de Bearn near Bayonne and the II battalion was in Orthez. The regiment was disbanded on 31 January 1944 and its manpower was posted to the SS-Training Ground at Heidelager to join the 14. Waffen-Grenadier-Division der SS (galizische Nr.1).

Kommandeur

Oberst der Schutzpolizei Heinz Hüber	29.09.1943–31.01.1944

Galizisches SS-Freiwilligen-Regiment 8 (Polizei) was formed on 31 January 1944 as the Galician Volunteer Replacement using men from the 6 and 7 regiments who were not suitable for Waffen-SS service. It was upgraded to regiment status in mid-1944.

Kommandeur

Oberstleutnant der Schutzpolizei Wilhelm Schwertschlager 25.10.1944–end

Polizei-Freiwilligen-Regiment 1 "Serbien" formed in May 1944 for police duties in Serbia. It consisted of Hilfspolizei Battalions V, VIII, IX, and IV which were used for battalions numbered I to IV. It was disbanded in April 1945.

Kommandeur

Oberstleutnant der Schutzpolizei Gottfried Saupe 15.07.1944–end

Polizei-Freiwilligen-Regiment 2 "Serbien" formed in May 1944 for police duties in Serbia. It used Hilfspolizei Battalions II, VII and III for its battalions I to III and was disbanded in April 1945.

Kommandeur

SS-Sturmbannführer und Major der
Gendarmerie Willi Pfeiffer 15.07.1944–20.10.1944
SS-Sturmbannführer und Major der Schutzpolizei
Gustav Zuschneid 20.10.1944–end

Polizei-Freiwilligen-Regiment 3 "Serbien" formed in May 1944 for police duties in Serbia. It used Hilfspolizei battalions X and VI for its first two battalions (I and II) and a further two battalions were newly created numbered III and IV. The regiment was dissolved in April 1945

Kommandeur

SS-Sturmbannführer und Major der Gendarmerie
Richard Graf 15.07.1944–end

Polizei-Selbstschutz-Regiment "Sandschak" formed in July 1944 in part of Yugoslavia that had been under Italien control until the autumn of 1943. It consisted of four battalions and was disolved in April 1945.

Kommandeur

Oberstleutnant der Schutzpolizei Otto Mechow 09.05.1944–15.07.1944
SS-Sturmbannführer und Major der Gendarmerie
Ernst Arndt 15.07.1944–end

Lettische-Freiwilligen-Polizei-Regiment 1 "Riga" formed on 1 August 1943 by order of the Befehlhaber der Ordnungspolizei for Ostland, Georg Jedicke. It consisted of four battalions formed from Schutzmannschaft Battalions 276, 277, 278 and 312. Originally named the Lettisches-Freiwilligen-Polizei-Regiment, it was renamed and numbered on 4 September 1943. It initially served in the Daugavpils area of Latvia on anti-partisan duties and, on 6 November 1943, it was sent to the front between the Necherdo and Yasno lakes with 8. Army Corps (General der Infanterie Gustav Höhne). It later served with the Waffen-SSand remainded with them until the end of the war and so impressed Himmler that he allowed them to wear their own cuffband titled "Lett.Polizei Reg.Riga" from March 1944.

Kommandeur

Waffen-Standartenführer Roberts Osis	01.08.1943–21.12.1943
Waffen-Obersturmbannführer Osvalds Meija	21.12.1943–end

Lettische-Freiwilligen-Polizei-Regiment 1 formed early in February 1944 and consisted of Schutzmannschaft Battalions 22, 25, 313 and 316. It was unofficialy known as as Regiment "Liepaja" and was involved in anti-partisan warfare in the Polotsk/Drissa area of Latvia until May 1944 when it was sent to the front. On july/august 1944 with Polizei-Kampfgruppe "Jeckeln" until it was disbanded by order of the Höhere SS und Polizeiführer for Ostland, Friedrich Jeckeln, on 18 August 1944. Its manpower posted to the 1. Latvian Volunteer Regiment.

Kommandeur

Waffen-Standartenführer Janis Grosbergs	02.1944–18.08.1944

Lettisches-Freiwilligen-Polizei-Regiment 2 formed at the beginning of September 1944 by order of the Höhere SS und Polizeiführer for Ostland, Friedrich Jeckeln, to replace the old 2 Regiment. It used men from the police and the home guard (Aizsargi) that had escaped to Riga from territory now occupied by the Soviet forces. It was also known as Polizei-Regiment "Kurzeme." Trained at the Seelager training ground, it was posted to the 15. Waffen-Grenadier-Division der SS (lettische Nr.1) (SS-Oberführer Herbert von Obwurzer) in Thorn during October 1944. By this time nearly 40% of its men had deserted and it was a virtual non-entity.

Kommandeur

Waffen-Obersturmbannführer Nikolajs Rusmanis	16.09.1944–end

Lettische-Freiwilligen-Polizei-Regiment 3 formed on 9 March 1944 by order of the Höhere SS und Polizeiführer for Ostland, Friedrich Jeckeln. It consisted of Schutzmannschaft Battalions 317, 318 and 321 and was used in anti-partisan warfare in the Polotsk/Drissa area of Latvia. After that it was assigned to Detachment "Krukenberg" under SS-Brigadeführer und Generalmajor der Waffen-SS Gustav Krukenberg for service at the front. It was disolved by order of Jeckeln on 18 August 1944 and its manpower posted to the 1. Lettische-Freiwilligen-Polizei-Regiment.

Kommandeur

Waffen-Obersturmbannführer Alberts Kleinbergs	09.03.1944–18.08.1944

Litauische-Polizei-Regiment 1 formed on 14 July 1944 in Kaunas from men of the Lithuanian Schutzmannschaft Bataillone. It did not undertake any police duties but was sent to the front to serve alongside the 5. Panzer-Division (General der Panzertruppen Karl Decker) in army Group Center area. It capitulated in Courland in May 1945.

Kommandeur

Oberstleutnant A. Spokevicius	14.07.1944–end

Estnische-Grenzschutz-Regiment 1 (Pol) was formed in March 1944. This Frontier Polizei-Regiment consisted of the Estonian Police Battalions 286, 288, 291 and 292 It served for Coastal Protection mainly with Division z.b.V 300 (Generalmajor Rudolf Höfer) and 207 Security Division (Generalmajor Bogislav Graf von Schwerin). The regiment was disbanded in September 1944 and its men posted to the 20. Waffen-Grenadier-Division der SS (Estn. Nr.1).

Estnische-Grenzschutz-Regiment 2 (Pol) was formed in February 1944. It consisted of 3 Estonian Police 37, 38 and 40. It served in coastal protection duties alongside 207 Security Division, 58, 227 Infantry Division (Generalleutnant Wilhelm Berlin) and Division z.b.V 300. The regiment was destroyed in september 1944 as part of Kampfgruppe "Höfer" in Southern Estonia.

Estnische-Grenzchutz-Regiment 3 (Pol) was formed in February 1944. It consisted of 3 battalions of estonians recruits. It served next to 207 Security Division then units from Armee-Abteilung Narwa (Generaloberst Johannes Friessner). It was disbanded in September 1944 whilst with Kampfgruppe "Höfer".

Estnische-Grenzschutz-Regiment 4 (Pol) was formed in March 1944. It consisted of 3 battalions. It served next to 207 Security Division, 300 Division z.b.Vin the area of Armee-Abteilung Narwa. It was disbanded whilst fighting with Kampfgruppe "Höfer".

Estnische-Grenzschutz-Regiment 5 (Pol) was formed in April 1944. It consisted of 3 battalions. It served next to 207. Security Division then with Kampfgruppe 87 Infantry Division (Generalleutnant Mauritz Freiherr von Stachwitz) in the area of army Detachment Narwa until it was disbanded in September 1944.

Estnische-Grenzschutz-Regiment 6 (Pol) was formed in June 1944. It consisted of 3 battalions. It served with 207. Security Division, Division z.b.V300 and 227 Inf. Division in the Narwa area. It was disbanded on September 1944.

Polizei-Freiwilligen-Regiment "Montenegro" was formed in February 1944. The I battalion was formed from the Hilfspolizei-Bataillon I and a II battalion was formed from volunteers on 19 April 1944 in Mährisch-Ostrau. From June 1944 he served under the Befehlhaber der Ordnungspolizei Belgrad (Generalmajor der Polizei Andreas May).

Kommandeur

Oberstleutnant der Schutzpolizei Hermann Stührmann	08.06.1944–end

Polizei-Freiwilligen-Regiment 1 (Kroatian) was formed in November 1943 without number. It received the designation "1" when a further four regiments were formed in 1944. Initialy it had ten battalions of four companies each. Each company had two German officers and ten German NCOs with the remaining three officers and 135 men being Volksdeutsche or Croatian. When the remaining regiments were formed in 1944 this regiment was reduced to three battalions (the first three of the original ten). The remaining seven battalions were reorganised as follows:

IV Battalion became the 4 Battalion under the Kommandeur der Ordnungspolizei in Sarajewo
V Battalion became the 5 Battalion under the Kommandeur der Ordnungspolizei in Banja-Luka
VI Battalion became the 6 Battalion under the Befehlhaber der Ordnungspolizei Kroatien in Esseg
VII Battalion became the 7 Battalion under the Kommandeur der Ordnungspolizei in Agram
VIII Battalion became the 8 Battalion under the Kommandeur der Ordnungspolizei in Agram
IX Battalion became the 9 Battalion under the Kommandeur der Ordnungspolizei in Esseg
X Battalion became the 10 Battalion under the Kommandeur der Ordnungspolizei in Agram
From October 1944 until January 1945, the 1 regiment served with the 2 and 3 regiments next to Kampfgruppe "Linden blatt" with 117. (Generalleutnant August Wittmann) and 118. Jäger-Division.(Generalmajor Hübert Lamey)

Kommandeur
Oberstleutnant der Schutzpolizei Erwin Plenio 20.11.1943–end

Polizei-Freiwilligen-Regiment 2 (Kroatien) formed in April 1944 with two battalions. A third battalion was added in May 1944 and the regiment was used for internal police duties in Croatia.

Kommandeur

Oberst der Schutzpolizei Heinz Hüber	04.1944–1944
SS-Sturmbannführer und Major der Schutzpolizei Gustav Zuschneid	1944–20.10.1944
SS-Standartenführer und Oberst der Schutzpolizei Richard Paust	20.10.1944–03.12.1944

Polizei-Freiwilligen-Regiment 3 (Kroatien) formed in March 1944 with three battalions. These battalions were formed as Railway Security Battalions (Eisenbahn Sicherungs Bataillons) numbered 11, 12, and 13 on 1 December 1943 from members of the Croat armed forces. The regiment remained responsible for railway security.

Kommandeur

SS-Sturmbannführer und Major der Gendarmerie Helmuth Grunow	03.1944–20.10.1944
Major der Schutzpolizei Walter Kege	20.10.1944–end

Polizei-Freiwilligen-Regiment 4 (Kroatien) formed in July 1944 with three battalions. Its I battalion came from the Police Volunteer Battalion 7 in Agram, the II battalion from Police Volunteer Battalion 10 in Agram and the III battalion from the Police Volunteer Battalion 15 in Agram.

Kommandeur
SS-Obersturmbannführer und Oberstleutnant der Schutzpolizei Walter Soosten
.07.1944–end

Polizei-Freiwilligen-Regiment 5 (Kroatien) The regimental staff was formed in August 1944. The I battalion was formed in September 1944, II battalion in January 1945 and III battalion in February 1945.

Kommandeur

Major der Schutzpolizei Detlef Ohrt	08.1944–20.10.1944
SS-Obersturmbannführer und Oberstleutnant der Schutzpolizei Gustav Zernack	20.10.1944–end

SS-Polizei-Regiment "Bozen" formed on 1 October 1943 in Bozen (Bolzano) as Polizei-Regiment "Südtirol," its name changing to "Bozen" on 29 October 1943. It was created in the southern Tyrol area that had been Italien until that country capitulated in October 1943. Its headquarters were in Innsbruck until February 1944 when it moved to Bolenzo. It became the SS-Polizei-Regiment "Bozen" on 16 April 1944. The I battalion originally in Meran moved to Abbazi in May 1944 and the II battalion was in Belluno for the whole of its existence. The III battalion originally in Gossensass moved to Rome in March 1944, to Bologna in September 1944 and to San Stefano di Cadore in December 1944. A IV battalion was formed in April 1944 in Gossensass and became the I./Polizei-Regiment "Alpenvorland" in May 1944

Kommandeur
Oberst der Schutzpolizei Alois Menschik 01.10.1943–end

Polizei-Regiment "Alpenvorland" formed in May 1944 using the IV./Polizei-Regiment "Bozen" as a nucleus. In June 1944 the regiment headquarters, II, and III battalions were in Schlanders with the I battalion in Gossensass. In December 1944 the regimental headquarters moved to Bolonzo, I battalion to Edolo, the II battalion to Feltre and the III battalion to Belluno. On 29 January 1945 the regiment became the basis for SS-Polizei-Regiment 9.

Kommandeur
Oberst der Schutzpolizei Hans Köllner 05.1944–29.01.1945

Miliz-Regiment de Maria (Pol) was formed at the end of 1943 in Prag. It consisted of I to XI battalions of the Italian Black Shirts Milice from Northern Italy with a ORPO staff of 66 officers and 350 NCO's. The unit was involved in anti partisans fighting. The unit became the 1 regiment of the Milizia Armata and served in February 1944 as a nucleus for the 1. Waffen-Grenadier-Brigade der SS (Italian) (SS-Brigadeführer Hansen).

Kommandeur
Colonello Paolo De Maria 11.1943 – 01.1944

Polizei-Regiment "Schlanders" formed from October 1944 to December 1944 in Schlanders (Silandro) in the Province of Bolenzo. It used a cadre of trained German policeman and the balance came from the local Volksdeutsche. The regiment consisted of three battalions.

Kommandeur
SS-Sturmbannführer und Oberstleutnant der Schutzpolizei
Georg Hahn 10.1944–end.

Polizei-Regiment "Brixen" formed from October to December 1944 in Brixen (Bressanone) in the Province of Bolzano. It had a cadre of trained German policeman and the balance came from the local Volksdeutsche. The regiment consisted of three battalions.

Kommandeur
SS-Obersturmbannführer und Oberstleutnant
der Schutzpolizei Ernst Korn 11.1944–end.

Polizei-Freiwilligen-Regiment "Belgien-Nordfrankreich" formed in August 1944 in Belgium under the control of the Befehlhaber der Ordnungspolizei, Kurt Wolter. It consisted of 3 battalions in Flemish area and 2 battalions in Wallonian area. It was disolved in September 1944.

Kommandeur
Major der Schutzpolizei Gerhard Vensler 08.1944–09.1944

Feuerschutz-Polizei-Regiment 1 "Sachsen" formed on 10 November 1939 as Feuerschutz-Polizei-Regiment "Sachsen" with three battalions (Abteilungen). The I.Abteilung was in Leipzig-Wiederitsch, the II. Abteilung in Heyrothsberge bei Magdeburg and the III. Abteilung in Beeskow in Mark Brandenberg. In September 1940 the regiment moved to Holland

and then to Brittany. The IV. Abteilung was formed in 1941 and the regiment moved to the Ploesti oil district in Roumania. The regiment was numbered 1 in 1941 and was abolished on 14 June 1943. Its staff became the Kommandostab der Feuerschutz-Polizei-Abteilung in Kappenberg über Lunen in Westfalen. Its Abteilungen were consolidated and renumbered 1 and 4, remaining in Ploetsi.

Kommandeur

SS-Brigadeführer und Generalmajor der Polizei Hans Rumpf	27.12.1939–03.1943
Oberstleutnant der Feuerschutzpolizei Hans Schmidt	03.1943–07.05.1943

Stellvertreter Kommandeur

Major der Feuerschutzpolizei Holstein	27.12.1939–14.06.1943
I Abteilung: Major der Feuerschutzpolizei Kirchner	12.1939–14.06.1943
II Abteilung: Major der Feuerschutzpolizei Harder	12.1939–14.06.1943
III Abteilung: Major der Feuerschutzpolizei Dabbert	12.1939–14.06.1943
IV Abteilung:	

Note: The commander of the Kommandostab in Kappenberg was Major der Feuerschutzpolizei Speil.

Feuerschutz-Polizei-Regiment 2 "Hannover" formed in January 1941 and served in the Warschau district of Poland. It moved to the Ruhr area in 1942 and was abolished on 14 June 1943. Its Abteilungen were consolidated and became Abteilung 2 and 5 in Hannover.

Kommandeur

Oberstleutnant der Feuerschutzpolizei Hans Schmidt	29.11.1940–14.06.1943

Feuerschutz-Polizei-Regiment 3 "Ostpreussen" formed in December 1941 for service in Ostpreussen. It was formed from the II./Feuerschutzpolizei-Regimenter 1 and 2. Abolished on 14 June 1943, its Abteilungen became Abteilungen 3 and 6 in Ostpreussen.

Kommandeur

SS-Obersturmbannführer und Oberstleutnant der Feuerschutzpolizei Curt Bolz	12.1941–14.06.1943

Feuerschutz-Polizei-Regiment "Niederlande" formed during the summer of 1943 for service in Holland and Belgium. Its manpower was recruited in Germany from among the professional firemen and it was abolished in July 1943.

Kommandeur

Oberstleutnant der Feuerschutzpolizei Hans Schmidt	14.06.1943–07.1943

Feuerschutz-Polizei-Regiment"Ukraine" formed during the summer of 1943 for service in the Ukraine.
It was abolished early in July 1943.

Kommandeur

Oberst der Feuerschutzpolizei Fiedler	14.06.1943–07.1943

Feuerschutz-Polizei-Regiment "Böhmen-Mähren" formed during December 1942 for service in the Protectorate. Its manpower was recruited in Germany and in the Protectorate. It was abolished early in July 1943.

Kommandeur	
Major der Feuerschutzpolizei Möbius	12.1942–07.1943

Polizei-Strassenbau-Regiment "Eifel" formed in February 1945. It had four battalions and was part of the Technische Nothilfe organisation used in road repair and construction in western Germany.

There were three Polizei-Regiments established in Greece under the control of the Befehlhaber der Ordnungspolizei, Hermann Franz. They were known as Evzonen-Regiments and although administered by the Germans they were under Greek command. On March 1944, 11 Freiwilligen numered I to IX were created with a german staff. After june 1944, I, II and III Freiwilligen Bataillonen were in action in Macedonia.

7.4 Technical Support of Field Units

7.4.1 The Police Signals units

At the outbreak of the war, signals platoons (Nachrichtenzug) were assigned to each of the Police Battalions in Poland. The strength of a signals platoon was 1 officer and 18 men and comprised 2 phone sections (motorised) and 2 radio sections (motorised). A report by Kurt Daluege about police forces dated August 1940, mentionned a Signals Battalion (3 officers and 390 men) station in General Government of Poland. This unit was the nucleus of platoons assigned to battalions and regiments. Within the battalion, an armoured platoon had its own signal unit. Following the Western campaign, Police Battalion 66 and 122 were stationed in occupied Lorraine in June 1940. A signals squad (Nachrichten Bereitschaft) consisting of 1 officer and 36 men headed by Hauptmann Abel was transferred from Mannheim to Metz. It was assigned to Kommando der SCHUPO Metz to provide communications between police units and the civil administration. For the Operation Barbarossa, the invasion of Russia, one police signals battalion was assigned to each Higher SS and Police Leader. They were disbanded in May 1942. Later in the war, the signals company became the standard for all signals units, they could have various assignements:

1 – Independant signals company: Polizei-Nachrichten-Kompanies under the juridiction of an HSSPF (i.e Polizei-Nachrichten-Kompanie 11 assigned to the Higher SS und Police Leader White Russia in November 1943).

2 – Signals companies attached to Polizei-Regiments: for example Polizei-Nachrichten-Kompanie attached to Polizei-Regiment "Nord" and a similar one attached to Polizei-Regiment 13 etc…

3 – Signals companies attached to Polizei-Kampfgruppen: for example Polizei-Nachrichten-Kompanie 112 attached to Kampfgruppe "von Gottberg", and Polizei-Nachrichten-Kompanie 41 attached to Kampfgruppe Reinefarth in Warsaw..

4 – Signals companies attached to Volunteers Police Units: for example a company attached to Freiwilligen-Polizei-Regiment in Serbia.

A police battalion was created to protect signals units (Polizei-Funkschutz-Bataillon). It was stationed in Posen in 1944.

7.4.2 The Police Artillery and Assault Guns units

Police Assault gun batteries were created in a series of Polizei-Regiments (Nrs 10, 11, 13, 16, 23, 24) in 1943.
In Polizei-Regiment 2, three assault gun batteries were organised into a police assault gun battalion (Polizei-Geschütz-Abteilung I) in September 1943. The unit, headed by Hauptmann der SCHUPO Heinrich Jagst, was involved in anti-partisan actions with Kampfgruppe "von Gottberg" in 1943/44. It came under the tactical command of von Gottbergs military adviser Generalleutnant der Polizei Walter Schimana. An artillery battalion was created and it was assigned to the Polizei-Gebirgsjäger-Regiment 18 and it saw action in Balkans and Greece. In the Croatian Police Volunteers corps, two police volunteer artillery batteries were created in 1943.

In March 1945, a Polizei-Artillerie-Abteilung consisting of 3 batteries was created and it was assigned to the Polizei-Brigade "Nordwest" in Netherlands. During the retreat through Poland, various artillery units were set up: In August 1944, an assault gun battery was created in Lublin but it was disbanded in October 44. In October 1944, two police assault guns batteries were set up in Galicia. An assault gun battalion consisting of 4 batteries served with the Kampfgruppe Hannibal which served under the 4. army in Northern Poland in January 1945. This Kampfgruppe also consisted of SS-Polizei-Regiment 4 which had four batteries of artillery assigned to it.

7.4.3 Police Engineer units

Only one engineer company was created in Polizei-Regiments. It was under the Polizei-Gebirgs-Regiment 18 and it was known as Polizei-Pionier-Kompanie "Alpenland". Of course engineer units were created within Militarized units of the Police (Police Divisions and Police Brigades). Engineers duties were supported by the Emergency Technical Corps (Technical Nothilfe). (see Chapter "Technische Nothilfe). During Anschluss, 1500 men of TENO were mobilised for the occupation of Österreich and in October 1938, technical commandos of TENO were formed as Special formations of the Wehrmacht. During the Poland campaign, technical units of TENO called "TN Technischen Kommando" or "TN Abteilungen" were involved in the engineering: maintenance of water, gas and electric power stations as welle as economic factories and companies dealing with sphere of life (food, car repair...). An order of battle from August 1940 stated that 9 technical commandos of a battalion size were still active in Generalgouverment for the reconstruction.

11 technical commandos and 9 motorized technical battalions were involved in the western campaign. TENO units saw action next to Police units as well the 3 arms of the Wehrmacht. The Einsatzgruppe "Luftwaffe West" of the TENO was involved in support in airports in occupied areas. TENO units next Kriegsmarine served in harbours and TENO units next engineers army battalions were involved into bridges reconstruction. For action in East in 1941, a TN Abteilung was attached to rear area of each HSSPF headed by a TN Feldeinsatzführer. TENO Abteilung Regiment Nord which became in 1942 TENO Abt TENO Abteilung Regiment Mitte which became in 1942 TENO Abt II TENO Abteilung Regiment "Süd" which became in 1942 TENO Abt III TENO Einsatz Abteilung z.b.V was split to become in 1942 TENO Abt IV and TENO Abt V. On 1942 a sixth TENO Abteilung was created. During the retreat in Russia, TENO Abt II, III and VI suffered losses and were disbanded in 1944. On 1941, a TENO Einsatzgruppe "Luftwaffe Ost" was created for the airfield purposes from Northern areas to Black see.

7.4.4 The Police Armoured units

The armoured units 1939 – 1942

Poland 1939

2 armoured units were involved in police actions:

an armoured platoon as part of the 2 Polizei-Regiments (Oberst Paul Worm) of the Group of Generalmajor Eberhardt (AOK 3) saw action in Danzig.

A second armoured police company was attached to Police Group 1 and engaged around Cracow in the area of the 14. army. Then it moved to Lodz.

After the creation of the General-Gouvernement in Poland, an armoured platoon was attached to the police battalions stationed in the following districts:

District of Warsaw: an armoured platoon next to the Police Battalion 301 in Polizei-Regiment "Warsaw"

District of Cracow: an armoured platoon next to the heavy company of the Polizei-Regiment "Cracow"

District of Radom: an armoured platoon next to the Police Battalions 51, 111, 305 and 309 in Polizei-Regiment "Radom"

District of Lublin: an armoured car unit next to Police Battalions 73 and 104 in Polizei-Regiment "Lublin"

Russia 1941

In the rear area of the German armies, the three Polizei Regiments were reinforced by armoured car units:
Polizei-Regiment "Nord" under the Higher SS and Police Leader Ostland had 2 platoons with 3 armoured cars in each. The units served in the Baltic area until July 1942 when the regiment was reorganised into Polizei-Regiment 15.
Polizei-Regiment "Mitte" under the Higher SS and Police Leader "Russland-Mitte" had 2 platoons with 3 armoured cars in each. These were combined with a reconnaissance armoured platoon to become the 10 Heavy Company. The unit served in Belarus. Polizei-Regiment "Süd" under the Higher SS and Police Leader "Russland-Süd" had 2 armoured platoons. The unit served in Ukraine.

Police armoured car in Poland (Panzerkampfwagen Steyr)

The armoured units 1942 – 1944

From July 1942, following the formation of the Polizei Regiments, the armoured troops were organised into armoured police companies (Polizei Panzer Kompanien) attached to Polizei Regiments or operating as independant units used in anti-partisans duties under the control of combat groups or the relevant BdO/SSPF.

Armoured units attached to Polizei Regiments:
1 Polizei-Panzer-Kompanie (Polizei-Regiment 2)
2 Polizei-Panzer-Kompanie (Polizei-Regiment 14)
3 Polizei-Panzer-Kompanie (Polizei-Regiment 15)
4 Polizei-Panzer-Kompanie (Polizei-Regiment 13)
5 Polizei-Panzer-Kompanie (Polizei-Regiment 10)
6 Polizei-Panzer-Kompanie (Polizei-Regiment 1 "Kroatien")
7 Polizei-Panzer-Kompanie (Polizei-Regiment 11)
13 Polizei-Panzer-Kompanie (Polizei-Regiment "Griese" later Polizei-Regiment 14)
14 Polizei-Panzer-Kompanie (Polizei-Regiment 3)
Polizei Zug (Polizei-Regiment 1)
Polizei Zug (Polizei-Regiment "Bozen")

Independant armoured companies were attached to combat groups operating against partisans in the East and in the South East.

8 Polizei-Panzer-Kompanie (Kampfgruppe "Jeckeln")
9 Polizei-Panzer-Kompanie (Kampfgruppe "von Gottberg")
10 Polizei-Panzer-Kompanie (Polizei Regiments 10 et 11)
11 Polizei-Panzer-Kompanie (Befehlhaber der Ordnungspolizei Kroatien)
12 Polizei-Panzer-Kompanie (Kampfgruppe "von Gottberg")
14 Polizei-Panzer-Kompanie (Befehlhaber der Ordnungspolizei Salzburg)
15 Polizei-Panzer-Kompanie (Befehlhaber der Ordnungspolizei Italien)
Polizei-Panzer-Kompanie Mitte (Kampfgruppe "von Gottberg")
Polizei-Panzer-Kompanie (SS und Polizeiführer Oberitalien West)
Cossacks Mounted Front Battalions 68, 72, 73 and 74 in Bielorussia
Cossack Mounted Troop in Cracow

South East

Several Mounted units are created in Balkans area:
A Police Mounted Battalion in Serbia with 4 squadrons
A Police Mounted Squadron in Greece as part of Police Volunteers Battalion Greece.
A Police Mounted Squadron in Croatia.

In May 1943, the Mounted Police Battalions were given the prefix "SS".

7.5 Ordnungspolizei in the German Protectorate of Böhmen-Mähren

The Versailles Treaty of 1918 established Czechoslovakia. It was created out of four former regions of the dismembered Austro-Hungarian Empire, Böhmen-Mähren, Slovakia, Carpathien, Ruthenia and part of Schlesien. Its President was Jan Maseryk. The population, Czechs, Slovaks and Böhmen-Mähren were Slavs but large numbers of ethnic Germans were left within the boundaries of the new state. These minorities were not always happy to accept their changed status and their reluctance turned to militancy with the rise of Hitler in Germany.

In 1910, a Pan-Austrian Workers Party had been formed in Wien and before the end of the Great War it had been renamed the German National Socialist Workers Party (DNSAP). A Czech section of this Party was created in November 1918. Despite the close similarity of their party labels the DNSAP and Hitler's Party were not directly connected although they shared many of the same pan-Germanic, anti-Slav and anti-Semitic sentiments. By 1929 the DNSAP had some 200,000 supporters among German speaking Czechs. Tension between the Czech state and its German subjects increased and led to the suppression of overt Nazi parties and political sports clubs like the Deutsche Turnverband (German Gymmnastic Association) which was led by Konrad Henlein. In October 1933 the DNSAP went into voluntary dissolution (one day before the official decree ordering it to do so came into effect). In the same year a Sudetendeutsche Heimatfront (Sudeten German Home Front) was formed under Henlein and in 1934, in order to conform with Czech regulations relating to political movements, the Front was changed into a Party and became known as the Sudentendeutsche Partei (Sudeten German Party).

Following the Austrian Anschluss a Sudeten Legion was raised to consist of members of the SA, Allgemeine-SS and SSVerfügungstruppen (later to become the Waffen-SS). At the same time the Freiwilliger Schutzdienst (Voluntary Protection Service) was created by Henlein as a para-military training unit for use by the Party. Given training from July 1938 by the German army at the Neuhammer training ground near Breslau, after the training was completed the trainees took an oath of loyalty to Hitler. The Sudeten Legion changed its name to the Sudetendeutsche Freikorps units (Sudeten Volunteer Corps) in July 1938 and units were established along the Czech/German border. The Sudetenland was ceded to Germany following the München Agreement of the 1 October 1938 and it was formerly incorporated into the Greater German Reich as a Reichsgau in January 1939 under Gauleiter and SS-Obergruppenführer Konrad Henlein.

The Germans took over the provinces of and Böhmen-Mähren in March 1939 and a Protectorate was established. Although, for all practical purposes a satellite of Germany, it was permitted its own civilian administration under a Czech president, Dr. Emil Hacha. However he served under the control of a Reichsprotector who held supreme authority. The remaining part of the old Czechoslovakia, Slovakia, was allowed to form an independent state under German 'guidance'. The first Reichsprotector was the former German Foreign Minister SS-Obergruppenführer Constantin Freiherr von Neurath. The former Minister of the Interior, Reichsleiter Wilhelm Frick, succeeded Neurath in August 1943. These two men only held symbolic power, actual power was vested in the Deputy Reichsprotector, SS-Obergruppenführer und General der Polizei Reinhard Heydrich. When he was assassinated in June 1942 this post was given to the former head of the Ordnungspolizei, SS-Oberst-Gruppenführer und Generaloberst der Polizei Kurt Daluege. As he was already suffering from a type of multiple sclerosis, a new post was created, in August 1943 called the German Minister of State in the Protectorate. This post was given to the Sudeten born Secretary of State, SS-Obergruppenführer und General der Polizei und Waffen- SS, Karl Hermann Frank who was since 1939 Höhere SS und Polizeiführer for the Protectorate. Frank held virtual dictatorial powers until the end of the war.

The German Ordnungspolizei was involved in the area from October 1938 when five Ordnungspolizei Abschnitte (districts) were created as follows:

Abschnitt I	SS-Gruppenführer und Generalleutnant der Polizei August Edler von Meyszyner
Abschnitt II	SS-Brigadeführer und Generalmajor der Polizei Paul Will (succeeded by Generalmajor der Polizei Josef Albert)
Abschnitt III	SS-Gruppenführer und Generalleutnant der Polizei Arthur Mülverstedt
Abschnitt IV	SS-Obergruppenführer und General der Polizei Karl Pfeffer-Wildenbruch
Abschnitt V	SS-Brigadeführer und Generalmajor der Polizei Wilhelm Roettig

These districts were abolished on 10 October 1938 and four IdO were appointed. Reichenberg as a supervisory command to oversee the others IdO as follows:

"Nord-Böhmen" covering the Aussig region
"Nord-Mähren" covering the Troppau region
"Egerland" covering the Karlsbad region

It was found that this structure was not necessary and the subordinate commands of Northern Böhmen-Mähren, Northern Böhmen-Mähren and Egerland were disbanded on 20 December 1938 and police matters were all put under the post in Reichenberg. This post was abolished on 30 September 1939 when the area was put under the post in Prague. Further details can be found under the IdO/BdO chapter. As the Protectorate was accorded its own civilian administration, it was allowed to retain its own police force. This was the old Czech Gendarmerie with only a very slight modification to its insignia and as an auxiliary to this force a Bereitschaftspolizei (Alert Police) was raised by voluntary enlistment in 1943. Its function was to fulfill the role of 'other ranks' to the Gendarmerie. All of were either commissioned officers or senior NCOs. Both forces wore a light grey uniform. Gendarmerie officers wore peaked caps, tunics and trousers with, in bad weather, capes, also grey but with a dark collar. The cap badge was the Protectorate coat of arms upon a square set at a 45% angle surrounded by a wreath of linden leaves. The old Czech Gendarmerie helmet continued to be worn but by NCO's only, officers wore a peaked cap. All ranks had red collar patches and red down the centre of the shoulder strap upon which rank was indicated by either one two or three stars (officers had five pointed stars and NCOs three pointed stars).

The stars were white metal for NCO' s and junior officers and gilt for senior officers. The Gendarmerie was equipped only with light weapons, officers had symbolic short sabres and a 7.65 mm pistol and NCO' s an 1895 model Mannlicher carbine with a bayonet. The Alert Police wore a similar uniform with a red band around a peaked cap that was rather similar in appearance to the old Tsarist army type. Rank was indicated by one, two, three and four white metal buttons on red shoulder straps. The Czech police also had a Traffic police who wore a dark blue uniform and a Water Police who had light blue instead of red down the centre of the shoulder strap. The Gendarmerie was used to tackle ordinary crimes, traffic control, air raid protection etc., in fact all duties where local knowledge and language were essential. Czech detectives went on courses on modern forensic methods and finger printing under the supervision of the German KRIPO. Any case involving a Reich citizen, or with a political dimension, had to be handed over to the German KRIPO or the Gestapo. According to SS-Brigadeführer Walter Schellenberg, Himmler was so impressed by the Czech police that he talked about recruiting them into the Waffen-SS. This must be partially put down to the efficient methods used by Reinhard Heydrich while he was in Prague. On the other side of the coin, the local knowledge of the Czech police allowed them to assist political resistors and Jews to escape arrest.

A Befehlhaber der Ordnungspolizei post was created in Prague in May 1939 to supervise operations of Polizei-Regiments 20 and 21 that were based in Böhmen-Mähren. This command did not have any control over the Czech Gendarmerie but the German authorities had to show some sort of supervising direction and for this purpose three new posts were established in July 1942 as follows:

Generalinspekteur der Uniformierten Protektorat Polizei Böhmen-Mähren (General Inspector of Uniformed Police)

SS-Gruppenführer und Generalleutnant der Polizei
Paul Riege 01.07.1942–15.09.1943
SS-Gruppenführer und Generalleutnant der Polizei
Ernst Hitzegrad 15.09.1943–15.02.1945
SS-Brigadeführer und Generalmajor der Polizei
Paul Otto Geibel 15.02.1945–09.05.1945

This command was split into two subordinate commands for the two separate provinces of Böhmen-Mähren in Prague and Böhmen-Mähren in Brünn as follows:

Inspekteur der Uniformierten Protektorat Polizei Böhmen-Mähren (Inspector of Uniformed Police)
SS-Standartenführer und Oberst der Schutzpolizei
Paul Baehren 18.07.1942–12.08.1942
SS-Brigadeführer und Generalmajor der
Polizei Anton Diermann 12.08.1942–06.09.1943
Oberst der Schutzpolizei Hans Georg Hirschfeld 06.09.1943–09.05.1945

Inspekteur der Uniformierten Protektorat Polizei Mähren
SS-Standartenführer und Oberst der Gendarmerie
Georg Attenberger 18.07.1942–15.02.1945
SS-Standartenführer und Oberst der Schutzpolizei
Josef Heischmann 15.02.1945–29.03.1945
SS-Standartenführer und Oberst der Gendarmerie
Georg Attenberger 29.03.1945–09.05.1945

As has been stated the Czech Gendarmerie did not officially come under the BdO in Prague but this was purely on paper as the General Inspector was also the BdO. The Inspectors in Böhmen-Mähren also commanded the two Polizei-Regiments based in those provinces with the exception of Josef Heischmann in Brünn, whilst he held the post as Inspector the regiment was commanded by SS-Obersturmbannführer und Oberstleutnant der Schutzpolizei Walter Danz. To supervise the detective force in the Czech police two Inspekteur der Nicht-Uniformierten Protektorat Polizei (Inspectors of non-uniformed Protectorate Police) were set up for Böhmen-Mähren.

Inspekteur der nicht-Uniformierten Protektorat Polizei Böhmen-Mähren
SS-Standartenführer, Regierung-und Krimininaldirektor

Friedrich Sowa	11.09.1942–31.12.1944
SS-Sturmbannführer, Regierung-und Kriminalrat	
Walter Odewald	01.01.1945–09.05.1945
Inspekteur der nicht-Uniformierten Protektorat Polizei Mähren	
SS-Sturmbannführer, Regierung-und Kriminalrat	
Konrad Nussbaum	18.07.1942–10.01.1945
SS-Sturmbannführer, Regierung-und Kriminalrat	
Kurt Geisler	19.01.1945–09.05.1945

These two commands came under the authority of the Befehlhaber der Sicherheitspolizei und SD, SS-Oberführer und Oberst der Polizei Dr. Erwin Weinmann, which was outside the authority of the Ordnungspolizei. Friedrich Sowa was the senior KRIPO officer in the Protectorate. The Protectorate also had all the relevant police services as in the Reich and details can be found under the relevant chapters.

7.6 Ordnungspolizei in the General Gouvernement of Poland

The campaign against Poland (Polenfeldzurg) from 1 September 1939 had, as its main objective, to destroy the Polish state. This would allow enlarging the German sphere of influence in the spirit of the "Lebensraum" the conquest of vital space.

Police groups of the Ordnungspolizei 01.09.1939 – 29.09.1939
In the rear area behind the front line, Police groups (Polizei-Gruppe) were set up led by a Befehlhaber der Ordnungspolizei attached to each Armee:

Polizei-Gruppe 1 attached to the 14. Armee (Silésia) led by SS-Oberführer Udo von Woyrsch. It moved from Böhmen-Mähren to the east of Polish Oberschlesien with five battalions numbered 63, 92, 82, 62,and 171.

Polizei-Gruppe 2 attached to the 10. Armee led by Generalmajor der Polizei Wilhelm Roettig, killed in a car crash in October 1939 and was succeeded by Generalmajor der Polizei Herbert Becker. It moved from Schlesien to Cracow with four battailons numbered 42, 71, 101, 102, and 103.

Polizei-Gruppe 3 attached to the 8. Armee led by Oberstleutnant der Schutzpolizei Hermann Franz moved from Schlesien to Warsaw/Lodz area with one battalion numbered 41.

Polizei-Gruppe 4 z.b.V attached to the military Commander Posen and led by Generalleutnant der Polizei Karl Pfeffer Wildenbruch moved from Brandenburg to Posen with one battalion numbered 61.

Polizei-Gruppe 5 attached to the 4. Armee led by Generalleutnant der Polizei Arthur Mülverstedt moved from Pommern with 1 battalion, numbered one and a mounted battalion.

Polizei-Gruppe 6 attached to the 3. Armee led by Oberst Curt Pohlmeyer moved from Ostpreussen with four battalions numbered 2, 3, 4,and 91.

Because of the swift progression of the army, Police battalions became involved in fighting in the front line. During the offensive of Polish army in Lutno, Polizei-Bataillon 41 led by Franz was engaged for the defence of the front line. Apart from this their main duties were protection of military buildings and control of the factories and production areas. During the military operations, BdO and battalion commanders were under the orders of the Senior SS and Police Leader attached to Commanders of the Armies. Losses: 83 killed (including General Roettig) and 117 wounded.

Military Administration 29.09.1939 – 25.10.1939

On 29 September 1939, a military Administration was set up under command of Generaloberst Karl von Rundstedt as Commander in Chief East (Oberbefehlhaber "Ost" or "Oberost"). The Nazi lawyer and Reichsleiter of the Party Hans Frank became Chief of Civil Administration alongside the "Oberost."
Poland was divided into districts with the following Police organisation:

Military district South BdO: Oberst der Gendarmerie Emil Höring in Krakau with two battalions.
Military district Middle BdO: Generalmajor der Polizei Herbert Becker in Lodz with ten battalions.
Military district Westpreussen BdO: Oberst der Schutzpolizei Leo von Falkowski in Danzig with one battalion and one mounted battalion.
Military district Posen BdO: Oberst der Schutzpolizei Oscar Knofe in Posen with two battalions.
Military district Südostpreussen BdO: Oberst der Schutzpolizei Curt Pohlmeyer, former IdO Ostpreussen in Königsberg with the Police forces from Wehrkreis I.
Military district Oberschlesien BdO: Generalmajor der Polizei Paul Riege, the IdO Breslau with two battalions.

Two decrees dated 8 October 1939 and 12 October 1939 divided Poland into two parts under different authorities. The western territories were incorporated into Gau Danzig that became Reichsgau Danzig-Westpreussen and Gau Schlesien that became Reichsgau Schlesien. On 1 February 1941 the area became independent Reichsgau Oberschlesien. The remainder of the western area became a new Reichsgau called Wartheland. North of the Carpathian Mountains, the Cracovia District, and Central Poland with the high plain of Lublin constituted the Generalgovernment of Poland. The Galician area of eastern Poland was given to the Russians as a result of von Ribbentrop's Nazi-Soviet pact of August 1939.

General Gouvernment of Poland: 25 October 1939 to 1945

Dr Hans Frank was appointed General Gouverneur by Führer decree dated 25 October 1939. He had authority over the autonomous territory and was directly responsible to Hitler. His headquarters moved from Lodz to Castel Wavel at Krakau. The former Senior SS und Police Leader attached to him as Oberost (SS-Obergruppenführer Friedrich Wilhelm Krüger) became Higher SS and Police Leader "East" (HSSPF Ost) and the former BdO of the Military district Middle (Lodz) became the first BdO for the Generalgouvernement.

Two charts drafted by Kurt Daluge for Himmler dated 25 September 1939 and 27 October 1939 showed that three Police Administrations were to be created. One in Krakau under SS-Gruppenfüher Karl Zech, one in Warschau under SS-Oberführer Günther Claassen and a third, planned but never set up, in Tschenschau in Obershlesien. This was to have been under the Breslau Police President, SS-Brigadeführer Albrecht Schmelt. A decree dated 1 November 1939 changed the whole organisation, the Police Administrations were disbanded and police matters were put under senior civil servants.

Befehlhaber der Ordnungspolizei

SS-Gruppenführer und Generalleutnant der Polizei
Herbert Becker 25.10.1939–31.10.1940
SS-Gruppenführer und Generalleutnant der Polizei
Paul Riege 31.10.1940–22.08.1941

SS-Brigadeführer und Generalmajor der Polizei	
Rudolf Müller-Bonigk	22.08.1941–01.09.1941 (i .V.)
SS-Gruppenführer und Generalleutnant der Polizei	
Gerhard Winkler	01.09.1941 – 01.05.1942
SS-Gruppenführer und Generalleutnant der Polizei	
Herbert Becker	01.05.1942 – 01.08.1943
SS-Brigadeführer und Generalmajor der Polizei	
Hans-Dietrich Grunwald	01.08.1943 – 08.03.1944
Generalmajor der Polizei Fritz Sendel	09.03.1944 – 23.03.1944
SS-Gruppenführer und Generalleutnant der Polizei	
Emil Höring	23.03.1944 – 19.01.1945

The BdO had authority over the territorial organisation of the Ordnungspolizei and coordinated the actions of four Polizei-Regiments set up in each of the new administrative districts. In July 1943 a decree changed the organisation of the Police Administration. This reform which was more favourable to the SS followed the appointment of the HSSPF to the civil servant rank of State Secretary for Security. The decree decided that a department "Polizeiverwaltung" was created for each SSPF to be responsible for police regulations and administration. The Schutzpolizei and Gendarmerie would serve as the executive arm.

At the level of the Landkreis the police authority remained with the Kreishauptmann under a department called "Polizei". At the level of the big towns the police authority remained with the Stadthauptmann with an executive civil servant with the title of "Stadtpolizeidirektor" in Krakau, Lublin, Radom, Kielce, Tschenschau and Lemberg. He operated as a Police Direktor. The status of Warsaw was unique. Police authority was taken away from the Stadthauptmann and was given to an independent Polizeipräsident. This post was combined with the SSPF post being held by the same man. It controlled a KdO and had a KRIPO Dienststelle.

Field organisation

The General government was divided into administrative districts (Distrikt) led by a chief (Distriktchef). This title was changed to Governor (Distriktgouverneur) on the 10 November 1939. A Commander of the Ordnungspolizei (Kommandeur der Ordnungspolizei or KdO) was appointed in each district. He was assisted by a Commander of Protection Police (KDR der Schutzpolizei) and a Commander of Gendarmerie (KDR der Gendarmerie) to co-ordinate action of the urban uniform police and rural police in the district. The KdO also held the post of KDR der Schutzpolizei of the district. Until 1942, the KdO was Commander of the Polizei-Regiment of its district. Order of battle 1939:

District Krakau

KdO and Kommandeur Polizei-Regiment "Krakau:" Oberst der Schutzpolizei Emil Höring

District Radom

KdO and Kommandeur Polizei-Regiment "Radom:" Oberstleutnant der Schutzpolizei Ferdinand Heske

District Warschau

KdO and Kommandeur Polizei-Regiment "Warschau:" Oberst der Schutzpolizei Max Montua

District Lublin

KdO and Kommandeur Polizei-Regiment "Lublin:" Oberstleutnant der Schutzpolizei Gerret Korsemann

In August 1941 following the attack on Russia, the Galician area of eastern Poland was annexed to the General government as the fifth district. A KdO was appointed in Lemberg.

District Lemberg

KdO: Obersteutnant der Schutzpolizei Joachim Stach

Polizei-Regiments in General Government (Polizeiregiments)

From 1942, the Polizeiregimenter were numbered to conform with all other regiments as follows:

Polizei-Regiment "Warschau" became Polizei-Regiment 22 covering Warschau, Lublin, Zamosz, and Krakau

Polizei-Regiment "Krakau" became Polizei-Regiment 23 covering Krakau, Lemberg, and Radom.

Polizei-Regiment "Radom" became Polizei-Regiment 24 covering Radom and Lemberg.

Polizei-Regiment "Lublin" became Polizei-Regiment 25 covering Lublin

As the war drew nearer the Polish borders, Polizei-Regiments became independent of the local KdO

The following Polizei-Regiments were also stationed in the General government:

Polizei-Regiment 4 (1944 Lemberg)

Polizei-Regiment 10 (1944 Galicia)

Polizei-Regiment 11 (1944 Galicia)

Polizei-Regiment 17 (1944 Warschau)

Police-Schützen-Regiment 34 (Warschau)

Galician SS-Volunteer Regiments (Galizische SS-Freiwilligen-Regimenter)

In 1943, SS-Volunteer Regiments were set up in Galicia. Regiments 1 to 3 served to form the 14. Waffen-Grenadier-Division der SS (galizische Nr.1) and regiments 4 to 7 were employed in similar fashion to the German Polizei-Regiments and designated Galizisches SS-Freiwiligen-Regimenter (Polizei). Staff was German and the troops were Volksdeutsche from Galicia. After training they were mainly engaged outside of Poland.

Auxiliary Police Forces

Himmler had asked that in towns with large populations a Polish Police Administration should be created with a Kommandeur der Polizei serving alongside the Distriktchef. Disciplinary control was to be vested in the German KdO. However nothing came of this idea. The BdO benefited from the support of auxiliary police forces:

Polish "Blue" police

With a strength of 8,000 men, it was under KdO orders in each district. In urban areas it was under the control of the Schutzpolizei and in countryside it came under the Gendarmerie. The Gendarmerie was responsible for economics matters in connection with the "Blue" police. This force was involved in traffic, administration and public safety. They kept their former uniforms with the addition of an armband "General government."

Ukrainian police

The Ukrainian community had its own police force. In 1942 the auxiliary police force had 1,800 members.

Eastern Voluntary Units (Schutzmannschaft)

Formed with a view to supplement the German police in control of the vast eastern territories and took part in the fight against partisans, Volenteer units were set up under control of the KdO:

Town units (Stadtschutzmannschaft).

Rural units (Landschutzmannschaft)

Field battalions (Schutzmannschaft-Bataillon)

Schuma Battalion 202 was the only unit created with Polish volunteers. Formed at Debica, it was transferred to Galicia in 1943. Ukrainians from Poland provided the staff for the following 14 battalions. Schuma Battalions 101 to 107 were created in Galicia in 1942, battalions 203 to 206 in 1943 and battalions 207 to 212 in 1944.These units were employed against partisans.

7.7 Organisation of the Commanders of the Ordnungspolizei

All posts created in occupied territories were titled BdO from their creation. All the officers listed below are shown with their final ranks.

Agram: This was the command that had been established in Esseg on 4 May 1943 to cover the state of Croatia. It moved its headquarters to Agram on 28 June 1943 and came under the control of the Höhere SS und Polizeiführer "Kroatien." It was given the FP No 47942.

Befehlhaber

SS-Standartenführer der Polizei Rudolf Hand 28.06.1943–21.09.1943

Generalmajor der Polizei Herbert Jilski 21.09.1943 – end

Athen: Established 15 September 1943 to cover Greece following the capitulation of the Italians. It controlled five Kommandeur der Ordnungspolizei in Athens, Saloniki, Larissa, Peloponnes, and Arta. The command came under the Höhere SS und Polizeiführer for Greece and was allocated FP No 11497. A winding up staff was established in Regensburg in March 1945.

Befehlhaber

SS-Brigadeführer und Generalmajor der Polizei Hermann Franz 15.09.1943–07.02.1945

Belgrad: Established on 17 February 1942 to cover the state of Serbia in Yugoslava. It took over the state of Montenegro in 1943 following the capitulation of the Italians. The command came under the Höhere SS und Polizeiführer Serbien, Sandschak, Montenegro and was allocated the same FP No 27085 as the HSSPF. A winding up staff was established in Graz in March 1945.

Befehlhaber

Generalmajor der Polizei Andreas May 05.01.1942 – .03.1945

Brüssel: Established on 16 August 1944 to cover the area of the military commander Belgien-Nord-Frankreich. It came under the control of the Höhere SS und Polizeiführer "Belgien Nord Frankreich." Prior to August 1944 uniformed police duties were under the direct control of the army. The post was allocated the FP No 00869 and was abolished in October 1944.

Befehlhaber

Oberst der Schutzpolizei Kurt Wolter	16.08.1944–01.10.1944

Budapest: Established on 26 March 1944 to cover the independent state of Hungary. It followed the German takeover of Hungary on 14 March 1944 (Operation "Margarethe") after that country had tried to negotiate its surrender to the Russians. The post came under the Höhere SS und Polizeiführer "Ungarn" and probably used the FP No 18686 that was allocated to the HSSPF. It was abolished in February 1945 when the country fell to the Russians.

Befehlhaber

Generalmajor der Polizei Joseph Matros	11.03.1944–09.10.1944
SS-Gruppenführer und Generalleutnant der Polizei Konrad Hitschler	09.10.1944–20.02.1945

Danzig: Established in September 1939 to cover Gau Danzig. On 21 September 1939 a "BdO beim Militärbezirk West-Preussen" was set up to cover the newly occupied territory which was added on to the Gau Danzig to form the Reichsgau "Danzig-Westpreussen." On 25 October 1939 the two posts were combinated to become BdO Danzig. It was controlled by the Höhere SS und Polizeiführer "Weichsel" and was allocated to the army Wehrkreis XX.

Inspekteure

SS-Brigadeführer und Generalmajor der Polizei Leo von Falkowski	20.9.1939–16.11.1943
SS-Brigadeführer und Generalmajor der Polizei Anton Diermann	16.11.1943–01.03.1944
Oberst der Schutzpolizei Walter Strehlow (iV)	01.03.1944–13.06.1944
SS-Beweber und Generalmajor der Polizei Dr. Hans Hachtel	13.06.1944–end.

Den Haag: Established on 4 June 1940 to cover the state of Holland. The German authorities put its own organisation in place from the time of the Dutch surrender. The country's police force was reorganised and unified as a communal police, stiffened by an infusion of politically reliable men. The command came under the Höhere SS und Polizeiführer "Nordwest" and it was allocated the FP No 47623. On 28 May 1943 the headquarters was moved to Nimwegen.

Befehlhaber

SS-Gruppenführer und Generalleutnant der Polizei Otto Schumann	30.05.1940–01.12.1942
SS-Gruppenführer und Generalleutnant der Polizei Dr. Heinrich Lankenau	01.12.1942–28.05.1943

Esseg: Established on 4 May 1943 from a Gendarmerie command that had been set up on 16 March 1943. It covered the independent state of Croatia, controlling five Kommandeure der Ordnungspolizei in Agram, Esseg, Sarajewo, Banja-Luca and Knin. It came under the control of the Höhere SS und Polizeiführer "Kroatien" and moved its headquarters to Agram on 28 June 1943. It was given the FP No 47942

Befehlhaber

SS-Standartenführer Generalmajor der Polizei	
Rudolf Handl	04.05.1943–28.06.1943

Kopenhagen: Established on 23 September 1943 to cover the occupied country of Denmark. Prior to 1943 the country ran its own affairs supervised by a German Reichskommissar, Dr. Werner Best. The only German police presence was SS-Brigadeführer und Generalmajor der Polizei Paul Kanstein who was responsible for police and security matters with the title of "Beauftragter der Reichsführer-SS für Inner Verwaltung für die Sicherheit der Deutschen Truppen in Dänemark." He was not from the Schutzpolizei but came from the Gestapo and SD. After civil unrest and a general strike in September 1943 the full panapoly of German control was imposed. A Höhere SS und Polizeiführer, Günther Pancke, was appointed as was a Befehlhaber der Sicherheitspolizei, SS-Standartenführer Rudolf Mildner, both to replace the discredited Kanstein. The staff of the BdO came from the Police Administration in Flensburg and the command was under the control of the Höhere SS und Polizeiführer. It was allocated the FP No 57880.

Befehlhaber

SS-Brigadeführer und Generalmajor der Polizei	
Erik von Heimburg	01.10.1943–10.08.1944
Oberst der Gendarmerie Werner Lorge i.V.	10.4.1944 – 10.04.1944
Unknown	10.4.1944 – 07.04.1945
Oberstleutnant der Schutzpolizei Gustav Englisch i.V.	07.04.1945–08. 05.1945

Krakau: The first police appointment in this area was the "BdO Grenzabschnitt Süd beim Militärbezirk Krakau" which was established on 21 September 1939. It was changed to Befehlhaber der Ordnungspolizei in Krakau on 25 October 1939 to include the command in Lodz and to cover the remains of Poland known as the Generalgouvernement. The district of Lemberg was added in June 1941 when it was captured from the Russians. This command was split into five Kommandeure der Ordnungspolizei for the districts of Krakau, Warschau, Lublin, Radom and Lemberg. Each of these was split into Kommandeure der Schutzpolizei and Kommandeure der Gendarmerie. The BdO came under the control of the Höhere SS und Polizeiführer "Ost" and it was allocated the FP No 18945. In February 1945 the command was abolished and a winding-up staff (Abwicklungsstelle) was set up in Prague.

Befehlhaber

SS-Gruppenführer und Generalleutnant der Polizei	
Emil Höring	01.10.1939–25.10.1939
SS-Gruppenführer und Generalleutnant der Polizei	
Herbert Becker	25.10.1939–31.10.1940
SS-Gruppenführer und Generalleutnant der Polizei	
Paul Riege	01.10.1940–22.08.1941
SS-Brigadeführer und Generalmajor der Polizei	
Rudolf Müller-Bonigk i.V.	22.08.1941–01.09.1941
SS-Gruppenführer und Generalleutnant der Polizei	
Gerhard Winkler	01.09.1941–01.05.1942
SS-Gruppenführer und Generalleutnant der Polizei	
Herbert Becker	01.05.1942–01.08.1943
SS-Brigadeführer und Generalmajor der Polizei	

Hans-Dietrich Grunwald	01.08.1943–08.03.1944
Generalmajor der Polizei Fritz Sendel (i.V.)	08.03.1944–23.03.1944
SS-Gruppenführer und Generalleutnant der Polizei Emil Höring	23.03.1944–19.01.1945

Lodz: On 21 September 1939 a position titled "BdO Grenzabschnitt Mitte beim Militärbezirk Lodz" was established in Lodz. The post was abolished on 25 October 1939 and its staff was incorporated in the command in Krakau.

Befehlhaber

SS-Gruppenführer und Generalleutnant der Polizei Herbert Becker	21.09.1939 – 25.10.1939

Nimwegen: Established on 4 June 1940 in The Hague to cover the state of Holland, it moved to Nimwegen on 28 May 1943. It remained under the control of the Höhere SS und Polizeiführer "Nordwest" and retained FP No 47623.

Befehlhaber

SS-Gruppenführer und Generalleutnant der Polizei Dr. Heinrich Lankenau	28.05.1943–06.01.1944
SS-Brigadeführer und Generalmajor der Polizei Helmut Mascus	06.01.1944–14.10.1944
Oberst der Schutzpolizei Walter Griep i.V.	14.10.1944–08.02.1945
SS-Brigadeführer und Generalmajor der Polizei Helmut Mascus	08.02.1945–08.05.1945

Oslo: Established on 20 April 1940 on the appointment of the Reichskommissar, Gauleiter Josef Terboven to cover the occupied country of Norway. This country was allowed a certain measure of self-rule and as such it was allowed to retain its own police force called the 'Statspoliti'. It was under the command of the Norwegian Colonel Sundlo who reported to the Norwegen Minister for Police, SS-Standartenführer Jonas Lie. Overall control was vested in the BdO. It came under the control of the Höhere SS und Polizeiführer "Nord" and was allocated the FPO No 40206.

Befehlhaber

SS-Gruppenführer und Generalleutnant der Polizei Paul Riege	20.04.1940–10.09.1940
SS-Gruppenführer und Generalleutnant der Polizei August Edler von Meyszner	10.09.1940–16.01.1942
SS-Gruppenführer und Generalleutnant der Polizei Emil Höring	16.01.1942–01.06.1943
SS-Obergruppenführer und General der Polizei Jürgen von Kamptz	01.06.1943–09.09.1943
Generalmajor der Polizei Lothar Mackeldey	09.09.1943–07.02.1945
SS-Brigadeführer und Generalmajor der Polizei Hermann Franz	07.02.1945–08.05.1945

Paris: Established on 26 May 1942 to cover the area of France governed by the Military Command in Paris that excluded Northern France which was under a similar post in Brussels. It was under the control of the Höhere SS und Polizeiführer "Frankreich" and it was given the FP No 03069, later changed to 65624. The post was abandoned in August 1944.

Befehlhaber

SS-Brigadeführer und Generalmajor der Polizei
Helmut Mascus 08.04.1942–01.05.1942
Oberst der Schutzpolizei Bodo von Schweinichen 01.05.1942–06.01.1943
SS-Gruppenführer und Generalleutnant der Polizei
Walter Schimana 06.01.1943–05.1943
SS-Gruppenführer und Generalleutnant der
Polizei Paul Scheer 05.1943 -01.08.1944

Posen: Established on 21 September 1939 as the "BdO beim Militärbezirk Posen," covering the new Reichsgau "Wartheland" in what had been the western part of Poland. Its name was changed to BdO Posen on 25 October 1939. It came under the control of the Höhere SS und Polizeiführer "Warthe" and was allocated to the army Wehrkreis XXI.

Befehlhaber

SS-Brigadeführer und Generalmajor der Polizei
Oskar Knofe 09.1939–30.06.1942
SS-Brigadeführer und Generalmajor der
Polizei Walter Hille 30.06.1942–14.12.1943
Generalmajor der Polizei Hans Podzun 14.12.1943–03.1944
SS-Brigadeführer und Generalmajor der Polizei
Dr. Walter Gudewill 03.1944 – end

Pressburg: Established in November 1944 to cover the independent state of Slovakia which had come under direct control of the German authorities following a revolt in August 1944. Before this date it had its own independent police force, with only anti-partisan duties coming under German control, being vested in the BdO in Salzburg. This was the only connection between the two forces. The post in Pressburg came under the control of the Höhere SS und Polizeiführer "Slowakien" and it was presumably allocated a FP number although this is not known. In March 1945 the command was abolished and its staff became part of the Kampfgruppe "Untersteiermark."

Befehlhaber

Oberst der Schutzpolizei Dr Alois Kühhas 01.12.1944–03.1945

Prag: Established in May 1939 to cover the Protectorate of Böhmen-Mähren. It controlled the Polizei-Regiments Böhmen-Mähren that later were numbered 20 and 21. The Protectorate kept its own uniformed police that was not subordinated to the BdO and it is the subject of a chapter of its own. The BdO took over responsibility for the former post in Reichenberg on 30 September 1939. The BdO in Prague came under the control of the Höhere SS und Polizeiführer "Böhmen-Mähren" and it was given the FP No 38690.

Befehlhaber

SS-Obergruppenführer und General der Polizei
Rudolf Querner 05.1939 – 12.6.1939
SS-Obergruppenführer und General der Polizei
Jürgen von Kamptz 12.6.1939–01.05.1941

SS-Gruppenführer und Generalleutnant der Polizei Otto von Oelhafen	01.05.1941–22.08.1941
SS-Gruppenführer und Generalleutnant der Polizei Paul Riege	22.08.1941–15.09.1943
SS-Gruppenführer und Generalleutnant der Polizei Ernst Hitzegrad	15.09.1943–15.02.1945
SS-Brigadeführer und Generalmajor der Polizei Paul Otto Geibel	15.02.1945–09.05.1945

Riga: Established on 22 June 1941 to cover the Baltic states of Lithuania, Latvia and Estonia and the area known as White Russia. It had four subordinate commands known as Kommmandeur der Ordnungspolizei, one for each state and one for White Russia and each one of these controlled a Kommandeur der Schutzpolizei. There was no Kommandeur der Gendarmerie, Gendarmerie units came directly under the relevant KdO. It lost the area of White Russia on 1 April 1943. That area was put under the Höhere SS und Polizeiführer "Russland-Mitte und Weissruthenien" and the Ordnungspolizei came under an independent Kommandeur der Ordnungspolizei based in Minsk, commanded by SS-Brigadeführer und Generalmajor der Polizei Eberhard Herf. The BdO in Riga came under the control of the Höhere SS und Polizeiführer "Ostland" and it was allocated the FP No 243. The post was abolished in February 1945 and the staff put under Kampfgruppe "Jeckeln" with the FP No 19216.

Befehlhaber

SS-Gruppenführer und Generalleutnant der Polizei Georg Jedicke	22.06.1941–01.03.1944
SS-Brigadeführer und Generalmajor der Polizei Otto Gieseke	01.03.1944–24.01.1945

Rowno/Kiew: Established in September 1941 in Rowno to cover the Ukraine. The headquarters moved to Kiev on July 1942 and moved back to Rowno during the late summer of 1943. It controlled a total of ten Kommandeur der Ordnungspolizei based in Luzk, Shitomir, Kiew, Nikolajew, Dnjepropetrowsk, Tschernigow, Charkow, Simferopol, Stalino and Rostow. The posts in Charkow, Rostow and Stalino were abolished in February 1943 while the posts in Nikolajew and Simferopol were put under a new BdO based in the Crimea in August 1943. The command in Rowno/Kiew came under the control of the Höhere SS und Polizeiführer "Russland-Süd" that, itself, came under the Supreme SS and Police leader "Ukraine." It was allocated the FP No 40550. A winding up staff (Abwicklungstelle) was set up in Breslau on 18 March 1944 and the command was abolished in September 1944.

Befehlhaber

SS-Gruppenführer und Generalleutnant der Polizei Otto von Oelhafen	01.09.1941–01.10.1942
SS-Gruppenführer und Generalleutnant der Polizei Adolf von Bomhard	01.10.1942–31.10.1943
Oberst der Gendarmerie Werner Lorge i.V.	31.10.1943–15.12.1943
SS-Gruppenführer und Generalleutnant der Polizei Karl Brenner	15.12.1943–06.06.1944
Oberst der Gendarmerie Werner Lorge	06.06.1944–09.1944

San Martino: Established on 7 March 1943 as "Sonderstab von Kamptz." On 16 March 1943 the title was changed to "Befehlhaber der Ordnungspolizei-Stab von Kamptz" and in January 1944 changed again to BdO Italien. It covered that part of Italy remaining under German control following the Italian surrender of 8 September 1943. Under the control of the Höhere SS und Polizeiführer "Oberitalien-West" until 23 September 1943, it then it came under the Supreme SS and Police Leader "Italien." It was allocated the FP No 58068.

Befehlhaber

SS-Obergruppenführer und General der Polizei Jürgen von Kamptz	07.03.1943–08.05.1945

Simferopol: Established in August 1943 to cover the Crimea and the Black Sea coast. It took over this area from the BdO in Rowno/Kiew and controlled the Kommandeure der Ordnungspolizei in Simferopol and Nikolajew. It came under the control of the Höhere SS und Polizeiführer "Schwarzes-Meer" and was allocated the FP No 42345. A winding up staff was set up in Wien and the command was abolished on the 14 September 1944.

Befehlhaber

SS-Gruppenführer und Generalleutnant der Polizei Konrad Hitschler	02.11.1943–14.09.1944
Oberst der Gendarmerie Werner Meltzer i.V.	20.11.1943 -07.02.1944

Triest: Established on 22 September 1943 to cover the Adriatic Coast area taken over when Italy surrendered. It controlled five Abschnittkommandos in Udine, Gorz, Pisino, Fiume and Triest. It was controlled by the Höhere SS und Polizeiführer "Adriatisches Küstenland." It initially had the same FP as the the HSSPF, 58068. In September 1944 it was given its own, FP No 48481.

Befehlhaber

SS-Oberführer und Oberst der Schutzpolizei Hermann Kintrup	22.9.1943–30.4.1945

Woroschilowsk: Established on 23 September 1942 to cover the Northern Caucasus. It came under the control of the Höhere SS und Polizeiführer "z.b.V. Kaukasien" and it was allocated the FP No 31199. The command was abolished in March 1943 and the staff moved to Sambor and Lemberg.

Militarized Units of the Ordnungspolizei

8.1 Waffens-SS Units of the Police

Within the Waffen-SS there were two divisions and five brigades using members of the Ordnungspolizei. They were all formed for service at the front alongside the army. As much has been written on the Waffen-SS and its campaigns our intention here is only to describe these units histories and organisation and not their campaigns.

4. SS-Polizei-Panzergrenadier-Division

01.10.1939	Polizei-Division
10.02.1942	SS-Polizei-Division
26.10.1943	SS-Polizei-Panzergrenadier-Division

This division was ordered in a Führerbefehl (Hitler Order) dated 18 September 1939 and the setting up of battalion staff was ordered by a decree of the Reichsführer-SS und Chef der Deutschen Polizei dated 1 October 1939. As a result of these orders 15,803 members of the Ordnungspolizei were selected as suitable material and were posted to the new division, many of these were young police reservists recalled to duty. The division underwent three months training at the Truppenübungsplatz (Troop Training Area) Wandern and it was then sent to the Upper Rhine area. It took a minor part in the Western campaign of 1940 and, after a period in reserve, it was transferred to Ostpreussen on the 27 June 1941. It served in Northern Russia from August 1941 to early 1943. It was then transferred to the training areas in Schlesien and Böhmen- Mähren for refitting as a Panzer-Grenadier Division. A remnant Kampfgruppe "SS-Polizei-Division" remained in Russia until the 21 May 1944 when it was disbanded. As refitting was completed elements were posted to Greece to participate in anti-partisan warfare. The whole division moved by rail to Serbia late in 1944 and to Stettin on the Baltic Coast on the 21 January 1945. It remained in this area until it capitulated to the US forces in April/May 1945 in the Wittenberg-Lenzen area.

When first formed the division was known as the "Polizei-Division"and although subordinate to the Reichsführer-SS it was in his capacity as Chief of the German Police. Its members were not forced to be members of the SS and were not obliged to pass the racial and physical requirements demanded of SS-men. The uniform consisted of the standard Ordnungspolizei uniform with those who were members of the SS wearing an SS-runes badge on the left breastpocket. An order issued by the SS-Führungshauptamt dated 10 February 1942 stated that the Division with all its elements were to come under direct SS-control with effect from 24 February 1942. From that date it was known as the SS-Police Division. After refitting the Division was numbered within the Waffen-SS numbering system and was re-designated a Panzer-Grenadier-Division, its new title being the 4. SS-Polizei-Panzergrenadier-Division. On its formation the Division consisted of three infantry regiments plus an anti-tank section, an engineer battalion and a cyclist squadron. It also received Artillerie-Regiment 300 from army Wehrkreis III and Signals Section 300 from army Wehrkreis IV.

Divisional staff

Police Infantery Regiment 1

I Battalion

II Battalion

III Battalion

13 Company

14 Company

Police Infantery Regiment 2
I Battalion
II Battalion
III Battalion
13 Company
14 Company

Police Infantery Regiment 3
I Battalion
II Battalion
III Battalion
13 Company
14 Company

The infantry regiments were known as Rifle regiments (Schützenregiments) until October 1942.

Artillery Regiment 300
I Battalion
II Battalion
III Battalion
IV Battalion

On the 9 August 1940 Artillery Regiment 300 was reformed as the Police Artillery Regiment and a new Artillery Regiment 300 was formed under the control of army Headquarters.

Police Artillery Regiment
I Battalion
II Battalion
III Battalion
IV Battalion

Police Anti-tank Battalion
Police Engineer Battalion
Police Cyclist Company
Signal Battalion 300

The Divisional Signals Battalion was reformed as the Police Division Signals Battalion in Nürnberg on 9 August 1940 and a new Divisional Signals Battalion 300 was formed under the control of army Headquarters. In July 1941 a Reconnaissance Battalion and an Anti-Aircraft Battalion were formed.

On 1 April 1941 a Police Replacement unit with three battalions was created in Holland. It was intended that the first replacement battalion would supply the first Polizei-Schützen-Regiment, the second battalion the second regiment, etc.

Police Replacement Units
Replacement Battalion I
Replacement Battalion II
Replacement Battalion III
Artillery Replacement Battalion
Heavy Grenade Projector Replacement Company
Motorised Troops Replacement Company
Infanterie Signals Replacement Company
Signals Replacement Company
Cyclist Replacement Section

With effect from 24 February 1942 the Division came under direct SS-control and its elements had SS applied to all titles. In February 1943 the regimental titles were changed again and each became an "SS-Polizei-Panzer-Grenadier-Regiment" On 22 October 1943 the regiments were re-numbered to fit into the new Waffen-SS numbering system. SS-Polizei-Grenadier-Regiment 1 became SS-Polizei-Panzer-Grenadier-Regiment 7. The second regiment was re-numbered 8 and the third re-numbered 9. The latter regiment was disbanded on 12 November 1943 to conform to the requirements of a Panzer-Grenadier-Division. Its II Battalion became the I./SS-Polizei-Panzergrenadier-Regiment 8 and III Battalion became the III./SS-Polizei-Panzergrenadier-Regiment 7. The old I/8 and III/7 had remained in Russia as part of the Kampfgruppe "SS-Polizei-Division". All other elements of the division were numbered 4. An armoured element was added to the division in July 1944 with the creation of the SS-Panzer-Abteilung 4.

Division Staff
SS-Police Armoured Grenadier Regiment 7
I Battalion
II Battalion
III Battalion
13 Company
14 Company
16 Company

SS-Police Armoured Grenadier Regiment 8
I Battalion
II Battalion
III Battalion
13 Company
14 Company
15 Company
16 Company

SS-Police Armoured Battalion 4
SS-Police Artillery Regiment 4
I Battalion
II Battalion
III Battalion
IV Battalion

SS-Police (Light) Armoured Battalion 4
SS-Police Assault Gun Battalion 4
SS-Police Reconnaissance Battalion 4
SS-Police Anti Aircraft Battalion 4
SS-Police Signals Battalion 4
SS-Police Tank Repair Battalion 4
SS-Police Armoured Engineer Battalion 4
SS-Police Supply troops 4
SS-Police Motorized Battalion 4
SS-Police Medical Battalion 4
SS-Police Economics battalion 4

Divisionals Commanders:

SS-Obergruppenführer und General der Waffen-SS und der Polizei Karl Pfeffer-Wildenbruch	10.10.1939–10.09.1940
SS-Gruppenführer und Generalleutnant der Polizei Arthur Mülverstedt	10.09.1940–10.08.1941 (Killed in action)
SS-Gruppenführer und Generalleutnant der Polizei Emil Höring	16.08.1941–18.08.1941
SS-Obergruppenführer und General der Waffen-SS und der Polizei Walter Krüger	18.08.1941–15.12.1941
SS-Obergruppenführer und General der Waffen-SS und der Polizei Alfred Wünnenberg	15.12.1941–10.06.194
SS-Brigadeführer und Generalmajor der Waffen-SS und der Polizei Fritz Schmedes	10.6.1943–05.07.1944
SS-Brigadeführer und Generalmajor der Waffen-SS und der Polizei Fritz Freitag (m.d.F.b)	18.08.1943–25.8.194
SS-Brigadeführer und Generalmajor der Waffen-SS und der Polizei Herbert Vahl (killed in a road accident)	13.07.1944–22.07.1944
SS-Oberführer Karl Schümers (m.d.F.b)	23.07.1944–17.08.1944 (Died of Wounds)
SS-Oberführer und Oberst der Schutzpolizei Helmut Dorner (m.d.F.b)	17.08.1944–21.08.1944
SS-Brigadeführer und Generalmajor der Waffen-SS und der Polizei Fritz Schmedes	22.08.1944–27.11.1944
SS-Standartenführer Walter Harzer	28.11.1944 – end

Ia -1 General Staff Officer:

Unknown	10.1939–01 01.1940
SS-Obergruppenführer und General der Waffen-SS und der Polizei Walter Krüger	01.01.1940–11.04.1940
SS-Brigadeführer und Generalmajor der Waffen-SS Nikolaus Heilmann	11.04.1940--1.09.1942

SS-Standartenführer Willy Braun	01.09.1942–30.01.1943
SS-Brigadeführer und Generalmajor der Waffen-SS	
Nikolaus Heilmann	30.01.1943–04.04.1943
SS-Standartenführer d. R. Hans Blume	04.04.1943–13.07.1943
SS-Standartenführer Rüdiger Pipkorn	13.07.1943–04.10.1943
SS-Sturmbannführer Helmut Kordts	04.10.1943–10.08.1944
Major i.G. (in General Staff) Otto Kleine	10.08.1944 -..1944
SS-Obersturmbannführer Wilhelm Radtke	1944–20.03.1945
Major i.G Otto Kleine	20.03.1945–end

35. SS-Polizei-Grenadier-Division

00.02.45 35. SS-Polizei-Grenadier-Division

This division was formed in February 1945 on the Oder front from SS-Polizei-Brigade "Wirth" and consisted of three infantry regiments plus an artillery regiment. A fusilier regiment was added in March 1945. The first two infantry regimentscame from the Polizei-Regiments z.b.V 1 and 2 from the brigade. They were re-titled SS-Polizei-Regiments 29 and 30. The third infantry regiment came from the SS-Polizei-Regiment 14 and it consisted of two battalions, the first being based in Gurkfeld in Steiermark and the second in Dahme in Steiermark. It was not re-numbered. A decree dated the 6 April 1945 ordered the re-numbering of the three infantry regiments to bring them into line with the general Waffen-SS numbering scheme. As a result their last designations were SS-Polizei-Grenadier-Regimenter 89,90 and 91. The Artillerie- Regiment was formed in March 1945 from an Abteilung of the Polizei Waffen School II in Dresden-Hellerau. It consisted of three Abteilungen each consisting of three batteries. The divisional leadership staff came from 120 graduates of the SS-Officers Training Schools and the manpower came from the Ordnungspolizei. The division served under the XXXX. Panzer-Korps (General der Panzertruppen Siegfried Henrici) in the 4. Panzer-Armee (General der Panzertruppen Fritz-Hübert Graser), it surrendered to the Russians in the Halbe area.

Divisional Staff
SS-Police Grenadier Regiment 89
I Battalion
II Battalion
III Battalion
SS-Police Grenadier Regiment 90
I Battalion
II Battalion
SS-Police Grenadier Regiment 91
I Battalion
II Battalion
SS-Police Füsilier Battalion 35
SS-Anti-Tank Battalion 35
SS-Police Artillery Regiment 35
I Battalion
II Battalion
III Battalion
SS-Police Engineer Battalion 35

SS-Police Signals Battalion 35
SS-Divisional Supply Regiment 35
Both the Füsilier Battalion and the Signals detachment were formed with personnel from the Police Weapons School II in Dresden-Hellerau.

Divisionals Commanders:

SS-Brigadeführer und Generalmajor der Waffen-SS und der Polizei Fritz Schmedes	14.02.12945–17.02.1945
SS-Oberführer und Oberst der Schutzpolizei Johannes Wirth	17.02.1945–03.1945 (Killed in Action)
SS-Standartenführer Rüdiger Pipkorn	03.1945–24.04.1945 (Killed in action)

Ia–1 General Staff 0fficer	
SS-Sturmbannführer Wilhelm Buethe	14.02.1945–end

SS-Polizei-Brigade "Wirth"

This brigade was formed during the summer of 1944 from the staff of the Police Waffen School in Dresden-Hellerau. Created for service on the Eastern Front, it consisted of two infantry regiments, Polizei-Infanterie-Regiments z.b.V.1 and 2. In February 1945 it was used as the basis for the new 35. SS-Police Grenadier Division.

Brigade Staff
Polizei-Regiment z.b.V. 1
Polizei-Regiment z.b.V. 2

Brigade Commanders:

SS-Oberführer und Oberst der Schutzpolizei Johannes Wirth	Summer 1944–17.02.1945
Polizei-Regiment z.b.V. 1	
SS-Standartenführer und Oberst der Schutzpolizei Friedrich Korff	Summer 1944–16.03.1945
Polizei-Regiment z.b.V. 2	
Oberstleutnant der Schutzpolizei Fritz Auschner	01.1945–16.03.1945

1. SS-Polizei-Jäger-Brigade

This Brigade was formed in February 1945 with a staff plus a signals and Panzer-Jäger-Kompanie. A placement listing for the 15 April 1945 shows that the Brigade consisted of the SS-Polizei-Regiment 8 with three battalions, the SS-Polizei-Jäger-Regiment 50 with three battalions, plus two companies from the SS-Panzer-Grenadier-Ersatz-Battalion 9. It served in the Stettin area.

Brigade Commander:

Oberst der Schutzpolizei Leo von Braunschweig	02.1945–end

Polizei-Brigade "Nordwest"

This Brigade was formed in March 1945 under the control of the Höhere SS und Polizeiführer in Holland, SS-Obergruppenführer und General der Waffen-SS und Polizei Hanns-Albin Rauter. It included the Police Artillery Detachment "Northwest" but nothing else is known of its organisation.

SS-Polizei-Brigade "Anhalt"

This Brigade was formed on the 15 July 1944 from the Polizeigruppe "Anhalt" and it was under the control of Korpsgruppe of the Höhere SS und Polizeiführer for Central Russia, SS-Obergruppenführer General der Waffen-SS und der Polizei Curt von Gottberg, for the anti-partisan operation "Frühlingsfest" in the Lepel-Usaci area. This operation was from 11 April to 10 May 1944, the Brigade being used in mopping up duties and to maintain security. It consisted of SS-Polizei-Regiment 2, SS-Polizei-Regiment 24 and Schutzmannschaft Battalion 62. It became involved in operations at the front under control of the 4.Armee and was dissolved in August 1944.

Brigade Commander:	
SS-Standartenführer Günther Anhalt	15.07.1944–.08.1944
1a–1 General Staff Officer:	
Major der Schutzpolizei Neumann	15.07.1944–.08.1944

8.2 Feldgendarmerie (Military Police Forces)

During the 1930's a German Military police force (Feldgendarmerie) was created to control the Military traffic at the rear of the front line. The organisation was initially composed of conscripted civil policemen mainly from the motorised Gendarmerie, this part of the ORPO had regularly served on maneuvers with the armed forces and were therfore used to army service. Complete platoons of motorised Gendarmerie moved to the Feldgendarmerie complete with their equipment and vehicles. A report dated 20.08.40 stated 280 officers and 7,879 men had been transferred from the ORPO to the provost corps. During the Polish campaign, a Feldgendarmerie Battalion was attached to each army. Among them, the Feldgendarmerie-Abteilung (mot) 682 led by Oberstleutnant Konrad Hitschler. This unit was attached to Heeresgruppe "Süd" from 3 September to 2 October 1939 and it was cited for outstanding service in a daily order of the Heersgruppe signed by Generaloberst Gerd von Rundstedt.

Organisation

The war placed greater demands upon the logistical support of the armed forces. The ranks of the Feldgendarmerie were augmented by the introduction of active non-commissioned officers and enlisted men without a police background. Following the conquest of Poland, those men selected for the Feldgendarmerie from the army underwent Military police training at one of the two Feldgendarmerie schools in Prague Czechoslovakia and Litzmannstadft-Gornau Poland. Upon successfull completion the graduates were then assigned to whichever units need manpower. Based upon Feldgendarmerie regulations from 29.07.40, the units were organised as follows:

army	one or more Feldgendarmerie battalions (3 companies, 3 platoons each)

Army Corps	a Feldgendarmerie company or Feldgendarmerie Troop
Division	a Feldgendarmerie company or Feldgendarmerie troop
Field Command	a Feldgendarmerie Group

Parts of the Feldgendarmerie units may be assigned to others duties for reinforcement or for special assignment. The commander of a Feldgendarmerie battalion had the same degree of authority as a regimental commander. Commanding officers of companies, troops and groups had the authority of a company commander.

Chain of Command

The Höhere Feldgendarmerie Offizier (Senior Feldgendarmerie Officer) was Oberst der Gendarmerie (later Generalmajor) Hans-Dieter De Niem. He was subordinated to Generalquartiermeister (Supply and Administration) in the army High Command (OKH). As a technical staff officer he was responsible for all Feldgendarmerie matters, mainly of personal matters in relation with Personal Office of the army and the SS (for Waffen-SS units). Technical advisors (sachbearbeiter) were attached to senior staffs to supervise the execution of the tasks regarding traffic discipline or discipline enforcement in the army's area of operations:
Heeresgruppe (army group) or Armeeoberkommando (army)

Ib Quartiermeister (Quarter Master)	Stabsoffizier der Feldgendarmerie (Staff Officer)

Commanding officers were assigned to lead a company or a troop within a unit or a rear area command:

Armee-Korps or Division (Army Corps or Division)	Führer der Feldgendarmerie Kompanie/Trupp (Co. or troop commander)
Feldkommandantur (rear area command)	Offizier der Feldgendarmerie (Feldgendarmerie officer)

The Stabsoffizier der Feldgendarmerie for the 6 army after it had been reformed in 1943 was Major Dorgerloh. The Stabsoffizier der Feldgendarmerie for the 3 Panzer army was Major Missmahl.

Status of Military Police members

Staff personnel transferred from the ORPO to the Feldgendarmerie were given comparative rank in the army:

ORPO ranks	Feldgendarmerie ranks
Rottwachtmeister	Obergefreiter
Wachmeister	Unteroffizier
Oberwachtmeister	Feldwebel
Hauptwachtmeister (Less than 12 years service)	Oberfeldwebel
Hauptwachtmeister (More than 12 years service)	Stabsfeldwebel
Meister	Leutnant
Obermeister	Leutnant

The officers of ORPO transferred to Feldgendarmerie with rank seniority in army based upon the pay group seniority similar to the police civil servants. Promotions for officers were dependent on the army High Command Personnel office in conjunction with the Reichsführer-SS (as Head of the German Police). Promotions for non-commissioned officers and enlisted men were based exclusively on merit and time-in-service/time-in-grade. An Unteroffizier was eligable for promotion to Feldwebel only after completing a total of five years service, of which three years must have been spent as Unteroffizier. A Feldwebel had to have performed seven years service with one year as Feldwebel before promotion to Oberfeldwebel. Given the fact that enlisted personnel who, had transferred to the Feldgendarmerie from the police were considered to be only 'temporarily' detached to the army, promotions in the Feldgendarmerie had no influence on their civil service police rank. Consequently one could be an Oberfeldwebel der Feldgendarmerie while still holdint the rank of Wachmeister der Schutzpolizei.

Since all members of the Feldgendarmerie were entrusted with the task of 'policeing' their fellow servicemen, their behaviour and conduct had to be above reproach. If an officer transgressed his officers code of honour he would be relieved of command and sent back to his home duty station in disgrace. Other ranks that transgressed would be immediately transferred out of the Feldgendamerie and they would suffer punishment commensurate with their crime.

Missions of the Feldgendarmerie

The Feldgendarmerie regulations dated 29 July 1940 stated that the most important Feldgendarmerie tasks were traffic control and duties in connnection with the maintenance of order and discipline in peace time and duties of air raid defence (Luftschutz).

The Feldgendarmerie officers could serve to supervise and control specific roads or traffic areas. Also for investigations in case of accidents when armed forces vehicles are involved.

Further tasks of the Feldgendarmerie were:

Disciplinary matters of members of the army forces in their location
Establishment of prisoners assembly points in the their area of operations
Giving assistance to the Geheime Feldpolizei (the "Gestapo" of the army)
Disarming and control of the civilian population in occupied areas

Feldgendarms assigned to Feldkommandantur in occupied countries were involved in the following duties:

Control of population and luggage
Mobilisation of civilians for public works (burial of a dead, road repair, supervision of those involved in measures taken in connection with the Luftschutz)

In the rear area behind the front line, Feldgendarmerie units could be attached to Wachbataillons or security regiments to protect lines of communications or command and logistic installations from sabotage as well partisan warfare.

Waffen-SS and Feldgendarmerie

The Feldgendarmerie of the Waffen-SS had similar functions to those of the army. Each major field unit of the Waffen-SS had its own Feldgendarmerie unit. They did not wear the police eagle on the left sleeve, they only had the orange waffen farbe. From 1942, a special cuff band "SS-Feldgendarmerie" was worn above the cuff band of the division. The Feldgendarmerie troop of the "LSSAH" was created in 1940 in Metz when the motorised regiment was expanded to Brigade size. In the divisional staff, the Feldgendarmerie troop held the number of the division, such as SS-Feldgendarmerie Trupp 1 for LSSAH. From 1942, some troops rose to company size. Records state that the first duty of Waffen-SS Feldgendarmerie was that of a provost coprs for the unit.

At corps level, the Feldgendarmerie unit held the number of the SS-Korps (Feldgendarmerie Trupp 113 for the XIII.SS Armee-Korps). Senior staffs, such as the Kommandostab "Reichsführer-SS," that controlled Waffen-SS units in operationsagainst partisans, had a Feldgendarmerie company. In foreign units of the Waffen-SS, Feldgendarmerie followed specific policy and for most units consisted of German personnel only. The SS-Feldgendarmerie unit of the 29. SS-Italian Division wore a special gorget with the legend " Feldgendarmeria". The following is a partial list of Feldgendarmerie units with commanders:

XIII. SS-Armee-Korps	SS-Hauptsturmführer Eduard Smolka
1. SS-Panzer-Division "Leibstandarte"	SS-Hauptsturmführer Bernhard Hildebrand
	SS-Obersturmführer Helmut Rosenstengel
2. SS-Panzer-Division "Das Reich"	SS-Obersturmführer Otto Kahn
4. SS-Polizei-Panzergrenadier-Division	Hauptmann der Schutzpolizei Baumel
12. SS-Panzer-Division "Hitler Jugund"	SS-Obersturmführer Kurt Buschhausen
28. Freiwilligen SS-Division "Wallonie"	SS-Obersturmführer Otto Bachinger
SS-Kavallerie Brigade	SS-Hauptsturmführer Franz Rinner

Luftwaffe and Feldgendarmerie

The ground combat units of the Luftwaffe were the only Luftwaffe units to include a Feldgendarmerie troop in their staff. These units were:

22 Luftwaffe Field Divisions
Six Fallschirmjäger Divisions (paratroops)
Fallschirm-Panzer-Korps "Hermann Göring" the elite armoured paratroop Army Corps of the Luftwaffe.

They didn't wear the police eagle on the sleeve but used the orange color of the Feldgendarmerie, a Feldgendarmerie army pattern gorget and cuff band. The duties were similar to army and Waffen-SS units.

Kriegsmarine and Feldgendarmerie

The Kriegsmarine had no Feldgendarmerie units but only a provost organisation on ships. In costal towns where naval forces were located, security duties were conducted by Marine Küsten Polizei under Kriegsmarine regulations. Members of this force were mainly former enlisted policemen.

Verkehrsregulungsbataillone and Feldgendarmerie

The traffic control battalions composed of two companies of 150 men and they were involved in the regulation of traffic mainly in difficult conjested areas. The Senior Feldgendarmerie Officer had authority over these units. The staff officers of Feldgendarmerie were responsible for training matters and employment.

Their main tasks were:
To control and supervise traffic during troops movements under military command
To regulate traffic of supply (convoys and in services areas)

They had the same regulations and instructions as the Feldgendarmerie and wore an armband "Verkehraufsicht" (traffic supervision). They had authority over all members of the Wehrmacht in these matters. Ten battalions were formed in October 1939 and they served during French Campaign and later on the Eastern front. These units were disbanded in 1942 and members were transferred to Feldgendarmerie.

Heeresstreifendienste and Feldgendarmerie

The army Patrolling Service served next to each army (Ameeoberkommando) under authority of Chief of General Staff. These units were involved in discipline inside army forces. From February 1941, these duties were enlarged to serve in all branches of German army. The army Patrolling Service (Heeresstreifendienste) later became the Wehrmacht Patrolling Service (Wehrmachtstreifendienste). Generalmajor Hartmann Freiherr von Ow auf Wachendorf served as Kommandeur der Wehrmacht Streifendiesnt beim Oberbefehlhaber Grenzabschnitt "Nord" 25 January 1944 to 16 October 1944 and was Kommandeur der Wehrmacht Streifendienst in Wehrkreis VII from 16 October 1944. The Waffen-SS had its own "SSS treifendienst." The Patrolling Service was considered part of the military Police Corps.

Feldjägerkorps and Feldgendarmerie

At the turn of the war in November 1943 a special force was set up to fight against the decline of morale, the Feldjägerkorps (Field Rifle Force). They operated behind the frontline with the task of preventing panic retreats, assembling quickreaction units, etc. In addition to these tasks, they were involved in traffic control with a view to keeping roads open for the passage of troops and supplies. The Feldjägerkorps was organised into three Feldjägerkorps commands including:

A Feldjäger regiment of 5 battalions
Each battalion included 3 companies of 50 patrols (streife)
A patrol had one officer and three NCO' s with front line experience

They were not a police force but served to preserve order. Feldjägerkommando II created in Breslau in May 1944 was led by General der Infanterie Karl von Oven, former chief of Staff of a Prussian Landespolizei Inspection in the 1930s and a holder of the Knight´s Cross of the Iron Cross.

The listing contains only the officers who held generals rank in the Ordnungspolizei. It includes those officers who were members of the technical branches of the Ordnungspolizei: the Fire Service and the Technical Emergency Service (TENO). It also includes those civil servants in the service of the Ordnungspolizei whose civil rank was equal to generals rank. Also shown are officers who held General rank in the Landespolizei until that force was incorporated in the army. These officers also transferred to the army. Finally there are five officers with generals rank who were "ausser Dienst", on the retired list.

The list will also show generals who retired before the end of the war. Those listed with (*) were reactived (General a W.) during the war and held important posts. Most of retired generals were given civil service posts with police connections and those in the SS retained their SS-rank. A decree dated 12.9.1940 changed the rank designation for police generals from "General der Ordnungspolizei" to "General der Polizei". SS-rank lists show other officers not listed here as generals of police. They were given such ranks due to their duties in the Security Police (SIPO) and Security Service (SD), also included are Inspekteur/Befehlhaber der SIPO/SD, Amtschef in Reichssicherheitshauptamt and SS-Leaders with HSSPF or SSPF posts. They were not entitled to wear Ordnungspolizei uniform and did not receive pay from the Ordnungspolizei.

The General Officer Corps of the Ordnungspolizei

9.1 Rank list of the General officers

Ordnungspolizei

Born	Rank Date	Joined NSDAP	Joined S.S.	Death
Generaloberst der Polizei				
Daluege Kurt				
15.09.1897	20.04.1942	12.03.1926	25.07.1926	23.10.1945(H)
General der Polizei				
Frank August				
05.04.1898	09.10.1944	01.02.1933	08.04.1932	21.03.1984
von Kamptz Jürgen				
11.08.1891	01.08.1944	01.08.1932	12.03.1938	12.08.1954
Pfeffer-Wildenbruch Karl				
12.06.1888	09.11.1943	01.11.1932	12.03.1938	29.01.1971
Querner Rudolf				
10.06.1893	21.06.1943	01.05.1943	22.05.1938	27.05.1945
Winkelmann Otto				
04.09.1894	15.03.1944	01.11.1932	01.07.1938	24.09.1977
Wünnenberg Alfred				
20.07.1891	01.07.1943	01.05.1933	01.01.1940	30.12.1963
Generalleutnant der Polizei				
Becker Herbert*				
13.03.1887	20.04.1942	01.05.1933	09.11.1938	03.01.1974
von Bomhard Adolf				
06.01.1891	01.07.1940	01.05.1937	20.04.1938	19.09.1973
Brenner Karl-Heinrich				
19.05.1895	01.01.1944	01.05.1933	11.07.1938	14.02.1954
Dillenburger Otto				
6.06.1880	1936	1936		16.03.1948
Göhrum Kurt				
27.03.1891	01.04.1944	01.05.1933	26.11.1943	11.04.1953
Hitschler Konrad				
21.12.1896	01.01.1945	01.05.1933	20.04.1941	20.02.1945 (K)
Hitzegrad Ernst				
26.12.1889	30.01.1944	01.02.1932	01.07.38	14.12.1976
Höring Emil				
01.12.1890	01.09.1943	01.05.1937	20.04.1939	02.06.1973
Jedicke Georg*				
26.03.1887	01.10.1941	01.10.1930	20.04.1939	10.03.1969
Klinger Otto*				
25.04.1886	01.10.1943	01.05.1937	20.04.1939	26.06.1986
Lankenau Dr. Heinrich				
11.10.1891	01.04.1943	01.05.1933	09.11.1938	16.04.1983
Liessem Reiner				

23.08.1890	01.06.1944	01.05.1933	15.08.1943	20.04.1973
von Meyszner August Edler				
03.08.1886	01.01.1942	31.01.1943	20.02.1935	24.01.1947 (H)
Meyer Dr. Johannes FS				
19.07.1890	01.04.1944	01.05.1933	16.01.1941	10.06.1980
Mülverstedt Arthur				
30.06.1894	01.09.1940	30.07.1932	12.03.1938	10.08.1941(K)
von Oelhafen Otto				
08.06.1886	01.10.1941	01.05.1937	20.04.1939	13.03.1952
Reinefarth Heinz				
26.12.1903	01.08.1944	01.08.1932	19.12.1932	07.05.1979
Retzlaff Dr. Carl				
07.05.1890	01.12.1943	01.05.1937	01.08.1939	23.04.1967
Riege Paul				
27.04.1888	01.11.1940	01.05.1933	20.04.1939	13.10.1980
Scheer Paul				
04.04.1889	01.01.1944	30.04.1933	01.08.1940	29.01.1946 (H)
Schimana Walter				
12.03.1898	01.09.1943	07.12.1926	01.07.1939	12.09.1948 (S)
Schmelcher Willy TN				
25.10.1894	01.11.1943	01.06.1928	17.06.1930	15.02.1974
Schreyer Georg*				
16.07.1884	01.11.1941	01.12.1931	01.07.1939	09.05.1961
Schumann Otto*				
11.09.1886	01.09.1943	01.04.1933	20.04.1939	08.11.1952
Siebert Theodor* TN				
05.10.1881	1940ch	01.04.1937	03.05.1945 K	
Wagner Gustav FS				
07.01.1888	Unknown	"-"		31.12.1956
Weinrich Hans TN				
05.09.1896	01.12.1942	15.03.1922	15.12.1936	23.12.1963
Winkler Gerhard				
30.10.1888	01.02.1944	01.04.1933	20.04.1939	18.04.1945 (S)

Generalmajor der Polizei

Abraham Walter				
25.10.1896	01.04.1944	01.05.1937	02.03.1944	24.06.1963
Albert Josef				
10.06.1885	01.01.1944	22.04.1933	"-"	02.05.1961
Asmus Georg *				
07.10.1888	01.01.1944	01.05.1933	30.01.1939	01.05.1944
Bader Dr. Kurt				
26.06.1899	01.04.1943	01.05.1933	20.12.1933	01.06.1959
Bahl Arthur				
09.08.1893	01.09.1944	01.05.1933	"-"	03.1966

Basset Walter				
09.07.1883	01.08.1942	01.05.1937	1943	11.09.1964
Buban Richard TN				
08.02.1880	21.07.1943	01.05.1933	”-”	04.11.1966
Bernaschek Paul FS				
09.07.1887	15.04.1945	”-”	”-”	08.05.1987
Crux Hermann				
31.08.1886	01.01.1944n	01.05.1933	01.06.1940	18.03.1944
Daeuwel Hans *				
25.08.1884	09.1943	01.05.1933	1942	29.06.1958
Denicke Wolfgang				
28.12.1889	1944	01.05.1933	1944	17.11.1962
De Niem Hans-Dieter				
13.12.1893	01.04.1944	01.05.1933	”-”	”-”
Diermann Anton				
25.02.1889	01.01.1944	01.05.1933	01.09.1942	2.07.1982
Dierske Ludwig				
08.03.1898	“-”	“-”	”-”	”-”
von Falkowski Leo				
23.05.1888	01.09.1943	01.05.1933	01.08.1940	27.07.1956
Fischer Karl				
16.04.1889	01.01.1944	01.05.1937	23.01.1939	08.10.1953
Flade Hans				
27.10.1898	01.06.1944	03.09.1939	20.04.1941	04.11.1978
Fornoni Hans TN				
24.01.1884	30.01.1945	01.05.1937	”-”	28.01.1954
Franz Hermann				
16.08.1891	01.08.1944	01.12.1937	01.08.1940	08.10.1960
Franz Karl				
15.02.1899	09.11.1944	“-”	”-”	18.03.1958
Freitag Fritz				
28.04.1944	20.04.1944	01.05.1933	01.09.1940	20.05.1945 (S)
Geibel Paul Otto				
10.06.1898	01.04.1944	01.12.1931	01.03.1938	12.11.1966
Gerloff Dr. Helmut				
21.09.1894	01.10.1941	01.05.1932	20.04.1935	17.03.1975
Geyer Waldemar TN				
14.03.1882	1934	03.1926	”-”	05.09.1947
Giesecke Otto				
24.03.1891	01.05.1944	01.05.1933	01.06.1940	21.07.1958
Goldbach Walter FS				
03.08.1898	01.12.1943	01.05.1933	20.04.1943	26.04.1945 (E)
Griphan Walter				
02.07.1893	01.04.1944	01.01.1933	01.06.1940	03.03.1947 S
von Grolman Wilhelm *				

16.07.1894	01.01.1942	01.05.1930	01.05.1930	20.06.1985
Grünwald Hans-Dietrich				
14.12.1898	20.04.1942	01.08.1932	01.07.1938	20.01.1925
Grussendorf Oskar				
16.07.1888	01.04.1943	01.05.1937	01.09.1940	23.05.1945
Gudewill Dr Walter				
28.12.1894	01.05.1944	01.05.1933	30.01.1939	11.01.1956
Hachtel Dr Hans				
25.10.1894	01.03.1945	01.05.1937	”-”	21.05.1993
Handl Rudolf				
17.04.1887	01.03.1944	01.05.1935	01.07.1939	01.02.1944
Hannibal Heinrich				
19.11.1889	20.04.1945	01.02.1932	01.05.1939	-1971
Hauser				
Unknown	”-”	”-”	”-”	-15.03.1943 (K)
von Heimburg Erik				
06.10.1892	01.06.1942	01.05.1937	01.07.1939	05.05.1945 (K)
Herf Eberhard				
20.03.1887	01.01.1942	01.09.1932	09.11.1941	30.01.1946 H
Herrmann Karl				
27.10.1891	21.06.1943	01.11.1932	28.01.1939	08.10.1960
Hille Walter				
24.05.1894	01.01.1944	01.05.1937	20.04.1943	06.05.19458 (S)
Himmelstoss-Maximilian				
16.06.1887	12.1943ch	07.06.1937	- 1943	26.06.1966
Hoffmann Karl				
07.08.1887	01.08.1943	01.05.1933	20.04.1939	20.12.1970
Jandl Johann				
04.10.1880	01.02.1944	“-”	“-”	18.04.1960
Janka Dr. Heinrich				
26.03.1880	07.10.1938	“-”	“-”	07.10.1958
Jilski Herbert				
27.08.1893	01.04.1944	01.05.1933	“-”	1945
Jünecke Walter TN				
22.06.1894	1943	“-”	“-”	08.10.1957
Karrasch Alfred				
26.01.1889	21.06.1944	01.05.1933	01.01.1940	30.08.1968
Keuck Walter				
06.02.1889	01.01.1944	17.02.1933	“-”	10.12.1972
Kleinow Gustav				
12.01.1877	Unknown	“-”	“-”	31.07.1945
Klinghammer Wilhelm				
16.09.1884	1944ch	“-”	“-”	1966
Knofe Oskar				
14.05.1888	01.12.1941	01.04.1933	01.03.1939	03.11.1978

Kowalski Curt				
01.06.1883	09.1942	"-"	"-"	05.05.1948
Krumhaar Bruno *				
21.08.1885	20.04.1942	01.05.1937	20.04.1939	27.09.1945
Kuschow Otto				
31.12.1880	21.06.1944	01.05.1933	15.07.1942	20.01.1945 (K)
Lichem von Löwenburg Dr. Arnold				
22.04.1892	"-"	"-"	"-"	26.05.1953
Lossen Dr. Oskar				
17.06.1887	01.1945 1942		01.07.1938	15.08.1964
Mackeldey Lothar				
06.05.1892	01.04.1944	"-"	"-"	23.12.1957
Mascus Hellmut				
30.03.1891	01.01.1944	01.05.1933	20.04.1938	17.12.1972
Matros Joseph				
13.03.1889	01.09.1944	01.05.1937	"-"	01.03.1949
Matt August				
30.04.1890	01.12.1944ch	01.05.1937	"-"	18.10.1967
May Andreas				
05.02.1891	01.09.1943	01.05.1937		15.04.1949 H
Merk Dr. Günther				
14.03.1888	01.08.1943	01.10.1932	01.11.1939	16.01.1947
Montua Max *				
18.05.1886	01.09.1943	04.05.1933	09.11.1941	20.04.1945 S
Mühe Ludwig				
27.03.1891	01.07.1944	01.05.1937	"-"	21.12.1958
Müller-Bönigk Rudolf				
27.04.1890	01.10.1942	01.05.1933	01.08.1940	09.05.1968
Münchau Dr. Kurt				
15.01.1887	01.04.1936	"-"	"-"	27.05.1938
Nowotny Hugo				
17.06.1886	01.01.1944	"-"	"-"	15.04.1964
Petersdorf Kurt				
24.08.1896	01.11.1944	01.05.1933	"-"	"-"
Podzun Hans				
09.09.1892	01.04.1944	01.05.1933	"-"	21.03.1946
Pohlmeyer Kurt *				
31.03.1887	01.11.1943	01.05.1933	20.04.1939	25.11.1955
Rauner Adolf *				
05.10.1880	09.1943	01 .05.1937	"-"	06.12.1954
Ritzer Konrad				
24.08.1893	01.01.1944	01.05.1933	21.11.1938	27.05.1979
Rode Ernst				
09.08.1894	21.06.1944	01.05.1933	01.07.1941	12.09.1955

Röthenmeier				
Dr. Ludwig TN	"-"	"-"	1944	"-"
Roettig Wilhelm				
25.07.1888	01.07.1938	20.04.1939		10.09.1939 (K)
Rumpf Hans FS				
07.03.1888	01.09.1943	01.05.1933	17.02.1944	05.11.1965
Ruoff Curt				
09.01.1883	28.03.1939ch	04.1933	31.03.1939	30.11.1970
Schlake Robert				
08.05.1893	01.01.1944	01.05.1937	20.04.1943	"-"
Schmedes Fritz				
07.10.1894	09.11.1943	01.05.1937	01.04.1942	07.02.1952
Schmiedel Oskar				
20.05.1897	20.04.1944	01.05.1933	21.01.1945	03.06.1954
Schnell Walter FS				
06.01.1895	01.06.1942	"-"	"-"	07.05.1967
Schroers Johannes				
07.01.1885	09.12.1941	01.08.1932	20.04.1939	08.06.1960
Schüberth Fritz				
04.10.1890	01.11.1944	01.05.1937	04.12.1942	10.04.1945 (K)
Schulze Christian				
15.07.1893	12.09.1941n	01.05.1933	01.01.1940	13.09.1941 (K)
Schuster Paul				
09.02.1888	1944	01.05.1933	01.05.1933	02.11.1952
Schweinle Karl				
16.09.1885	30.04.1938ch	14.05.1929	"-"	10.10.1954
Sendel Fritz *				
19.12.1885	01.09.1943	01.05.1933	01.12.194	31.10.1963
Seyffarth Franz				
12.06.1884	1943	01.05.1933	1942	"-"
von Thaden Wilhelm				
31.10.1888	01.05.1944ch	01.05.1937	"-"	1944
Wenzel Franz TN				
07.10.1879	1944	01.05.1937	"-"	"-"
Wieder Georg				
19.07.1887	01.10.1943	01.05.1933	"-"	15.11.1943 (K)
Will Paul				
16.08.1888	01.11.1942	01.05.1937	20.04.1939	30.09.1943
Wolfstieg Dr. Friedrich *				
12.09.1887	01.09.1943	01.04.1933	01.12.1943	10.1950
Worm Paul				
13.02.1893	01.05.1944	01.12.1932	01.07.1938	01.05.1946
Zaps Dr. Otto FS				
13.01.1898	1945	"-"	"-"	"-"

Ritter von Zottmann Maximilian

27.09.1892	01.04.1943	14.05.1937	"-"	17.01.1966

Generalarzt der Polizei

Becker Dr. Fritz				
28.06.1891	01.02.1943	01.05.1937	12.12.1944	12.11.1954
Hock Dr. Oskar				
31.01.1898	01.09.1943	01.09.1928	01.08.1936	24.06.1976
Hoffmann Dr Kurt				
24.11.1899	01.11.1944	01.05.1933	01.07.1938	"-"
Jüttner Dr. Viktor				
08.04.1880	01.02.1943	"-"	31.08.1945	"-"
Karehnke Dr. Gerhard				
15.07.1895	20.04.1945	01.05.1933	01.04.1942	01.03.1981
Kloster Dr. Wilhelm				
22.08.1891	01.04.1935	"-"	"-"	29.08.1942
Wenzel Dr. Ernst				
08.06.1891	01.02.1942	01.05.1937	08.09.1934	21.04.1945 S
Wrobel Dr. Karl				
26.02.1882	01.03.1944	"-"	"-"	30.09.1948

Generalveterinär der Polizei

Dasch Dr. Alfred				
Unknown	1944	"-"	"-"	"-"
Kries Dr. Wilhelm				
21.09.1887	01.07.1942	1933	"-"	20.09.1953
Magerl Dr. Heinrich				
02.08.1882	"-"	01.04.1938	"-"	03.03.1971

Beamten mit Generalsrang

Bracht Werner				
05.02.1888	09.11.1940	01.05.1933	31.10.1938	21.09.1980
Scheidel Rudolf				
31.12.1884	01.05.1940	01.03.1933	"-"	"-"

Generalmajor der Gendarmerie

Schoepplenburg Paul (3)				
19.03.1879	03.1933	"-"	12.12.1935	"-"

(1) All these officers had applied to join the SS and had been given the rank of SS-Bewerber (SS-candidate) with no SS-number. Investigations would be conducted into each mans background before acceptance.
(2) This officer was charged with showing "homosexual tendencies" March 1944. Found guilty he was imprisoned and dissmissed from the SS & Police. Sentence was quashed on appeal in October 1944.
(3) Former chief of the department "Landjägerei" and after January 1934 "Gendarmerie" in Ministry of Interior, he was the only Police general to hold the rank of General of Gendarmerie (rural police).

Generalmajor der Landespolizei who transferred to the army

LAPO **Born**	**To the** **Rank Date**	**Final** **army**	**army** **Rank**	**Death** **Rank Date**
Baltzer Richard				
01.06.1886	15.08.1933	16.03.1936	Gen Lt 01.10.1939	10.05.1945 (K)
Bertram George				
31.08.1882	01.04.1935	15.10.1935	Gen Lt 01.08.1939	27.10.1953
Doehla Heinrich				
03.11.1881	01.06.1933	01.08.1936	Gen Lt 01.02.1941	14.07.1956
von dem Knesebeck George				
25.07.1881	19.12.1933	15.10.1935	Gen Lt 01.02.1941	02.06.1955
Niehoff Heinrich (1)				
20.11.1882	01.04.1933	02.1936	Gen Lt 30.01.1938	19.02.1946
Poten Georg				
14.12.1881	03.10.1932	16.03.1936	Gen Lt 01.06.1941	
Ritter von Reiss-Josef				
03.03.1872	15.03.1926	30.09.1939	Gen Maj	01.09.1942
Schmidt-Logan Wolfgang				
08.09.1884	1935	01.04.1936	Gen Lt 01.03.1941	04.05.1945 S
Stieler von Heydekampf Hans				
24.08.1880	01.12.1932	01.02.1937	Gen Lt 01.02.1941	31.12.1946
Strecker Karl (2)				
20.09.1884	01.04.1934	14.06.1935	Gen d Inf.	01.04.1942
Wecke Walter (3)				
30.09.1885	1935	1935	Gen d Lw 01.12.1942	16.12.1943
von Zepelin Ferdinand				
12.04.1886	1934	01.10.1935	Gen Lt	01.06.1942

(1) transferred to the Luftwaffe as Major-General February 1936. Retired 31 March 1938. Recalled to the army February 1941 as Lieutenant General.

(2) served in Stalingrad and it is said he was proposed for Colonel General rank but was captured before the promotion went through.

(3) transferred to the Luftwaffe as Major-General 1935. He remained in that arm. Ranked Gen lt on 1.8.1940 then promoted General der Lw on the z.v. (at disposal) list 1 December 1942.

Generalmajor der Landespolizei on the pensioned list

	Date of birth	Rank date	Death
Caspari Walter	26.07.1877	1933	
von Padberg Wolfgang	19.10.1878	1933	06.11.1958
Graf von Poninski Bernhard	12.12.1872	1933	21.01.1955
Pirner Christian (1)		1933	
Ritter von Seisser Johann (2)	09.12.1874	1927	

(1) he was commander of the landespolizeiamt in Bayern during the München Putsch of November 1923. Dismissed March 1924, he was recalled by the end of 1924.

(2) he held the rank of Ministerialrat and served as referent for Landespolizei matters in the Bayern Ministry of the Interior during the München Putsch.

Abreviations

FS: Feuerschutzpolizei
TN: Technische Nothilfe
ch: characterisiert (brevet rank)
n: nachtraglich (posthumous promotion)
E: executed by the Nazi's
H: hanged by the allies
K: killed in action
S: committed suicide

Only one officer was executed by the Nazi's, Walter Goldbach, a fire service officer, who attempted to return fire engines to Berlin in April 1945 against the orders of Dr. Josef Goebbels in his capacity as Gauleiter of Berlin. Goldbach was shot by the SS on 26 April 1945. Of those hanged by the Allies, Daluege was hanged by the Czechs, Meyszner by the Yugoslavs, Scheer and Herf by the Russians and May by the Greeks.

SS-Membership

On 17 June 1936, Reichsführer-SS Heinrich Himmler was given the added title of Chief of the German Police. As a result, he began to formulate the complete merger of the SS and Police into a single "Staatsschutzkorps" (state protection corps). This was to be achieved by the reorganisation of the Police Service and by the absorbtion of Police personnel into the SS. It was quickly realised that not all members of the Police were politically, racially and physically suitable for membership and Himmler refused to abandon usual qualifications to admit policemen "en block". He modified his original aim to one of having effective control over the police network without assimilating the whole corps into the SS. Historians admit that the Ordnungspolizei was only thinly penetrated numerically by the SS but they consider that the command "had been effectively captured and co-ordinated (gleichgeschaltet) by the ambitious in "top ranks" (1). This is confirmed by the fact that all heads of departments were SS-members and most major field commands were held by SS-members. The formation of the Inspection of Ideological Training (Inspektion für die Weltanschauliche Erziehung) in October 1939 re-inforces this view.

This office was responsible for providing SS ideological training to all new Police members and the first Inspector, Dr. Joachim Caesar, was an SS-Oberführer from the Race and Settlement Office.

To qualify for SS membership applicants had:
to have joined the Party by 1933,
to be racially sound,
to withdraw from any church affiliation,
to have a settled family life (divorce and re-marriage were borderline cases)
and did not belong to any proscribed groups like Freemasonary.

Himmler issued a rank parity decree on 26 June 1938 which laid down the following provisions:
A) members of the Police could be accepted into the SS providing they fulfilled general SS-recruiting conditions (see above)
B) Reichsführer-SS reserved to himself the right to authorise the acceptance of those outide the criteria in (1). This included many Police generals who would have been rejected due to age.
C) acceptance into the SS would take place according to the Police rank held.
D) civilians employees could join the SS with rank corresponding to their civil service rank.
E) rank parity promotions would take place as required.

A typical example of the above provisions in action occurs in the personal file of Oskar Grussendorf. A letter from SS-Personal Hauptamt signed by its chief Walter Schmitt to Himmler's personal staff dated 3 September 1940, requesting the admission of four officers into the SS. There were Colonel Oskar Grussendorf, Lieutenant Colonel Hermann Kölle, Oberbaurat Richard Gribow and Major Willy Bachstein. In the margin of the letter Himmler has written "Ja" by the names of Grussendorf and Kölle and "Nein" by the names of Gribow and Bachstein. Documents in the Personal files of Dr. Hans Hachtel dated 12 January 1945 from the SS-Kinship Office in Danzig to the SS Race and Settlement office show he was SS-Bewerber. They confirm his family and health status and are evidence that such checks were made even at this late date. There was resistance from the Police officer corps to forced incorporation into the SS. The Police was traditionaly close to the army in its outlook, nationalist and at the service of the state rather than a political party. It had a tradition of "neutrality" like the army and this was hard to break. Senior officers who joined did so for personal reasons, better chance of promotion and provision of a good job after retirement. Some were accepted in spite of problems in their backgrounds like Walter Griphan a freemason and Fritz Schüberth who had a poor racial background, as shown in item (2) in the rank parity decree shown above. Until 1942, Police officers wore uniforms similar to the army with branch of service colours (Truppenfarbe) to identify them. These were under the shoulder rank badges and the collar insigna and were allocated as follow:

Colour	**Branch of Uniformed Police**
Green	Schutzpolizei
Yellow	Gendarmerie
Bright yellow	Wasserschutzpolizei
Carmine	Feuerschutzpolizei
Cornflower Blue	Medical
Light Grey	Administrator (civil service rank)
Black	Veterinary

Other differences were that the police had the national badge (eagle and swastika) on the left upper arm rather than over the left breast and their cap badges were the Police Badge surmounted by the national cockade rather than the oakleaf surrounded cockade surmounted by the Eagle and Swastika. All members of the SS wore an SS-runes badge on the lower left breast. On 22 July 1942, Himmler issued an order stating that all Police Generals should change the "Arabian style" collar patch for new SS-rank badges whilst retaining their old Truppenfarbe.

Police rank	SS-Pattern	SS-Equivalent
Generalmajor der Polizei (Major-General of Police)	Three Oakleaves	SS-Brigadeführer
Generalleutnant der Polizei (Lieutenant General of Police)	Three Oakleaves and 1 star	SS-Gruppenführer
General der Polizei (General of Police)	Three Oakleaves and 2 stars	SS-Obergruppenführer
Generaloberst der Polizei (Colonel General of Police) (*)	Three Oakleaves and 3 stars	SS-Oberst-Gruppenführer

(*) This rank was created on 20 April 1942 for Kurt Daluege who was promoted to the new rank of Oberst-Gruppenführer in the Allgemeine-SS at the same date. Daluege was the only police officer to hold such rank in SS. A total of four SS-leaders reached that rank: Daluege and Reichsleiter Franz-Xavier Schwarz, Reich Party Treasurer on 20 April 1942 and two leading figures of the Waffen-SS, Sepp Dietrich in August 1944 back dated to 20 April 1942 and Paul Hausser on 1 August 1944. The obvious reason for this change was to bring the rank badges of the police into line with the other sectors of the SS and to visibly show the general public that the police was part of the SS. A majority of the Generals in the Ordnungspolizei were in the SS due to the restrictions imposed by Himmler as listed above and the resistence from a minority of Police generals. Himmler was not able to achieve full joint membership. Figures for Police Generals who were members of the SS as follows:

Ranks	SS	Non SS	% in the SS
Generaloberst	1	0	100 %
Generals	6	0	100 %
Lieutenant Generals	25	3	89 %
Major-Generals	49	46	51 %
Major-Generals (medical)	4	5	4 %
Major-Generals (veterinary)	0	3	0 %
Major-Generals (officials)	1	1	50 %
Total + (Average)	86	58	(62%)

In the senior ranks (Lieutenant General to Colonel General): 91 % were SS-members. The resistance to SS came from wartime promoted generals whose abilities overcame their political views, only 51 % of Major-Generals were SS-members. Some interesting facts can be gained from looking at the Police Generals rank list. Shown are the inroads made by the SS into the police hierarchy. The most important was the head of the Ordnungspolizei Kurt Daluege who had no police background. He had been a Berlin City engineer and was Himmler rival in that city in the late twenties. An early member of the General SS (Allgemeine-SS), he was given the Police post to bind him to the SS/Police structure. August Frank was a full time Allgemeine-SS staff officer who specialised in administration. He has served in the SS-Economic and Administration Headquarters from 1935 and was brought into the Police after Himmler's had been appointed Minister of the Interior to bring Police ideology in line with general SS-thinking. Heinz Reinefarth was a part time Allgemeine-SS officer who joined the Police after winning the Knight´s Cross as an army Sergeant. Willy Schmlecher, an Allgemeine-SS field officer with Police Presidency experience was brought into the Police specifically to take over the TENO office from the disgraced Hans Weinreich. Dr. Oscar Hock had served in the SA then Allgemeine-SS Medical Departments. He came to the Police from the Waffen-SS medical service. Oskar Schmiedel has been a regular army Officer and a transport specialist. He was posted to the Police to supervise transport matters and joined the SS as late as January 1945. As has been mentioned, it was Himmler's intention that Police officers who joined the SS would have rank parity. This rule was generally followed but there were exceptions. Gerhard Winkler was promoted Lieutenant-General of Polizei in February 1944 but he remained an SS-Brigadeführer. Dr. Kurt Hoffmann, a Major-General from November 1944 only achieved the SS-rank of SS-Oberführer. Dr. Oskar Lossen a Major-General since January 1945 and Walter Goldbach a Fire Service Major-General from December 1943 never rose above the SS-rank of Standartenführer. Five Police generals ended the war as Höhere SS und Polizeiführers: Rudolf Querner for Wehrkreis XI based in Braunschweig, Walter Schimana for Wehrkreis XVII covering Österreich, Heinz Reinefarth for Wehrkreis XXI covering the part of Poland known as Wartheland, Otto Winkelmann for Hungary and August Edler von Meyszner for Serbia. Finally, one Police Major-General, Hans Dieter De Niem, transferred to the army as Major-General on 1 April 1944. He had served as Higher Field Gendarmerie Officer in the army High Command from 1940.

Pay Structure covering Police Generals

By a Führer decree of 19 March 1937 which came into effect from 1 April 1937 all police officers and officials were integrated into the Reichsbesoldungsgesetz (Reichs Civil Service Salaries Law) organised in Besoldungsgruppen (Pay Groups). This was the result of the unification of the uniformed police into the" Ordnungspolizei" corps. This consisted of the Schutzpolizei, Gendarmerie,Feuerschutzpolizei,Sanitäts und Veterinär and Verwaltungspolizei (Urban police, rural police, Fire Service, Medical Veterinary and Administration, this also covered the TENO (Technical Services Organisation), its chief and deputy chief were ranked Lieutenant-General and four of the Landesführer reached the rank of Major-General, the remainder holding the rank of Colonel. In 1936 when the Landspolizei was disbanded, the whole of the General corps joined the Wehrmacht and as a result Daluege had to create a new Generals corps. From this small start the corps grew to total 144 members by the end of the war.

Table of Paygroups (Befehlsblatt der Chef der Ordnungspolizei 1944/1945)

Besoldungsgruppen (old Pay Groups)	**Wehr Besoldungsgruppen (war pay groups)**	**Ranks**	**Annual Basic Salary***
B2	W2	Generaloberst	unknown
B3a	W3	General	24,000 DM
B4	W4	Generalleutnant and Ministerialdirektor **	19,000 DM
B7a	W5	Generalmajor, Generalarzt, Generalveterinär and Ministerialdirigent**	16,000 DM

(*) the basic salary could be augmented by various other payments; senority, lodging allowance, childrens allowance, foreign service allowance etc.

(**) The pay group W4 also covered the Police President of Berlin no matter what his rank. The pay group W5 also covered the Police President of Hamburg.

(1) Koehl page 174

9.2 Biographies Of The Police Generals

BERNASCHEK Paul

Generalmajor der Polizei.

Born on 9 July 1887 in Österreich. After schooling he studied at university and achieved a Diploma in Engineering. After service in the Great War he joined the Fire Service. From 1941 until March 1944 he served as Kommandeur der Feuerwehr und Feuerschutzpolizei in Wien and was given the rank of Oberst der Feuerschutzpolizei. He was promoted Generalmajor der Polizei on 15 April 1945. Died on 8 May 1987.

BUBAN Richard

Generalmajor der Polizei.

Born on 8 February 1880 in Bautzen (Sachsen). Studied at the Technical Institute in Chemnitz. Joined the Imperial Navy on 1 October 1901 and studied at the Imperial Marine Engineers school, and the Technical High School in Berlin-Charlottenburg and then spent four years in ship construction. During the Great War he served in submarines and ended the War as a Torpedo-Stabsingenieur. He joined the Technische Nothilfe (TENO) on its formation in 1919 and served in the Landesbezirk Troppau. On 1 January 1941, he was appointed Landesführer der TENO for the Bereich Elbe and Leiter der TENO Reichschule in Dresden. He was given the rank of Oberst der Schutzpolizei on the 20 April 1943 and was promoted Generalmajor der Polizei on the 21 July 1943. Joined the Party on the 1 May 1933. He was also a member of the Party Welfare Organisation. He was a married man with one son.Died on the 4 November 1966

DASCH Dr. Alfred

Generalveterinär der Polizei.

Little is known about this officer, evidence exists that he was born in Österreich. He studied veterinary medicine at university and graduated with a Doctorate. He served in the Austrian state service in veterinary service and rose to the rank of Hofrat. He was ranked Oberstveterinär der Schutzpolizei in 1943 and was appointed to the staff of the BdO in Krakau. Promoted Generalveterinär der Polizei in 1944.

DENICKE Wolfgang

(char) Generalmajor der Polizei.

Born on 28 December 1889. After service in the Great War, he joined the Schlesienn Schutzpolizei. In 1936, he moved from Gleiwitz to Magdeburg as Kommandeur der Schutzpolizei. Promoted Oberstleutnant der Schutzpolizei in 1936. He was transferred to the staff of the Regierungspräsident in Arnsberg on 1 June 1938 as Kommandeur der Schutzpolizei. Later he was appointed as Kommandeur of the Schutzpolizei beim Gruppenkommando Mitte in Wien. He was retired with the rank of Oberst in 1944. On retirement he was given the rank of brevet Generalmajor. He joined the Party on 1 May 1933.

Died on 17 November 1962.

DILLENBURGER Otto

Generalleutnant der Polizei

Born on 16 June 1880 in Castel beim Mainz (Hessen). After service in the Great War, he joined the Schutzpolizei in Kiel. Promoted Major in November 1920, he was involved in the organisation of the Schutzpolizei in Schleswig Holstein. From 1921 to 1922, he served as chief of the Personal Office of the Prussian Schutzpolizei in Prussian Ministery of Interior then he was appointed as Gruppenkommandeur in the Schutzpolizei in Berlin. He was ranked Oberst der Schutzpolizei in 1926. From 1929, he took over as head of the Police Officers Association. He was retired in 1936 with the rank of Generalleutnant. He later served in the Reichsministerium der Luftfahrt (Air Ministry). Died on 16 March 1948.

FALKOWSKI Leo von

SS-Brigadeführer und Generalmajor der Polizei

Born on 23 May 1888 in Metz (Lorraine). He attended the Prussian army main cadet school at Berlin-Lichterfelde until 1907 and then served in the artillery until August 1919. Commissioned Leutnant 18 August 1908, he was promoted Oberleutnant on 25 February 1915, and Hauptmann on 6 November 1917. He joined the Schutzpolizei in Kattowitz as Hauptmann on 28 August 1919. He served in Berlin and Halle until October 1935. Then, he was appointed Kommandeur der Schutzpolizei in Erfurt. Promoted Major der Schutzpolizei on 20 April 1927 and Oberstleutnant in August 1936. IdO Magdeburg from 15 September 1936 to 4 May 1938. Promoted Oberst der Schutzpolizei on 20 April 1938. Kommandeur der Schutzpolizei in Nürnberg from 4 May 1938 until 6 October 1940. BdO Danzig-Westpreussen from 20 September 1939 to 16 November 1943. Ranked brevet Generalmajor der Polizei on 30 January 1943 and confirmed on 1 September 1943. He was placed in retirement with effect from 1 November 1943. Joined the Party on 1 May 1933 and the SS as Standartenführer with effect from 1 August 1940. Promoted Oberführer on 30 January 1942 and Brigadeführer on 9 November 1942. Appointed Leiter der Werkluftschutz-Bereichsstelle Wartheland der Reichsgruppe Industrie from 22 August 1944 to the end of the war. He was responsible for air raid protection for all factories in the Wartheland. He was a married man with one son and one daughter. He died in Holzminden on 27 July 1956.

FISCHER Karl

SS-Brigadeführer und Generalmajor der Polizei.

Born on 16 April 1889 in Schauenstein bei Hof (Bayern). Studied science at school and gained a certificate before joining the Royal Bayern army on 18 October 1906. Served in the Great War as an armaments specialist in the artillery ending the war as Feuerwerkoberleutnant. He joined the Bayern Landespolizei on 3 October 1919. Served first as a technical specialist in weaponry then transferred to the Schutzpolizei in June 1936 as Major. Served in the technical office in Amtsgruppe-Kommando I of the Hauptamt Ordnungspolizei until December 1940. Promoted Oberstleutnant der Schutzpolizei on 1 September 1937, and Oberst on 6 October 1940. Leiter Gruppe Waffen und Geräte in Amtsgruppe Kommando I Hauptamt Ordnungspolizei from December 1940 to 15 September 1943. His status rose to that of Inspekteur from 15 September 1943. Its task was to supervise weapons and munitions for the Ordnungspolizei. Promoted Generalmajor der Polizei on 14 January 1944. Joined the Party on 1 May 1937 and the SS as Obersturmbannführer on 23 January 1939. Promoted Standartenführer on 9 November 1940, Oberführer on 20 April 1943 and Brigadeführer on 14 January 1944. He was a married man with one son. He died on 8 October 1953.

FORNONI Josef

Generalmajor der Polizei.

Born on 24 January 1884 in Stuhlingen (Baden). Graduated from a technical high school. Served in the army from October 1904 to September 1905 and from August 1914 to November 1918. He was commissioned Leutnant in the Landwehr on 18 April 1915. Joined the Technische Nothilfe on 1 October 1919 and served as Organisation leader for the Landesbe zirk Baden-Württemberg until April 1921. Leiter des Landesbezirks Berlin until April 1929. Then he headed Abteilung I (Organisation und Technische Dienst) in Reichsamt Technische Nothilfe until 1 January 1943. Then, he served as Inspekteur ür das Ausbildungswesens der Technische Nothilfe. He was promoted Landesführer der Technische Nothilfe on the 12 March 1941. He was later given the equivalent rank of Oberst der Schutzpolizei. He was placed in retirement as a result of heart disease on 24 January 1944 and was promoted Generalmajor der Polizei on 30 January 1945. He served in the SA Reserve from January 1934 until December 1935 and joined the Party on 1 May 1937. He died on 28 January 1954.

FRANK August

SS-Obergruppenführer General der Waffen-SS und der Polizei.

Born on 5 April 1898 in Augsburg (Bayern). Served in the Bayern artillery during the Great War rising to the rank of Wachtmeister. Joined the Landespolizei in Passau on 14 October 1920. Promoted Rottmeister der Landespolizei on 1 December 1920. He moved to Augsburg in January 1921 and was promoted Wachtmeister on 1 April 1921 and Oberwachtmeister on 14 November 1922. He passed his exams as a paymaster in March 1921 and was posted, as a paymaster, to the Bayern Ministry of the Interior until 30 April 1930. Promoted Verwaltungssekretär der Landespolizei on 1 July 1927. Left the Police on 30 April 1930 and became self-employed until April 1932 when he took up paid work in the SS. Joined the SS on 8 April 1932 as SS-Mann and joined the Party on 1 February 1933. Served as an administrator in various SS commands until April 1939 when he took over Amt IV (Verwaltung) in SS-Hauptamt. Commissioned Sturmführer in Verwaltungswesens on 9 November 1933 he had risen to the rank of Oberführer by 1938. Served as standing deputy to the head of SS Administration from 1 March 1938. Chef des Verwaltungsamts in Hauptamt Haushalt und Bauten from 20 April 1940 until 1 February 1942. Promoted Brigadeführer on 20 April 1940, he was given the rank of Generalmajor der Waffen-SS with effect from the same date. Chef Amtsgruppe A (Truppenverwaltung) in SS-Wirtschafts und Verwaltungshauptamt and standing deputy to the head of the Hauptamt (Oswald Pohl) from 1 February 1942 until 16 September 1943. Promoted Gruppenführer and Generalleutnant der Waffen-SS on 30 January 1943. Chef der Wirtschaftsverwaltungsamt in Hauptamt Ordnungspolizei from 16 September 1943 until the end of the war. He was given the rank of Generalleutnant der Polizei on 16 September 1943. He also served as Chef der Heeresverwaltungsamt beim OKH from 18 August 1944 and was promoted Obergruppenführer and General der Waffen-SS und der Polizei on 9 November 1944. Awarded the German Cross in Silver on 13 December 1944. He was a married man with two daughters. Died in Karlsruhe on 21 March 1984.

FRANZ Karl

Generalmajor der Polizei

Born on 15 February 1899. Served in the Great War and then joined the Schutzpolizei. Promoted Oberst in 1941 and appointed IdO Königsberg from July 41 until March 1942. He retired but was reactived as Oberst der Schutzpolizei a.W. He moved to Wiesbaden where he remained until July 1942. Then he was appointed to Hauptamt Ordnungspolizei. In mid 1942, he was given the brevet rank of Generalmajor der Polizei a.W and was confirmed as Generalmajor der Polizei a.W. on 9 November 1944.Died on 18 March 1958.

GERLOFF Proffessor Dr. Helmuth

SS-Brigadeführer und Generalmajor der Polizei.

Born on 21 September 1894 in Magdeburg (Prussian Sachsen). Attended a technical high school from 1912 until the 1914. Served in the Great War in the engineer corps being commissioned Leutnant der Reserve in June 1916. After the war he completed his studies and gained a diploma in engineering in 1920. Achieved a Doctorate in 1933. Served as Referent in Reichsamt TENO from 1921 to 1924. Then worked in private industry, in teaching and in the war ministry until 1941. He served in the TENO from 1936 to 1939 as Landesführer der Landesgruppe Kurmark. Kommandeur der Technische SS und der Polizei Akademie Berlin from 1941 to September 1944. Promoted Generalmajor der Polizei on 30 January 1942. Retired from the police in March 1945. Joined the Party on 1 May 1932 and the SS on 1 March 1933 as SS-Anwärter. Served as an engineering specialist with various SS-Standarten until September 1937 being commissioned Untersturmführer on 20 April 1935. Promoted Obersturmführer on 20 April 1937, Hauptsturmführer on 30 January 1938 and Sturmbannführer on 30 January 1939. His next promotion was to Brigadeführer on 30 January 1942 bypassing the intervening ranks. He was a married man with one son and two daughters. Died in Hannover on 17 March 1975.

GOLDBACH Walter

SS-Standartenführer, Generalmajor der Polizei

Born on the 3 August 1898 in Königstelt. Served in the Great War and then joined the Fire Service in Hannover. Served as Oberbaurat until March 1937 and was promoted Ministerialrat in November 1939. Gruppenleiter und Sachbearbeiter in Hauptamt Ordnungspolizei from March 1937 until November 1937. Leiter Amt Feuerschutzpolizei in der Kommandoamt Hauptamt Ordnungspolizei from 25 November 1937 to 1943. Given the rank of Oberst der Feuerschutzpolizei on 31 July 1940 and was promoted Generalmajor der Polizei on 1 December 1943. Chef der Feuerschutzpolizei und Feuerwehren der Hauptstadt Berlin from the end 1943 to April 1945. Joined the Party on 1 May 1933 and the SS on 20 April 1943 as Standartenführer. He was a married man with two children. Ordered out of Berlin by the Gauleiter Dr. Josef Goebbels at the end of April 1945 he refused to leave and was arrested. He tried to commit suicide, failed and was shot by the SS on 26 April 1945.

GRUNWALD Hans-Dietrich

SS-Brigadeführer und Generalmajor der Polizei

Born on 14 December 1898 in Beuthen (Upper Schlesien). Served in the army from the 27 November 1915 until the 1 September 1920. Commissioned Leutnant on the 12 October 1916. Joined the Schutzpolizei on the 1 September 1920 as Leutnant and was promoted Oberleutnant on the 1 December 1923 and Hauptmann on the 1 May 1928. Transferred to the Prussian Landjägerei in December 1928, he was promoted Major on 27 October 1933. Transferred back to the Schutzpolizei on the 16 March 1935. Served in the police department in the Ministry of the Interior until June 1936 and then in the Hauptamt Ordnungspolizei until October 1939. Kommandeur der Polizeioffizierschule in Berlin-Köpenick from October 1939 until September 1942. Promoted Oberst der Schutzpolizei on 1 September 1939 Leiter Amtsgruppe Kommando I in Hauptamt Ordnungspolizei from 1 October 1942 to 31 July 1943 and then served as BdO in Krakau until 8 March 1944. Promoted Generalmajor der Polizei on 20 April 1942. Joined the Party on 1 August 1932 and the SS as Obersturmbannführer on 1 July 1938. Promoted Standartenführer on 1 April 1940, Oberführer on 20 April 1942 and Brigadeführer on 9 November 1942. He was brought up before an SS-Court in München on charges of conduct unbecoming an SS and police officer on 21 April 1944. The charge was that he had showed homosexual tendencies by staying the night with another man after a party. Although he was found guilty and was sentenced to a term of imprisonment and was dismissed from the SS and Police, he appealed and the sentence was reduced because the evidence was only circumstantial. However he was not allowed back into the SS because the case had brought it into disrepute. He had opposed Hans Frank's Jewish policies and it is thought that this was the reason behind the trial. He was a married man with two sons. Died in Bad Tölz on 20 January 1975.

HACHTEL Hans

Generalmajor der Polizei

Born on 25 October 1894 in Kusel (Saarpfalz). Attended the Humanities Gymnasium in Würzburg until October 1913 when he joined the Royal Bayern army. Served in the Great War in the infantry being commissioned Leutnant der Reserve on 23 June 1916. He joined the Bayern Landespolizei on 27 November 1919 as Leutnant. He served in Nürnberg until 31 March 1929 when he transferred to the Gendarmerie. Promoted Oberleutnant der Landespolizei on 1 August 1922 and Hauptmann der Gendarmerie on 1 May 1929. Served as a Staff officer in the Hauptamt Ordnungspolizei in Berlin from July 1937 until 15 September 1942. Promoted Major der Gendarmerie on 1 April 1937, Oberstleutnant on 1 April 1939 and Oberst der Gendarmerie on 1 June 1942. Appointed Kommandeur der Ordnungspolizei in Lithuania based in Kauen on 15 September 1942 serving until 11 November 1944. Inspekteur der Ordnungspolizei beim Höhere SS und Polizeiführer Weichsel in Danzig from 13 June 1944 until the end of the war. Promoted Generalmajor der Polizei on 1 March 1945. Joined the Party on 1 May 1937 and was appointed SS-Bewerber on 12 January 1945. Died on 21 May 1993.

HEIMBURG Erik von

SS-Brigadeführer und Generalmajor der Polizei

Born on 6 October 1892 in Karlsruhe (Baden). His brother Heino served in the Navy rising to the rank of Vizeadmiral. Attended army cadet schools and joined the army as Fahnenjunker 14 March 1911. Served in the infantry until February 1915 when he transferred to the Flying Service as an Observer. Commissioned Leutnant 22 May 1912. Promoted Oberleutnant 1 October 1919. Left the army and joined the Schutzpolizei in Hamburg as Hauptmann 16 December 1919, promoted Major 1 October 1924 and Oberstleutnant 1 July 1935. Kommandeur der Schutzpolizei in Essen from 1937 until 1 July 1939. Promoted Oberst der Schutzpolizei 1 December 1937. Kommandeur der Schutzpolizei and Chef Abteilung C in Staatsverwaltung Hamburg from 1 April 1939 to 5 December 1941. IdO Stettin 30 May 1940 to 20 February 1942. Kommandeur der Ordnungspolizei in Charkow from December 1941 to 28 February 1942. Returned to his post in Hamburg and served until 1 October 1943. Promoted Generalmajor der Polizei 1 June 1942. BdO Kopenhagen from 1 October 1943 to 10 August 1944 and then served as Kommandeur der Schutzpolizei in Berlin until the end of the war. Joined the Party 1 May 1937 and the SS as Standartenführer 1 July 1939. Promoted Oberführer 18 August 1942 and Brigadeführer 9 November 1942. He was a married man with three daughters. Missing believed killed in Berlin on 5 May 1945.

HITZEGRAD Ernst

SS-Gruppenführer und Generalleutnant der Polizei

Born on 26 December 1899 in Fraustadt (Grenzmark). Served in a machine-gun company during the Great War being commissioned Leutnant der Reserve on 26 April 1916. Joined the Schutzpolizei in Cologne on 10 January 1919 and served there until 1 August 1933. Promoted Hauptmann der Schutzpolizei on 1 July 1925. Transferred to the Landespolizei on 1 August 1933 until 1 January 1934. Then moved to the Ministry of Interior and was promoted Major der Landespolizei on 1 January 1934. Ranked Oberstleutnant der Landespolizei on 1 June 1936. Returnded to the Schutzpolizei as Amtsleiter in the Kommandoamt of the Hauptamt Ordnungspolizei from 1 October 1936 until 1 April 1940. Promoted Oberst der Schutzpolizei on 1 March 1938. IdO Berlin from 1 April 1940 to 16 February 1942. Promoted brevet Generalmajor der Polizei on 9 November 1941 and was confirmed in that rank on 22 December 1941. IdO Dresden from 23 February 1942 until 1 September 1943. BdO Prague and Generalinspekteur der Uniformierten Protektorat Polizei from 1 September 1943 until 1 February 1945. Promoted Generalleutnant der Polizei on 1 December 1943. Joined the Party on 1 February

1932 and the SS as Standartenführer on 1 July 1938. Promoted Oberführer 9 November 1941, Brigadeführer 9 December 1941 and Gruppenführer 30 January 1944. He was a married man with one son. Spent eleven years in a Czech prison from 1950. Died on 14 December 1976.

JANDL Johann

Generalmajor der Polizei.

Born on 4 October 1880. Served in the Great War and then joined the Schutzpolizei. Rose to the rank of Generalmajor der Polizei by 1 February 1944. Retired from the police on the 1 February 1944. He died on 18 April 1960.

JANKA Dr. Heinrich

Generalmajor der Polizei

Born on 26 March 1880. Served in the Great War and then joined the Schutzpolizei. Rose to the rank of Generalmajor by 7 October 1938. Died on 7 October 1958.

JUNECKE Walter

Generalmajor der Polizei

Born on 22 June 1894. Served in the army during the Great War and then studied engineering. Joined the Technische Nothilfe and rose to the rank of Landesführer and Generalmajor der Polizei by 1943. Landesführer der Landesgebiet XVII Ostmark-Nord with his headquarters in Wien. He died on 8 October 1957.

UTTNER Dr .Viktor

Generalarzt der Polizei

Born on 8 April 1880. He attended university medical school and achieved a Doctorate. After he served in the Great War he joined the Prussian state service as a medical official. He served as Leitender-Arzt (head of medical services) der Polizeipräsidium Berlin in 1934. Promoted Generalarzt der Polizei on 1 February 1943, he was later retired. Died on 31 August 1945.

KEUCK Walter

Generalmajor der Polizei

Born on 6 July 1889 in Kassel (Hessen Nassau). Attended a Realgymnasium in Arolsen and passed his abitur. Served in the army in the Great War during which he was wounded eight times. Transferred to the Sicherheitspolizei which later became the Schutzpolizei with the rank of Oberleutnant on 3 June 1920. Promoted Hauptmann der Schutzpolizei on 13 July 1921. Joined the Party on 17 February 1933. Promoted Major on 1 October 1931, he served in the Police Administration in Breslau until 1936 when he was transferred to the Anhalt state service. Served as IdO in Dessau from 1 September 1936 until 1 July 1937 when the post was abolished. Promoted Oberstleutnant on 1 September 1937 and transferred to the Police Administration in Frankfurt am Main. Promoted Oberst on 1 April 1940. Served as Kommandeur der Schutzpolizei in Litzmannstadt until 1 May 1943. Then he was appointed Kommandeur der Schutzpolizei in Wuppertal. Served as BdO in Wehrkreis XI in Hannover from 11 May 1943. He was promoted Generalmajor der Polizei on 1 January 1944. Joined the Party on February 1933. A married man, his wife was a member of the Frauenschaft in Frankenstein in Schlesien and his eldest son served in the army Medical Corps. Died on 10 December 1972.

KLINGHAMMER Wilhelm

(char) Generalmajor der Polizei.

Born on 16 September 1884. After service in the Great War he joined the Schutzpolizei. By 1934, he was on the staff of the Schutzpolizei in Berlin. Promoted Oberst der Schutzpolizei on 1 January 1934. He led the Gruppenkommando Mitte of the Schutzpolizei Berlin until his retirement in 1944. He was given the brevet rank of Generalmajor on his retirement. Died in 1966.

KOHLEPP Dr. Arnulf

Generalarzt der Polizei.

Born on 14 September 1884 in Weinheim (Bayern). He attended university where he studied medicine. Passed his state exams and graduated with a Doctorate in 1917. Served in the army during the Great War as Oberarzt der Reserve. Left the military on 28 February 1920 and practised as a physician in Rosenheim in Oberbayern until 1936 being accredited to the local general hospital. Joined the police medical service on 1 November 1936 as Leitender Polizeiarzt der Polizeiverwaltung München und Polizeiartzlicher Referent im Bayerischen Staatsministerium der Innern (Leading police doctor in München and police medical official in the Bayern Interior ministry). He was given the rank of Oberstarzt der Polizei on 20 April 1938. He joined the Party in 1921 and left after the München Putsch of November 1923, he did not rejoin. Served as Ortsgruppenarzt der NSFK (National Socialist Flying Corps) in Rosenheim from 1933 until 8 December 1936. Served as Leitender Sanitätsoffizier beim Höhere SS und Polizeiführer in Wehrkreis VII–BdO from 1939. Leitender Arzt der SS und der Polizei beim Höhere SS und Polizeiführer Süd from 13 October 1943 until the end of the war. Promoted Generalarzt der Polizei on 1 April 1944. He was a married man with one son. Died on 13 August 1955.

KOWALSKI Curt

(char) Generalmajor der Polizei.

Born on 1 June 1883. After service in the Great War he joined the Prussian Landjägerei. As Oberstleutnant, he commanded Landjägereischule Allenstein in 1931. Promoted Oberst der Gendarmerie in 1934. Kommandeur der Gendarmerie Potsdam I from 1934 until September 1936. Appointed IdO in Königsberg on 15 September 1936, he remained there until 5 April 1939. Transferred to Potsdam as Kommandeur der Gendarmerie in April 1939 and was then transferred to Berlin as IdO on 23 February 1942. He was retired as Oberst in October 1942 and was given the rank of brevet Generalmajor. Died on 5 May 1948.

Breslau 1940, Left to right, Udo von Woyrsch, Franz Breithaupt, unknown, Gauleiter Karl Hanke

Polizei Präsident Bochum, SS-Brigadeführer Walter Oberhaidacher

MACKELDEY Lothar

Generalmajor der Polizei.

Born on 6 May 1892. He joined the army and was commissioned Leutnant on 22 June 1912. Served in the Great War and was promoted Oberleutnant on 20 June 1918. After the war he joined the Prussian Landjägerei and was promoted Hauptmann on 1 December 1920. He was promoted Major on 1 October 1928 and appointed Kommandeur der Landjägerei Schneidemühl. Transferred to the Gendarmerie in 1934. Kommandeur der Gendarmerie in Schneidemühl. Promoted Oberstleutnant der Gendarmerie on 1 April 1937. Appointed Kommandeur der Gendarmerie in Merseburg in January 1936 and was transferred to Posen in 1940. Promoted Oberst der Gendarmerie on 1 November 1940. On 7 February 1943, he was transferred to Norway as BdO in Oslo and remained there until February 1945. Promoted Generalmajor on 1 April 1944. Joined the Party on 1 November 1941. He was a married man with one child. Died on 23 December 1957.

MATT August

(char) Generalmajor der Polizei

Born in Bogen on 30 April 1890. After service in the Royal Bayern army during the Great War he joined the Bayern Gendarmerie as Oberleutnant and served in the Gendarmerie Abteilung in Oberbayern. Promoted Hauptmann der Gendarmerie on 1 February 1921 and Major on 1 September 1932. Served as Kommandeur der Gendarmerie in Regensburg until 1940 when he was transferred to the same post in Kattowitz. Promoted Oberstleutnant der Gendarmerie on 1 May 1937 and Oberst on 1 October 1940. He was transferred back to Regensburg in 1943. From 15 December 1943 to 14 January 1944, he served on the staff of the BdO in Münster. A Member of the Bayern Volkspartei in 1922 he joined the National Socialist Party on 1 May 1937. He served as BdO in Kassel from January to August 1944 and he held the same post in Erfurt until 9 August 1944. He was promoted brevet Generalmajor der Polizei on 1 December 1944. Died on 18 October 1967.

MEYER Dr. Johannes

SS-Gruppenführer und Generalleutnant der Polizei

Born on 19 July 1890 in Schneverdingen (Prussian Sachsen). Served in the railways transportation arm of the army from 1 October 1910 to November 1918. Commissioned Leutnant der Reserve on 22 March 1915. Studied engineering at the University of Hamburg from 1919 to 1924. Graduated with a Doctorate in Engineering in 1924. Joined the Fire Service in Hamburg on 1 April 1920. Served in Hamburg, Bremen, Lübeck and Karlsruhe until 1928. Landesbranddirektor in the Thüringen Interior Ministry from 1928 to 14 June 1936. Generalinspekteur der Feuerlöschwesens in Hauptamt Ordnungspolizei from 14 June 1937 to 15 September 1943. Given the rank of Generalmajor der Polizei 1 November 1939 and promoted brevet Generalleutnant der Polizei on 18 August 1942. Generalinspekteur des Feuerwehrschulen, Werkfeuerwehren und Brandschau in Hauptamt Ordnungspolizei from 15 September 1943 to the end of the war. Confirmed as Generalleutnant on 1 April 1944. Joined the Party on 1 May 1933 and the SS as Brigadeführer on 16 January 1941. Promoted Gruppenführer on 21 June 1944. He was a married man with one son and one daughter. Died in Deutsch-Evern bei Lüneburg on 10 June 1980.

Strassbourg 1940, Gauleiter Robert Wagner speaks to the Polizei Präsident SS-Ober-führer Carl Engelhardt

MÜHE Ludwig

Generalmajor der Polizei.
Born on 27 March 1891. He joined the army and was commissioned Leutnant on 30 October 1912. Served in the Great War and then joined the Schutzpolizei. Promoted Oberleutnant der Schutzpolizei on 1 October 1919, Hauptmann on 1 April 1920, Major on 20 October 1933. Ranked Oberstleutnant on 1 July 1937 while serving in Schutzpolizei München. By 1939 he was serving in the Bayern State Ministry in München and in the same year he was posted to the Police Administration in Stuttgart. Promoted Oberst on 1 November 1939. Appointed BdO in München on 1 February 1944, he remained in this post until the end. Promoted Generalmajor der Polizei on 1 July 1944. He joined the Party on 1 May 1937 and was a married man with one child. Died on 21 December 1958.

MÜLLER-BOENIGK Rudolf

SS-Brigadeführer und Generalmajor der Polizei.
Born on 27 April 1890 in Landeck (Westpreussen). Served in the Prussian army from 1 October 1911 to 1920. Commissioned Leutnant on 27 July 1912 and was promoted Oberleutnant 18 October 1918. Joined the Prussian Landjägerei in 1920. Promoted Hauptmann on 1 October 1920, Major 1 April 1929. Posted as Inspekteur der Landjägerei in Münster in 1931. Later Kommandeur der Gendarmerie in Postdam. IdO Darmstadt from 26 October 1936 to June 1938. Promoted Oberstleutnant der Gendarmerie on 1 June 1936 and Oberst on 1 March 1938. Kommandeur der Gendarmerieschule in Hildesheim from 31 October 1938 to 22 August 1941. BdO Krakau to 1 March 1942. IdO Königsberg to 15 December 1943. Promoted brevet Generalmajor der Polizei on 20 April 1942. BdO Königsberg to 5 August 1944. Confirmed as Generalmajor der Polizei on 1 January 1944. BdO Erfurt from 9 August 1944 to the end of the war. Joined the Party 1 May 1933 and the SS as Standartenführer on 1 August 1940. Promoted Oberführer on 20 April 1942 and Brigadeführer on 9 November 1942. He was a married man with one son and one daughter. Died in Krefeld on 9 May 1968.

NOWOTNY Hugo

Generalmajor der Polizei
Born on 17 June 1886. After service in the army during the Great War, he joined the Gendarmerie and held the rank of Oberst by 1939. He served as Kommandeur der Gendarmerie in Steiermark. Promoted Generalmajor on 1 January 1944. Died on 15 April 1944.

OELHAFEN Otto von

SS-Gruppenführer Generalleutnant der Polizei
Born on 8 June 1886 in Würzburg (Bayern). Served in the Great War and then joined the Landespolizei in Bayern in 1920. Served in Bamberg until 1931 then München. Promoted Major der Landespolizei in 1928 and Oberstleutnant in 1933. Kommandeur der Schutzpolizei in München from 1933 to 1 November 1937. After the SA Putsch of June 1934, he served as deputy Police President in München from 30 June 1934 to 15 April 1936. Promoted Oberst der Schutzpolizei on 30 January 1936. Kommandeur der Schutzpolizei Dresden from 1 November 1937 to 16 December 1939. BdO Nord Böhmen-Mähren on 1 October 1938 to 20 December 1938. IdO Königsberg from 1 January 1940 to 1 May 1941. Promoted Generalmajor der Polizei on 6 October 1940. BdO Prague from 1 May 1941 to 22 August 1941. BdO Ukraine in Rowno-Kiew from 1 September 1941 to 1 October 1942. Promoted Generalleutnant der Polizei on 9 December 1941. IdO then BdO München from 1 October 1942 to 1 February 1944. Retired from the police on 1 April 1943. Joined the

Party on 1 May 1937 and the SS as Standartenführer on 20 April 1939. Promoted Oberführer on 20 April 1940, Brigadeführer on 30 January 1941 and Gruppenführer on 30 January 1942. He was a married man with two sons. Died in Lichtenfels (Franken) on 13 March 1952.

PETERSDORFF Kurt

Generalmajor der Polizei.

Born on 24 August 1896. He joined the army in 1914 and was commissioned Leutnant on 22 May 1914. Served in the Great War and then joined the Prussian Landjägerei as Leutnant. Promoted Oberleutnant on 19 January 1921 and Hauptmann on 1 December 1924. As Kommandeur der Gendarmerie District Göttingen, he was promoted Major der Gendarmerie on 1 July 1934. Served with the Gendarmerie in Hannover until 1940 when he was posted to the staff of the IdO in Mark Brandenburg for duty at the Gendarmerie School in Hildesheim. Promoted Oberstleutnant der Gendarmerie on 1 January 1940. Posted to Linz as Kommandeur der Gendarmerie in 1943. Promoted Oberst der Gendarmerie on 1 April 1943. Took over the post of BdO in Stuttgart on 1 January 1944 and remained there until the end of the war. Promoted Generalmajor on 1 January 1944. He joined the Party on 1 May 1933. He was a married man with two children.

PFEFFER-WILDENBRUCH Karl

SS-Obergruppenführer und General der Waffen-SS und der Polizei.

Born on 12 June 1888 in Kalkberge/Rudersdorfer (Berlin). Joined the army on 7 March 1907 and served in the artillery and then as a staff officer. Commissioned Leutnant on 1 August 1908, promoted Oberleutnant on 28 November 1914 and Hauptmann on 18 April 1916. Joined the Schutzpolizei in Münster on 16 August 1919 as Hauptmann. He served in Osna brück and Magdeburg until 1 February 1928 and was promoted Major on 6 July 1920. Emigrated to Chile on 1 February 1928 and served as a Gendarmerie Instructor in Santiago until 31 March 1930 when he returned to Germany. Served in Berlin and then transferred to the Landespolizei in 1932. Promoted Oberstleutnant der Landespolizei on 1 April 1933 and Oberst on 1 April 1934. Transferred to the army on 1 April 1936 and commanded an infantry battalion. Returned to the Schutzpolizei at the request of Kurt Daluege on 1 August 1936. Generalinspekteur der Polizeischulen in Hauptamt Ordnungspolizei from 1 June 1936 to 31 August 1943. Promoted brevet Generalmajor der Polizei on 21 October 1936 and confirmed on 1 May 1937. Kommandeur der Polizei-Division from 1 October 1939 to 10 September 1940. Promoted brevet Generalleutnant der Polizei on 20 April 1939 and confirmed on 15 November 1939. Chef des Kolonialpolizeiamtes in Hauptamt Ordnungspolizei from 14 January 1941 to March 1943. He was given the rank of Generalleutnant der Waffen-SS on 27 September 1943. Kommandierender-General der VI SS-Freiwilligen-Armee-Korps from 8 October 1943 to 11 June 1944. Promoted General der Waffen-SS und Polizei on 9 November 1943. Befehlhaber der Waffen-SS in Hungary from 1 September 1944 to 1 November 1944. Kommandierender-General der IX Waffen-Gebirgskorps der SS (Kroatisches) from 5 December 1944 to 11 February 1945. Festungskommandant Budapest in February 1945. Joined the Party on 1 November 1932 and the SS as Oberführer on 12 March 1938. Promoted Brigadeführer 20 April 1939, Gruppenführer on 20 April 1940 and Obergruppenführer on 9 November 1943. He was a married man with two sons, the eldest was killed in action near Tobrück on 25 June 1941 and the youngest was killed in France in June 1944. Badly wounded in Budapest, he was captured by the Russians on 12 February 1945. He returned from captivity on 9 October 1955 and died in Bielefeld on 29 January 1971.

RAUNER Adolf

Generalmajor der Polizei.

Born on 5 October 1880. After service in the Great War he joined the Gendarmerie in Bayern. By 1936 he had reached the rank of Oberst. Served as Kommandeur der Gendarmerie in Nürnberg from 1 October 1936 until 1 August 1937. After he retired, he was reactived as Generalmajor der Polizei a.W. in September 1943. He served as Sachbearbeiter für Gendarmerie Angelegenheiten beim Bayerische Staatsministerium der Innern in München (Staff Officer for the Gendarmerie in the Bayern Interior Minstry) throughout the war. Joined the Party on 1 May 1937. Died on 6 December 1954.

RITZER Konrad

SS-Brigadeführer und Generalmajor der Polizei

Born on 24 August 1893 in Trams (Mecklenburg). One of his sisters later married the Knight's Cross winner SS-Oberführer and Oberst der Schutzpolizei Friedrich-Wilhelm Bock. After attending University he joined the army on 4 August 1914. Served in the infantry until February 1918 and then in the Flying Corps. Commissioned Leutnant on 20 March 1916. Joined the Schutzpolizei in Hamburg on 1 October 1919 (He joined with the later Generalleutnant Dr. Carl Retzlaff). Promoted Oberleutnant on 16 December 1919, Hauptmann der Schutzpolizei on 1 January 1921, Major on 17 March 1930. He served in Hamburg until 16 March 1935 when he transferred to Berlin. Promoted Oberstleutnant on 1 June 1936. Kommandeur der Polizeioffizierschule in Berlin-Köpenick from 11 March 1938 to 21 February 1939. Kommandeur der Schutzpolizei in Danzig from 21 February 1939 to 1 October 1939 and then took over command of the Polizei-Schützen-Regiment 1. Taken ill in Northern Russia in June 1941 and was convalescent until February 1942. Promoted Oberst der Schutzpolizei on 1 April 1939. IdO then BdO Stettin from 20 February 1942 to the end of the war. Promoted brevet Generalmajor der Polizei on 30 January 1943 and was confirmed in that rank 1 January 1944. Joined the Party on 1 May 1933 and the SS as SS-Mann on 21 November 1938. Commissioned Obersturmbannführer on 23 February 1939. Promoted Standartenführer on 20 April 1939, Oberführer on 21 December 1942 and Brigadeführer on 30 January 1943. He was a married man with two daughters. Died in Innsbruck on 27 May 1979.

RODE Ernst-August

SS-Brigadeführer und Generalmajor der Waffen-SS und der Polizei.

Born on the 9 August 1894 in Wustewaltersdorf (Schlesien). Joined the army on 10 August 1914 and served in the artillery until 25 July 1919. Ended with the rank of Vizewachtmeister. Joined the Schutzpolizei as Wachtmeister on 1 June 1920. Served in Liegnitz, Berlin, Breslau, Waldenburg and Dortmund until 20 January 1936. Commissioned Leutnant der Schutzpolizei 1 December 1924 and was promoted Oberleutnant on 1 April 1928, Hauptmann on 1 October 1934 and Major on 1 September 1938. Taktiklehrer der Polizeioffizierschule Berlin-Köpenick from 20 January 1936 to 1 March 1940. Operations Offizier (Ia) to the BdO in Oslo from 21 April to 31 August 1940. Served with the Polizei-Regiment Mähren then with Police Battalion 315 until May 1941. Transferred to the Kommandostab Reichsführer-SS on 22 May 1941, he became Chief of Staff on 30 January 1942. Promoted Oberstleutnant der Schutzpolizei on 1 April 1942 and Oberst on the 1 October 1942. On 24 August 1943, he was appointed liaison officer for the Waffen-SS with the army General Staff. Chef der Stabes der Bandenkampfverbände from Summer 1944 until the end of the war. Promoted Generalmajor der Polizei on 13 August 1944. Joined the Party on 1 May 1933 and joined the SS as Sturmbannführer on 1 July 1941. Promoted Obersturmbannführer on 30 January 1942, Standartenführer on 9 November 1942, Oberführer on 9 November 1943 and Brigadeführer on 21 June 1944. Awarded the German Cross in Silver on 20 February 1945. He was a married man with two sons and one daughter. Died on 12 September 1955.

ROETTIG Wilhelm

SS-Brigadeführer und Generalmajor der Polizei.

Born on 25 July 1888 in Mülhausen (Alsace). Served in the Great War and then joined the Prussian Landjägerei as Hauptmann. Promoted Oberstleutnant on 7 July 1930. Commander of the Landsjägerie in the District Breslau in 1931. From 1933 to 1935, transferred to the Landespolizei. Then returned to the Gendarmerie as Kommandeur der Gendarmerieschule Bad Ems. Appointed IdO in Stettin from 15 September 1936 to 1 August 1937. Promoted Oberst der Gendarmerie in January 1937. Generalinspekteur der Gendarmerie und Schutzpolizei der Gemeinden in Hauptamt Ordnungspolizei from 6 April 1937 to 10 September 1939. BdO beim AOK 14 from 1 September 1939 to the 10 September 1939. Promoted Generalmajor der Polizei on 1 July 1938. Joined the SS as Oberführer on 15 August 1939. Promoted Brigadeführer posthumously on 7 November 1944 with senority from the 21 June 1939. He was killed in a car crash north of Opoczow near Tamaszow (Poland) on 10 September 1939.

RUMPF Johannes "Hans"

SS-Brigadeführer und Generalmajor der Polizei.

Born on 7 March 1888 in Zimmern (Thüringen). Joined the army on 2 June 1908 and served until 11 February 1919. Commissioned Leutnant in 1909. He left the army as Hauptmann and joined the Fire Service in Königsberg on 15 May 1919. He rose to command the service in Königsberg by March 1930. Kommandeur und Branddirektor in Leipzig from March 1930 until 1 December 1939. Kommandeur der Feuerschutz-Polizei-Regiment 1 "Sachsen" from 10 September 1939 to March 1943. Generalinspekteur für das Feuerlöschwesen (Feuerschutzpolizei, Freiwillige Feuerwehren) in Hauptamt Ordnungspolizei from 1 September 1943 to the end of the war. Given the rank of Generalmajor der Polizei on 1 September 1943. Joined the Party on 1 May 1933 and the SS as Staffelmann on 17 February 1944. Promoted Brigadeführer on 24 August 1944. He was a married man with no children. Died in Elmshorn in Schleswig-Holstein on 5 November 1965.

RUOFF Curt

Generalmajor der Polizei.

Born on 9 January 1883 in Ludwigsburg (Württemberg). Joined the army in July 1902 as Cadet. Promoted Leutnant on 27 January 1902, Oberleutnant on 27 January 1912 and Hauptmann on 8 November 1914. Served in the army during the Great War as a Staff Officer. Released from army as brevet Major on 30 September 1920. Joined the Schutzpolizei in Baden as Hauptmann. Ranked Major on 1 July 1923. Appointed Kommandeur der Schutzpolizei Stuttgart and promoted Oberstleutnant on 1 October 1932. Transferred to Landjägerei as Commander of the Württemberg Corps on 2 October 1933 with the rank of Langjägerieoberst. Then from 1934 to 1937 he served in the Württemberg Gendarmerie. Inspekteur der Ordnungspolizei in Stuttgart from 1 April 1937 to 1 April 1939. Retired from the police with the brevet rank of Generalmajor der Polizei on the 31 March 1939. Joined the Party in April 1933. Died on 30 November 1970.

SCHEIDEL Rudolf

Ministerialdirigeant.

Born on 31 December 1884 in Oberrod in Kreis Schleusingen (Thüringen). Attended the Technical High School in Berlin from 1905 to 1909 where he studied building construction. He joined the Prussian Ministery of the Interior in June

1921 and was appointed Regierungsrat in 1922. Promoted Oberregierungsrat in 1925 and Ministerialrat in 1929 in the Abteilung II (Polizei). Joined the Ordnungspolizei Hauptamt in June 1936. Promoted Ministerialdirigent on 20 April 1940. Head of the Amtsgruppe VuR III in Hauptamt Ordnungspolizei from 1 December 1940 to 15 September 1943. Generalinspekteur für das Unterkunftswesens in Hauptamt Ordnungspolizei from 1 January 1942 to 15 September 1943 and Amtsgruppenleiter W III in Hauptamt Ordnungspolizei from 15 September 1943 until the end of the war. From 31 December 1942 he was a senior official in the Kameradschaftbund Deutscher Polizeibeamgen. He joined the Party on 1 May 1933.

SCHLAKE Robert

SS-Brigadeführer und Generalmajor der Polizei.

Born on 8 May 1893 in Karlsruhe (Baden). Served in the army signals department from 16 April 1914 to 1 November 1919. Commissioned Leutnant with senority from 18 March 1913 and was promoted Oberleutnant on 18 October 1918. Joined the Schutzpolizei as Leutnant on 1 November 1919. Promoted Hauptmann der Schutzpolizei on 22 December 1921. Served in Breslau and Berlin and then in the police signals section in the Ministry of the Interior. Referent for Signals of Landespolizei from 1933 to 1935. Ranked Major on 1 January 1934. Then Leiter Gruppe "N" (Nachrichtenwesens) in Amtsgruppe Kommando I der Hauptamt Ordnungspolizei to 1 September 1943. Promoted Oberstleutnant on 1 April 1937, and Oberst der Schutzpolizei on 1 July 1940. Inspekteur der Nachrichtenwesens der Kommandoamt Hauptamt Ordnungspolizei to the end of the war. Promoted Generalmajor der Polizei on 1 January 1944. Joined the Party on 1 May 1937 and the SS as Standartenführer on 20 April 1943. Promoted Oberführer on 16 October 1943 and Brigadeführer on 14 January 1944. He was not married but had a daughter born in 1923.

SCHMEDES Fritz

SS-Brigadeführer und Generalmajor der Waffen-SS und der Polizei.

Born on 7 October 1894 in Schwarme (Hannover). Served in the artillery from 20 February 1913 to April 1920. Commissioned Leutnant with senority from 7 October 1912 and promoted Oberleutnant on 18 October 1917. Joined the Schutzpolizei in June 1920 as Oberleutnant. Served in Mülhausen, Brieg, Naumburg, Wiesenfels, Berlin and Erfurt to April 1939. Promoted Hauptmann der Schutzpolizei on 13 July 1921, Major on 1 April 1929 and Oberstleutnant on 1 June 1936. Kommandeur der Schutzpolizei in Erfurt from 15 September 1936 to March 1939. Ia beim IdO Kassel to 4 June 1941. Kommandeur I Bataillon der Polizei-Artillerie-Regiment to 1 December 1941. Kommandeur Polizei-Artillerie-Regiment to 10 June 1943. Promoted Oberst on 1 April 1942. Joined the SS as Obersturmbannführer und Obersturmbannführer der Waffen-SS on 1 April 1942. Promoted Standartenführer und Standartenführer der Waffen-SS on 20 April 1942. Kommandeur der 4. SS-Polizei-Panzergrenadier-Division to 27 November 1944. Promoted Oberführer on 20 April 1943 and Brigadeführer on 9 November 1943. Promoted Generalmajor der Waffen-SS und der Polizei on 9 November 1943. Führer 35. SS-Polizei-Grenadierdivision from 14 February 1945 to 17 February 1945. Taktischer-Führer 36. Waffen-Grenadier-Division from 17 February 1945 to 29 April 1945. Joined the Party on 1 May 1937. He was a married man with two sons and one daughter. Died in Springe/Deister on 7 February 1952.

SCHULZE Hans Christian

SS-Brigadeführer und Generalmajor der Polizei (nachträglich).

Born on 15 July 1893 in Schwartenbeck (Holstein). Served in the infantry from August 1912 to 1 October 1919. Commissioned Leutnant March 1914. Joined the Schutzpolizei in Hamburg with the rank of Leutnant on 1 October 1919. Promoted Oberleutnant der Schutzpolizei in 1921, Hauptmann in 1921 and Major in 1 January 1925. Transferred to the Landespolizei Hamburg from 16 March 1933 to October 1935. Promoted Oberstleutnant in June 1934. Left the police and joined the army as Major on October 1935. Rejoined the Schutzpolizei in May 1938. Served in Hamburg again to 5 December 1941. Kommandeur der Schutzpolizei Hamburg 31 August 1940 to 5 December 1941. Kommandeur Polizei-Schützen-Regiment 2 from 2 October 1939 to 13 September 1941. Promoted Oberst der Schutzpolizei 30 January 1940 and Generalmajor der Polizei (posthumously) on 12 September 1941. Joined the Party on 1 May 1933 but left it in October 1935. Joined the SS as Standartenführer 1 January 1940. Promoted Oberführer 12 September 1941 (posthumously) with senority from 11 September 1941 and Brigadeführer 12 September 1941 (posthumously). He was awarded the Knight's Cross posthumously on 11 September 1941. He was a married man with no children. Fatally wounded by grenade splinters in the stomach in fighting on the River Luga in Northern Russia on 12 September 1941. Died in hospital on 13 September 1941.

SCHUMANN Otto

SS-Gruppenführer und Generalleutnant der Polizei.

Born on 11 September 1886 in Metz (Lorraine). Joined the army as Leutnant. Served in the infantry during the Great War and then joined the Schutzpolizei in 1921. Served in Hannover until June 1935. Kommandeur der Schutzpolizei in Weisenfels from 1 June 1935 to 1 March 1936. Promoted Oberstleutnant der Schutzpolizei on 1 January 1936. Kommandeur der Schutzpolizei in Stettin to 1 August 1937. Promoted Oberst der Schutzpolizei on 1 August 1937. IdO Stettin to 30 May 1940. Promoted Generalmajor der Polizei in May 1940. BdO Den Haag to 1 December 1942. IdO Münster to 1 September 1943. Promoted Generalleutnant der Polizei on 1 September 1943. Retired from the police on 1 November 1943. Recalled as Generalleutnant der Polizei a.W in February 1944. BdO Wien from 27 February 1944 to 1 October 1944. Joined the Party on 1 April 1933 and the SS as Standartenführer on 20 April 1939. Promoted Oberführer in 1940, Brigadeführer on 30 January 1941 and Gruppenführer on 27 August 1943. Died in Detmold on 8 November 1952.

THADEN Wilhelm von

(char) Generalmajor der Polizei.

Born on 31 October 1888. After service in the Great War he joined the Schutzpolizei. Promoted Oberstleutnant in 1937. Kommandeur der Schutzpolizei in Lübeck until March 1938 and then took over the post in Kassel. He exchanged posts with Joachim Petsch. Promoted Oberst der Schutzpolizei in 1942. He was retired in 1944 with the brevet rank of General major on 1 March 1944. Joined the Party on 1 May 1937.

WAGNER Gustav

Generalleutnant der Polizei

Born on 7 January 1888. He graduated as an engineer. He joined the fire service and was appointed Branddirektor in the City Administration in Berlin. He was a member of the Prüfungsstelle in Abteilung III of the Police Administration in Berlin from 1934. He had served as an expert at the Court in Potsdam in 1933 during the trial of those connected with the

Reichstags fire. Promoted Oberbranddirektor in 1935. Kommandeur der Feurschutzpolizei in Berlin until he was succeeded by Walter Goldbach. Died on 31 December 1956.

WIEDER Gerhard

Generalmajor der Polizei.

Born on 19 July 1887. After service in the Great War he joined the Schutzpolizei. As Major he served as Staff Officer attached to the Regierungspräsident Magdeburg in 1931. Served on the staff of the Police Administration in Hannover until 1936 when he was transferred as Kommandeur der Schutzpolizei in Koblenz. Appointed Kommandeur der Schutzpolizei in Karlsruhe in 1937 and promoted Oberstleutnant. Promoted Oberst by 1941. Appointed standing deputy as IdO in Stuttgart on 15 August 1941 then as Kommandeur der Schutzpolizei in Stuttgart on 23 February 1942. Promoted Generalmajor der Polizei on 1 October 1943. Posted as Chief of Staff of the BdO in Riga in 1943. Joined the Party on 1 May 1933. He was killed in action on 15 November 1943.

WINKLER Gerhard

SS-Gruppenführer und Generalleutnant der Polizei.

Born in Belzig (Mark Brandenburg) Joined the army as Fahnenjunker on 10 March 1910. Served in the engineers, as a staff officer and in the artillery until 1919. Commissioned Leutnant in 1914. Promoted Oberleutnant in 1917 and Hauptmann on 18 September 1918. Joined the Schutzpolizei in Berlin in June 1919. Served in Berlin and Brandenburg to May 1927. Transferred to the Prussian Landjägerei with the rank of Hauptmann in May 1927. Served in Köslin then Allenstein to 1 April 1928. Promoted Major 1 April 1928. Kommandeur der Landjägerei (from 1934 Gendarmerie) in Stettin from 1 April 1928 to 1 July 1936. Transferred back to the Schutzpolizei with the rank of Major on 16 March 1935. Promoted Oberstleutnant der Schutzpolizei on 1 April 1936. Leiter Amt "Organisation" in Kommandoamt in Hauptamt Ordnungspolizei from 1 July 1936 to 1 April 1939. Promoted Oberst der Schutzpolizei on 30 January 1937. IdO Stuttgart to 15 August 1941. Promoted brevet Generalmajor der Polizei in May 1940 and was confirmed in that rank on 6 October 1940. BdO Krakau from 1 September 1941 to 1 May 1942. IdO Stuttgart to 1 January 1944. Promoted brevet Generalleutnant der Polizei on 30 January 1944 and confirmed on 1 February 1944. Retired from the police on 1 April 1944. Luftschutzoffizier beim Luftgaukommando VII München from 1 January 1944 to 1945. Luftschutzoffizier der Luftgaukommando XVII in Wien to 15 April 1945. Joined the Party on 1 April 1933 and the SS as Standartenführer on 20 April 1939. Promoted Oberführer on 20 April 1940 and Brigadeführer on 30 January 1941. He committed suicide in Salzburg on 15 April 1945.

WOLFSTEIG Dr Friedrich

Generalmajor der Polizei.

Born on 12 September 1887. After service during the Great War he joined the Schutzpolizei and rose to the rank of Major der Schutzpolizei by 1934. Referent in Abteilung II "Polizei" in the Prussian Ministry of the Interior from 1934 to the 1 May 1935. Promoted Oberstleutnant in 1935. Served as Kommandeur der Schutzpolizei for the Industrial Upper Schlesien in Gleiwitz from 1 May 1935. Promoted Oberst in 1939. Kommandeur der Schutzpolizei in Dresden from 1939 until 1 October 1942. Kommandeur der Polizei-Regiment 4 from 16 September 1939 to January 1940. IdO and later BdO for Berlin from 1 October 1942 to March 1945. Promoted Generalmajor on 1 September 1943. Retired with effect from 1 December 1943. Joined the Party on 1 April 1933. Died on 10 October 1950.

WORM Paul

SS-Brigadeführer und Generalmajor der Polizei.

Born on 13 February 1893 in Russenau (Ostpreussen). Joined the army as Fahnenjunker in March 1912. Served in the infantry to 20 October 1914 when he was wounded. After recovery he transferred to the Flying Corps as an Observer in May 1915. Commissioned Leutnant on 19 November 1913 and was later promoted Oberleutnant. Left the army as Hauptmann on 9 October 1919. Joined the Landespolizei and served in Marienwerder, Elbing, Oberhausen, Altona, Köslin, Berlin, Luneburg then Gumbinnen. In 1935, transferred to the Schutzpolizei as Major. Gruppenleiter in Personalabteilung der Hauptamt Ordnungspolizei from 17 June 1936 to April 1938. Promoted Oberstleutnant der Schutzpolizei on 1 Janu ary 1937. Kommandeur der Schutzpolizei Stuttgart to 15 April 1939. Kommandeur der Polizei-Regiment "Mähren" to 13 February 1940. Kommandeur der Polizei-Regiment "Radom" from 25 October 1940 to 24 June 1942 then Polizei-Regiment 13 to 27 January 1943. Promoted Oberst der Schutzpolizei on 1 August 1940. Badly wounded in action against partisans on 27 January 1943, he did not serve actively again and retired from the police due to ill health on 1 September 12944. Promoted Generalmajor der Polizei on 1 May 1944. Joined the Party on 1 December 1932 and the NSFK in January 1935. Transferred to the SS as Obersturmbannführer on 1 July 1938. Promoted Standartenführer on 9 November 1940, Oberführer on 9 November 1943 and Brigadeführer on 1 May 1944. He was a married man with no children. Died as a Russian prisoner on 31 May 1956.

WROBEL Dr. Karl

Generalarzt der Polizei .

Born on 26 February 1882. After schooling he attended a university medical school studying medicine. Passed his state exams and graduated as a Doctor. Served as Leitender-Arzt der Polizeipräsidium in Berlin in succession to Dr. Viktor Juttner. Promoted Generalarzt der Polizei on 1 March 1944. Died on 30 September 1949.

ZAPS Dr. Otto

Generalmajor der Polizei.

Born on 13 January 1898. He joined the professional fire service (Beruffeuerwehr) in Hamburg in 1907. Served in the army during the Great War and was awarded the Iron Cross 1 and 2 Class. Studied engineering at University and was awarded a Doctorate in 1927. Served as Landesbranddirektor der Feuerwehr Thüringen from 1925 to 1928 and then returned to Hamburg. Leiter der Feuerwehr Hamburg from 1 February 1937 to September 1939. Kommandeur der Feuerschutzpolizei Hamburg from September 1939 to the end of the war. Awarded bars to his Iron Crosses. He held the rank of Oberbranddirektor until September 1939. When following the decree of 27 September 1939 he was given the rank of Oberst der Feuerschutzpolizei. Promoted Generalmajor der Polizei in 1945. Surrended to the British in Hamburg in April 1945.

Bibliography

Institutions

Bundesarchiv Koblenz , Berlin	B.A.
U.S. Berlin Document Center later Bundesarchiv Berlin	B.D.C.
Institut für Zeitsgeschichte Munchen	I.f.Z.
Bibliothéque de Documentation	
Internationale Contemporaine Paris	B.D.I.C.
U.S. National Archives Washington D.C.	USNC

Unpublished Sources
B.A.

Personal Documents Police officers and SS officers
Bestand R 19 (Ordnungspolizei)
Befehlsblatt der Chef der Ordnungspolizei 1940 – 1945
Preussische (from 1936 Reich und) Ministerialblatt der Innern 1933 – 1945
Dienstalterslisten der SS der NSAP 1934 – 1944
Reichsranglisten der Offiziere der Ordnungspolizei 1941, 1943,
SS-Personalverfügungen, SS-Personalveränderungsblatt, SS-Stabsbefehl, SS-Befehlsblatt (1932 to 1945)
Taschenbuch f ür Verwaltungsbeamte 1933 – 1942 Berlin

U.S. B. D. C.

Personal Documents of SS-officers

U.S. N. A.

Personal Document SS-Officers
Serie " RFSS und Chef der Deutschen Polizei "T 175 Rolls 41, 145, 158, 191, 196, 201, 204, 205, 209, 222, 223, 232, 238, 240

Published Sources (prior 1945)

Magazines

Die Deutsche Polizei	Magazine of the German Police 1933 – 1944 (from 1943 SIPO and Ordnungspolizei issues)
Der Deutscher Feuerschutz	Magazine of the german fire service
Illustrierte Beobachter	Illustrated magazine of the Party 1933 – 1944
Das Schwarze Korps	Magazine of the SS-1935 – 1945

Books

Bader	Aufbau und Gliederung der Ordnungspolizei 1943
Best	Die Deutsche Polizei Berlin 1940
Daluege	Tag der Deutschen Polizei 1934
-	Das Deutsche Führer Lexikon Berlin 1934
Du Prel	Das General Gouvernement Polen 1942
Gauweiler	Deutsches Vorfeld im Osten (Bildbuch über das Generalgouvernement Polen) 1941
-	Die Deutsche Polizei (Werbeschrift) 1939
-	The German Police. A report issued by Supreme Headquarters Allied Expeditionnary Force. April 1945
Kehrl	Jahrbuch der Deutschen Polizei Berlin 1936
Kienast	Der Grossdeutsche Reichstag 1936, 1938, 1943
Koroschke	Jederzeit einsatzbereit (Ein Bildbericht von der Neuen Deutschen Polizei) 1939
Koroschke	Polizeireiter in Polen 1940
	Polizei greift ein! Berlin 1941
	Die Deutsche Polizeibeamte 1936, 1937
	Die Deutsche Polizei 1937
	Lautenschläger Handbuch für den Hilfspolizeibeamten 1940
Ley	Nationalsozialistisches Jahrbuch 1942
Ragener	Werist 1935 (german who' who)
Roden	Polizei greift ein (Bildokumente der Schutzpolizei) Berlin 1934
Richter	Einsatz der Polizei (Bei den Polizeibataillonen in Ost, Nord und West) Berlin 1943
Richter	Ordnungspolizei. Auf den Rollbahen des Ostens. (Bildbericht Einsatz der Ordnungspolizei in Sommer 41 im Osten) Berlin 1942
	Reichsband Adressenwerk der Party 1941/42
Rumler	Freigemachtes Grenzland (Polizei Bataillonen in Luxemburg u Lothringen) 1942
	Reichsrangliste der Offiziere der Ordnungspolizei 1943, 1944 Berlin
Schmitt	Der Einsatz der Schutzpolizei im Aufruhrgebiet 1933
	Taschenkalender für die Schutzpolizei des Reiches und der Gemeinden und die Verwal tungspolize Taschenkalender für die Technische Nothilfe 1942, 1943
	Taschenbuch für Verwaltungsbeamten 1933 – 1943 Berlin
Wirth	Schutzpolizei im Kampfeinsatz. Handbuch der taktik des Polizeibataillons 1942

Published Sources (after 1945)

Books

Angolia	Cloth Insignia of the NSDAP and SA. San Jose 1985
Birn	Die Höheren SS und Polizeiführer (Himmlers vertreter im Reich und in den besetzen Gebieten) Düsseldorf 1986
Lohalm,	
Wildt	Der Dienstkalender Heinrich Himmler 1941/1942 Hamburg 1999
Böckle	Feldgendarmen, Feldjäger, Militärpolizisten Stuttgart1987
Broszat T	he Hitler State. Harlow 1991
	Anatomy of the SS-State. London 1968
Browder	Hitler Enforcers Oxford 1996
Browning	Ordinary Men, Reserve Police
	Battalion 101 and the Final Solution in Poland 1992
Campbell	The SA Generals. University of Kentucky Press-1998
Castellan	Le réarmement clandestin du Reich Paris 1954
Davis	Badges and Insignia of the Third Reich 1933 – 1945. London 1992
Fangmann	Parteisoldaten Die Hamburger Polizei im III Reich Hamburg 1987
Foedrowitz	euerwehrfahrzeuge im Einsatz 1939 – 1945, Erlangen 1995
Foltmann	Opfergang der Generale Berlin 1957
Franz	Gebirgsjäger der Polizei Bad Nauheim
Gihl	Feuerwehr Hamburg (125 Jahre
	Berufsfeuerwehr Hamburg) Hamburg 1997
Goldhagen	Hitler's Willing Executionners. Ordinary Germans and the Holocaust 1997
Grieser	Himmlers Mann in Nürnberg. Stadtarchiv Nürnberg 1974
Guicheteau	Marseille 1943. La fin du Vieux-Port (14 SS-PolizeiRgt) Marseille 1973
Höffkes	Hitler Politische Generale. Tübingen 1986
Höhne	The Order of the Death Head. Hamburg 1966
Husemann	Die Guten Glaubens waren 2 volumes Osnabrück 1973
Ingressi	Die Ordnungspolizei. Les forces de police sous le 3e Reich. Pulnoy 1996
Hampe	Der Zivile Luftschutz im Zweiten Weltkrieg Frankfurt am Main 1963
Huck, Neufeld &Tessin	Zur Geschichte der Ordnungspolizei Koblenz 1957 Kannapin,
Tessin, Bruns	Waffen-SS und Ordnungspolizei im Kriegeinsatz Osnabrück 2000
	Landeshauptstadt Düsseldorf und die Polizei (50 jahr Polizeipräsidium) Düsseldorf
Lankenau	Polizei im Einsatz während des Krieges 1939 – 1945 1957

Keilig	Das Deutsche Heer 1939 – 1945 Bad Nauheim
Koehl	The Black Corps University of Kentucky Press-1983
Koehl	R.K.F.D.V. German Resettlement and Population Policy 1939-1945 1957
Krätschmer	Die Ritterkreuzträger der Waffen-SS. Preuss. Oldendorf 1982
Klee, Dressen	Those were the days. Frankfurt a Main 1988
Kurowski	Hitlers Last Bastion. Atglen. Pennsylvania 1998
Lenfeld, Thomas	Die Eichenlaubsträger 1940 – 1945. Wiener Neustadt 1983
Lessmann	Die Preussiche Schutzpolizei in der Weimarer Republik. Düsseldorf 1989
Lian	The Berlin Police Force in the Weimar Republic. Los Angeles 1970
Lichtenstein	Himmlers grüne Helfer " Die Schutz und Ordnungspolizei im III Reich " 1990
Löhken	Die Polizei-uniformen in Preussen 1866-1945 Bad Nauheim 1986
Lumsden	Himmlers Black Corps 1923 – 1945. Stroud 1997 Mc Donald.
Kaplan	Prague in the shadow of the Swastika. Prague 1995
Mehnert	Die Waffen-SS und Polizei 1939 – 1945 Norderstedt 1995
Padfield	Himmler London 1990
Patzwall	Die Ritterkreuzträger des Kriegsverdienstkreuzes 1942 – 1945 Hamburg 1984
Hass & Hocke	Die Preussische Polizei (dargestellt durch die von 1920 bis 1935 in Flensburg stationierte Polizeibereitschaft) 1986
Hogg	German Order of Battle 1944. 1975
V. Preradovich	Österreichs Höhere SS-Führer Berg am See 1987
Regenberg	Panzerfahrzeuge und Panzereinheiten der Ordnungspolizei 1936 – 1945 Preuss. Oldendorf 1999
Retlinger	The SS alibi of a nation 1922 – 1945 1956
Riege	Kleine Polizei Geschichte 1954
Schreibert	Die Träger des Deutschen Kreuzes in Gold Mark Die Deutschen Kreuzes in Silber. Markt.
Smelser	Die Braune Elite II (21 biographies of NS leaders –Daluege-) 1993
Siggermann	Die Kasernierte Polizei 1918 – 1933 Frankfurt a Main 1980
Stockhorst	Funftausend Köpfe
Stolz	Geschichte der Polizei in Schleswig Holstein 1978
Taugourdeau	Les Organisations Nationales Socialistes 1991
Tessin	Deutsche Verbände und Truppen der deutschen Wehrmacht und Waffen-SS 1939 1945. Osnabrück 1974 Deutsche Verbände und Truppen 1918 – 1939.

	Osnabrück 1974
Wember	Umerziehung im Lager. Koblenz 1991
Williamson	German Military Police Units 1939 – 1945
Witter	Chain Dogs (The German army Military Police of World War II (volume I) 1994 (volume II) 1996
Yerger	Allgemeine-SS Atglen Pennsylvania 1997 Waffen-SS Commanders (2 volumes) Atglen Pennsylvania 1997
Thesis	Riding East. Atglen Pennsylvania 1996
Boehnert	A sociography of the SS-Officer Corps 1925 – 1939 London
Browder	Foundations of the Nazi Police State University Press of Kentucky 1989
Eisenblätter	Grundlinien der Politik des Reich Gegenüber dem Generalgouvernement 1939-1945 1969
Shalka	The "General SS" in Central Germany 1937 – 1939 Un. of Wisconsin 1972
Wilhelm	Die Württembergische Polizei im dritten Reich Stuttgart 1988
Wheeler	The SS and the administration of the nazi occupied eastern Europe 1939 – 1945 Oxford 1981

Articles

Boehnert	The Jurist in the SS-Führerkorps
Jamin	Zur Rolle der SA im NS Herrschaftssystem
Jerome	Ordnungspolizei en Moselle 1940. 39/45 Magazine December 1999 Selbstchutzverein 1939 – 1940 Guerres Mondiales July 1991
Le Gouvernement	General de Pologne 1939 – 1945 39/45 Magazine October 2001

Glossary

a.D	(Ausser Dienst) retired from active service
Abschnitt	Regional district of the territorial organisation (land level in feuerwehren, district command in feuerschutzpolizei)
Abteilung	**Branch of of an office (Amt), unit of the size of a bataillon (Technische Nothilfe,Feldjägerkorps...) or territorial area of the gendarmerie**
Adjutant	**Staff officer attached to a senior officer dealing with routine and administrative matters**
Amt	**Office (subdivision of an amtsgruppe in a Main Office)**
Amtsgruppe	Branch of a main office of Hauptamt Ordnungspolizei
Ausbildung	Training matters
Aussendienststelle	Outpost of criminal police (staff over 10)
Aussenpost	Outpost of criminal police (staff under 10)
Bahnschutzpolizei	**Railways protection police with the status of special police (sonderpolizei)**
bandenkampfverband	**Tactical command composed of army, Waffen-SS and police units operating against anti partisans**
Baurat der Feuerwehr	Construction councillor: professional fire brigade officer rank equivalent to Major der SCHUPO
Beauftragter	Representative
Befehl	Order (Befehlsblatt) or Command (Befehlhaber)
Befehlhaber der Ordnungspolizei	Commander of the Uniformed Police in occupied countries under HSSPF and in Germany after 1943
Behörde	Authority in the german administration
Bereitschaft	**Police unit (i.e.Umfall Bereitschaft: Accident brigade or barrack unit of motorized gendarmerie)**
Bevollmächtigter	Plenopotentiary
Bezirk	Subdivision of an district in Fire Protection Police
Bürgermeister	**Mayor of a middle size and small towns**
Chef der Ordnungspolizei	Chief of the Uniformed Police Main Office under chief of the German Police in the Ministery of Interior
Chef der Zivilverwaltung	Head of a civil administration attached to an army in 1939 and 1940 then in an 1 annexed territory (Bialystok, Luxemburg, Alsace, Lorraine…)
Dienststelle	Administrative office
Einheit	Unit
Einsatzgruppe	Action group of the technische nothilfe in East and West in during polish and western campaign
Einsatzkommando	Detachment of an action group
Freiwillige	Voluntary (in Hilfspolizei or Feuerwehr)
Führer z.V	**Officer at disposal**
Führungsamt	Operations department of a Main office (i.e. Hauptamt Ordnungspolizei)
Führungsstab	Operation staff (i.e. for anti partisan war)
Funk	**Radio**
Gauleiter	**Regional leader of the NSDAP head of a gau.**

Gemeinde	Municipality
Gendarmeriekreis	Gendarmerie district (40 gendarms) covering several gendarmerie detachments
Gendarmerieabteilung	Detachment of 15 gendarms
General Government	German administration in the Central Poland from 1939 till 1945 headed by a General Gouverneur
Gewerbepolizei	**Branch of the administrative police in charge of trade matters in a Police Administration** or a municipal police
Grenzpolizei	Frontier Police controlled by Gestapo. Personnel was supported by SCHUPO in various border areas.
Grenzpolizeikommissariat	Regional frontier office of the Frontier Police
Gruppe	**Departement of an office in ORPO Main Office**
Hauptabteilung	**Main departement in an office**
Hauptamt	**Main office of the NSDAP or state administration**
Hauptmannschaft	**Company of gendarmerie of about 150 men**
Hoheitsabzeichen	**National police badge worn of the cap and left arm**
Höhere	**Polizeibehörde senior civil authority in police at the level of Land or Pro vince in Preussen**
Höhere SS und Polizeiführer	**Senior SS and Police leader in a wehrkreis or an occupied territory**
Ia	**Operation officer in the staff of major unit (brigade, division...)**
Inspekteur der Ordnungspolizei	**Regional commander of the uniformed police in Germany from 1937**
Kampfkommandant	**Commander of the garrison of a town inthe front line**
Kommandeur der Ordnungspolizei	Area commander of the Uniformed Police in occupied countries under BdO
Kommandoamt der ORPO	Office responsible for the Operation control of the branches of the Uniformed police
Kommissarische	**Temporary head of an office or an unit, usually given the permanent position**
Konteradmiral	**Navy rank equivalent to a Major-General**
Kreis	Administrative district (Landkreis) also gendarmerie district (Gendarmeriedistrikt)
Kreishauptmann	Head of a district in Sachsen (from 1939t Regierungs Präsident) also in Generalgouvernement of Poland
Kriminal(ober)	Sekretär ranks for the lower officer class-equivalent to 2nd lieutenant
Kriminaldirektor	Rank for the upper officer class-equivalent to major or lieutenant colonel
Kriminalinspektor	Rank for the lower officer class-equivalent to captain
Kriminalkommissar	Rank of the upper officer class-equivalent to lieutenant
Kriminalpolizei	Branch of security police in charge of the repression of crimes.
Kriminalrat	Rank of the upper officer class-equivalent to major
Landeskriminalpolizeiamt	**Central office of the prussian criminal police up to 1937**
Landespolizei	Militärized barrack police created in 1933 in Preussen then in whole germany. Disbanded in 1935 after the law for conscription
Landkreis	**Rural administrative district**
Landrat	**Head of a rural or urban administrative district**

Landwacht	Auxilliary rural police force established in 1942 to assist gendarmerie or municipal police in small towns
Luftschutzpolizei	Air raid police force formed in 1942 from personnel of the Sicherheitund Hilfsdienst
Marktpolizei	**Branch of the administrative police in charge of the markets and fairs in a Police Administration or a municipal police**
m.d.U	**Mit der Uniform: allowed to wear the uniform of a police general rank usually given to a police president**
Ministerialblatt der Innern	Official gazette of the Ministery of the interior dealing with all legal and administrative police regulations
Ministerialdirektor	**Senior civil servant head of a main departement in a ministry equivalent to a lieutenant general**
Ministerialdirigeant	**Senior civil servant head of a departement in a ministry equivalent to a major general**
Ministerialrat	**Senior civil servant equivalent to a colonel**
Ministerpräsident	**Prime minister of a Land gouvernement**
Nachrichtenführer	Signal officer
NSKK motorgruppe	**Senior administrative region of the NS motorised corps**
Oberabschnitt	**Administrative region for the Allgemeine-SS**
Oberamt	**Administrative district in south länders (Württemberg, Baden)**
Oberbaurat der Feuerwehr	**Senior Construction councellor: professional fire brigade officer rank equivalent to Oberstleutnant der SCHUPO**
Oberbürgermeister	**Major of a large town**
Oberlandrat	**Head of German administration in a district of the Reich protectorate Böhmen-Mähren**
Oberpolizeirat	**Senior austrian police rank**
OberPräsident	**Senior administrative official in a prussian province**
Oberregierung und Kriminalratsenior	**Criminal councillor equivalent to a lieutenant colonel**
Ortpolizeibehörde	**Local civil police authority**
Polizei-Bataillon	Main mobile unit of the Uniformed police in occupied territories from 1939 became part of Polizei-Regiments after 1942.
Polizei-Regiment	Command staff for Police bataillons up to 1942 then main mobile unit of the Uniformed police
Polizeidirektion	**Police Administration in a middle size town**
Polizeigefängnis	**Prison under authority of police (no part of the KL network) guards could be SS, Gestapo and ORPO men i.e.**
Polizeipräsidium	**Police Administration in large towns**
Polizeirat	**Head of a polizeiamt in polizeiverwaltung**
Polizibehörden	**Civilian Police authorities at Land, kreis and Ort levels headed by Reich statthalter, RegierungsPräsident, Landrat or Bürgermeister**
Provinz	**Land Preussen was divided into provinces, headed by an Oberpräsident who was often a Gauleiter**
Referent	**Head of a referat (administrative subdivision of an abteilung or a Gruppe)**
Regierungsdirektor	**senior administrative and police official equivalent to a lieutenant colonel**

Regierungspräsident	**Senior administrative official, head of an main administrative district (regierungsbezirk) in a Land or a province**
Reichsgau	**Region formed in annexed territories and heade by a Reich governor**
Reichskommissar	**Head of the german administration in former occupied russian territories and western occupied countries**
Reichskriminaldirektor	Chief of the criminal police
Reichskriminalpolizeiamt	**Central office of all german criminal police forces from 1937**
Reichsleiter	**Reich leader of a party branch of the NSDAP**
Reichstatthalter	**Governor acting as the representative of the Reich in each Land or Reichsgau which enlarged powers**
Sachbearbeiter	**Officer responsible of a duty in an administration (sachbearbeiter für SCHUPO ...)**
Schutzmannschaft	**Auxilliary uniformed police recruited in the eastern occupied territories organised in batallions to maintain public order.**
Schutzpolizei	**Protection police force with state or municipal status serving in revier ser vice, traffic control** or public security in mobile units
Sicherheits und Hilfsdienst	Security and assistance service with status of auxilliary police in charge of air raid protection up to 1942
SS-Schulungsamt	**Office of the SS-Main Office in charge of education**
SS-Standortführer	**Chief of garrison of the Allgemeine-SS units in a main town**
Staatskommissar	**State commissionners appointed by the nazis next to Land ministries in 1933**
Staatsminister	**Head of government in small landers or land minister in larger länder**
Stab	**Staff of a main office or a field unit**
Stadtkreis	**Urban administrative district**
Stadtwacht	Auxilliary municipal police force established in 1943 to assist protection police
Standortkommandant	**Commander of a garrison of the Waffen-SS in a large town**
Stellvertreter	**Deputy head**
Übungsplatz	**Training camp for army or Waffen-SS**
Verband	Formation
Verbindungsoffizier	Liaison officer
Verwaltung	**Administration**
Vollzugspolizei	**Executive branch of the police (SCHUPO, Gendarmerie, Gestapo, KRIPO...)**
Wehrkreis	Military district in germany
Wehrwolf	**Special force created at the end of the war to resist to invasion of germany by allied**
z.b.V	**At special disposal**
Zugführer	**Platoon leader in german army and Waffen-SS**

Appendix

Polizei Präsident Dortmund, SA-Gruppenführer Otto Schramme

Polizei Präsident Karlsruhe, SA-Gruppenführer Hanns Lundin

Polizei Präsident Königsberg, SA-Obergruppenführer Heinrich Schöne

Polizei Präsident Kiel, SA-Gruppenführer Joachim Meyer-Quade

Polizei Präsident Duisburg, SA-Gruppenführer Heinz Knickmann

Polizei Präsident Königsberg, SA-Gruppenführer Adolf Kob

Polizei Director Regensburg SA-Gruppenführer Hans Georg Hofmann

Polizei Präsident Wiesbaden, SA-Gruppenführer Franz von Pfeffer

Polizei Präsident Halle an der Saale, SA-Ogruf. Wilhelm Jahn

Polizei vice President Berlin
SS-Oberführer Paul Kanstein

28 september, 1938 Wien, Oberst der Gendarmerie Dr. Arnold Licken von Lowenburg, SS-Oberführer Otto Steinhäusl, SS-Oberführer Josef Fitzthum, SS-Gruppenführer Dr. Ernst Kaltenbrunner

Polizei Präsident Flensburg, Konrad Fulda

Polizei Präsident Breslau, SS-Brigadeführer Albrecht Schmelt

Polizei Präsident Mülhausen, SS-Ostubaf. Ulrich Weist

SS-Brigadeführer Walter Oberhaidacher Polizei Präsident Dresden

Polizei Präsident Duisburg SA (later SS) Oberführer Karl Gutenberger

Berlin 1933, SS-Stubaf. Peter Johannsen, SS-Obergruppenführer Josef Dietrich, SS-Oberführer Walter Stein, SS-Brigadeführer Max Henze

Polizei Präsident Dortmund, SS-Oberführer Georg Altner

Polizei Director Salzburg, SS-Ostubaf. Dr. Benno Breitenberg-Zellenberg

SS-Oberf. Otto Steinhäusl Pol Pdt Wien and Pdt of International Criminal Police Commission

Polizei Präsident Augsberg, SS-Oberführer Rolf von Humann-Hainhofen

Polizei Präsident Kassel, SS-Oberführer Max Henze

Polizei Präsident Weimar, SS-Oberführer Walter Ortlepp

Polizei Präsident Essen, SS-Brigadeführer Karl Zech

Polizei Präsident Magdeburg, SS-Brigadeführer Andreas Bolek

Polizei Director Ulm SS-Oberführer Wilhelm Dreher

Polizei Präsident Saarbrücken and Metz, SS-Brigadeführer Christoph Diehm

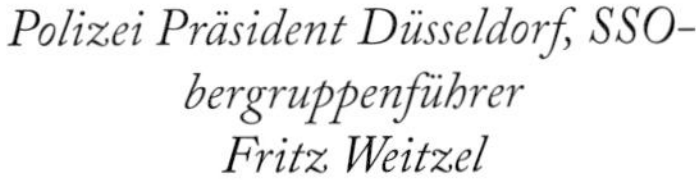

Polizei Präsident Düsseldorf, SSO-bergruppenführer Fritz Weitzel

Polizei President Bremen, Generalmajor der Polizei, Johannes Schoers

Polizei President Dessau, SS-Standartenführer Nils-Otto Wiese

Polizei Präsident Leipzig, Generalmajor der Polizei Wilhelm von Grolman

Polizei Director Tilsit, SS-Standartenführer Heinz Thieler

Polizei Präsident Wiesbaden, Generalmajor der Polizei Anton Diermann

Polizei Präsident Münchenm SS-Obergruppenführer Philipp Bouhler

Polizei Director Marburg am Drau, SS-Ostubaf. Dr. Adolf Wallner

Polizei Director Wittenberg, SS-Ostubaf. Erwin Wickert

Polizei Präsident Reichenberg, SS-Standartenführer Karl Jäger

Polizei Director Bitterfeld, SS-Sturmbannführer Kurt Mainz

Polizei Präsident Lübeck, Oberst der SCHUPO, Joachim Petson

Polizei Präsident Danzig, Oberst der SCHUPO, Erich Rottmann

Polizei Präsident Gotenhafen, SS-Obersturmbannführer Helmut Muller

Polizei Director Cuxhaven, SS-Standartenführer Karl D'Angelo

Polizei Director Znaim, SS-Sturmbannführer Dr. Alfred Kottek

Polizei Präsident Saarbrücken and Metz, SS-Oberführer Willy Schmelcher

Oberst der Gendarmerie Dr. Hans Hachtel

Polizei Director Jena, SS-Obersturmbannführer Walter Schmidt

Polizei Director Graudenz, SS-Sturmbannführer Heribert Kammer

Generalmajor der Polizei Oskar Schmiedel

Polizei Director Baden-Baden, Oberreigerungsrat Dr. Hebold (1st right)

SA-Gruppenführer Richard Wagenbauer PP Karlsruhe

Oberst der SCHUPO August Edler von Meysener

Generalleutnant der Polizei Adolf von Bomhard

Generalmajor der Polizei Herbert Becker

Generalleutnant der Polizei, Otto Schumann accompanies Frau Gertrud Seyss-Inquart to a toy fair in the Hague 1940

Mannheim 1940, Generalmajor der Polizei Georg Jedicke and Major der Schutzpolizei Walter Soosten

Wiesbaden 1940, left to right, Oberstleutnant der Gendarmerie Fritz Schüberth, Generalmajor der Polizei Georg Jedicke, Hauptmann der SCHUPO Matthes, Hauptmann der SCHUPO Günther Rumler, Oberst der SCHUPO Paul Worm.

General der Polizei, Alfred Wünnenberg greets Members of the fire service during an inspection in the Ruhr. Behind him stands Generalmajor der Polizei Kurt Gohrum

Oberst der SCHUPO Hermann Kintrup

Generalmajor der Polizei Theodor Siebert

Generalmajor der Polizei Karl Fischer

Tivoli 1941, General Gazzola inspector of the Italian Police School in Tivoli with Oberst Josef Heismann

Berlin 1945, Left to right, Generalleutnant Walter Schmid-Dankward, Generalarzt der Polizei Dr. Ernst Wenzel, General der Artillerie Helmuth Weidling, Generalleutnant Kurt Woytasch, Oberst Reifior

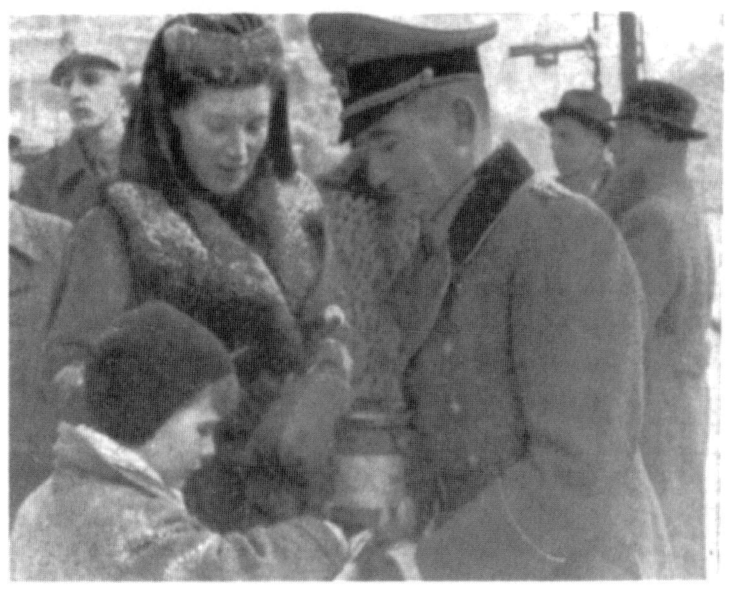

Ministerialdirektor Werner Bracht during a collection day from the german police 1942

Preussen 1933. Minister President of Preussen Göring as senior chief of the Landespolizei with Daluege Commander of the Landespolizei

Members of Municipal Police on Exercise

Police signals unit radio network

Major der Gend. Walter Schimana receives a Gendarmerie standard from IdO Wien Oberst der SCHUPO August Edler von Meyszner

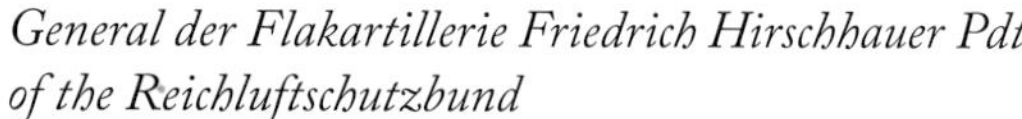

General der Flakartillerie Friedrich Hirschhauer Pdt of the Reichluftschutzbund

SS-Oberführer Paul Werner

Generalmajor der Polizei Otto Zaps Commander of Fire Police Hamburg

Oranienburg Castle, the seat of the colonial police school

Cavalryman at the police riding school Rathenow

Police signals unit in South Steiermark 1941

An SS-man as auxiliary policeman takes his dog on patrol with a Schutzpolizei man

SS-Oberf. Carl Zenner PP Aachen

Polizei Präsident Berlin, SA-Gruf. Wolf Graf von Helldorf

Reichführer SS, Heinrich Himmler as Polizei Präsident München 1933

SS-Oberführer Fritz Schlessmann Polizei Präsident Essen

Polizei Präsident Bromberg, SS-Oberführer Otto von Proeck

SA-Obergruppenführer August Schniedhüber PP München

SS-Brigaf. Wilhelm Graf von Wedel, PP Potsdam

1933 meeting of the Prussian state council. SA-Gruppenführer Georg von Detten (Pol Pdt Dresden), SS-Gruppenführer Siegfried Seidel-Dittmarsch with Himmler

SS-Gruf. Theodor Eicke and SS-Gruf. Karl Alfred Rodenbucher

SS-Obergruf. Fritz Weitzel, PP Düsseldorf

Genmajor der Polizei Gerhard Winkler

SS-Brigaf. August Korreng, PP Düsseldorf

SS-Brigaf. Rudolf Weiss, PP Metz

Female Auxilian of the police signals section

Police Signals unit in Russia 1941

Oberst der Polizei
Ferdinand Heske

Generalleutnant der Polizei
Ernst Hvitzegrad

SS-Brigaf. Otto Ullmann

München 1944 Reichsleiter Franz Ritter von Epp,General der Flieger Emil Zenetti, Gauleiter Paul Giesler, SS-Obergruppenf ührer Karl Freiherr von Eberstein

A Police Assault Gun in action in Russia 1943

SS-Gruppenführer Carl Graf von Puckler-Burghauss,
Generalleutnant der Polizei Ernst Hitzegrad

Police Panzerkampfwagen Renault R-35 in action in Boenia 1942

A Police Battalion machine-gun unit in action in Belurussia

Polizei Präsident Münster
SS-Brigadeführer
Otto Heider

Holland 1941, SS-Brigadeführer Kurt Knoblauch, Generalmajor der Polizei, Otto Schumann, Reichskommissar Arthur Seyss-Inquart

Generalmajor der Polizei Robert Schlake

SS-Oberführer Dr. Josef Plakolm

SS-Brigaf. Alfred Karrasch

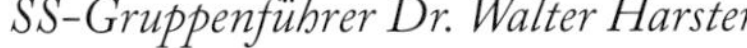

SS-Gruppenführer Dr. Walter Harster

SS-Obergruppenführer Philipp Bouhler

Generalmajor der Polizei Wilhelm Roettig

Pol pdt Breslau SS-Brigadeführer Franz Breihaupt

SS-Gruppenführer Lothar Debes SS-Brigadeführer Rolf Humann-Hainhofen

SS-Oberführer Alfred Borchet

Pol Pdt Bremen SS-Brigadeführer Curt Ludwig

PP Dresden SS-Brigadeführer Karl Pflomm

Oberst der Polizei Johannes Wirth

Reichsführer Heinrich Himmler, SS-Obergruppenführer August Heissmayer, SS-Brigadeführer Christoph Diehm

SS-Brigadeführer Andreas Bolek Pol Pdt Magdeburg

Polizei Präsident Strassburg SS-Oberf. Carl Engelhardt

SS-Oberführer Georg Langosch

Generalmajor der Polizei Paul Will

Generalmajor der Polizei Kurt Gohrum

Generalmajor der Polizei Helmuth Mascus

Oberst der SCHUPO Otto Schumann

1st left SS-Oberführer Emil Klein 6 left SS-Oberführer Michael-Faist 8 left SS-Obergruppenführer Karl von Eberstein 13 left SA ObergruppenführerWilhelm Schepmann, 15 Left SS-Brigadeführer Carl Zenner, right SS-GruppenführerTheodor Berkelmann

1938 Generalmajor der Polizei Arthur Mulverstedt and Oberfeldarzt der SCHUPO Dr. Kurt Hoffmann

Generalmajor der Polizei Dr. Carl Retzlaff

Gen. Major der Pol Heinz Reinefarth

SS-Obergruppenführer Rudolf Querner

Prague 1940 SS-Obstubaf Horst Bohme, SS-Gruf. Karl Hermann Frank, SS-Ostubaf Robert Ries, SS-Oberf. Julien Scherner SS-Staf Hans Ulrich Geschke

SS-Gruppenführer und General-leutnantder Polizei Karl Heinrich Brenner

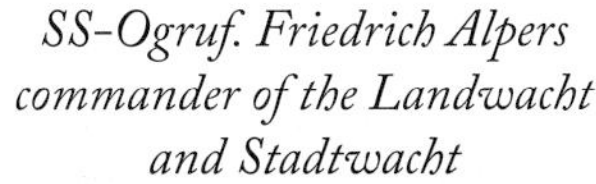

Generalmajor der Polizei, Walter Keuck

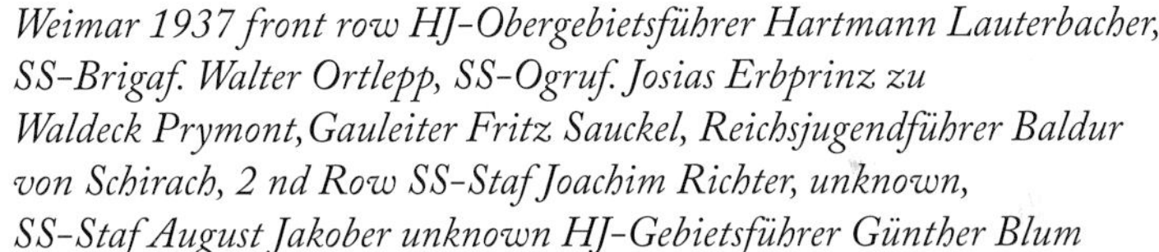

Weimar 1937 front row HJ-Obergebietsführer Hartmann Lauterbacher, SS-Brigaf. Walter Ortlepp, SS-Ogruf. Josias Erbprinz zu Waldeck Prymont, Gauleiter Fritz Sauckel, Reichsjugendführer Baldur von Schirach, 2 nd Row SS-Staf Joachim Richter, unknown, SS-Staf August Jakober unknown HJ-Gebietsführer Günther Blum

SS-Ogruf. Friedrich Alpers commander of the Landwacht and Stadtwacht

Oberst der Polizei Hans Griep

Poland 1939. SS-Brigaf. Odilo Globocnik, Generalmajor der Polizei Herbert Becker

Generalmajor der Polizei Leo von Falkowski

Oberst der Polizei Hans Griep

Left to right SS-Gruf. Richard Glücks, SS-Ogruf. August Frank, SS-Ogruf. Oswald Pohl, SS-Gruf. Georg Lorner, SS-Gruf. Dr. Hans Kammler

Generalmajor der Polizei Eberhard Herf Commander of the ORPO in Minsk

SS-Brigadeführer Berthold Maack inspects the Landespolizei in Danzig 1937

Generalmajor der Polizei Hermann Crux

Oberts der Polizei Hans Muller-Brunckhorst

Generalmajor der Polizei Franz Scryffart

German Police Day Nuremburg 1942 Left to right Adjutant E.G.Schultze SS-Brigaf. Franz Fischer SS-Staf. Wiilibald Faust,Heinz Schlosser, unknown Generalmajor Paul Will unknown SSGruppenführer Dr. Benno Martin Generalmajor Otto Kuschow (Source Jost Schneider)

Treptow 1935. Gen der Pol Daluege, SS-Staf. Willy Luckner (head of the Police veterans association), Gauwart Ludwig, SS-Ostubaf. Kurt Knoblauch, SS-Stubaf Fritz Teufel.

Winter Sports Meeting 1937 Reinhard Heydrich, Emil Mazuw, two unknown SA